STRUCTURE, ROLE, AND IDEOLOGY
IN THE HEBREW AND GREEK TEXTS
OF GENESIS 1:1–2:3

SOCIETY
OF BIBLICAL
LITERATURE

DISSERTATION SERIES
David L. Petersen, Old Testament Editor
Pheme Perkins, New Testament Editor

Number 132

STRUCTURE, ROLE, AND IDEOLOGY
IN THE HEBREW AND GREEK TEXTS OF GENESIS 1:1–2:3

by
William P. Brown

William P. Brown

STRUCTURE, ROLE, AND IDEOLOGY IN THE HEBREW AND GREEK TEXTS OF GENESIS 1:1–2:3

Scholars Press
Atlanta, Georgia

STRUCTURE, ROLE, AND IDEOLOGY IN THE HEBREW AND GREEK TEXTS OF GENESIS 1:1–2:3

William P. Brown

Ph.D., 1991
Emory University

Advisors:
Carol A. Newsom
John H. Hayes

© 1993
The Society of Biblical Literature

Library of Congress Cataloging in Publication Data
Brown, William P., 1958–
    Structure, role, and ideology in the Hebrew and Greek texts of
Genesis 1:1–2:3/ William P. Brown.
        p. cm. — (Dissertation series/ Society of Biblical
Literature; no. 132)
    Dissertation (Ph. D.)—Emory University, 1991.
    Includes bibliographical references.
    ISBN 1-55540-759-5 (alk. paper). — ISBN 1-55540-760-9 (pbk.:
alk. paper)
    1. Bible. O. T. Genesis I, 1–II, 3—Criticism, interpretation,
etc. 2. Bible. O. T. Greek—Versions—Septuagint—Criticism,
Textual. 3. Water in the Bible.   I. Title.   II. Series:
Dissertation series (Society of Biblical Literature); no. 132.
BS1235.2.B76 1993
222'.11048—dc20   93-17786
                                                       CIP

Printed in the United States of America
on acid-free paper

Contents

PREFACE

It must be admitted at the very outset that in light of the unusual cross-fertilization of disciplines represented in this study, many students of these disciplines will no doubt be disappointed after reading this dissertation. On the one hand, text critics can justifiably criticize the study for not having gone far enough in exploring the textual history of Gen 1:1–2:3. On the other hand, criticism that this study fails to examine fully the complex socio-ideological matrix from which certain textual variants arose can be leveled by the socio-literary critics. Nevertheless, despite the flaws inherent in a project such as this, the author hopes to establish a modest link between these seemingly unrelated disciplines in the attempt to answer the question of the relationship between the Old Greek and Masoretic textual traditions of Gen 1:1–2:3.

This study examines what is generally considered to be a resolved text-critical issue and suggests that the recent *communis opinio* be rejected. It is generally assumed that the Greek text represents a harmonizing translation of the Hebrew. However, I hope to demonstrate that the textual basis of the Greek tradition does not stem from a concern to produce a harmonized text but rather is the result of socio-ideological concerns that are markedly different from that of the MT of Gen 1:1–2:3.

The points of difference between the LXX and the MT come into sharp focus with regard to (1) the differing cosmogonic roles the waters are assigned by the respective texts and (2) the prominence of a heptadic structure in the MT. From an ideological perspective, these differences suggest a textual relationship in which the LXX preserves the more difficult text (*lectio difficilior*) relative to the MT. This study demonstrates that the Hebrew *Vorlage* of the LXX, which can be reconstructed with some confidence in light of Qumran findings, represents an earlier textual tradition than that preserved by the Masoretes.

Chapter One deals with the methodological issues concerning the literary relationship between form and ideology and suggests how an ideological investigation can fit within the working principles of the text-critical enterprise. As for the literary relationship between form and ideology, the sociological poetics of M. M. Bakhtin and the dramatistic method of K. Burke are particularly helpful. As for exploring a heuristic alliance between socio-ideological criticism and text criticism, I draw essentially from the recent discussions of P. K. McCarter and E. Tov.

Chapter Two contains a translation of the LXX of Gen 1:1–2:3 and a descriptive analysis of its structure, within which the respective roles of the earth and the waters are defined. Chapter Three does the same for the MT text.

Chapter Four reconstructs a probable Hebrew retroversion of the LXX for Gen 1:1–2:3 and examines the textual relationship between the Hebrew *Vorlage* of the LXX and the MT. It is suggested that the VorLXX of Gen 1:1–2:3 is prior to the MT in light of (1) the different role the waters assume within the formal structure of the VorLXX and (2) the intricate heptadic structure the MT exhibits.

Chapter Five examines the Greek, ancient Near Eastern, and Israelite traditions relating to the role of the waters in creation. The first area is crucial from a traditio-historical perspective, since it could be argued that the prominent and positive role the waters are given in the LXX is the result of Hellenistic influence during the time in which the Greek translation of the Pentateuch was produced. An investigation into the Greek cosmogonies, however, yields inconclusive results, whereas the positive and productive role of the waters depicted in the VorLXX suggests a Mesopotamian and/or Egyptian background. Furthermore, the negative role the waters often assume in Ugaritic, Babylonian, and Israelite traditions sufficiently establishes the traditio-historical context of the MT's revision of the VorLXX.

Lastly, Chapter Six examines both texts in terms of their socio-ideological differences and settings.

A study of this type that involves a cross section of interests and disciplines naturally involves a diverse group of people who have been instrumental in the development of the thesis. For the methodological impetus behind this dissertation, I wish to thank Professor Gene Tucker, the first to spark my interest in form and ideological criticism. At the other extreme, for leading me through the intricacies of preparing the manuscript, I am deeply grateful to Dr. Patrick Graham of the Pitts Theological Library at Emory University and Ms. Sally Hicks of Union Theological Seminary in Virginia for the time and energy they generously spent reading and checking the "penultimate" drafts. Thanks also go to Scholars Press, particularly David L. Petersen, editor of the Series, and Darwin M. Melnyk, Associate Manager for Publications.

Somewhere in between the theoretical and the practical, special words of thanks go to my two advisors, Professors Carol A. Newsom and John H. Hayes. Their support at every step of the way and their invaluable insights have been indispensable in the development of my work. In different ways both have become my mentors.

Given the nature of this text-critical study, I must also express my gratitude to Professor James Davila, who has generously corresponded with me the past two years with regard to the results of his work on the Qumran fragments of Genesis 1. His openness sets an example for all who have worked closely with the Qumran documents.

Finally, I wish to thank Gail King Brown, my spouse, for her confidence in me and for all the sacrifices she has made during my research. I dedicate this work to her.

ABBREVIATIONS

AB   Anchor Bible

AEL   *Ancient Egyptian Literature*, I, II, III (M. Lichtheim; Berkeley: University of California, 1975, 1976, 1980)

AGRL   Aspects of Greek and Roman Life

AJSL   *American Journal of Semitic Languages*

ANET   *Ancient Near Eastern Texts Relating to the Old Testament* (3rd edition, ed. J. B. Pritchard; Princeton: Princeton University, 1969)

AO   Analecta Orientalia

APAW   Abhandlungen der preussischen Akademie der Wissenschaften

ASR   Aids for the Study of Religion

ASTI   Annual of the Swedish Theological Institute

AUSTR   American University Study Series: Theology and Religion

AzKG   Arbeiten zur Kirchengeschichte

BAG   *A Greek-English Lexicon of the New Testament* (W. Bauer; ed. W. F. Arndt and F. W. Gingrich. Chicago: University of Chicago Press, 1958)

BAS   Biblical Archaeological Society

BASOR   *Bulletin for the American Schools of Oriental Research*

BHS   *Biblia hebraica stuttgartensia*

BIOSCS   *Bulletin of the International Organization for Septuagint and Cognate Studies*

BJRL   *Bulletin for the John Rylands Library*

BM   *Beth Miqra'*

BS   *Bibliotheca Sacra*
BSR   Bibliothèque de sciences religieuses
BT   *The Bible Translator*
BWANT   Beiträge zur Wissenschaft vom Alten und Neuen Testament
BZ   *Biblische Zeitschrift*
BZAW   Beihefte zur ZAW
CAB   Christianisme antique bibliothèque
CB OTS Coniectanea Biblia: Old Testament Series
CBQ   *Catholic Biblical Quarterly*
CBQMS   CBQ Monograph Series
CPSSV   Cambridge Philological Society Supplementary Volume
CST   Concepts in Social Thought
CTA   *Corpus des tablettes en cunéiformes alphabétiques découvertes à Ras Shamra-Ugarit de 1929 à 1939* (ed. A. Herdner; Paris: Imprimerie Nationale, 1963).
CTSRR   College Theology Society Resources in Religion
CWS   Classics of Western Spirituality
Diels   *Die Fragmente der Vorsokratiker* (7th edition; H. Diels and W. Kranz; Berlin: Weidmann, 1954)
EJ   *Encyclopedia Judaica*
ET   *Expository Times*
FRLANT Forschungen zur Religion und Literatur des Alten und Neuen Textaments
GAG   *Grundriss der Akkadischen Grammatik* (W. von Soden; Rome: PIB, 1969)
GBS   Guides to Biblical Scholarship
GHAT   Göttingen Handbuch zum Alten Testament
G-K   *Gesenius' Hebrew Grammar* (ed. E. Kautzsch, trans. A. E. Cowley; 2nd edition; Oxford: Clarendon Press, 1910)
HR   History of Religions
HSM   Harvard Semitic Monographs
HTR   *Harvard Theological Review*
HUCA   *Hebrew Union College Annual*
IBHS   *An Introduction to Biblical Hebrew Syntax* (B. K. Waltke and M. O'Connor; Winona Lake: Eisenbrauns, 1990)
ICC   International Critical Commentary
IDB   *Interpreter's Dictionary of the Bible* (ed. G. A. Buttrick; Nashville: Abingdon, 1962)
IDBSV   *Interpreter's Dictionary of the Bible Supplementary Volume* (ed. K. Crim; Nashville:Abingdon, 1976)
IESS   *International Encyclopedia of the Social Sciences* (ed. D. L. Sills; New York: Macmillan and Free Press, 1968)

IRT	Issues in Religion and Theology
JAOS	*Journal of the American Oriental Society*
JANES	*Journal of the Ancient Near Eastern Society of Columbia University*
JBL	*Journal of Biblical Literature*
JBTh	*Jahrbuch für biblische Theologie*
JCS	*Journal of Cuneiform Studies*
JJS	*Journal of Jewish Studies*
JNSL	*Journal of Northwest Semitic Languages*
JPSTCS	Jewish Publication Society Torah Commentary Series
JQR	*Jewish Quarterly Review*
JSOT	*Journal for the Study of the Old Testament*
JSOTSS	*JSOT* Supplement Series
JSS	*Journal of Semitic Studies*
JTS	*Journal of Theological Studies*
KB	*Lexicon in Veteris Testamenti Libros* (ed. L. Koehler and W. Baumgartner; Leiden: E. J. Brill, 1985).
KTU	*Die keilalphabetischen Texte aus Ugarit*, Teil 1: Transkription (ed. M. Dietrich, O. Loretz, J. Sanmartin; AOAT 24/1; Kevelaer/Neukirchen-Vluyn: Butzon und Bercker/Neukirchener Verlag, 1976)
LAPO	Littératures anciennes du Proche-Orient
LCL	Loeb Classical Library
LS	*A Greek-English Lexicon* (ed. H. G. Liddell and R. Scott; Oxford: Clarendon Press, 1968)
LXX	Septuagint or Old Greek text
MHUCA	Monographs of *HUCA*
MT	Masoretic text
NICOT	New International Commentary on the Old Testament
NRSV	New Revised Standard Version
NTT	*Norsk Teologisk Tidsskrift*
OAW	Österreichische Akademie der Wissenschaft
OBO	Orbis Biblicus et Orientalis
OS	*Oudtestamentische Studiën*
OTP	*The Old Testament Pseudipigrapha*, 2 vols. (ed. J. H. Charlesworth; Garden City: Doubleday & Company, 1983, 1985)
PE	*Preparatio Evangelica* (Eusebius)
PEQ	*Palestine Excavation Quarterly*
PIB	Pontificium Institum Biblicum
RB	*Revue Biblique*
SBS	Stuttgarter Bibelstudien
SBT	Studies in Biblical Theology
SCS	Septuagint and Cognate Studies

SH	*Scripta Hierosolymitana*
Smyth	*Greek Grammar* (H. W. Smyth; Cambridge: Harvard University Press, 1956)
SPSH	Scholars Press Studies in the Humanities
ST	*Studia Theologica*
SVF	*Stoicorum Veterum Fragmenta* (ed. I. von Arnim; Leipzig: Teubner, 1905-24)
TDNT	*Theological Dictionary of the New Testament* (ed. G. Kittel and G. Friederich; Grand Rapids: William B. Eerdmans Publishing Company, 1964-76)
TU	Texte und Untersuchungen zur Geschichte der altchristlichen Literatur
Ugaritica V	*Ugaritica V* (J. Nougayrol, *et al.*; Paris: Imprimerie Nationale, 1968)
Ugaritica VI	*Ugaritica VI* (Paris: Mission Archèologique de Ras Shamra, 1969)
Vg	Vulgate text
VT	*Vetus Testamentum*
VTG	Vetus Testamentum Graecum
VTS	Vetus Testamentum, Supplements
WAW	Writings from the Ancient World
WBC	Word Bible Commentary
WMANT	Wissenschaftliche Monographien zum Alten und Neuen Testament
YES	Yale Egyptology Series
ZAW	*Zeitschrift für die alttestamentliche Wissenschaft*
ZTK	*Zeitschrift für Theologie und Kirche*

INTRODUCTION

Die Welt ist nicht gegeben, aber aufgegeben.[1]
— Hermann Cohen

What sort of creative power is that which brings
forth nothing but numbers and names?[2]
— Julius Wellhausen

FORM AND IDEOLOGY

The priestly account of creation in Gen 1:1–2:3[3] is without a doubt one of the most structured and highly formalized texts in the Hebrew Bible. The consistent structure of the passage is evident from the text's regular repetition of certain formulaic elements within the movement from divine word to creative event for each act of creation. Since H. Gunkel,[4] commentators have attempted to describe the structure of the creation account, specifically the Hexaemeron (Gen 1:1–31), and its significance for exegesis. Yet a multitude of divergent descriptions have resulted in little consensus in the history of exegesis of Gen 1–2:3. This is perhaps partly due to the disproportionate amount of attention given within the last few decades to the mythological antecedents of the priestly account, namely from Sumerian, Akkadian, Egyptian, and Ugaritic sources. Though such pursuits have been fruitful, insufficient attention to the text's unique form and structure has left many "stones unturned." The methodological supposition of this study is that the formal contours of Gen 1:1–2:3 that have eluded modern exegetes contribute decisively to the ideological significance of the Hebrew and Greek texts of the creation account.

If any biblical text invites a formalistic analysis, it is Genesis 1:1–2:3. Such an analysis, however, can be conducted in a variety of ways, employing diverse methodologies ranging from semiotics and structuralism to traditional form criticism. However, one literary method that is recently (re)gaining wide attention among modern literary critics but has not yet made its full impact upon biblical studies is the "sociological poetics" of M. M. Bakhtin (1895–1975). Though highly critical of the formalism of his day (i.e., Russian Formalism), Bakhtin laid the foundations of a new literary method that incorporated much of the formalistic enterprise.

Russian Formalism designates a particular movement that developed in reaction to the ideological approach of socialism. The movement flourished in the 1920s and included a group of young Leningrad literary critics, as well as Roman Jakobson and other Moscow linguists.[5] Their rallying principle was that the text was inherently more than simply a mirror reflecting the economic conditions of society. To the contrary, the text was to be treated as a disembodied entity distinct from the external world that produced it. In short, Russian Formalism conceived of the literary text as a result of impersonal forces at work within the system of the literary language itself. The text was considered free of all values except those unique to literary discourse.[6] In the U.S. such a brand of formalism was most closely allied with New Criticism. But the Russian Formalists went further than their American counterparts by entirely banishing content as something external to literariness.[7] Form was considered as representative of the totality of the literary work. Consequently, Formalism disregarded authorial intent, social effect, ideology, and even the perceiver's role in contributing to the meaning of the text. Instead, the "autonomy of the text" was the catchword, and the text was the sum total of its literary devices.[8]

M. M. Bakhtin and his circle[9] were Russian Formalism's most ardent yet constructive critics. While despising an exclusively ideological approach, which he frequently called "vulgar ideologism,"[10] Bakhtin sought to criticize Russian Formalism from within. For Bakhtin, texts are by nature *dialogical*. Meaning is not the lonely product of an intention willed by a sovereign ego. Rather, meaning arises in discourse with others. One's voice can have meaning, but only in conjunction with others: "The word is a two-sided act. It is determined equally by whose word it is and for whom it is meant. A word is territory shared by both addressor and addressee, by the speaker and his interlocutor."[11] In short, meaning is in essence a *social construction.*

Bakhtin's approach was in effect a drawing together of ideological and formalistic criticisms. He was quick to point out that literature never directly reflected an ideological system. To claim that it did was blatant reductionism. Rather, Bakhtin claimed that literature reflected the living processes by which ideologies were formed, since ideology was the totality of the discourses by which meaning was made.[12] Indeed, Bakhtin criticized the Marxists for omitting all the relevant factors that mediated between socioeconomic forces and the individual literary work.[13] Two of these mediating factors were, according to Bakhtin, the ideological horizon and the literary environment.[14]

Bakhtin maintained that an effective approach had to be oriented towards literary history. The problem with the current Marxist approaches of his day was their inability to reveal the sociological nature of literary phenomena *from within* literary forms.[15] The means and aims of Bakhtin's "sociological poetics," on the other hand, were unapologetically literary: specification, description, and analysis.[16] That is, the goal was to isolate the literary work as such, to reveal its structure, to determine possible forms and variations of this structure, and to define its elements and their functions.[17] Inseparable from this formal pursuit, however, was the ideological pursuit of exposing the values concealed in the form and structure. For Bakhtin, language was not a monolithic system but an arena of ideological generation and contention.

In short, Bakhtin recognized the invaluable contribution of Russian Formalism to modern literary-critical pursuits, especially in his attack against narrow Marxist literary approaches. Bakhtin could not deny that Formalism recognized the relationships the text generates within itself, the structures that reveal the text's hidden meanings. Yet these hidden meanings, according to Bakhtin, were not the unique prerogative of the text or unrelated to the social world. As Sternberg rightly notes: "Form has no value or meaning apart from the communicative (historical, ideological, aesthetic) function."[18]

The Formalists, on the other hand, drove a wedge between form and social content, a separation they felt justified since they regarded literature as uniquely poetic. Poetic language, the Formalists argued, had its own form as its object of representation, whereas practical language was exclusively defined by its content. The Bakhtinian circle contested such a division: Practical language was dependent on form as much as meaning in literature was subject to content.[19] Consequently, "poetic language" was not composed of unique linguistic forms.[20] Indeed, all language was made up of the same form/content totality for its object of representation; neither form nor content could be severed to serve independently as the basis for identifying genres.[21] To use the extreme example of sound in poetry, Bakhtin observed: "It is not the physical sound or the psychophysiological act of its pronunciation and perception that is artistically organized. What is organized is the socially meaningful sound, the ideological body of social intercourse."[22] In other words, literature cannot be defined merely by how it is made from a technical perspective; it must also be defined by how it is constructed and what it produces *socially*.[23]

In short, Bakhtin condemned the Formalists for regarding literary works as similar to physical objects rather than as repositories of socially constructed meaning.[24] Yet, as noted above, Bakhtin's severe critique of the Formalists was not without a modicum of respectful appreciation of their positive contributions to the art and science of literary analysis. Bakhtin condemned the Formalists, at best, for being too narrow in their approach and, at worst, for establishing artificial, meaningless constructs as the means of literary representation. Conversely, Bakhtin condemned the Marxists, on the one hand, for failing to meet the Formalists on their own ground, and, on the other, for reducing ideology to simplistic and meaningless mechanisms. Whether he realized it or not, Bakhtin paved the way for a synthesis of the best of both formalistic and ideological approaches to the literary text, thereby laying the foundation for a significantly different and inclusive methodology in literary criticism.

Recently Fredric Jameson has developed and refined the methodology of such a synthesis. Jameson is particularly sensitive to the interface between structure and the historical factors formative in the development of the text. He champions the study of the "ideology of form," which he defines as the analysis of "the linguistic, narrative, or purely formal ways in which ideology expresses itself through and inscribes itself in the literary text."[25] Quite often, the structure and the contents clash: Whereas the contents of a text would tend to conceal the historical precursors of the text, the structure reveals the hidden dynamics that constitute the written material.[26] For Jameson, history is for the most part accessible only in textual form,[27] and ideology is an integral historical force evident in the production of texts.

What precisely is this "ideology" that is so indissolubly connected to the form of literary texts? Paul Ricoeur traces the development of its definition in Marx, Althusser, Mannheim, Weber, Habermas, and Geertz. Agreeing with Habermas, Ricoeur notes:

> Ideology is not the distortion of communication but the rhetoric of basic communication. There is a rhetoric of communication because we cannot exclude rhetorical devices from language; they are an intrinsic part of ordinary language. In its function as integration, ideology is similarly basic and ineluctable.[28]

Coupled with ideology's integrative function is its power of confrontation: "Integration without confrontation is pre-ideological."[29] "Ideology operates at the turning point between the integrative function and resistance."[30] The term "ideology" thus can no longer be used in the pejorative sense of designating a falsehood or fiction.[31] For Jameson, the term is a "mediatory concept" that in no way presupposes "cut-and-dried sociological stereotypes like the notion of the 'bourgeois' or the 'petty bourgeois.'"[32] Here, Jameson is clearly standing upon the shoulders of Bakhtin, since Bakhtin himself similarly distanced his critical methods from "vulgar ideologism." Eagleton, too, reflects such a distancing when he defines ideology in appropriately broad terms: "The largely concealed structure of values which informs and underlies our factual statements."[33] In short, ideology deals with the structure of material values expressed in and by the text.

Formal ideological analyses of texts have the advantage of being able to uncover layers of meaning, from the explicit to the implicit. This, in part, is reflective of the separation identified by some literary theorists between the communicative intention of a text and the motives behind the text.[34] As M. Brett suggests: "Instead of constructing a *dichotomy*, for example, of motives and communicative intentions, we could perhaps think of a *continuum* from the most explicit and conscious layer of communication down to the most hidden and sub-conscious layer of motives."[35] Such a continuum of textual meaning can only be discerned by judiciously moving from the most explicit layers of meaning towards the less explicit or concealed levels. Consequently, constructing the ideological motives of a text without considering the surface structure, genre, content, and communicative intentions of the text can only result in contrived conclusions. In short, a formal approach should constitute an integral part of every ideological investigation of the text.

With regard to Gen 1:1–2:3, how a formalistic analysis is to be undertaken appears both deceptively simple and frustratingly complex. Given the highly structured nature of the text, one does not lack sufficient material for describing the text's formal contours. The structural components of the text immediately rise to the surface in the initial reading. However, the structured nature of the text is of such high density that it is possible to construct a multitude of structural models by which to describe the text's form, as the history of scholarship has demonstrated.[36] However, attempts at describing the text's dense structure have usually been done without taking seriously the nature of literature as ideologically active in the general cultural and social world in which it is embedded.

To be sure, exploring the ideological side of the formal structure and content of Gen 1:1–2:3 places one on uncertain grounds. The reason a literary critic like Jameson can ideologically analyze Honoré de Balzac's novels with such confidence stems from the accessibility of abundant resources for reconstructing nineteenth-century French culture and history.[37] Such is not the case with the priestly account of creation. Many exegetes have conducted extensive comparisons with ancient cosmogonic texts, thereby attempting to reconstruct a general cultural milieu of the ancient Near East for the text. In so doing, most have noted the comparatively unique features of the priestly cosmogonic account in relation to the mythological accounts of ancient Israel's neighbors. In a similar fashion, one could conduct a comparative examination of texts that more closely resemble the rational tenor of Gen 1:1–2:3, such as the Greek philosophical creation texts, of which there are abundant examples. In either case, however, one must by necessity begin with the particular text, for the text itself provides the basic framework for discerning the ideological motives behind it.

A helpful way to begin to uncover the motives behind texts is demonstrated in Kenneth Burke's "dramatistic" method. Burke has noted that literature is inherently dramatic, since language itself is an action that exhibits purpose and conflict as part and parcel of social relations.[38] Much of Burke's literary-critical program is to restore to the literary text its value as *activity* and its meaning as a gesture and a response to a determinate situation.[39] Burke calls his method of analysis "dramatism," which he defines as a "critique of terminology designed to show that the most direct route to the study of human relations and human motives is via a methodological inquiry into cycles or clusters of terms and their functions."[40] The term "act" is key to the dramatistic approach to a text, for from it are derived the "dramatistic pentad": act, scene, agent, agency, and purpose.[41] In other words: "Any complete statement about motives will offer *some kind of* answers to these five questions: what was done (act), when or where it was done (scene), who did it (agent), how he did it (agency), and why (purpose)."[42] However, these terms can be interchangeable, depending upon the context. For example, an agency can be an agent: The term "war may be treated as an agency, insofar as it is a means to an end . . . [but] in mythologies war is an agent, or perhaps better a super-agent, in the figure of the war god."[43] Similarly, the scene is traditionally the "container" of the act, yet it can also supply the motivation for the act: "there is implicit in the quality of a scene the quality of the action that is to take place within it,"[44] or, more succinctly, "scene is to act as implicit is to explicit."[45] Such distinctions can easily become blurred, given the pervasive nature of "act" in language. Moreover, Burke makes the trenchant observation that "theological notions of creation and re-creation bring us nearest to the concept of total acts," whereby features of the agent (e.g., nature, attitude, motive) and scene (e.g., structure of the universe) are derived from the nature of the act.[46] In short, the dramatistic approach treats language as a mode of action for the purpose of discerning the ideological motives that engender its usage.

Although Jameson faults Burke for not taking account of the role of the unconscious in the formation of ideological structures, he notes that "drama . . . is the very source of the ideology of representation and . . . of that vanishing point from which spectacles—whether of culture, of everyday life or of history itself—fall into place as metaphysically coherent meanings and organic forms."[47] Though Burke intends to view drama as an all-pervasive dimension of language, his insight is particularly useful for examining Gen 1:1–2:3. In the priestly creation account there is one major agent, namely, *ʾĕlōhîm*, which, according to the formal structure of the text, commands, creates, observes, approves, and blesses. Yet there are at least two other active agents in the narrative text, namely *hāʾāreṣ* and *hammayim*. These two secondary agents also warrant critical attention. Analyzing them as active characters in the narrative structure of creation will reveal certain clues about the ideology of the text as a whole, or, as Burke puts it, the "motivations" behind the text; that is, the reasons *why* the text was written.

In light of Burke's dramatistic method, the Genesis text, as with any literary text, must be analyzed as a progression of meaning. As Eagleton puts it, "a word or image which is repeated does not mean the same as it did the first time, by virtue of the very fact that it is a repetition."[48] In the priestly cosmogony the repeated key terms *hāᵓāreṣ* and *hammayim* are nuanced in different ways as they occur in the Genesis text. Far from being static entities within the movement of the text, they assume new functions in every "scene" or day-section in which they appear, not unlike actors on the stage. An examination of their respective roles within the formal structure of the priestly cosmogony lends an important clue for discerning the ideological motives of the text.

An examination of the formal structure of Gen 1:1–2:3 with special attention to certain terms that assume active roles is the point of departure for examining the dialogical relationship between two very similar texts of Gen 1:1–2:3, namely, the MT and the Hebrew *Vorlage* of the LXX. It is hoped that such a formal ideological study will cast new light on their respective differences and, consequently, their textual relationship. The methodological overview discussed above is helpful in such textual investigations, since its starting point, the Bakhtinian notion of language as inherently dialogical, is most clearly exemplified by the way in which different closely related texts are produced, excluding, of course, identifiable scribal mistakes.

In most cases of textual comparison, this dialogical relationship has been examined in the context of translation, as, for example, from Hebrew to Greek. It is a truism that translation is interpretation,[49] no matter how accurate the translation purports to be.[50] When B translates A, B necessarily takes up the "pre-owned" words, images, concepts, and structures of A *as B understands them in relation to B's world view and presuppositions* and publicly disseminates these words, images, concepts, and structures *now appropriated by B* into a different language, culture, and social situation. Hence, translation is a process of interpretation that begins with a dialogical relationship between B and A. As C. R. Taber describes it, B in effect "restructures" A into B's language, the receptor language.[51] In the process of translation correlative accuracy and understanding are often, but not necessarily, the *professed* principles.

The dialogical relationship, however, can be more pronounced between two texts of the same language, for here translation as an exercise in correlative precision need not come into play. The Samaritan Pentateuch, for instance, exhibits some 6000 differences in comparison with the MT, most of which are orthographic,[52] and thus are "translative" in nature.[53] However, with this level of textual variation accounted for, many remaining variants reflect sharp ideological differences. In these instances, those who produced the Samaritan Pentateuch had no intention of reproducing the texts that were later preserved by the Masoretes. At certain points the SP textual tradition revised pre-Masoretic texts to suit its own ideological needs (or vice versa?). As M. J. Mulder points out, such differences "prove that in a fairly constant text, alterations may have been made in the Hebrew by either party, in corroboration of its own, theologically biased, position, and detracting from that of the other side."[54]

This study claims to find similar deliberate revision between the MT and the *Vorlage* of the LXX, specifically with regard to the passage Gen 1:1–2:3. To get to the textual and, in due course, ideological differences between the MT and the *Vorlage* of the LXX, the principles of textual criticism necessarily apply. It will be shown that ideological criticism can complement the discipline of textual criticism in the study of textual relationships.

Textual Criticism

The principles of modern text-critical research of the Bible have deep roots that can no doubt be traced back to Origen and Jerome; however, many of the methodological principles acknowledged today began to be formulated by J. A. Bengel (1687–1752) in his work on the New Testament.[55] One of his most widely accepted principles was, in Bengel's Latin, *proclivi scriptioni praestat ardua* ("the difficult is to be preferred to the easy reading").[56] In addition, Bengel was one of the first to recognize the need to classify manuscripts into families, later known as *recensions*.[57] J. Semler (1725–1791) continued Bengel's program, formulating no less than fifteen axioms, including the principle that the shorter reading is to be preferred to the longer, later known as *brevior lectio potior*.[58] These two rules, the shorter and the more difficult readings are to be preferred, have been stereotyped as the two most important rules in text-critical research,[59] despite the fact that the former has been subjected to some criticism.[60] It is commonly recognized among modern textual critics that there are no irreducible principles that apply in every case of textual variation; instead, every case must be examined individually with reason and logic.[61] As A. E. Housman maintains:

> We must have no favourite method. An emendator with one method is as foolish a sight as a doctor with one drug. The scribes knew and cared no more about us and our tastes than diseases care about the tastes of doctors; they made mistakes not of one sort but of all sorts, and the remedies must be

of all sorts too. . . . Criticism requires a mind as various as its matter, nimble, flexible, empty of prepossessions and alert for every hint.[62]

Yet as with any discipline, basic principles must be provisionally and tentatively made. The following examines two of the most recent attempts at describing the text-critical program.

Standing on the shoulders of the great textual critics of the New Testament, P. K. McCarter has neatly reduced the textual critical enterprise to two basic rules:

1. *Difficilior lectio potior* ("the more difficult or distinctive reading is preferable").
2. *Utrum in alterm abiturum erat?* ("which would have been more likely to give rise to the other?").[63]

McCarter observes that both are actually two sides of one rule. Undoubtedly there is a close connection; however, I would hazard to suggest that the latter rule, rather than providing a particular criterion like the first rule, represents the overarching *modus operandi* behind the text-critical enterprise. McCarter collapses the two by spelling out what "rule 2" signifies: "A common, familiar reading is unlikely to have given rise to an unusual, elegant, distinctive equivalent; the reverse is more likely to have been the case."[64] But what do "unusual," "elegant," and "distinctive" mean? Clearly they are terms that invite subjective interpretation. A good example is the Targumim, which quite often provide very "unusual," even "elegant" readings of the Hebrew texts. Yet an ironclad application of "rule 2," as McCarter defines it, would require ascribing priority to many Targumic texts over and against the MT. The only exception McCarter gives to the rule is the case of textual accident: "the more difficult reading is not to be preferred when it is garbage."[65]

Part of the problem is that McCarter equivocates when he elucidates his two "rules" by collapsing them on the same level. "Rule 2" is not a rule proper but rather the essential, determinative question of the textual critic, of which "rule 1" provides one guideline among others.[66] In conjunction with this guiding principle is the additional goal McCarter finds intrinsic to the text-critical enterprise: "The goal is the recovery of an earlier, more authentic—and therefore superior—form of the text."[67]

However, apart from scribal mechanical corruptions, what makes the earlier text "superior?" The frequently expressed preference for the earlier, and "therefore superior form of the text" in the exegetical enterprise among textual critics has led to a disregard for the less "superior" yet equally meaningful texts. E. Tov addresses this issue more explicitly than McCarter.

Tov describes the two-fold aim of text-criticism of the Hebrew Bible as follows: "The work of textual criticism proper may be divided into two stages. The first deals with collecting and reconstructing Hebrew variants, while the second is concerned with that of evaluation."[68] Tov is correct in stressing that these two stages must remain separate.[69] The process of evaluation is to be separated from the correction-by-emendation method, since emendation applies "if one regards MT as the *only* witness of the biblical text."[70] With regard to examining the text of the Septuagint, one must first establish an accurate Hebrew retroversion. This part of the text-critical enterprise involves "some objective aspects," Tov claims.[71] Once retroverted, all variant readings are to be treated equally in the evaluative stage. Tov warns against the past history of textual research, which has been consumed with the desire to establish the "original" or "archetypal" reading of the OT as a whole. Such a reconstruction is problematic. Tov does, however, concede the legitimacy of the enterprise with regard to *individual* instances in which it is legitimate "to reconstruct the 'original' reading, which is supposedly superior to all other readings."[72] Yet this second stage of the enterprise, namely evaluation, necessarily involves some subjectivity, despite the methodological rules scholars have formulated: "In these matters objectivity is impossible, and the use of abstract rules which by themselves are correct does not render the evaluations more objective,"[73] and, "While some objective aspects are involved in the *retroversion* of variants, their *evaluation* is completely subjective."[74] Yet Tov takes pains to outline such rules, the most important one being "the appropriateness of the reading in its context."[75] Tov is fully aware that this rule often clashes with the rule that the more difficult reading is to be preferred: "The application of this rule is so subjective that it can hardly be called a textual rule. For what is linguistically or contextually difficult for one scholar, might not be for another."[76] Lastly, Tov observes that textual sources can preserve some vestiges of earlier stages of the *literary* growth of biblical books. A good example is the Greek text of Jeremiah, which differs from the MT not only in length but also in the arrangement of material. In light of the evidence of 4QJer[b], Tov suggests that the LXX does not reflect a different textual recension of Jeremiah, but an earlier *edition* or redaction of the book.[77] Such a comparison should not be evaluated by the usual textual criteria, because they were not created in the process of mechanical textual transmission. In such cases, no one reading should be preferred to another.

> While on the textual level one is allowed to prefer one detail to another, in the realm of literary analysis one does not prefer details or stages. . . . Literary criticism may express a judgment on the priority of a certain stage, stratum or story to another one, but it does not speak in terms of preference as textual criticism does.[78]

Hence, it is methodologically problematic, according to Tov, to follow the *BHS* when it suggests that Jer 27:22b-b is an addition to the text because it is lacking in the LXX: "this minus forms part of a *large body* of minuses from which it cannot be singled out"[79] (italics added). In other words, the *BHS* mistakenly evaluates such variants individually and not as instances of a coherent network of textual differences that mark different stages in the literary growth of the work.

In sum, Tov describes the aims of text-critical research by delineating the boundaries between textual and literary-critical readings: Texts whose variants constitute a larger coherent body of variants are to be evaluated by the literary-critical method (e.g., redaction) rather than by the methods of text-criticism. Such a delineation, however, appears a bit too neat. Tov discusses the two *editions* of the Book of Jeremiah, whose evaluation, he maintains, lies beyond the text-critical domain. However, it must be pointed out that coherent patterns of textual variants certainly exist in literary units smaller than those of books (e.g., Jeremiah) and canons (e.g., Samaritan Pentateuch). By working backwards *ad absurdum*, it is possible to reduce the text-critical enterprise to the examination of a single, isolated textual variant. As Tov has delineated the boundaries, patterns of textual variants whose parameters are defined by units smaller than whole books or extensive passages comprise a grey area between isolated textual variants, on the one hand, and broad literary stages, on the other, in the study of textual transmission. Clearly, what Tov calls literary criticism, an umbrella term that includes numerous exegetical disciplines, must be seen as working hand in hand with textual criticism if the latter enterprise is to involve anything more than examining mechanical scribal mistakes, whose number in the Hebrew Bible pales in comparison to the number and variety of other textual differences.

Furthermore, with regard to intentional textual differences, the boundary between textual and literary criticism begins to blur; their respective domains of focus begin to merge. As in the case of Jeremiah, textual criticism does indeed shed light on the literary or redactional process of biblical books.[80] Textual and redaction criticism must be seen as complementary disciplines working toward the common goal of discerning the relationships of texts.

Fishbane has uncovered the extent to which scribal activity appropriated and transformed the texts and traditions of ancient Israel. Scribes did much more than passively transmit texts.[81] To the contrary, Israelite scribes "not only copied what came to hand but also responded in diverse ways to the formulations which they found in earlier manuscripts."[82] Such "diverse ways" evidently ranged from simple corrections to elaborate exegetical interpretations.[83] Consequently, the ancient texts "were not simply copied, studied, transmitted, or recited. They were also, and by these means, subject to redaction, elucidation, reformulation, and outright transformation."[84] In short, if the transmission of texts involved a whole range of scribal activities, even including "authorial" activity, then any comprehensive study of textual transmission would necessarily warrant a complementary merging of diverse disciplines such as text-criticism and redaction criticism. The fact that scribal activity involved literary activity necessarily precludes atomistic applications of textual and literary methodologies in discerning the relationships of textual variants. Moreover, the fact that ancient scribal activity can be to some degree located on the social-historical plane invites ideological analyses of the produced texts.[85]

Given the diverse and active nature of scribal work in ancient Israel, another methodological implication for text-critical study is that one cannot in comparing texts indiscriminantly attach the label of "superior" to one text and "inferior" to another, except in cases of clear scribal mistakes or corruptions. Each variant text exists in its own right and contains its own authentic "structure of values." That is to say, each variant text must be examined as a whole in comparative textual investigations.

Such equal treatment, however, does not preclude one from giving *temporal* priority to one text in relation to another. Indeed, as both McCarter and Tov are in agreement, the question as to which text would be more likely to give rise to the other is the determinative aim of textual criticism. In order to achieve that aim, "literary criticism," to use Tov's label, is integral to the text-critical enterprise when dealing with *patterns* of textual variants. Thus, in order for the text-critical enterprise to be sufficiently comprehensive in its examination of textual relationships, the

door must be open for employing an ideological criticism that acknowledges the dialogical character of texts.

What is also clear in the text-critical enterprise as outlined by Tov is
an inescapably subjective element in the text-critical program, an element
that comes to the fore at the most crucial juncture of the process, namely
the evaluation stage. McCarter relies ultimately on that final and nebu-
lous arbiter, *common sense*,[86] while Tov stresses the subjectivity of any
evaluative methodology. Yet neither one views this as a total liability
within the discipline. Indeed, the discipline invites developing inductive,
coherent, and rational ways by which to construct the historical relationship among versions, ways that are not limited to the mechanics of
explaining textual corruption.

In short, textual criticism of the Hebrew Bible, with its aim of collecting and reconstructing Hebrew variants, provides many of the necessary
tools for comparative work. Yet ultimately it is up to the exegete to
decide whether variant texts are the result of different literary or redactional stages or simply scribal corruptions. The critical factor in deciding
one way or another depends on whether the particular variations can be
accounted for on the level of isolated instances of accidental scribal
"corruption" (e.g., dittography, haplography, parablepsis, homoioarkton,
homoioteleuton, graphic confusion, metathesis, etc.) or whether they
point to larger, meaningful complexes or patterns that constitute literary
or redactional stages. As for the latter, the kind of ideological criticism as
inaugurated by Bakhtin fits nicely within the goals of text-criticism, since
such an approach can work specifically to highlight and examine the
dialogical differences between texts.

HISTORY OF SCHOLARSHIP

It is the basic premise of this dissertation that many of the textual
differences between the MT and the Hebrew *Vorlage* of the LXX of Genesis
1:1–2:3 are not the result of mechanical scribal corruptions, that is, of
isolated alterations, whether accidental or intentional. Rather, many of
the variant readings are better explained by coherent literary or redactional stages, characterized by a shift in ideological viewpoints, which
can only be gleaned from an examination of the respective formal
structures of the variant texts.

Many exegetes who have done comparative textual analyses of the
MT and LXX of Gen 1:1–2:3 have described the latter text as more
structurally consistent, thereby harmonizing the apparent structural

discrepancies evident in the MT. Indeed, this appears to be the most recent consensus.[87] On the other hand, those who favored the LXX in their exegesis of the creation text have attributed unintentional scribal corruption to the MT, because little sense could be made of the structural inconsistencies of the Hebrew text.[88] In only one instance has the case been made that the MT represents a conscious revision of the *Vorlage* of the LXX.[89] This study maintains that an examination of both texts in light of their dialogical relationship, most particularly with respect to their differing ideologies, will provide a more accurate assessment of their relationship. I hope to demonstrate that the Masoretic tradition represents a later systematic revision of the priestly creation account that ideologically resists the implications the *Vorlage* of the LXX manifests with regard to the relationship between *ʾĕlōhîm* and the created order.

The key to unlocking the dialogical relationship between these two text-forms and to disclosing their ideological contentions is an examination of their respective formal structures and the "dramatic" roles (à la Burke) that certain key terms ("actors") assume within the structures. As suggested in the first section, the formal ideological analysis suggested by Bakhtin in his critique of Russian Formalism best suits such a textual comparison. It is hoped that such a formal ideological investigation of the Greek and Hebrew texts of Gen 1:1–2:3 will shed new light on their textual as well as socio-historical relationships.

NOTES

[1] Quoted from K. Clark and M. Holquist, *Mikhail Bakhtin* (Cambridge: Harvard University, 1984) 59.

[2] J. Wellhausen, *Prolegomena to the History of Ancient Israel* (1885 translation; Gloucester: Peter Smith, 1983) 361.

[3] Instead of the typical documentary source division between Gen 2:4a and 4b, the unit division of Gen 1:1–2:3 is preferred in light of the observations of F. M. Cross (*Canaanite Myth and Hebrew Epic: Essays in the History of the Religion of Israel* [Cambridge: Harvard University Press, 1973], 302); S. Tengström (*Die Toledotformel und die literarische Struktur der priesterlichen Erweiterungsschicht im Pentateuch* [CB OTS 17; Lund: CWK Gleerup, 1981] 54-58); R. Rendtorff (*Das überlieferungsgeschichtliche Problem des Pentateuch* [BZAW 147; Berlin: Walter de Gruyter, 1977] 112-42; *idem., The Old Testament: An Introduction* [Philadelphia: Fortress Press, 1986] 132); and B. S. Childs (*Introduction to the Old Testament as Scripture* [Philadelphia: Fortress Press, 1979] 145, 149), who all agree that Gen 2:4 introduces the next block of material. Whether P is an independent source or a redactional layer still remains an open question and need not depend on the literary status of Gen 2:3–4. Indeed, the two alternatives are perhaps too sharply drawn.

4 Gunkel cites the work of K. D. Ilgen (1798) as his point of departure for describing the thematic structure of the Hexaemeron of Genesis 1 (*Genesis* [GHAT 1; Göttingen: Vandenhoeck & Ruprecht, 1917] 118).

5 Clark and Holquist, 186.

6 Clark and Holquist, 186.

7 W. Godzich, "Foreword," in M. M. Bakhtin/P. N. Medvedev, *The Formal Method in Literary Scholarship: A Critical Introduction to Sociological Poetics*, trans. A. J. Wehrle (Cambridge: Harvard University Press, 1985) xi.

8 Clark and Holquist, 188-89.

9 The authorship of many works attributed to Bakhtin and others in his circle remains problematic (see Clark and Holquist, 151, 165, 169-70). Unless otherwise noted, the works cited here are considered to have come essentially from Bakhtin without denying the possibility of contributions from others within Bakhtin's circle.

10 Bakhtin/Medvedev, 26.

11 V. N. Volosinov/M. M. Bakhtin, *Marxism and the Philosophy of Language*, trans. L. Matjeka and I. P. Titunik (New York: Sernium Press, 1973) 188.

12 Bakhtin/Medvedev, 7-15, 19.

13 Bakhtin/Medvedev, 17.

14 Bakhtin/Medvedev, 26.

15 Bakhtin/Medvedev, 30.

16 Bakhtin/Medvedev, 33.

17 Bakhtin/Medvedev, 33.

18 M. Sternberg, *The Poetics of Biblical Narrative: Ideological Literature and the Drama of Reading* (Bloomington: Indiana University Press, 1987) xii.

19 Bakhtin/Medvedev, 95-103.

20 J. Tarlin, "Thinking in Circles: A Brief Introduction to the Work of Bakhtin and Company" (forthcoming) 7. As will be seen in the analysis of Genesis 1, the vague term "mythopoeic," used frequently by commentators to describe the form of the priestly cosmogony of Gen 1:1–2:3, fails to account for many meaningful elements relating to the content of the creation story (see Chapter Six).

21 Tarlin, 8.

22 Bakhtin/Medvedev, 102.

23 Tarlin, 7.

24 Tarlin, 9.

25 F. Jameson, *The Ideologies of Theory: Essays 1971-1986, Volume 1: Situations of Theory* (Minneapolis: University of Minnesota Press, 1988) 139.

26 F. Jameson, *The Political Unconscious: Narrative as a Socially Symbolic Act* (Ithaca: Cornell University Press, 1981) 280.

27 Jameson, *The Political Unconscious*, 33.

28 P. Ricoeur, *Lectures on Ideology and Utopia*, ed. G. H. Taylor (New York: Columbia University Press, 1986) 259.

29Ricoeur, 259.

30 Ricoeur, 266.

31 Cf. C. Geertz, "Ideology as a Cultural System," in *The Interpretation of Cultures: Selected Essays* (New York: Basic Books, 1973) 208-10.

32 Jameson, *The Ideologies of Theory*, 140.

33 T. Eagleton, *Literary Theory: An Introduction* (Minneapolis: University of Minnesota Press, 1983) 14.

34 Cf. Q. Skinner, "Motives, Intentions, and the Interpretations of Texts," *New Literary History* 3 (1972) 393-408; M. G. Brett, "Motives and Intentions in Genesis 1," *JTS* 42 (1991) 1-16. The distinction between communicative intention and motives is illustrated in the distinction between *"what* an author is trying to say" and *"why* it is being said" (Brett, 5).

35 Brett, 16.

36 Probably the most extreme example of the numerous structures one can discern in Genesis 1 is P. Beauchamp's thorough work *Création et séparation: Étude exégétique du chapitre premier de la Genèse* (BSR; Paris: Desclée de Brouwer, 1969) 17-148.

37 Jameson, *The Political Unconscious*, 169-205.

38 K. Burke, *A Grammar of Motives* (Berkeley: University of California Press, 1969) 510-12.

39 Jameson, *The Ideologies of Theory*, 139.

40 K. Burke, "Dramatism," in *IESS*, vol. 7, 445.

41 Burke, "Dramatism," 445.

42 Burke, *A Grammar of Motives*, xv.

43 Burke, *A Grammar of Motives*, xx.

44 Burke, *A Grammar of Motives*, 6-7.

45 Burke, *A Grammar of Motives*, 7.

46 Burke, *A Grammar of Motives*, 19-20.

47 Jameson, *The Ideologies of Theory*, 151.

48 Eagleton, 116.

49 George Steiner effectively reverses the truism by observing that all interpretation, indeed, all communication is an act of translation (*After Babel: Aspects of Language and Translation* [New York: Oxford University Press, 1975] 47).

50 See C. R. Taber, "Translation as Interpretation," *Interpretation* 32 (1978) 131.

51 Taber, 143.

52 J. D. Purvis, *The Samaritan Pentateuch and the Origin of the Samaritan Sect* (HSM 2; Cambridge: Harvard University Press, 1968) 52.

53 For example, the increased use of the letters *waw* and *yod* as *matres lectionis* rendered the Hebrew words more intelligible with fuller spelling.

54 M. J. Mulder, "The Transmission of the Biblical Text," in *Mikra: Text, Translation, Reading and Interpretation of the Hebrew Bible in Ancient Judaism and Early Christianity*, ed. M. J. Mulder and H. Sysling (Philadelphia: Fortress Press, 1988) 96.

55 See B. M. Metzger's discussion in *The Text of the New Testament: Its Transmission, Corruption, and Restoration* (New York: Oxford University Press, 1964) 112-3.

56 Metzger, *The Text of the New Testament*, 112; J. Finegan, *Encountering New Testament Manuscripts: A Working Introduction to Textual Criticism* (Grand Rapids: William B. Eerdmans Publishing Company, 1974) 61.

57 Finegan, 61.

58 Finegan, 62; Metzger, 161.

59 E.g., J. H. Hayes describes them as the "two general principles which certainly must be employed in biblical textual criticism" (*An Introduction to Old Testament Study* [Nashville: Abingdon, 1979] 80-1).

60 For example, A. C. Clark argued for the principle *longior lectio potior*: "A text is like a traveller who goes from one inn to another, losing an article of luggage at each halt" ("The Primitive Text of the Gospels and Acts: A Rejoinder," *JTS* 16 [1915] 233).

61   P. K. McCarter, Jr., *Textual Criticism: Recovering the Text of the Hebrew Bible* (GBSOTS; Philadelphia: Fortress Press, 1986) 19.

62   A. E. Housman, ed., *M. Manilii Astronomicon*, vol. 1 (2nd ed; London: Cambridge University Press, 1937) liii-liv.

63   McCarter, 21.

64   McCarter, 21.

65   McCarter, 73.

66   Cf. McCarter, 72-74.

67   McCarter, 12.

68   E. Tov, *The Text-Critical Use of the Septuagint in Biblical Research* (Jerusalem: Simor Ltd., 1981) 34.

69   Tov, *Text-Critical Use*, 277.

70   Tov, *Text-Critical Use*, 34 n. 4.

71   Tov's phraseology is understandably tentative (281). However, I would even deny that there is such a thing as an "objective retroversion." As M. H. Goshen-Gottstein aptly puts it: "There can be no such thing as 'objective retroversion.'. . . The true difference in this case is not between objective facts and subjective attempts to get rid of those alleged facts, but between what I shall call for lack of better terms *mechanical* and *interpretive* retroversion, both of which are in general equally 'subjective.'" ("Theory and Practice of Textual Criticism: The Text-Critical Use of the Septuagint," *Textus* 3 [1963] 133).

72   Tov, 34 n. 4.

73   Tov, 284.

74   Tov, 281.

75   Tov, 288.

76   Tov, 292.

77   See also R. W. Klein's discussion of Jeremiah in *Textual Criticism of the Old Testament: The Septuagint after Qumran* (GBSOTS; Philadelphia: Fortress Press, 1974) 20-21, 30-35, 42.

78   Tov, 308.

79   Tov, 208.

80   Klein, 42.

81   See M. Fishbane, *Biblical Interpretation in Ancient Israel* (Oxford: Clarendon Press, 1985) 23-43.

82   Fishbane, *Biblical Interpretation in Ancient Israel*, 23.

83   Fishbane organizes his study along a continuum of increasing scribal activity, from scribal corrections to mantological exegesis (*Biblical Interpretation in Ancient Israel*, 44-524).

84   Fishbane, *Biblical Interpretation in Ancient Israel*, 543.

85   See, for example, Fishbane, *Biblical Interpretation in Ancient Israel*, 32-37.

86   McCarter, 21.

87   E.g., J. Cook, "Genesis I in the Septuagint as Example of the Problem: Text and Tradition," *JNSL* 10 (1982) 25; G. J. Wenham, *Genesis 1–15* (WBC 1; Waco: Word Books, 1987) 6; C. Westermann, *Genesis 1–11*, trans. J. J. Scullion (Minneapolis: Augsburg Publishing House, 1984) 78; M. Alexandre, *Le commencement du livre Genèse I-V* (CAB 3; Paris: Beauchesne, 1988) 45-46; Beauchamp, *Création et séparation*, 26; H. Gunkel, *Genesis*, 108; B. Jacob, *Das Erste Buch der Tora: Genesis* (New York: KTAV, 1934) 39.

88 G. J. Spurrell, *Notes on the Hebrew Text of the Book of Genesis* (Oxford: Clarendon Press, 1887) 7-8; A. Dillmann, *Genesis Critically and Exegetically Expounded*, trans. W. B. Stevenson (Edinburgh: T. & T. Clark, 1897) 59. W. H. Schmidt, *Die Schöpfungsgeschichte der Priesterschrift* (WMANT 17; Neukirchen-Vluyn: Neukirchener Verlag, 1964) 56; O. Steck, *Der Schöpfungsbericht der Priesterschrift: Studien zur literarkritischen und überlieferungsgeschichtlichen Problematik von Genesis 1,1–2,4a* (FRLANT 115; Göttingen: Vandenhoeck & Ruprecht, 1975) 41-43; E. A. Spieser, *Genesis* (AB 1; Garden City: Doubleday and Company, 1964) 6-7; and B. Vawter, *On Genesis: A New Reading* (Garden City: Doubleday and Company, 1977) 43, 45.

89 J. Cook, "The Exegesis of the Greek Genesis," in *VI Congress of the International Organization for Septuagint and Cognate Studies: Jerusalem 1986* (ed. C. Cox, SCS 23; Atlanta: Scholars Press, 1987) 91-110. His thesis is entirely opposed to his earlier article (see n. 87 above). Although helpful, Cook's most recent analysis is imprecisely formulated and inaccurate in some cases. Cook's article, however, will serve as a point of departure for discussing the respective ideological slants of the textual versions (see Chapter Six).

2

The Septuagint Text of Genesis 1:1–2:3

Historical Background

The origins of the Septuagint (lxx) began with a translation of the Pentateuch in Alexandria, Egypt, around the mid-third century bce. Evidence of this comes primarily from the legendary Letter of Aristeas[1] and a fragment attributed to the second century bce Jewish philosopher Aristobulus,[2] both of which mention the commissioning King Ptolemy II (Philadelphus, 285-247 bce). Conjectures as to the date of the letter itself range from 250 bce to 100 ce.[3] Indeed, as early as Jerome, the authenticity of the letter was questioned.[4] One glaring example of historical inaccuracy is the fact that Demetrius of Phalerum, who according to Aristeas prompted the king to commission the translation, was never chief librarian at Alexandria.[5] Many modern commentators have considered the letter a Jewish apologia whose intended audience was Greek, but V. Tcherikover makes the case that the letter was probably written for a Jewish audience.[6] Most probably, the letter did not exclude either cultural group, which existed side by side in Hellenistic Alexandria.[7] In either case, the author's aim was primarily apologetic, since much of the letter was a defense for a particular Greek translation of the Pentateuch.[8] Reduced to its core, the letter suggests that a Greek translation of the Pentateuch was produced sometime in the third century bce and that Egypt was its place of origin.

P. Kahle argued vigorously against the letter's claim that such a translation was ever produced in the third century BCE, concluding that the letter was written between 130 and 100 BCE as a piece of propaganda, and as such, "we can be quite sure that the translation with which it deals was finished at about the time when the letter was written."[9] Thus, according to Kahle, the recension of the Greek Pentateuch was carried out in the second half of the second century BCE.

Wevers, among others, has identified problems with Kahle's translation of the letter[10] and notes that had the Greek revision been made as late as ca. 100 BCE, it is unusual that the work would have been limited to the Pentateuch and would not have included the "Law and the Prophets and the rest of the books," as mentioned in the prologue of Ben Sirach.[11]

The historical claim of the letter is also vindicated by one crucial piece of external evidence, namely the chronological system worked out by Demetrius the Hellenist, who flourished in the late third century BCE.[12] His work on biblical chronology reflected for the most part the Genesis chronology of the LXX.[13] As J. Hanson points out, "Demetrius is the first witness to the use of the Septuagint, or at least of the Greek Pentateuch."[14] Indeed, Demetrius' work is the only independent attestation for Aristeas' claim that the LXX was in existence by the middle of the third century BCE. In addition, Wevers supports such a dating and provenance for the LXX Pentateuch by internal evidence: Linguistically the books of the Greek Pentateuch share much in common with "what is known from papyri to fit third century usage," and the Greek language reflects Egyptian usage.[15] Contemporaneous with the author of the letter (ca. 170 BCE?), the LXX was evidently one of several translations by the early second century BCE.[16]

With the Egyptian provenance for the Greek translation well established, F. M. Cross has suggested that the Hebrew recension associated with the *Vorlage* of the LXX was in fact indigenous to Egypt, and that two other recensions originated in Palestine and Babylon. Cross claims that the *Vorlage* of the LXX "separated from the Old Palestinian textual tradition no later than 400 BC."[17] As Gooding has pointed out, confusions in terminology have mired Cross's attempts to demonstrate this.[18] Cross readily admits that the evidence from Qumran bears striking similarity to retroverted reconstructions of the Greek text. However, as G. Howard observes, "in almost any given instance, the LXX, as we have it today, can be equated with one of the Palestinian recensions which have turned up at Qumran."[19] Such an observation also applies to two Genesis fragments from Cave 4.[20] Thus, for now, the provenance of the LXX's *Vorlage* remains an open question. In Tov's words, "the LXX does not reflect any Hebrew text which was characteristic of Egypt."[21]

MANUSCRIPT SOURCES FOR THE LXX OF GENESIS 1:1–2:3

The manuscript tradition of the LXX is extensive. A. Rahlfs has enumerated over 1,500 complete and fragmentary manuscripts.[22] Fortunately, it is fairly easy to establish the LXX text of Gen 1:1–2:3, for significant textual variations are not extensive. Since neither Codex Vaticanus nor Codex Sinaiticus contains the passage, the manuscript most important for Genesis 1 is that of Codex Alexandrinus (fifth century CE), the basis of the Cambridge edition.[23] Other codices containing Gen 1:1–2:3 include D (fifth/sixth century CE), M (seventh century CE), and E (ninth/tenth century CE).[24] The pertinent minuscules are too numerous to mention but are equally valuable as the extant uncials. Of note is Wevers's observation that no Lucianic group can be detected in Genesis.[25]

The Codex Alexandrinus (A) departs from Rahlfs's and Wevers's reconstructed text most significantly in 1:11 and 14. In 1:11, A adds after the second *kata genos* the term *eis homoiotēta*. A wealth of minuscules, however, counts against this addition as part of an earlier reading.[26] In 1:14, A (along with D) seemingly adds between *tēs gēs* and *diachorizein* ("to divide") the words *kai archein tēs hēmeras kai tēs nuktos* ("to rule the day and the night"), which can easily be explained as an expansion along the line of 1:16. In both of these variants (in 1:11 and 14), the contextual and textual considerations clearly outweigh A, hence, Wevers's preference to view A as containing later deviations in these two verses. It must be admitted, however, that the Göttingen text of Genesis, which Wevers edited, is undeniably a reconstructed, eclectic text that relies on no single manuscript, in contrast to the Cambridge edition. With the exception of the variations noted in vv 11 and 14, A is for the most part identical to the eclectic Göttingen edition.[27]

Also of note is the fact that only very few of the manuscripts correspond to the *structure* of the MT for Genesis 1. Only the Hexaplaric and Catena groups ("chains" of comments compiled from writers such as the early church fathers, Philo, and Josephus)[28] add the transition marker at the end of 1:7, along with what Wevers identifies as the s and t families of texts, both clearly influenced by Origen.[29] Only manuscript 75 deletes 1:9b in accordance with the MT. However, influence from the MT is not consistent: Manuscript 75, along with 508 and its Old Latin translation, codex 111, adds the transition marker *kai egeneto houtōs* at the end of 1:26 between the last divine command and fulfillment, contrary to both the MT and the LXX traditions.[30] The fact that the transition marker occurs in 1:30 in all other manuscripts suggests that these three manuscripts are the work of a later harmonizing hand.

In summary, it is clear that the LXX textual history represents a *fairly* consistent tradition, despite minor variant attestations, for Gen 1:1–2:3. Although any reconstructed early LXX text is inescapably conjectural, one can assuredly arrive at a text, be it conjectured or represented by the Codex Alexandrinus, that represents a textual tradition significantly different from that of the MT.

The following section consists of translation, discussion of exegetical issues, and analysis of the structure of the Septuagint text for Gen 1:1–2:3. The issue of structure will prove most helpful in underscoring the textual differences between the MT and the reconstructed *Vorlage* of the LXX. This chapter ultimately serves only as a means to that end. However, an appreciation of the Greek text as it stands will best enable the exegete to reconstruct the Hebrew *Vorlage* of the LXX and its relationship to the MT.

TRANSLATION OF THE SEPTUAGINT TEXT
OF GENESIS 1:1–2:3

1:1   In the beginning[31] God made the heaven and the earth.

1:2   Yet[32] the earth was invisible[33] and unformed,[34] and darkness was[35]over the unfathomable deep, while the breath[36] of God was floating[37] upon the water.

1:3   And God said, "Let light come into being," and light came into being.

1:4   And God saw the light, that it was good, and God separated between[38] the light and between the darkness.

1:5   And God called the light day, and the darkness he called night. And evening came and morning came, day one.[39]

1:6   And God said, "Let a firmament in the midst of the water come into being, and let it separate[40] between water and water." And it came about as follows:[41]

1:7   God made the firmament and God[42] divided between the water, which was under the firmament, and the water above the firmament.[43]

1:8   And God called the firmament heaven. And God saw that it was good. And evening came and morning came, the second day.

1:9   And God said, "Let the water below the heaven be collected into one collection,[44] and let the dry land appear." And it came about as follows:

The water under the heaven was gathered into their collections, and the dry land appeared.[45]

1:10 And God called the dry land earth and the (various) consolidations[46] of waters he called seas. And God saw that it was good.

1:11 And God said, "Let the earth produce[47] plants of the pasture,[48] reproducing[49] seed according to genus[50] and according to likeness,[51] and fruitful trees of wood[52] that produce fruit, whose seed is in it[53] according to genus[54] upon the earth." And it came about as follows:

1:12 The earth brought forth[55] plants of the pasture, reproducing seed according to kind and according to likeness, and fruitful trees of wood that produce fruit, whose seed is in it according to kind upon the earth. And God saw that it was good.

1:13 And evening came and morning came, the third day.

1:14 And God said, "Let there come into being celestial luminaries in the firmament of heaven for illumination[56] of the earth,[57] to divide between the day and the night, and let them be for signs and for seasons and for days and for years.

1:15 And let them be for illumination in the firmament of heaven so as to shine upon the earth." And it came about as follows:

1:16 God made the two great celestial luminaries, the greater celestial luminary for regulating[58] the day and the smaller celestial luminary for regulating the night, and the stars.

1:17 And God placed them in the firmament of heaven so as to shine upon the earth,

1:18 and to rule over the day and the night and to divide between the light and the darkness. And God saw that it was good.

1:19 And evening came and morning came, the fourth day.

1:20 And God said, "Let the waters[59] bring forth[60] sea creatures[61] (consisting) of[62] living souls and winged creatures that fly[63] upon the earth toward the firmament of heaven." And it came about as follows:

1:21 God made the great sea-monsters and every soul of the living sea creatures, which[64] the waters brought forth according to their genus, and every winged creature according to genus. And God saw that they were good.

1:22 And God blessed them, saying, "Increase and multiply and fill the waters in the seas, and let the winged creatures multiply upon the earth."

1:23 And evening came and morning came, the fifth day.

1:24 And God said, "Let the earth bring forth the living soul according to genus, quadrupeds and reptiles and wild animals of the land[65] according to genus." And it came about as follows:

1:25   God made the wild animals of the land according to genus and the herds[66] according to genus[67] and all the reptiles of the land according to genus.[68] And God saw that they were good.

1:26   And God said, "Let us make a human creature according to our[69] image[70] and likeness, and let it rule over the fish of the sea and the winged creatures of heaven and the herds[71] and all the land and all the reptiles that crawl upon the land."[72]

1:27   And God made the human creature, according to God's image, he made it, male and female he made them.

1:28   And God blessed them saying, "Increase and multiply and fill the land and exercise dominion over it, and rule over the fish of the sea and the winged creatures of heaven and all the land and all the reptiles that crawl upon the land."[73]

1:29   And God said, "See, I hereby give to you every sowable field plant[74] that reproduces seed, which[75] is above the ground, and every tree (of wood), which has in itself fruit of sowable seed, to you it shall be for eating,

1:30   and to all the wild animals of the land and all the winged creatures of heaven and every reptile that crawls upon the land, that has in itself the soul of life, even every field plant for food." And it came about as such.[76]

1:31   And God saw all the things, as many as he had made, and, indeed, they were very good. And evening came and morning came, the sixth[77] day.

2:1   And heaven and earth were completed and all the order thereof.

2:2   And God completed on the sixth day his works, which he had done, and he rested[78] on the seventh day from all of his works, which he had done.

2:3   And God blessed the seventh day and sanctified it, because on it he rested from all his works, which God had begun[79] to do.

STRUCTURE IN GENESIS 1:1–2:3 OF LXX

Formal Structure

Even a cursory glance can discern a tightly woven structure in the LXX of Gen 1:1–2:3. At the broadest level an inclusio marked by similar language in 1:1 (*en archē̦ epoiēsen ho theos*) and 2:3 (*hōn ērxato ho theos poiēsai*) demarcates this passage as a whole. The last verb in 2:3 (from *archomai*) is related etymologically to the temporal noun in 1:1 (*archē*). In fact, the translator probably chose this verb in 2:3 to divide the unit between 2:3 and 2:4, since any corresponding Hebrew verb for *ērxato* is not present in the MT.

Most striking from a structural standpoint, however, is the material in 1:3-31, in which certain formulaic elements are consistently repeated.

This major section is formally set off from the surrounding material. The material preceding and following this unit does not present creation as formally described in 1:3-31, but consists of a descriptive condition (1:2), a summary statement (2:1-2a), and a report of divine actions in relation to the sabbath (2:2b-3). Gen 1:1, though a creation statement of sorts (see below), is formally set apart from vv 3-31 by the absence of a corresponding *Wortbericht* and the addition of the temporal phrase *en archę*.

In contrast, the material in vv 3-31 is replete with formulaic repetitions. Marking off the largest units within this block are the repeated day-enumeration formulas (*kai egeneto hespera kai egeneto prōi, hēmera X*), which conclude each day-section. Furthermore, within each day-section are found repeated elements. The most common elements include in typical order:

1. Divine command
2. Transition formula (*kai egeneto houtōs*)
3. Fulfillment of the command
4. Divine naming
5. Divine approbation
6. Day enumeration

These elements can be recognized as formal components merely by virtue of their repeated use throughout the six days of creation. There are two day-sections in the LXX that incorporate all of these elements: the creation of the firmament on the second day (vv 6-8) and the collection of the waters on the third day (vv 9-10), in which the day-enumeration formula is deferred to v 12. The MT, on the other hand, has no day-section that incorporates all of the elements listed above (see Chapter Three).

Variations of this repeated pattern represent, naturally, variations in content. For instance, the divine naming formula is absent in the creation account beginning with the creation of vegetation (vv 11-13), thereby underscoring the first three acts of creation (light, firmament, seas, and land) as distinct from all that follows. Also a new component is introduced in the fifth and sixth days, namely that of blessing in 1:22 and 28. In addition, the section concerning the first day reverses the typical order of divine naming and approbation. How these formal elements are arranged throughout each day-section (in 1:3-31) in contrast to the surrounding material is illustrated by the following structural outline of

Gen 1:1–2:3. The outline seeks to highlight the more formulaic components of the passage with only limited reference to content.

Outline of the Formal Structure of Genesis 1:1–2:3

Formal Structure of the Hexaemeron[80]

Again, one can easily see how the unit 1:3-31 is formally set apart
from the surrounding material, given the highly formulaic language in
which it is cast. This tightly structured unit reports divine activity (divine
speech and action) within the formal context of six days and the thematic
context of creation. An inclusio is formed around the six days, since *ho
ouranos* and *hē gē* are terms common to 1:1 and 2:1 in identical order.
Verse 2:2a is inextricably linked to the previous verse by the common
verb and its summarizing force (in contrast to the MT!). Thus 2:1-2a must
be considered a summarizing unit concluding the six days of creation.

What comes after 2:2a is different both in form and content. The
seventh day-section does not report any creation. On a formal level, one
notes the absence of the day-enumeration formula in the seventh day-
section. Moreover, the last day-section lacks the divine speech/act
correlation typical of the Hexaemeron. Thus the divine action described
in 2:2b-3 is on formal grounds "non-creative." This corresponds to the
fact that nothing material is created on the seventh day. Similarly, Gen

1:1 must also be considered *formally* a "non-creative" statement, although it does describe the creation of something (see below).

Most of the formal components of 1:3-31 within each day-section bear clearly defined roles by virtue of their consistent positions relative to each other. Every command, for instance, has its corresponding fulfillment report and vice versa. The divine approbation formula consistently appears in every day-section, with the final approval (1:31) applying to all the preceding acts. Most of these components function unambiguously. The function of the phrase *kai egeneto houtōs*, however, is not so clear at first glance, and therefore merits further attention.

In his examination of the Masoretic text, Coats designates the phrase as an "execution formula,"[81] similar to H. Holzinger's "Einleitung zur Ausführung des Befehls,"[82] O. Loretz's "Vollzugsbestätigung,"[83] W. Schmidt's "Geschensformel,"[84] and P. Beauchamp's and M. Alexandre's "formules d'accomplissement."[85] Coats notes that the formula usually serves as the link between two dependent parts. "Its peculiar structural intention is to show the interaction between the command and fulfillment."[86] As to the kind of "interaction," Coats neither specifies nor notices that in fifty percent of the cases *in the* MT (1:7, 9, and 30) this formula does not stand between "command" and "fulfillment." Without realizing it, Coats appears to have formed conclusions more appropriate to the LXX, which uses this formula more consistently than the MT.

It is clear that the formula's function in the LXX serves to make the transition from command to realization, from word to act. Broken down into its syntactic structure, the phrase *kai egeneto houtōs* points both backwards and forwards. The impersonal subject of the predicate clearly refers back to the content of the command. The adverbial particle *houtōs* points forward to the realization and can be rendered "*and it came about as follows.*" Hence, the formula serves double duty by both concluding the divine command and introducing the fulfillment. Whereas all other formulas vary according to content and theme, the transition formula invests each day-section with a sense of familiarity and methodical progression.

The last instance of this transitional phrase bears a different nuance in 1:30. Its context is similar to all its other attestations in that it occurs after a divine declaration, and thus serves to conclude the divine word. However, the divine word in 1:29 is not a command but a decree (*Idou dedōka* . . .), since it does not anticipate another act of creation. Thus the "transition marker" in this context assumes the concrete realization of the decree, namely, the permission to eat certain types of food. The fulfillment is understood as contained within the transitional phrase. The transition marker's unique context is dictated by the fact that a decree and not a command is what is fulfilled.

However, justifying its placement at this position does not explain why the formula is missing between the command and creation of humans beings (1:26-27). Its additional function as a "decree execution formula" seems natural enough, but its absence between 1:26 and 1:27 remains anomalous. In sum, the appearance of this phrase is thoroughly consistent from the second to seventh acts of creation. Its anomalous absence in the first and last acts of creation (light and human beings) in the LXX sets these particular creations apart from the rest of the creative acts and, as will be shown below, can be explained on the basis of the overall *thematic* structure of the Hexaemeron.

The Introduction

Since 1:3-31 describes the formal progression of creation beginning with the creation of light and ending with that of human beings, the material in 1:1-2 evidently describes something other than formal creation. As suggested above, the first verse depicts a creation of heaven and earth, since the following verse is a continuation of 1:1 as implied by the force of the postpositive particle *hē* in 1:2. In other words, 1:1, though introductory, does not function as a superscription or title to the passage as a whole but depicts the first "creation," namely that of heaven and earth, an incomplete cosmos. The second verse then qualifies the kind of earth created, namely unformed and invisible, an "aformal" creation, as it were. Therefore verses 3-10 depict, in part, the actual formation of the earth or land. Indeed, nowhere is it said that the earth was created (*poieō*) except in 1:1. In vv 9-10 it appears or literally "becomes seen" (from *horaō*).

In short, the LXX construes the first verse as an initial step in the creative process, but a step that remains apart from the formal creation reported in 1:3-31. It is a creation that lacks form (1:2). By implication, the LXX leaves open the possibility of interpreting the first verse in terms of a *creatio ex nihilo*, as was done by early Christian exegetes,[87] although the doctrine is nowhere explicit in the LXX.

Excursus: Creatio ex nihilo?

It is difficult to locate when the doctrine of *creatio ex nihilo* first emerged in Jewish-Christian thought and literature. In his study of the development of this doctrine in Jewish and early Christian theology, G.

May finds in the Christian gnostic Basilides in the second half of the second century CE the first unambiguous reference to creation out of nothing, while acknowledging the possibility of the concept's having antecedents.[88] The first Christian theologian to expound the doctrine was Theophilus of Antioch, whose work suggests that it was already a traditional Christian perspective.[89] May suggests that the concept of *creatio ex nihilo* can be pushed as far back as the beginning of the second century CE in Antioch.

Another more disputed text comes from *Genesis Rabbah* 1.9.1, which describes the response of Rabban Gamaliel II (ca. 100 CE) to a "philosopher's" suggestion that God was a great artist who had good materials to help him. The variety of materials the philosopher names comes from Gen 1:2: *tōhû, bōhû, ḥōšek, mayyim, rûaḥ,* and *tĕhômôt*. Gamaliel responds by claiming that "all of them are explicitly described as having been created by (God)." D. Winston[90] and May both argue that Gamaliel's response reflects only an isolated incident and arose from the "Erfordernissen aktueller Diskussionen."[91] J. Goldstein, on the other hand, views it as a bona fide claim of *creatio ex nihilo*.[92]

Isolated or not, the account betrays a diversity in early Jewish thought with regard to creation, as also reflected in the Babylonian Talmud *Hagiga* 12a and the midrash *Shemoth Rabba* 15:22, in contrast to Wis 11:17 and *Genesis Rabbah* 10.3.1, which imply the contrary. In addition, the debated text of 2 Macc 7:22-29, which Origen took as the first unequivocal statement in scripture espousing the doctrine of *creatio ex nihilo*, makes, at least, progress towards the development of the doctrine, even if it cannot be considered an explicit formulation of the teaching.[93]

Given the consensus among the Greek philosophers beginning with Thales (sixth century BCE) concerning preexistent material and the lack of unambiguous textual evidence asserting the contrary before the Common Era, it is hard to imagine the LXX expounding the doctrine of *creatio ex nihilo*. However, G. Stead refers to several texts from Eudorus of Alexandria (ca. 25 BCE), Simplicius, and Alexander of Aphoridisias, which all suggest a minority, albeit late, view within classical Greek circles that favored *creatio ex nihilo*.[94] Furthermore, Cicero's proof that God could not have created anything without preexistent material as quoted by Lactantius (*The Divine Institutes* 2.9) suggests that the contrary view was popular as early as the first century BCE. In fact, the strong insistence among most Greek philosophers of the preexistence of material could imply contact with an opposing view.[95]

Similarly, another *crux interpretum* in scholarship is the issue of whether Philo endorsed such a doctrine or was even aware of it.[96] Indeed, frustration over the investigation is expressed by Winston: "Philo's descriptions of preexistent matter appear to be almost deliberately vague."[97] To be sure, Philo's work is replete with passages that refer to God "bringing," "leading," "creating," or "calling"[98] into existence from the non-existent (*ek tou mē ontos* [or *ontōn*]). One typical statement that seems to come close to the doctrine of *creatio ex nihilo* is found in Philo's *De Somnis* 1.76:

> God gave birth (*gennēsas*) to all things (*ta panta*), not only brought them into sight, but also made (*epoiēsen*) things that before were not (*ha proteron ouk ēn*), not just handling material as an artificer (*dēmiourgos*), but being himself its creator (*ktistēs*).

As H.-F. Weiss has pointed out, the key word *ktistes* normally refers in Philo's work to God as a "*Städtegründer*," and thus "Nichtvorhandensein einer dieser Schöpfung gegenüber primären Materie wird an dieser Stelle überhaupt nicht reflektiert!"[99] Winston claims that the passage "may simply mean that God . . . established the very structure of matter, thereby bringing into being forms that did not exist before."[100] Indeed, this seems to be the case in Wis 1:14: *ektisen gar eis to einai ta panta*, in which "bringing into existence" does not at all imply *creatio ex nihilo* (see Wis 11:17: *kai ktisasa ton kosmon ex amorphon hylēs*). Elsewhere Philo explicitly posits the reality of shapeless matter (*amorphos hylē*), from which God creates all things (*panta egennēsen* [*De specialibus legibus* 1, 328-29]), and in another passage claims that *ek tou mē ontos ouden ginetai* (*De aeternitate mundi* 5). In addition, Philo's account of the creation of manna describes God as simply "changing around the elements" (*metabalōn ta stoicheia* [*De vita Moses* 2.267]) so that the air rather than the earth would carry (*phere*) food (see also *De. spec. leg.* 2.225). The above passages would seem to imply that for Philo *to mē on* or *ta mē onta* does not necessarily imply *nihilo* in any formal sense.

Yet Philo is insistent that God alone is uncreated (*Legum allegoriarum* 2.1.2). God is the creator of ideas in the same way an architect creates a plan for a city (*Opf.* 16-22). As Wolfson correctly points out, Philo ascribes the creation of the Forms to God, whereas for Plato they are ungenerated.[101] With regard to the LXX text, upon which he was dependent, Philo uses the first three verses of Genesis as a description of God's creation of the world of ideas or forms: *prōton oun ho poiōn epoiēsen ouranon asōmaton kai gēn aoraton, kai aeros idean, kai kenou* (*Opf.* 29). Light, for instance, is an "incorporeal pattern" (*asōmaton en kai noēton . . . paradeigma*). Thus, one must concede that "logically, of course, God is for Philo, indirectly the source of pre-existent matter."[102] Philo's unsystematic creation philosophy, if pressed hard enough by later standards of philosphical thought, would very well begin to posit the *creatio ex nihilo* doctrine. However, as May puts it, the conception concerning the creation out of the non-existent (things) is not the

> Antitheses zur Annahme einer ewigen Materie und zum Prinzip 'ex nihilo nihil fit' zu verstehen, sondern es handelt sich hier um unreflektierte, alltagssprachliche Wendungen, die zum Ausdruck bringen sollen, daß durch den Schöpfungsakt bisher nicht Existierendes entstanden ist.[103]

Thus, Philo can and does say, like Rabban Gamaliel, that God created everything, but this does not necessarily imply a *creatio ex nihilo*, given his statements on non-existence elsewhere. In sum, Philo's philosophical and exegetical investigations into the scriptural account of creation employed language that later came to contain some of the trademarks of the doctrine of *creatio ex nihilo* as first theoretically expounded by several of the Ante-Nicene Fathers. However, Philo himself, at least a century earlier, never quite made the precise formulation.

In sum, no concrete instance can be cited that proves that the doctrine existed by the time the LXX was written. In fact, more evidence to the contrary can be marshalled. Furthermore, some of the earliest Christian commentators, in their effort to reconcile Platonic philosophy and biblical exegesis, claimed a creation from shapeless matter (e.g., Justin Martyr *First Apology* 59) or at least allowed it as a legitimate interpretaton (e.g., Athenagoras *The Resurrection of the Dead* 3). Yet, conversely, one cannot claim that the doctrine of *creatio ex nihilo* suddenly came upon the scene in the second century CE via the Christian struggle with Gnosticism.[104] Indeed, its conceptual precursor, namely the claim that God created every *thing* (that is, whatever has concrete form), is attested prior to the second century CE. Thus, at most one can say that the LXX endorses neither *creatio ex nihilo* nor *ex aliquo*, yet due to its differing grammatical construal of the Hebrew MT of Gen 1:1-3 (see chapter 3), the Greek translation nevertheless helped facilitate the development of the doctrine of *creatio ex nihilo* when it did emerge. The LXX shifts the focus away from the *creatio ex aliquo* of the Hebrew and towards a *creatio de omnibus*.

It took three centuries before Theophilus took the silence of Gen 1:1 a simple step further to formulate the doctrine of *creatio ex nihilo* (*ex ouk ontōn poiein* [*Ad Autolycum* 2.4; see also 2.10]). Theophilus cast the doctrine in terms echoing his Jewish predecessors (as did also Tatian *Ad Graecos* 5; Irenaeus *Against the Heresies* 2. 10.3,4; and Tertullian *Against Hermogenes* 34). Similarly, Tertullian argued precisely from the "silence" of the LXX:

> For in the case of what is made out of nothing, it is clear that it was made out of nothing from the very fact that it is not shown to have been made out of something (*quoniam, quod fit ex nihilo, eo ipso, dum non ostenditur ex aliquo factum, manifestatur ex nihilo factum*).[105]

From Ambrose to the Latin authors of the Middle Ages, Gen 1:1 alone was considered sufficient and irrefutable means for refuting the Platonic doctrine of the eternity of matter.[106] However, such exegetical arguments for *creatio ex nihilo* based exclusively on the silence of the Greek translation of Gen 1:1 simply begged the question.

Double Creation and Form in Gen 1:1-3

What is implied, then, in Gen 1:1-3 of the LXX is a "double creation": Heaven and earth are the created "aformal" substances from which the entities *named* "heaven" and "earth" are fashioned in vv 6-8 and 9-10, respectively, within the formal creation account of six days.[107] The formal structure of 1:3-31, thus, coincides with the content of creation in that creation is given definitive form. How that is depicted is best highlighted by examining the *thematic* structure of 1:3-31.

Corresponding Thematic Structure

Introduction

In contrast to the formal structure described above, which centers on the repetition of stock phrases, there is another structure evident in Gen 1:3-31 that corresponds in part to the formal structure. For lack of a better description, I shall call this the "thematic structure." Specifically, this structure is formed around the content of the different *acts* of creation in relation to three spatial divisions. Attempts to describe the overall structure of the Hexaemeron from this perspective have in common the recognition that the structure consists of two parallel "triads of days" that progress from heaven to water to earth.[108] Naturally, all attempts heretofore have focused on the Masoretic textual tradition,[109] but it will become evident that the LXX version exhibits its own tightly woven thematic structure.

If one were simply to line up the list of creation sections as they are formally divided along two parallel lines, each comprising three days, not much correspondence would be discernible.

1. Light	2. Heaven	3. Seas and land	4. Vegetation
5. Luminaries	6. Sea and winged creatures	7. Land animals	8. Human beings

However, all the creative acts can be arranged under the major spatial categories of "heaven," "water," and "earth." The winged creatures, for instance, fall under the category of **water**, since they are in part produced by the waters (see translation note on 1:20 and below). In addition, the luminaries bear a direct relation not only to the creation of light on the first day but also to the firmament on the second day (vv 14, 15 and 17). With these correlations in mind, it can be shown that the LXX displays a highly organized thematic structure arranged in part according to the formal divisions of labor and organized under three spatial main headings:

Heaven	Waters	Earth
1. Light and 2. Firmament	3. Seas and land	4. Vegetation
5. Luminaries	6. Marine and winged creatures	7. Animals and 8. Human beings

With this structural outline, one observes a point-by-point correlation between each of the three sections arranged in two parallel rows. The two rows designate two halves of the sequential order of the creative process. As Gunkel pointed out, this intended structure explains why the celestial luminaries are not created until after the plants.[110]

The connection between the luminaries, on the one hand, and the creation of light and the firmament, on the other, is obvious in terms of both the location and function (1:14-18) of the luminaries. The parallelism of the middle section is established by the fact that the water is commanded to "bring forth" *both* the aquatic and winged creatures in the divine command of 1:20.[111] The reason "land" is included under the category of waters is due to the causal relation described in v 9 between the collection of waters and the "appearance" (from *horaō*) of dry land (*xēra*): The emergence of land takes place as a result of the horizontal separation of the waters. This causal relation is also confirmed by the formal combination of water and land in 1:9-10. Thus, the creation of land (*xera*), sea, and winged creatures is dependent upon the actions of the waters, according to the LXX. Only after the dry land (*xēra*) is named "earth" (*gē*) in v 10 does the land constitute an independent and productive spatial category (1:11-12, 24).

In short, all the creative acts can be grouped under three major categories that serve as the basic spatial constituents of the cosmos.

1. Heaven is the name designated for the firmament (v 8). It provides the spatial location for the luminaries and is related to the transcendent quality of light itself.

2. Water is the constitutive element that makes up the seas and is instrumental in a passive sense in producing the land and more actively in creating the marine and aerial creatures.

3. The earth serves in part to create both plants and animals and is the principal domain for human beings.

The verbal parallels giving rise to such a thematic structure are listed below.

Light and Heaven (vv 3-5, 6-8; 14-18)

Day 1 (vv 3-5)	Day 4 (vv 14-18)
phōs (vv 3, 4)	*phōsteres* (vv 14, 16)
diechōrisen ho theos ana meson	*diachōrizein ana meson*
tou phōtos kai ana meson	*tou phōtos kai ana*
tou skotous (v 4)	*meson tou skotous* (v 18)
*to phos **hēmeran**, to skotos . . .*	*diachorizein ana meson*
nukta (v 5)	*tēs **hēmeras** kai ana*
	*meson tēs **nuktos*** (v 14)
	*eis archas tēs **hēmeras***
	(vv 16, 18 <*archein*>)
	*eis archas tēs **nuktos***
	(vv 16, 18 <*archein*>)
Day 2 (vv 6-8)	
stereōma (vv 6, 7, 8)	*en tǭ stereōmati tou*
to stereōma ouranon (v 8)	*ouranou* (vv 14, 15, 17)

It is clear that the fourth day-section finds parallels not only with the first, but also with the second day, given the location of the luminaries "in the firmament of heaven." This location is repeated three times as part of the function of illumination (1:15 and 17): The luminaries' role in illuminating the earth is made possible by the fact that they are located in the firmament (*hōste phainein*; Hebrew: *lĕhāʾîr*). In addition, a strong parallel between days one and four is found in 1:18, in which one function of the luminaries repeats almost verbatim 1:4. Whereas God originally divided between light and darkness on the first day, the sun, moon and stars take over this divine role as part of their function.

Water (vv 9-10; 20-22)

Day 3a (vv 9-10)	Day 5 (20-22)
Synachthētō **hydor**	*Exagageto ta* **hydata** . . .
to hypokato tou ouranou (v 9)	*peteina petomena epi tēs gēs*
	kata to stereoma tou ouranou
	(v 20)
ta hydata (v 10)	*ta hydata* (vv 20, 21, 22)
thalassas (v 10)	*en tais thalassais* (v 22)

The connection between the first half of the third day and the fifth day is established by the identical subjects in the respective commands in vv 9 and 20, namely water. In v 20, the waters are called upon to "bring forth" both sea and "winged creatures that fly." Other than God in v 21, water is the primary subject connecting these two sections. In addition, there is a conceptual link between vv 9 and 20. Both verses reflect a common spatial point of reference, namely underneath heaven. This is literally expressed in v 9 in order to distinguish between the waters above and below the firmament/heaven. Verse 20 in part describes the creation of the "winged creatures" whose area of movement is bracketed by the land and the firmament, hence, also below heaven (*kata to stereoma tou ouranou*). Thus, both sections are linked with this expressed point of spatial reference. In short, day five is inextricably tied to the first half of the third day and not in any significant manner to the creation of the firmament as argued by Gunkel and others for the MT (see Chapter Four).

Earth (vv 11-12; 24-25, 26-30)

Day 3b (1:11-12)	Day 6 (1:24-25)
Blastēsato **hē gē** *botanēn*	*Exagageto* **hē gē** *psychen*
chortou (v 11)	*zōsan kata genos* (v 24)
exēnegken hē gē botanēn	*epoiēsen ho theos ta thēria*
chortou (v 12)	(v 25)
kata genos epi tes ges	*thēria tēs gēs* **kata genos**
(vv 11, 12)	(vv 24, 25)

herponton epi tēs gēs (v 26)

plērōsate tēn gēn (v 28)

archete . . . pases tēs gēs (v 28)

botanēn **chortou, speiron** **sperma** (vv 11, 12)	*chorton sporimon* **speiron** **sperma** (v 29)
xylon *karpimon poioun* *karpon ou to sperma autou* *kata genos epi tes ges* (vv 11, 12)	*pan* **xylon**, *ho echei en* *eauto karpon spermatos* *sporimou* (v 29)

As with the parallel sections concerning water, the second subsection of the third day and the sixth day are linked from the outset by the identical subject in the command, namely the earth or land. Despite the different verbs employed, the land animals and plants correspond as objects of the earth's productivity as rendered in the commands (vv 11, 24).

A major change, however, occurs in the actual fulfillment: The earth no longer figures in the creative process; rather, it is God who creates the living animals in 1:25. This change of subjects in the command and fulfillment is also paralleled in the preceding section concerning the waters' creation of the sea and winged creatures in 1:20 and 21. The waters are commanded to "bring forth" creatures, yet God figures as the creator in the fufillment.

Another point of contact between the creation of plants and the creation of animals is the way in which the term for land (*gē*) is used predicatively. With regard to the creation of the plant world, the seeds of the fruit trees are described as "upon the earth," a locative phrase probably also meant to apply to seeds of vegetation in 1:11a and 12a. The earth creates "upon" itself as opposed to within itself or above itself (as in the case of the sea). Conceptually the earth creating "upon" itself is also presupposed in what the earth is commanded to produce in 1:24, namely land animals of many sorts, including the *thēria tēs gēs*, a *terminus technicus* for wild animals. The reptiles in 1:25 are also described as "of the land," as well as "crawling upon the land" (*epi tēs gēs*). Thus plants and animals, though radically different in composition, are described similarly in relation to the land or earth. In sum, the latter half of day three and former half of day six are correlative sections from a thematic perspective.

The creation of human beings in the latter half of day six is also associated with the land, not so much in their actual creation (although this is conceptually presupposed) as in their commission and blessing in 1:28 and 29. The human beings are commanded to fill the earth in exactly the same way as the sea creatures were commanded to fill "the waters in the seas." Thus the acknowledged domain for human beings is the land, and the principal source of sustenance for them comes from the land in the form of vegetation and trees. The earth produces on its own only the plant world, the primary source of nourishment for human beings.

Again, formal distinction is matched by content. The genesis of the plants are formally characterized by the fact that the earth is subject in both the command and fulfillment, whereas animals and human beings are distinguished from plants in that God is described in the fulfillment as their creator. Indeed, one can observe a deliberate progression when one compares the respective subjects mentioned in the command and fulfillment of the creations connected in one way or another to the land.

Plants	Animals	Human Beings
Command: earth	Command: earth	Command: God
Fulfillment: earth	Fulfillment: God	Fulfillment: God

The formal distinctions between these three creations are reflected in the nature of each creation. Land animals (like the sea and winged creatures) have "souls" (*psychai*); human beings, on the other hand, are distinguished from both plants and animals in that they bear resemblance to the divine image (*eikōn*). Yet given these very different products of creation, earth provides the basis for this whole range of life.

Light and Human Beings

In view of the overall symmetrical thematic structure of the LXX described above, there is some tension evident in the first and last acts of creation. The creation of light and that of human beings stand out as special acts on the formal structural level, and thus correspond to each other in some degree. As noted above, only in the sections dealing with the creation of light and human beings does one find the transition marker (*kai egeneto houtōs*) enigmatically missing from its typical location.[112] Thus a tighter connection is forged between command and fulfillment without the formal intermediate step. This structural anomaly alone separates the first and last acts from the rest of creation. In addition, the creation of light is set in relief from the rest of creation in that light is described as having been created impersonally (*kai egeneto phōs*), that is, without divine action in the fulfillment report. In contrast, all other parts of creation are described as created either by God (firmament, luminaries, sea and winged creatures, land animals, and human beings) or by another part of creation (vegetation and the sea and winged creatures).

The creation of human beings is also set apart in several ways. First, the divine command is in some sense self-directed.[113] Indeed, 1:26 is the only instance of a self-exhortation in the creation account. Secondly, in place of the standard nomenclature for distinguishing species (i.e., *kata genos* and variants thereof), human beings are described as created *kat' eikona hēmeteran kai kath' homoiōsin* (v 26) and *kat' eikona theou* (v 27). Whereas all other creatures are organized by their shared characteristics to one another, human beings are set apart by virtue of their resemblance to the divine. Lastly, God blesses human beings with the command to rule over limited aspects of the three basic elements of the cosmos: "over the fish of the *sea* and the winged creatures of *heaven* and the herds and all the *earth* and all the reptiles that crawl upon the *earth*" (vv 26, 28). Each reference to a basic, constitutive part of creation is, however, qualified. For instance, of the marine animals only the fish (*ichthys*) are mentioned as subject to human rule (v 21).

In addition, the mention of heaven in relation to the winged creatures does not imply that human beings have control over the firmament. The creation of the winged creatures described in v 20 makes clear that they are not indigenous to heaven. Indeed, they are commanded to "multiply on the earth" in v 22; hence, the term *peteina tou ouranou* is conceptually awkward. This can be explained from the fact that the Hebrew language base from which the Greek version was translated contained no word for atmosphere or air. Furthermore, the term "heaven" could have been chosen with reference to winged creatures in order to complete the tripartite structure of the cosmos over which human beings are to rule in some limited sense. Of all the living creatures, those that fly are spatially closest to the firmament. Thus, human beings are affirmed to have some relationship, albeit very indirect, to heaven/sky. In short, human rule touches in some limited extent upon all three spatial constituents of the cosmos. In addition, human rule over the land is limited by the fact that the one category of animals inimical to human beings, *thēria tēs gēs*, is not mentioned in vv 26 and 28.[114] Rather, this particular category of animal is not explicitly placed under human rule until Gen 9:2-3, which for the first time grants to human beings the animals for food.

In summary, both light and human beings, the first and last creative acts, are held in tension within the overall structure of creation and set somewhat apart from the rest of the creative acts. Both have a special relationship to the divine, the former created solely by divine fiat, that is, exclusively by the occasion of divine speech; the latter created solely by God to resemble the divine. Formally, both sections resemble each other in that the descriptions of their respective geneses lack the transition marker or "execution formula," *kai egeneto houtōs*, thereby forging a tighter link between command and fulfillment. Thus a more accurate presentation of the overall thematic structure of the Hexaemeron can be outlined as follows:

Heaven	Water	Earth
2. Firmament	3. Seas and land	4. Plants
1. Light ←	→	8. **Human beings**
5. Luminaries winged creatures	6. Marine and	7. Land animals

With the different acts of creation grouped around the three spatial constituents of creation, both light and human beings stand out as special acts of creation, while at the same time retaining their associations with the "heaven" and "earth," respectively.

The Respective Roles of Earth and Water

Compared with other versions, the LXX of the Hexaemeron is characterized by balance and symmetry both in terms of its overall structure (formal and thematic) and in the arrangement of the component parts within each day-section. This consistent structure is also reflected in part within the respective roles of both the earth and the water throughout the creative process. Second to God, the earth and the waters are the most active "agents" in the creation process. They are present in the following three sections:

Command:	Earth produces (*Blastanō*) vegetation	1:11
Fulfillment:	Earth brings forth (*ekpherō*) vegetation	1:12
Command:	Waters bring forth (*exagō*) sea and winged creatures	1:20
Fulfillment:	a) God creates (*poieō*) sea monsters and every soul of living creepers	1:21
	b) Waters bring forth (*exagō*)	1:21
Command:	Earth brings forth (*exagō*) the living soul . . .	1:24
Fulfillment:	God creates (*poieō*) the wild animals . . .	1:25

Only with regard to the botanical realm does a part of creation, namely the earth, assume the *exclusive* role of creating (1:11-12). Elsewhere, the divine commands summon the earth and the waters to "bring forth" (*exagō*), while the fulfillments depict God as creating (*poieō*). In the last two sections the earth and the waters are co-equal with regard to their creative function in producing animals. The relative clause in 1:21 repeats the waters' creative contribution mentioned in the command but now in relation to *divine* creation. Indeed, the actual act of creation described in 1:21 turns out to be rather complex, since God emerges as the main *actant*: God creates (*poieō*) "the great sea monsters and every soul of the living sea creatures . . . and every winged creature." Yet the waters still have a part in the process: They are described as having "brought forth" (*exagō*, as in the command) the "sea creatures" (*herpeta*). It is also possible that the end of 1:21 is elliptical and, if filled out, would read: *kai pan peteinon, ho exēgagen ta hydata kata genos*, that is, with the waters also having "brought forth" the winged creatures. The major point of difference between divine and aquatic activity seems to depend on the difference in the Greek verbs *poieō* and *exagō*, the former applied exclusively to divine action.

The exegetical issue at stake is one of temporal priority: Does God "fashion" the final form of the sea creatures once they are "produced" by the waters (thus, *exēgagen* would be translated as a pluperfect), or does God "create" the creatures that the waters then "bring forth"? Since *poieō* is attested in Greek literature often with regard to manufactured objects from raw material (e.g., Herodotus 4.22) as well as divine creation (Hesiod *Opera et Dies* 110), the issue is not resolved. The verb *exagō*, whose root meaning is "lead out," is only infrequently attested with reference to actual creation, as in Sophocles *Fragmenta* 834. Most commonly the object is a person, an animal or a group that is brought out from one location (*cum genitivo loci*) to another. Indeed, this is confirmed in the LXX usage of the verb: Noah brings forth the animals out of the ark in Gen 8:17 and Terah leads his family out of the land of the Chaldees into Canaan (Gen 11:31). Only in a few instances is the verb employed in relation to creating: Psalm 103 (104):14 (*kai chloen tē douleią tōn anthrōpōn tou exagagein arton ek tēs gēs*), Job 10:18 (*Hinati oun ek koilias me exēgages*), Wis 19:10 (*pōs anti men geneseōs zōōn exēgagen hē gē sknipa*), Jer 10:18; 28:16 (*kai exēgage phōs ek tōn thēsaurōn autou*). In all of these cases, except possibly Psalm 103, the verb involves "bringing forth" something already existing: the light from God's treasure, the embryo from the womb, and the flies from the land.

Examining the common uses of *exagō* in context, then, establishes in all probability the temporal sequence of the waters' engagement in the creative process: God creates that which the earth and the waters subsequently "bring forth." Though it is clear that neither the earth nor the waters has a hand in the initial genesis of what they bring forth, both are instrumental in the result. The terminology employed by the philosopher who argues with Rabban Gamaliel II in *Genesis Rabbah* 1.9 may be more on the mark in describing the LXX's treatment of the waters: Both the waters and the earth *actively assist* God in producing certain parts of creation. This understanding of *exagō* is also consonant with the term's semantic cousin *ekpherō* in 1:11 and 12, in which it is understood that the earth does not create *per se* the plants (*blastanō, exagō*) but brings forth what is dormant in the form of seed.

It is clear, then, that the LXX treats the earth and the waters almost as co-equals with regard to their respective contributions to the creative process. Furthermore, their respective origins are similar. The earth or land (*gē*, unnamed as *xēra*) arises passively in that its appearance is brought about by the gathering of "water . . . into their collections" (1:9). The emergence of land is the result of action imposed upon water. The key word to describe the land's genesis is *ōphthē*, aorist passive of *horaō*: "and the dry land *appeared*." Before the earth can be commanded to act (1:11), the "dry land" (*xēra*) must first be named *gē*. Consequently, a contrast is established between the passive emergence of the dry land and the earth actively "producing" vegetation (1:11) and animals (in the command in 1:24).

It is noteworthy that the earth is not commanded to come into being (*egeneto*). Indeed, the thought behind the "creation" of the land in v 9 is that it makes its appearance by being uncovered by water. Hence earth, or at least its constitutive basis, has prior existence in some form within or underneath water. This is confirmed in v 2, in which *gē*, though functioning as a more inclusive term, is described in its primordial state as "unseen" or "invisible" (*aoratos*). Indeed, the choice of this adjective seems to have been governed by the way in which land appears (*horaō*) in v 9.

Similar to land, water has "primordial" existence, since it is also mentioned in v 2: "The *pneuma* of God floated upon the water." The choice of the verb *epipherō* to describe the movement of the divine spirit upon water depicts water in a passively supportive role as a ship carried by the sea.[115] Both *gē* and *hydor* frame the sentence describing the primordial, yet created state of the cosmos, but whereas the earth is the subject in 2a, the water is an indirect object.

Water, similar to the earth, also has its initially passive stage: It must be acted upon, namely, divided (*diachorizō*) and gathered (*synagō*). This inert condition only lasts until v 9. From then on water actively contributes to creation, similar to the earth's role. Thus, a critical change in the role of the water occurs beginning in 1:10. The quantitative change from singular *hydor* to plural *hydata* is matched by a qualitative change from passive to active interaction with the creative process. With the new name *thalassai*, water is transformed from its inert, passive role to the "waters" that participate with the divine in producing life (vv 20, 21). In short, both "land" and "water" are transformed from passive to active participants in the creative process when they are conferred their respective names in v 10. Whereas the land is changed from a passive, undifferentiated entity to an active one, the waters undergo a more profound change. Indeed, as "water" they dominate the condition of initial creation as an inert entity; hence, their transformation is more sharply drawn once they contribute actively in the creative process in 1:20-21.

In sum, the basic elements of earth and water bear similar roles in the creative sweep of the six days. Both have a primordial base and are at first passive: The earth emerges once the waters are collected, and water is initially described as an inert mass. Water must be acted upon, that is, differentiated before it can actively contribute to the creative process. According to the LXX, water takes on this active role in its diversity, as the "waters in the seas" (1:21), rather than as a single, formless body.

Conclusion

A descriptive analysis of the structure of the LXX of Gen 1:1–2:3 has demonstrated that the text exhibits both a consistent formal structure and a balanced thematic arrangement for the six days of creation (1:3-31). Both structures highlight the equally active roles of the earth and the water in the cosmogonic process. Indeed, these active elements can be regarded as assisting God in the formation of various life forms (plants, winged and sea creatures, and land animals).

The symmetry evident in both the formal and thematic structures, as well as in the parallel roles of earth and water, provides a critical point of comparison between the Greek text and the Hebrew text preserved by the Masoretes.

NOTES

[1] The most recent translation is by R. J. H. Shutt, "Letter of Aristeas," in *OTP*, ed. J. H. Charlesworth (2 vols; Garden City: Doubleday & Company, 1985), 2. 12-34.

[2] See translation of fragment 3 (Eusebius *PE* 13.12.1-2) by A. Y. Collins, "Aristobulus, in *OTP*, 2. 839. Aristobulus, in order to prove that Plato imitated Jewish "legislation," claimed that Greek translations of the "parts concerning the exodus of the Hebrews, . . . the conquest of the land, and the detailed account of the entire legislation," were in existence prior to the translation directed by "Demetrius Phlaterus." Collins points out that though there are a number of verbal similarities between Aristobulus and the Letter of Aristeas, there is insufficient evidence for literary dependence. Instead, "the two authors could have known the legend independently" (Collins, "Aristobulus," 835). S. Jellicoe, on the other hand, agrees with Schürer and others that Aristobulus actually cited from Aristeas (*The Septuagint and Modern Study* [Oxford: Clarendon Press, 1968] 49). In either case, the letter's claim that a Greek translation of the Pentateuch was conducted under Ptolemy II is also supported by Aristobulus.

[3] For a breakdown of the suggested dates along with their adherents, see Jellicoe, *The Septuagint and Modern Study*, 48, n. 1.

[4] In *Praefatio in Pentateuchum* Jerome claimed that the letter's account of the seventy separate cells at Alexandria in which the translators wrote the same words was a fiction (Cf. W. Schwarz, "Discussions on the Origin of the Septuagint," in *Studies in the Septuagint: Origins, Recensions, and Interpretations*, ed. S. Jellicoe [New York: KTAV, 1974] 110-37). Jerome's criticism was directed against the principle of inspirational translation as defended by Augustine rather than against the claim that a Greek translation was produced under Ptolemy II. For example, in his *Hebraicae Quaestiones in Genesin* Jerome claimed that the seventy translators deliberately concealed from Ptolemy II the meaning of all the passages in which the coming of Christ was promised (Schwarz, 124).

[5] J. Wevers, "Proto-Septuagint Studies," in *Studies in the Septuagint*, 62.

[6] V. Tcherikover, "The Ideology of the Letter of Aristeas," in *Studies in the Septuagint*, 181-207.

[7] Shutt, "The Letter of Aristeas," 11.

[8] Jellicoe, *The Septuagint and Modern Study*, 54.

[9] P. Kahle, *The Cairo Geniza* (London: Geoffrey Cumberlege, 1941) 135.

[10] A major crux in translation is paragraph 30 of the letter. See also Shutt, 14, n. e.

[11] Wevers, "Proto-Septuagint Studies," 63-65.

[12] See J. Hanson's discussion and translation of "Demetrius the Chronographer," in *OTP*, 2. 843-854; B. Z. Wacholder, *Eupolemus: A Study of Judaeo-Greek Literature* (MHUC 3; Cincinnati: Hebrew Union College Press, 1974) 99.

[13] Wacholder, *Eupolemus*, 99.

[14] Hanson, "Demetrius the Chronographer," 844.

[15] J. W. Wevers, "An Apologia for Septuagint Studies," *BIOSCS* 18 (1985) 18.

[16] There was at least one rival translation from Leontopolis (Jellicoe, *The Septuagint and Modern Study*, 50; Shutt, 14, n. e.).

[17] F. M. Cross, "The History of the Biblical Text," *HTR* 57 (1964) 295, 297.

[18] D. W. Gooding, "An Appeal for a Stricter Terminology in the Textual Criticism of the Old Testament," *JSS* 21 (1976) 16-24.

[19] G. Howard, "The Septuagint: A Review of Recent Studies," in *Studies in the Septuagint*, 64.

[20] J. Davila, "New Qumran Readings for Genesis One," in *Of Scribes and Scrolls: Studies on the Hebrew Bible, Intertestamental Judaism, and Christian Origins*, ed. H. W. Attridge, J. J. Collins, T. H. Tobin (CTSRR 5; Lanham: University Press of America, 1920) 7-12.

[21] Tov, *The Text-Critical Use*, 260.

[22] E. Würthwein, *The Text of the Old Testament*, trans. E. F. Rhodes (Grand Rapids: William B. Eerdmans Publishing Company, 1979) 68.

[23] A. E. Brooke, and N. McLean, eds., *The Old Testament in Greek according to the Text of the Codex Vaticanus. Volume I, The Octateuch. Part I, Genesis* (Cambridge: Cambridge University Press, 1906) 1-4.

[24] J. Wevers, *Septuaginta: Genesis*, (VTG 1; Göttingen: Vandenhoeck & Ruprecht, 1974) 9-13.

[25] J. W. Wevers, *Text History of the Greek Genesis* (Göttingen: Vandenhoeck & Ruprecht, 1974) 158-75.

[26] Brooke and McLean, 2, n. 11.

[27] See Chapter Four for a comparison of the possible retroverted word counts between the Göttingen text and Codex Alexandrinus.

[28] Klein, *Textual Criticism of the Old Testament*, x.

[29] Wevers, *Text History of the Greek Genesis*, 96, 137.

[30] Cook, "Genesis I in the Septuagint as Example of the Problem," 28.

[31] The introductory phrase *en kephalaiō* in several manuscripts containing Hexaplaric notes (135, 78, 413, 343, 344 [see Aquila's translation]) lends a markedly different nuance to the first verse. Based on a pseudo-etymological rendering of the Hebrew (*rēʾšît* from *rōʾš*), the Greek translation takes on non-temporal implications in the first verse. The prepositional phrase often denotes "in summary" in classical Greek (e.g., Xenophon *Institutio Cyri* 6.3.18 and Plato *Timaeus* 26C), thereby setting the first verse off as a summary statement to the creation account (see also Alexandre, 67). What temporal implications the word *kephalaios* does infrequently have in classical literature point in the opposite direction of *archē*, that is, in the sense of "completion" (*LS* 945).

In the LXX the lack of the article may correspond to its absence in Hebrew (*bĕrēʾšît*), but in *koine* Greek *en archē* can denote determinate time as, for example, in John 1:1 and Phil 4:15 (see Alexandre, 66). In addition, Greek syntax does not require the presence of an article to denote the definiteness of the object of a preposition.

[32] In general Greek usage of the postpositive particle *de* usually appears in parallel with its correlative particle *men* in order to introduce a contrastive clause. But this convention is surprisingly rare in the LXX (F. C. Conybeare and St. G. Stock, *Grammar of Septuagint Greek* [Peabody: Hendrickson, 1988 (reprint of Boston: Ginn and Company, 1905)] 39). The particle *de* generally marks a transition from what precedes by denoting slight contrast, weaker than *alla* but stronger than *kai*. Indeed, the adversative use of *de* (without *men*) can mark a "silent contrast" at the beginning of speeches, in answers, and in corrections (H. W. Smyth, *Greek Grammar* [Cambridge: Harvard University Press, 1956] 2834). Thus the particle establishes for v 2 a slight contrast in relation to v 1 within a continuous temporal sequence. Consequently, 1:1 must be

regarded as a creation statement rather than as a summary statement or introductory clause, thereby, implying a "double creation" in context with 1:3 (see below). Indeed, a double creation is clearly evident in Symmachus' translation of 1:2: *hē de gē egeneto argon kai adiakriton* ("Yet the earth *became* idle and indistinguishable").

33 J. B. Schaller, in his unpublished dissertation, identifies the key words *aoratos* and *akataskeuastos* as one of the few examples in which the Greek translator clearly betrays himself as an exegete, since "die Vorstellung vom Tohuwabohu der Erde griechischem Denken fremd ist" (*Gen. 1.2 im antiken Judentum* [Unpublished dissertation: Göttingen Universität, 1961] 12). Despite his sweeping claim, Schaller is correct in that the Greek translation tendentiously interprets the Hebrew in this case. The first term *aoratos* appears only twice elsewhere in the LXX. In Isaiah 45:3 *aoratos* is synonymous with *apokryphos* ("hidden") and *skoteinos* ("dark"). 2 Macc 9:5 refers to an "invisible" and incurable plague striking Antiochus. In classical literature the term figures prominently in the works of Plato (*Phaedo* 85E; *Sophist* 246AB, 247B; *Theaetetus* 155E), usually referring to the world of ideas which cannot be perceived by the senses. Indeed, Philo draws from the Platonic use of the term (e.g., *Opficio Mundi* 29-34). For Philo, *aoratos* is an essential quality of the incorporeal and intelligible creation (34). Josephus, on the other hand, takes Gen 1:2 in a purely physical sense (*Jewish Antiquities* i.27): *tautēs d' hyp' opsin ouk erchomenēs, alla bathei men kryptomenēs skotei*, that is, the earth is hidden by darkness, thus it is invisible. Josephus' interpretation seems more appropriate to the meaning behind the LXX rendering in Gen 1:2. Indeed, the choice of *aoratos* by the Greek translator forms a nice parallel with the description of the land's appearance (*ōphthē hē xēra*) in 1:9 (see below), a clear case of contextual interpretation.

34 The term *akataskeuastos* is rare in Greek literature. It is a *hapax legomenon* in the LXX, and in Jewish-Hellenistic literature it occurs only a few times: e.g., 1 Enoch 21:1, 2, in which the Greek term corresponds to the Ethiopic "where nothing is done." In classical literature it occurs in Theophrastus *Historia Plantarum* 9.16.6 and refers to an improperly prepared medicine (*pharmakon*) and much later in Pseudo-Plutarchus *Vita Homeri* 218 (after second century CE). The term's frequently attested verbal base *kataskeuazō* ("furnish, construct") occurs thirty times in the LXX, most commonly corresponding to the Hebrew verbs *bārā'*, *yāṣar*, and *'āsāh*. As Schaller has observed, the verb is often used to describe the creative works of God (Schaller, 10). Thus the context of 1:2 implies an earth that is "unformed" or "unprepared." For Josephus the sense of 1:2a is that of an earth hidden (*kryptomenes*) by darkness (see n. 31). Consequently, Josephus places more stress on the first quality (*aoratos*) and interprets the second quality by it. Philo, on the other hand, invests the sense of the term with the Platonic notion of incorporeality (*asōmatos*, see n. 31). Since the term is never a *terminus technicus* in the Platonic writings for the world of ideas, it is best to view its use in Gen 1:2 in a materialistic sense.

35 Although most minuscules render this clause as nominal (as in the MT), several provide the verb *ēn* (e.g., 569, 246, 75, 730).

36 The meaning of *pneuma* expands in different directions when one moves from Greek mythology and philosophy through Philo to the early church fathers. In light of the LXX's historical-cultural context and the literary context of Gen 1:2, the meaning denotes not so much "spirit," as it would later come to mean in the eyes of Christian commentators, as "wind."

The term's basic and earliest meaning was "wind" or "breath," given its deriva-
tion from the verb *pneō*, as attested in Aeschylus (e.g., *Prometheus Vincius* 1086) and
Herodotus (7. 16a [*anemōn pneumata*: "gales of wind"]). Indeed, Plato used the term
pneuma only in the context of natural science (H. Kleinknecht, *"pneuma"* in *Theological
Dictionary of the New Testament*, ed. G. Kittel [10 vols; Grand Rapids: Eerdmans, 1964]
6. 343). Within the field of science *pneuma* denoted that substance between earth and
heaven which permeated all of nature, both organic and inorganic (Hippocrates *De
Flatibus* 3.4.15). Yet in a figurative sense the term could denote "spirit" in early Greek
poetry in the context of divine/human relations (Euripides *Hercules Furens* 216
[Kleinknecht, 336]), but even this "spiritual" side was situated in the "etymological
idea of a powerful, material, moving breath" (Kleinknecht, 337). Indeed, in similar
fashion Diogenes of Apollonia (ca. 440 BCE) viewed air (*aēr*) as the primary substance,
endowing it with mind, divinity, the principle of soul, and all-disposing power (see
Simplicius *Physica* 152, 2ff.). Thus the term denoted something as "palpable" as "in
the case of the snorting animal," yet could also signify an invisible, even divine, albeit
material, force (Kleinknecht, 337).

The term's divine cosmological significance in Greek philosophy reached its
height in Stoicism, in which *pneuma* denoted a cosmic and universal power or
substance, denoting even the manifestation of the deity (Aëtius *Placita* 1.6). This
cosmic wind was often depicted as having a generative potency (Pliny *Naturalis
Historia* 2. 116). In Stoicism *pneuma* was regarded as a substance of its own which
united *pyr* and *aēr*. It was the divine source of the four elements (Chrysippus
Fragments 414), and was of invisibly fine corporeality (Cleanthes *Fragments* 484).
Indeed, Cleanthes, the head of the Stoa from 263 to 232 BCE, seems to have been the
first to define God as *pneuma* (*Fragments* 1093). Yet *pneuma* was always conceived in a
material sense, since *sōma* was also predicated of God (Kleinknecht, 358). It was this
Stoic use of *pneuma* that the Ante-Nicene fathers found objectionable (Tatian *Ad
Graecos* 4; Theophilus *Ad Autolycum* 1.4; 2.4). Yet the break from a materialistic view
of *pneuma* was not altogether clear cut. Theophilus used the term materialistically by
likening *pneuma* to water and situating it between heaven and water to nourish the
water and the earth (*Ad Autolycum* 2.13). On the other hand, Clement of Alexandria
repudiated the Stoics by claiming that God could not be of material *pneuma* (*Stromata*
5.89.2), rather, God could only be called *pneuma* in its true sense of *asōmatos*
(Kleinknecht, 358). Furthermore, Origen, in his reply to Celsus (6,70) makes clear that
scripture describes God's spirit in a figurative sense that does not imply materiality
(*sōma*)

In between the Stoics and the later Christian Apologists, Philo's use of the term
illustrates the varied meanings the term had in Hellenistic Judaism. Philo was fully
aware that *pneuma* in connection with Gen 1:2 could only mean the air (*aēr*) which
"rides upon the waters" (*epochoumenon hydati* [*De gigantibus* 22]) but in other passages
could mean "pure knowledge" (*akeratos episteme*) and the antithesis of flesh (*sarx*), (*De
gigantibus* 22-30). Indeed, Philo elsewhere states that the *pneuma theou* "is not a
movement of air but intelligence and wisdom" (*Questiones et solutiones in Genesin*
1.90). Thus Philo concedes the standard materialistic view of *pneuma theou* in Gen 1:2,
but elsewhere clearly intends the term to mean more by having it denote divine
inspiration, the substance of the soul, and the nature of the divine in connection with
the divine *logos* (see M. Weaver, "Pneuma in Philo of Alexandria" [Unpublished
dissertation: University of Notre Dame (Ann Arbor: University Microfilms, 1973)] 74-

75, 95-96). Although Weaver and more so H. Orlinsky ("The New Jewish Version of the Torah," *JBL* 82 [1963] 254-258) overstate their case with regard to Philo's interpretation of Gen 1:2 (it is nowhere clear that Philo means anything more than what he says in *De gigantibus* 22 about the term *with respect to Gen 1:2*), it is clear that Philo represents a turning point in the history of the term's usage by expanding its semantic range and anticipating the way in which later Christian apologists invested *pneuma* with a radically spiritual (i.e., incorporeal) meaning.

In short, the LXX's translation of the Hebrew *rûaḥ* seems to share the meaning that Philo *explicitly* gives it, namely that of wind or breath, since the more spiritual connotations are not fully developed until later, although they begin to find their roots elsewhere in Philo's writings. As noted above, the early usage of the term is frequently attested in creation accounts. Thus, the "wind" of God seems to refer materially to divine creative power, despite the fact that it is nowhere mentioned again in the creation account.

37 The closest parallel to this use of *epipherō* is found in Gen 7:18 of the LXX: *epephereto hē kibōtos epanō tou hydatos* ("the ark floated upon the water"). Given its middle form and the context of the flood story, the verb is best rendered resultative. The LXX translator of Gen 1:2 evidently used this verb, which customarily describes the relation of a ship to the water (cf. Herodotus 2.96), to portray metaphorically the relationship of the *pneuma* of God to the primordial water.

38 The repetition of the common two-word prepositional phrase *ana meson* (literally "midway between") in vv 4, 6, 7, 14, 18 is the result of a literal Greek translation of the original Hebrew *ben . . . ben*.

39 The temporal phrase *mian hēmeran* can also be rendered "single day." Based on the Hebrew *yōm ʾeḥād*, the cardinal number *mian* is used by the Greek translator instead of the expected ordinal number (*prōtē*), despite the fact that ordinal numbers are used for all other day-sections. The early Greek commentators made much of this choice in terminology, which sets the "first" day apart from the other days of creation. Philo, for example, treats the first day as the occasion for the creation of the intelligible, non-sensible creation (*Opificio Mundi* 26-35).

40 The construction *estō diachōrizon* is periphrastic, thereby highlighting the particular function of the firmament (see Smyth 1857) as well as replicating the syntax of the Hebrew *wîhî mabdîl* ("so that it will be a divider").

41 The adverb *houtōs* can refer either to what precedes or to what follows (*BAG* 597-98). Since in almost all cases the Greek text brackets the formula *kai egeneto houtōs* with the command and fulfillment, the phrase is clearly transitional and the adverb must therefore point forward to the fulfillment of the command. Such a construction renders the following *kai* (1:7) pleonastic in meaning. Of note is the omission of the transition formula in the Complutensian Polyglott (1514 CE).

42 Three minuscules (44, 508, 527) omit *ho theos* in accordance with the MT. This simply corrects a redundancy in subject or is perhaps traceable back to the MT.

43 In contrast to 1:6, many minuscules add the transition formula to 1:7 in accordance with the MT. With few exceptions these variants comprise the s, t, and *Catena* groups, all of which are interrelated and bear affinities to hexaplaric material such as the Syro-Hexapla (Wevers, *Text History*, 67, 95-96, 100, 136-37).

44 Two minuscules 72 and 129 read *eis tas synagōgas autōn* ("into their collections"), a clear case of harmonization with the fulfillment in 1:9b. A correction of minuscule 56 renders the confusing text: *en tais synagōgais mian* ("in the collections, one").

45 Minuscule 75 lacks the fulfillment account in accordance with the MT. Three manuscripts from the Catena group (57, 73, 413) and three from the s group (343, 344, 127) bear the obelos sign.

46 The root meaning of *systēmata* is a "whole compounded of several parts or members" (*LS* 1735). The word functions in Greek literature in a variety of contexts, from politics to the metric system, but in most instances denotes a social organization of some sort. The word is employed here to denote the various collections of waters in definable, localized entities. Schaller attributes the change in terminology between vv 9 (*synagōgē*) and 10 (*systēmata*) merely to stylistic reasons (Schaller, 13) and thereby misses the special nuance resulting from such a change. "Systems" or "consolidations" of water imply a discernible geographical organization. Furthermore, the plural rendering in v 10 makes better sense than the MT (*lĕmiqwēh hammayim qārāʾ yammayîm*). The change from singular to plural in the Greek results in a change of perspectives: The command in v 9 stems from a "microcosmic" perspective (*eis synagōgēn mian*), whereas the fulfillment and the naming (v 10) depicts a wider, more global perspective by virtue of the plural terminology (*eis tas synagōgas autōn, ta systēmata tōn hydatōn*). In so doing, vv 9b and 10 imply a sort of "diasporic" transformation of water into separate waters.

47 Literally "cause to grow" (*blastanō*; *LS* 317). B. Paradise points out that the translator chose a verb that had a more active sense than similar words (e.g., *phuō*). "The creative agency of the earth is the important aspect" ("Food for Thought," in *A Word in Season: Essays in Honor of William McKane*, ed. J. D. Martin and P. R. Davies [JSOTS 42; Sheffield: Sheffield Academic Press, 1986] 188). In addition, witnesses from Chrysostomus and Epiphanius, as well as Symmachus' translation, replace the verb with *exagō*, thereby terminologically linking the creative actions of the earth and water (cf. 1:20).

48 The general Greek usage of the term *chortos* seems to be restricted to "fodder" or "hay," that is, to animal foodstuffs or to a parcel of land for growing such crops (*LS* 2000). Given its genitival relation to *botanē*, the latter meaning is preferable. Paradise points out that Gen 1:29-30, as well as Gen 9:3, intends the term to include plants for human consumption and concludes that *chortou* is an artificial Greek translation, which "for anyone who did not know the Hebrew text, [has taken the connotation of the Hebrew *ʿēśeb*] too far in the direction of animal foodstuffs" (Paradise, 191). Thus the Greek translator has artificially broadened the semantic borders of the term, according to Paradise. But Paradise offers no reason to account for the use of a common animal foodstuff term specifically intended for human consumption in Gen 1:29 (*Idou dedōka hymin pan chorton . . .*). It seems that by choosing *chortos* over a more general term for vegetation, such as *chloē* and *phyton*, the Greek translator intended to stress the nature of the original vegetarian diet of human beings by depicting the diet as overlapping the herbivorous animal diet, in contrast to the postdeluvian age in which meat was first introduced into the human diet (Gen 9:3). The translator makes the point that animals and human beings primarily shared a common diet before the flood, namely the produce from field crops and pastures. Thus, the seemingly strange choice of *chortos* in 1:11, 29, 30 and 9:3 was deliberately made to highlight the exclusively vegetarian diet for human beings during the primeval age.

49 Since neither *chortos* nor *botanē* is neuter, normal Greek syntax demands that the participle *speiron* modify *sperma*, rendering the phrase: "Let the earth produce plants of the pasture, seeds which reproduce . . . ." However, it is also possible that the

neuter was chosen to modify *chortos* (and thus *botanē* by extension), since the masculine form normally designates a human sower (Paradise, 193). The same construction applies to Gen 1:29.

⁵⁰ Genus or species (Alexandre, 128-29).

⁵¹ The phrase *kath homoiotēta* signifies resemblance in nature. Alexandre notes that *homoiotēta* functions in the same way as *homoiosis* and *eikona* in Gen 1:26 and considers *kath homoiotēta* a gloss or "double traduction" of the Hebrew *mîn* (Alexandre, 129). The latter claim, however, is questionable (cf. Chapter Five).

⁵² The term *xylon* normally means in Greek "wood" or "timber." Only rarely does it designate a "live tree" (*LS* 1191-92). A more appropriate term would have been *dendron* or *hylē* for designating fruit-bearing trees (Paradise, 194). What seems to be emphasized by the translator is the utilitarian quality of trees not only for their fruit-production but also for building material and fuel.

⁵³ Verse 11 is beset with numerous textual variants, but most of them are sparsely attested. One notable exception is the addition, on the one hand, of *eis homoiotēta* after *en autō* in eleven minuscules and *kath homoiotēta* by several other minuscules, on the other. However, both sets of variants can be explained as simple harmonizations with the preceding clause, which refers to the seeds of the plant fodder reproduced *kata genos kai kath homoiotēta*. The addition of *eis homoiotēta* evidently bears some relationship with **A**'s (Codex Alexandrinus) addition (see following note).

⁵⁴ The prepositional phrase *kata genos* is lacking in the original reading of the Codex Alexandrinus as well as in twelve other minuscules and in most of the Catena group. The absence in this case is clearly dependent on the Origen Recension (Wevers, *Text History*, 92) and corresponds to the MT. The Codex Alexandrinus adds *eis homoiotēta* after the second *kata genos*. However, a wealth of minuscules count against this reading as early.

⁵⁵ Three minuscules (16, 56 [with correction], and 129) have *exēgagen* instead of *exēnegken*, thereby matching the first verb in the divine command of 1:20. Any difference in meaning is negligible.

⁵⁶ Instead of *eis phausin* (absent in the MT but present in the SP), two minuscules have *hōste phainein epi* (75 and 509). The latter reading is simply a repetition of the phrase in 1:15 and 17.

⁵⁷ An inclusio is formed with 1:16 by the addition of *kai archein tēs hēmeras kai tēs nyktos* by codices Alexandrinus and Cottonianus (with slight modification: *archetosan*), not to mention minuscules 129, 75, 392 (*archēn*) and 59. However, codices Bodleianus and Coislinianus, in addition to the numerous remaining minuscular attestations, count against the reading as early. Its secondary nature is clear from harmonistic reasons (cf. 1:16 and 18).

⁵⁸ This form from *archē* is the accusative plural. Its semantic range includes both political and celestial authority (*BAG* 112; *LS* 252). Note for instance that Philoponus 193s replaces the term with *exousian*. The plural form can be explained as an "abstract plural," which refers to single cases or manifestations of the idea expressed by the abstract noun (Smyth 1000.3), thus suggesting with respect to the luminaries' respective domains the concrete alternations of night and day. Alexandre notes that the Greek term also has the built-in ambiguity of meaning "to begin," as rendered by the Old Latin version (*in initium*) (Alexandre, 139).

⁵⁹ At first glance, the Greek term for water seems inconsistently translated from the consistently Hebrew plural *hammayim*, since it is rendered throughout the

creation account in some instances as a singular and in other instances as a plural. In this verse and in 1:21b, the term is plural with a singular predicate. There is, however, a consistent method employed by the Greek translator. The term *hydor* remains singular in 1:2, 6 (three times), 7 (twice) and 9 (twice). After 1:9 the plural is consistently attested throughout (vv 10, 20, 21, 22). Schaller attributes this to the work of two translators (Schaller, 11), since vv 9 and 10 also render different translations for the Hebrew *miqwēh*. However, Schaller fails to consider the underlying logic for the shift. The reason lies in v 9, in which water is reported to have been gathered "into their collections." From then on, water is depicted as multiple *bodies* of water once they are horizontally separated into their respective places in v 9. Thus, the juncture between vv 9 and 10 marks the transition between water as an undifferentiated, primordial substance and waters as separated bodies of water. The phenomenon of a plural Greek neuter with a singular predicate, as in 1:20 and 21b, is commonly attested in Greek syntax.

60 With the verb *exagō* to describe the action of the waters, the LXX renders the Hebrew verb *šāraṣ* transitively and establishes a parallel with the productive actions of the earth in 1:24 (Alexandre, 144).

61 The common meaning of *herpeton* is "reptile" (cf. 1:24). However, the semantic range of the term in general Greek usage includes everything from snakes to four-footed animals (*LS* 691). Indeed its verbal base *herpō* means to "move slowly" (*LS* 692) or "to crawl." In the context of 1:20-21, the term evidently refers in a general sense to sea-creatures (other than fish [*enalios* or *ichthys*]?). Psalm 103 (104):25 of the LXX clearly employs the word as an umbrella term to designate the whole range of creatures living in the sea. Thus, the term probably refers to all sea-creatures (see Alexandre, 145).

62 Genitive of material or contents.

63 The syntax consists of an object followed by a participle (*peteina petomena*). Surprisingly, all Greek texts are in agreement, except Eusebius Caesariensis VIII 1.383, which renders the text *peteina tou ouranou*, thereby indirectly confirming the LXX syntax as early, since *peteina* remains the object of the verb. Thus, according to the Greek, the waters "bring forth" two types of creatures: the sea creatures and the winged creatures.

This observation did not remain unnoticed among early commentators, contrary to many modern commentators (for instance, Schaller's otherwise detailed textual comparison of the MT and LXX texts misses it). Philo explains their common origin from the waters by virtue of the fact that both fish and birds "float" (*nēkta*, or "swim") (*Opf.* 63). Theophilus of Antioch observes that marine animals and birds are of one nature (*ek mias physeōs*) and explains it allegorically (*Ad Autolycum* 2. 16). Tertullian observes: "Thus from the earth originated the grass and the fruits and the cattle and the human form itself, so from the waters the swimming and flying animals" (*ex aquis natatiles et uolatiles animae* [*Against Hermogenes* 33]). Ambrose, Basilus Magnus, Philoponus, and Augustine all observe this peculiar role of the waters. Augustine, for example, explains the watery origin of "flying things" (*volatilia*) by suggesting that moist air was "included under the name of the waters" (*De Genesi ad litterarum liber imperfectus* 14.45 [see translation by R. J. Teske, *Saint Augustine on Genesis* (Washington: Catholic University of America Press, 1991) 177]). F. E. Robbins falsely attributes the origin of this view to Plato's *Sophist* 220B (*The*

Hexaemeral Literature: A Study of the Greek and Latin Commentaries on Genesis [Chicago: University of Chicago Press, 1912] 32 n. 3) (see Chapter Five).

64 The antecedent of the relative pronoun is clearly the sea creatures (*herpeta*), in accordance with 1:20, and possibly the "great sea monsters" (*ta kētē*). On the other hand, God creates the *psyche*.

65 A host of minuscules add (*kai ta ktene kai*) *panta ta herpeta tēs gēs*. Despite such extensive textual support, the presence of this additional category of animals can be attributed to harmonization with the fulfillment in 1:25.

66 The term for domesticated animals (*ktēnē*) parallels the *tetrapoda* of 1:24, whereas the MT employs the same term in both cases (*běhēmāh*). Schaller attributes the unusual shift in terminology to two originally independent translations, using as evidence, "daß im Buche Genesis bis auf Gen. 34,23 stets die Übersetzung **ktēnos**, hingegen in den Büchern Exodus und Leviticus allgemein **tetrapous** verwendet ist" (Schaller, 14). However, Schaller misrepresents the evidence. Granted, *tetrapous* is used in Genesis only in 1:24 and 24:23 amid a plethora of attestations of *ktēnos* for the same Hebrew word (19x), but *ktēnos* is also widely attested in the books of Exodus and Leviticus for translating the same Hebrew word (34x), exceeding the attestations of *tetrapous* (10x). Thus, both terms overlap considerably in their semantic range to the extent that they can be used interchangeably. One need not posit different translations.

67 All of the **d** group as well as eight other minuscules omit any reference to domestic animals (*kai ta ktēnē kata genos*) in accordance with its absence in the command in 1:24. Evidently domestic animals were considered to be subsumed under the category *thēria tēs gēs* or more likely *herpeta tēs gēs*.

68 A large number of witnesses (most from the Catena group, all of the **d** group, plus six other minuscules) omit this third category of animals. As a result, this omission stresses only two mutually exclusive categories of created animals, into which presumably all animals would fall, namely wild and domestic (as in *Marcus Antoninus* 5.11).

69 The possessive adjective gives greater emphasis than the possessive pronouns.

70 The term *eikōn* denotes something concrete whether it refers to pictures and statues or mirror images and phantoms (Aeschylus *Septem contra Thebas* 559; Euripides *Medea* 1162; Lucianus *Dialog Mortuorum* 16.1). For Schaller, the Greek usage introduces a "Mittlergestalt" (Schaller, 15), which humans are created to resemble. However, such a claim is reading too much into the text.

71 A significant but sparsely distributed number of witnesses add at one position or another *tōn theriōn*. This is significant in that this addition collapses any difference concerning the extent of human rule over the created order with the description in Gen 9:2-5, in which human beings are to be a terror (*ho tromos hymōn kai ho phobos*) to the wild animals of the earth (*theriois tēs gēs*) and are granted the right to eat meat.

72 Only minuscules 75, 508, and Latin Codex 111 add the transition formula at the end of 1:26. This is fully consonant with the way in which the formula is used elsewhere in the LXX, namely to act as a bridge between command and fulfillment.

73 Miniscule 59 is the only manuscript that adds the approbation formula after the divine speech.

74 As noted above, the term *chortos* refers primarily to animal fodder in general Greek usage, even though the context stipulates that it be intended for human consumption. This does not present a problem, since both the Hebrew and Greek texts view the primeval age as characterized by a vegetarian diet, which is altered

only after the flood (see Gen 9:3). Thus the Greek translator viewed human beings as members of the Herbivora in this ancient age and stressed this common diet by choosing a term normally relegated solely for animal consumption to describe the human diet. This observation has not gone unnoticed among several early commentators. Theophilus of Antioch notes in conjunction with this verse that animals and human beings were to have the same diet, namely "the seeds of the earth," (*Ad Autolycum* 2.18). Tertullian discusses the widespread recognition of the change in prescription between this verse and the passage in Gen 9:2-5 and explains it as a change towards freedom (*On Fasting* 4).

75 The relative pronoun (neuter singular) refers to "seed."

76 The transition formula *kai egeneto houtōs* must be rendered in English differently from how it is attested elsewhere in Genesis 1, since the phrase is not immediately followed by a fulfillment of creation (see below).

77 Two Hexaplaric miniscules (17 and 135) plus two from the **s** group (127 and 344 [?]), along with the Hexaplaric Codex Coislinianus, have *hebdome* ("seventh").

78 The translator here used the intransitive verb *katapauein* for the Hebrew *šābat* (P. Walters, *The Text of the Septuagint: Its Corruptions and Their Emendation*, ed. D. W. Gooding [Cambridge: Cambridge University Press, 1973] 320).

79 The phrase *ērxato ho theos poiēsai*, unattested in the Hebrew, can be easily explained by the inclusio it establishes with 1:1 (*en archē epoiēsen ho theos*), thereby making clear that 2:4 introduces the next creation passage. Schaller, on the other hand, claims the phrase is used to mark the transition into the second creation report, thus pointing forwards (Schaller, 17). To the contrary, the phrase clearly refers back to the first verse.

80 The Greek term *hexaēmeron* refers to the six-day scheme of creation, first coined by Philo (G. May, *Schöpfung aus dem Nichts* [AzKG 48; Berlin: Walter de Gruyter, 1978] 61 n. 86).

81 G. W. Coats, *Genesis with an Introduction to Narrative Literature* (FOTL 1; Grand Rapids: William B. Eerdmans Publishing Company, 1983) 46.

82 H. Holzinger, *Genesis* (Freiburg: J. C. B. Mohr, 1898) 6.

83 O. Loretz, *Schöpfung und Mythos: Mensch und Welt nach den Anfangskapiteln der Genesis* (Stuttgart: Katholisches Bibelwerk, 1968) 54.

84 Schmidt, 56.

85 Beauchamp, 21; Alexandre, 45.

86 Coats, 46.

87 So Tatianus *Ad Graecos* 5; Theophilus *Ad Autolycum* 2.4.10; Augustine *Confessiones* 12.8 and *De genesis contra Manich.* 1.10.

88 G. May, 78.

89 G. May, 78.

90 D. Winston, "The Book of Wisdom's Theology of Cosmogony," *HR* 11 (1971) 191.

91 G. May, 23.

92 J. Goldstein, "The Origins of the Doctrine of Creation Ex Nihilo," *JJS* 35, 2 (1984) 133.

93 J. Goldstein, *II Maccabees* (AB 41A, New York: Doubleday, 1983) 307-11; and G. Schuttermayr, "'Schöpfung aus dem Nichts' in 2 Makk 7, 28? Zum Verhältnis von Position und Bedeutung," *BZ* 17 (1973) 203-28.

94 G. Stead, "Review of *Schöpfung aus dem Nichts*," *JTS* 30 (1979) 548.

95 Goldstein, 127.

96 See, for example, the sharp disagreements between H. A. Wolfson, *Philo: Foundations of Religion Philosophy in Judaism, Christianity, and Islam* (2 vols; Cambridge: Harvard University Press, 1947) 1. 295-315; and D. Winston, "Philo's Theory of Cosmogony," in *Religious Syncretism in Antiquity: Essays in Conversation with Geo Widengren*, ed. B. A. Pearson (Missoula: Scholars Press, 1975) 157-71.

97 D. Winston, *Philo of Alexandria: The Contemplative Life, The Giants, and Selections* (CWS; New York: Paulist Press, 1981) 9.

98 Cf. Schuttermayr, 212 n. 54.

99 H.-F. Weiss, *Untersuchungen zur Kosmologie des Hellenistischen und Palästinischen Judentums* (TU 97; Berlin: Akademie-Verlag, 1966) 56-7.

100 Winston, "Philo's Theory of Cosmogony," 160.

101 Wolfson, 305; see also Winston, "Philo's Theory of Cosmogony," 165.

102 Winston, "Philo's Theory of Cosmogony," 167-68.

103 G. May, 21.

104 So Winston, "The Book of Wisdom" 191, 199-200.

105 Tertullian *Against Hermogenes* 21.

106 See Robbins, *The Hexaemeral Literature*, 11.

107 The double creation described in Genesis 1 is explained by Philo in (*Opf.* 29). For Philo, Gen 1:1-5 describes the incorporeal creation. Light in v 3, being the seventh entity named, is of particular importance in that it constitutes the incorporeal (*asōmatos*) pattern (*paradeigma*) for the luminaries. This *asōmatos kosmos* or *noētos kosmos* described in vv 1-5 thus becomes the pattern for the creation of the solid, three dimensional firmament (*Opf.* 36), and the darkness and the deep (*abyssos*) are respectively the ideas of air and space (*Opf.* 29). This is confirmed by the use of the cardinal number *mian* in contrast to the ordinal numbers employed throughout the rest of the creation account, thereby highlighting the uniqueness of the intelligible, invisible world (*Opf.* 35). The firmament or "heaven" of the second day is the first of the visible things (*tōn horatōn*) or corporeal creation (*Opf.* 37).

Theophilus of Antioch also develops this line of reasoning, but is more sensitive to the formal structure of the introduction (Gen 1:1-3): He marks off only the first two verses as designating a sort of initial creation, with light as the "beginning of creation" (*archē tēs poiēseōs*, [*Ad Autolycum* 2.11]). However, in contrast to Philo, Theophilus designates Gen 1:1 as describing the creation of matter (*hylē*), with v 2 providing a description thereof. Theophilus states that this matter from which God made (*pepoieken*) and fashioned (*dedēmiourgēken*) the cosmos, "was *in a way* created" (*tropō tini* [*Ad Autolycum* 2.10]). Thus, Theophilus correctly senses the tension between vv 1-2 and the formal creation passage beginning in v 3. The contrast between heaven in v 1 and heaven in v 4 is set up by the contrast between invisibility and visibility. Indeed, there are two heavens: one that serves as a boundary, a firmament; another that is "invisible to us" (*peri heterou ouranou tou aoratou hēmin ontos* [*Ad Autolycum* 2.13]). By contrast, the earth, similarly invisible in its original state, becomes visible once the water is gathered. Thus, for Theophilus there are two "heavens" but one earth.

With this line of reasoning pressed further, Origen treats Gen 1:1 as including the creation of rational creatures (*rationabilium creaturarum vel intellectualium* [*De Principiis*, 2.9.1; cf. Jubilees 2:2]). The creation described in Gen 1:1 is distinguished from the later creation of the firmament and dry land, which only "borrowed (their) names" (*Certum est enim quia non de 'firmamento' neque de 'arida' sed de illo caelo ac terra dicatur, quorum caelum hoc et terra quam videmus vocabula postea mutuata sunt* [2.9.1]). Indeed, according to Origen, Moses introduces Gen 1:1 "rather secretively" (*lantentius*). Origen sharply distinguished the rational or incorporeal realm from the corporeal, visible nature (3.6.7). In his *Homilies on Genesis*, two "heavens" are described: one that is spiritual (*ex spiritu*) and acts as God's throne (from Isaiah 66:1) and one corporeal, namely, the firmament. Both correspond to the spiritual and exterior natures of human beings (*Homilies on Genesis* 1.2).

In contrast, Tertullian rejects a rational, as opposed to sensible, creation. Yet he also considers Gen 1:1 as a creation statement: After the earth "was made, waiting to be made perfect, it was in the meantime invisible and unfinished" (*Postea ergo quam fact est, futura etiam perfecta, interim erat inuisibilis et rudis* [*Against Hermogenes* 29]). This "earth" was made "invisible," "waiting to appear" (*uideri sustinebat*) as the dry land (*arida*) until its "separation from the water" (*ex diuortio humoris*) took place (29). Tertullian makes clear that the earth mentioned in v 1 is the same as in v 9: "'Appear,' he says, not 'be made'" (*videatur, inquit, non fiat* [29]). However, Gen 1:2 ("the earth was invisible and unfinished") "refers to that earth which God made separately along with the heaven" (*terra autem erat inuisiblis et rudis ad eam pertinet, quam deus cum caelo parauit* [29]). Similarly, the heaven in both vv 1 and 7 are identical (*et uocauit deus firmamentum caelum, ipsum, quod in primordio fecerat* [26]). Crucial for Tertullian is the *coniunctiva particula* of the Greek, which he renders as *autem*. The particle, thus, connects the two sentences together (*ad connexum narrationi adpositum est* [26]) and has the force of identifying the "earth" and "heaven" of 1:1 with what follows. In sum, Tertullian presents a strictly sequential development of creation without maintaining any rigid distinction between the first two verses with the rest of the creation account. Of all the early patristic interpretations, Tertullian's explanation seems to be the most congruent with the sense of the LXX: not a "double creation" in the sense of two separate worlds, one intellectual and one sensible, but a sequential creation from start (v 1) to finish (v 31). Nevertheless, both the structure and content of the LXX, as Theophilus notes, seem to maintain a distinction between Gen 1:1-2 and 3-31, a distinction between an "aformal" and a "formful" creation. It is understandable that this *structural tension* within the text has prompted many early commentators to separate the two sections as descriptions of two independent creations.

[108]   B. W. Anderson, "A Stylistic Study of the Priestly Creation Story," in *Canon and Authority*, ed. G. W. Coats and B. O. Long (Philadelphia: Fortress Press, 1977) 155-159.

[109]   See Chapter Three for a survey of the failed attempts to describe a thematic structure of corresponding creation acts for the MT.

[110]   Gunkel, *Genesis*, 118. Cf. Philo *Opf.* 45-6 and Theophilus *Ad Autocylum* 2.15.

[111]   See translation above.

[112]   Augustine perceptively notes this in his discussion of the creation of humans in *De Genesi ad litteram libri duodecim* 3.20.31:

> Dixit enim Deus, 'Faciamus hominem ad imaginem et similitudinem nostran', etc. Ac deinde non dicitur, 'Et sic est factum'; sed jam subinfertur, 'Et fecit Deus hominem ad imaginem Dei'; quia et ipsa natura scilicet intellectualis est, sicut illa lux, et proptera hoc est ei fieri, quod est agnoscere Verbum Dei per quod fit.

For God said, "Let us make humanity to our own image and likeness," etc. And then the sacred writer does not go on to say, "And so it was done," but he proceeds immediately to add, "And God made humanity in the image of God." Since the nature of this creature is intellectual, as is the light previously mentioned, its creation is identified with its knowing the Word of God through whom [humanity] was made.

The rationale is complex. Augustine identifies the creation of light as the creation of rational creatures by eternal light (2.8.19). The formulas *et sic est factum* and *et fecit Deus* are used only with regard to irrational creatures, whose creation begins in the "mind of a rational creature" (*in cognitione rationalis creaturae*) and is fulfilled as an existing irrational creature (*in aliqua creatura, quae rationalis non esset*, 3.20.32). *Et sic est factum* refers to the angels' intellects' having received knowledge of the essence of the particular creature to be made (2.8.19). Thus Augustine sees creation as having an epistemological component: The creation of humans is equivalent to its "knowing the Divine Word through whom it was made" (*hoc est ei fieri, quod est agnoscere Verbum Dei per quod fit*). On the other hand, "bodies or irrational souls" (*sive corpora sive irrationales animae*) are created in a two-step process. Thus the creation of light and human beings is described without the transition formula because God gives both angels and human beings a knowledge of themselves in the utterance of the command.

[113] The issue of whether the hortatory subjunctive implies the existence of other divine beings or is exclusively a form of self-address is not pertinent to the argument at hand, for in either case God is included in the command and responds accordingly in the fulfillment.

[114] The term *thēria* is well explicated by Theophilus of Antioch (*Ad Autolycum* 2.17). He describes the wild animals as "evil or poisonous" (*kaka . . . ē iobola*), although he believes that they were originally tame before the fall:

> *hopotan oun palin ho anthropos anadramē eis to kata physin mēketi kakopoion, kakeina apokatastathēsetai eis tēn hemrotēta*

> Whenever human beings again return to their natural state and so no longer do evil, they (i.e., the animals) too will be restored to their original tameness.

Clearly, Theophilus had Isa 11:6-9 in mind.

[115] See translation note for 1:2.

3

THE MASORETIC TEXT
OF GENESIS 1:1–2:3

BACKGROUND

The text of the Hebrew Bible is often called Masoretic because its final form is based on the masora.[1] Masoretic activity on the Hebrew text flourished between 500 and 1000 CE, during which the masora was codified.[2] The masora's final authority can primarily be attributed to the activity of the so-called "Tiberian Masoretes," specifically the Ben Asher family, whose five generations can be dated between ca. 780 and 930 CE.[3]

The consonantal text of the MT, however, is undoubtedly much earlier. Goshen-Gottstein places the stabilization of the MT text in the early first century BCE,[4] in which the MT was beginning to become the dominant Hebrew text. Cross has suggested in light of the Qumran discoveries that the text preserved by the MT had its origins in Babylon, which he admitted could only be ascertained by a process of elimination.[5]

The theory of "local texts" has been seriously undermined by the fact that, as in the case of the book of Jeremiah, at least two textual traditions existed side by side at Qumran: 4QJer[b], which resembles the shorter LXX text, and 4QJer[a], which resembles the longer MT.[6] In light of this, the problem of provenance for the MT (as well as for the Hebrew *Vorlage* of the LXX[7]) cannot presently be resolved. Against Kahle's view that the MT was created by 100 CE, Tov points out that scrolls from places in the

Judean desert other than Qumran (Murabba'at, Naḥal Ḥever, Nahal Tse'elim and Masada [70 CE–130 CE]) "represent almost exclusively the Massoretic text," thereby suggesting that already in the late first century the MT had replaced other textual traditions.[8] Most decisive, however, are the manuscripts found at Qumran that reflect the "proto-Masoretic" tradition. Thus, Tov concludes, "the Massoretic text was not created in the first two centuries A.D., but this text existed already in the last two centuries B.C."[9] In short, the most that can be said presently is that the textual tradition that culminated in the MT already existed in disseminated form by the second century BCE. Indeed, one can discern possible signs of editorial activity in the development of the MT textual tradition of the Pentateuch and Former Prophets from the early Maccabean period.[10]

TRANSLATION OF THE MT TEXT OF GENESIS 1:1–2:3

1:1   When God began[11] to create the heaven and the earth,[12]

1:2   (the earth, moreover,[13] having been a hodge-podge,[14] with darkness upon the deep[15] and the divine wind[16] sweeping[17] over the waters),

1:3   God said, "Let there be light." So there was light.

1:4   And God saw that the light was good, and God divided between the light and the darkness.

1:5   God called the light day, and the darkness he called night. There was evening and then morning, day one.

1:6   Then God said, "Let there be a firmament in the midst of the waters so that[18] it may be a constant divider[19] between the waters."

1:7   So God made the firmament and divided between the waters that were under the firmament and the waters that were above the firmament. And so it was.

1:8   God called the firmament heaven. There was evening and then morning, a second day.

1:9   Then God said, "Let the waters under the heavens be gathered[20] into one place so that[21] the dry land can appear." And it happened as such.

1:10   God called the dry land earth and the collection of waters he called seas. And God saw that it was good.

1:11   Then God said, "Let the earth cause wild vegetation[22] to sprout: plants[23] bearing seed, fruit-trees bearing fruit according to their kinds[24] whose seed is inside it upon the earth." And it came about as follows:

1:12 The earth brought forth wild vegetation: plants bearing seed according to their kinds and trees bearing fruit whose seed is inside it, according to their kinds. And God saw that it was good.

1:13 And there was evening and there was morning, a third day.

1:14 God said, "Let there be luminaries in the firmament of the heavens for separating between the day and the night and let them be for signs, for seasons, for days, and years.

1:15 And let them be as luminaries in the firmament of heaven to give light upon the earth." Thus it happened as follows:

1:16 God made the two great luminaries: the greater luminary for ruling over the day; and the smaller luminary for ruling over the night; and also the stars.

1:17 And God placed them in the firmament of heaven to give light upon the earth,

1:18 To rule the day and the night, and to divide between the light and the darkness. And God saw that it was good.

1:19 There was evening and then there was morning, a fourth day.

1:20 God said, "Let the waters produce[25] swarms of living creatures and let winged creatures fly[26] about above the earth up to the surface of the firmament of heaven."

1:21 So God created the great sea monsters and every living creature that moves, of which the waters produced swarms,[27] according to their kinds, and every winged creature according to its kind. And God saw that it was good.

1:22 And God blessed them, saying, "Be fruitful and multiply and fill the waters in the seas, and let the winged creatures increase on the earth."

1:23 And it was evening and then it was morning, a fifth day.

1:24 And God said, "Let the earth bring forth living creatures according to their kind: domestic animals,[28] crawlers,[29] and wild animals,[30] according to their kinds." And it happened as follows:

1:25 And God made the wild animals according to their kinds, domestic animals, and every animal that crawls on the ground according to their kinds, and God saw that it was good.

1:26 And God said, "Let us make human beings[31] in our image, according to our likeness so that they may rule[32] over the fish of the sea, and the winged creatures of the sky, over the domestic animals, and over all the land,[33] and over every creature that crawls upon the ground."

1:27 So God created the human beings in his image, in the image of God he created them; male and female he created them.

1:28 And God blessed them and God said to them, "Be fruitful and multiply and fill the earth and subdue it and rule over the fish of the sea and over the winged creatures of the heavens and over every creature that crawls on the ground."

1:29   And God said, "See here! I hereby give[34] to you every plant that bears seed upon the surface of the whole land and every tree on which the tree's fruit bears seed. You shall have it for food.

1:30   And to every wild land animal, to every winged creature of the heavens, to every creature that crawls on the ground in which there is the breath of life [I hereby give] all the vegetative plants[35] for food." And so it was.

1:31   And God saw everything that he had made, and, indeed, it was very good. And there was evening and there was morning, a sixth day.

2:1   Thus the heaven and the earth and all their host were completed.[36]

2:2   On the seventh day God had completed his work that he had done and rested on the seventh day from all his work that he had done.

2:3   And God blessed the seventh day and made it holy, because on it he rested from all his work that God had done in creation.[37]

Exegetical Issues

Genesis 1:1

The Lexical Argument: bĕrēʾšît

The exegetical literature concerning the syntax of the first verse is, to put it mildly, immense. The issues at stake are the verse's syntactical relation to 1:2 and the structural relationship between the first two verses and the formal creation account beginning in 1:3. The vigor with which both ancient and modern commentators have argued opposing positions betrays the fact that more than simply syntactical precision is at stake; there are also deep-seated theological conflicts over the way in which God is to be viewed in relation to the cosmos.

The translation adopted here is the one argued by Rashi (d. 1105), who states that "its plain sense" (pĕšûtô) should be interpreted as bĕrēʾšît bĕrîʾat, that is, by interpreting the finite verb as a substantive to which the prepositional phrase is in construct, rendering it adverbially.[38] Rashi cites a similar example in Hos 1:2 in which the noun tĕhillat is clearly in construct with the following clause. Rashi supports his argument by claiming that rēʾšît is found elsewhere only in construct and cites the examples of Jer 27:1, Gen 10:10, and Deut 18:4.

Such an interpretation, however, did not begin with Rashi, contrary to the opinions of most exegetes who have attempted the formidable task of recounting the history of interpretation of this verse.[39] P. Schäfer has uncovered some historical precursors to Rashi's interpretation.[40] One of the oldest midrashim, the Mekilta, claims that the LXX translators changed the meaning of the first verse:[41]

> This is one of the passages which they changed when writing the Torah for King Ptolemy. Likewise they wrote for him: 'God created in the beginning' (ʾĕlōhîm bārāʾ bĕrēʾšît).[42]

This allegation against the Greek translation is also picked up in *Tanhuma B Shemot* 1.19, which lists ten such changes including Gen 1:1.[43] Such a Hebrew retroversion from the "Torah for King Ptolemy" would preclude the possibility of translating Gen 1:1 as a dependent clause in the "original" Hebrew. In addition, early rabbinical texts unambiguously claim light as the first created substance (*Beresit Rabbah* 3:1; *Shemot Rabbah* 15:22; *Pirqe* 3), the last two of which favor the order given in Ps 104:2 over and against that of Gen 1:1-3.[44] Thus, it is clear that Rashi's reading was not entirely innovative.

In short, Rashi has only proved that the syntactical construction is possible, but is it probable? Or is it more probable that Gen 1:1 constitutes an independent sentence, as rendered by the ancient translations? Beginning with H. Ewald, much of modern scholarship has focused on this issue.[45] In light of the most recent discussions, however, it is no longer sufficient to defend Rashi's interpretation by simply stating that bĕrēʾšît lacks an article and thus is in construct to the following finite verb, as LaSor confidently claimed in 1956.[46]

As for the recent discussion, one must begin with P. Humbert's ground-breaking article (1955), in which he investigated the use of rēʾšît and discovered that of the fifty-one times the word is used, only twelve instances could be considered "proprement temporel."[47] From these only one instance could be found in the absolute state, namely Isa 46:10 (*maggîd mērēʾšît ʾaḥărît*), which, however, has relative meaning, according to him:

> Le sens même de rēšît dans Es. 46,10 est au fond relatif, même si la construction ne l'est pas et si rēšît est à l'état absolu.[48]

Humbert's support comes from the LXX's adverbial rendering of the word (*anaggelōn proteron ta eschata*) and the Hebrew correlation between mērēʾšît and ʾaḥărît, which indicates a "terminus a quo et terminus ad quem d'un certain laps de temps."[49] Humbert's suggestion has led to intense scrutiny of Isa 46:10. W. Lane reinforces Humbert's argument by pointing out that ʾaḥărît is always used with relative rather than absolute meaning.[50] So, according to Lane, the verse simply states that Yahweh "continually announces things before they happen."[51] In addition, bĕrēʾšît is elsewhere consistently used in construct (Jer 26:1; 27:1; 28:1; 49:34; Hos 9:10 [with suffix]).

Humbert's lexical investigation has met criticism on two fronts. Eichrodt extended the lexical investigation to the whole range of words related to rēʾšît, focusing mainly on rōʾš and citing Isa 40:21; 41:4; and Prov 8:23. The last example proves that "mērōʾš is unequivocally determined by the preceding mēʿôlām."[52] One need only point out, however, that Eichrodt's analysis oversteps the bounds of strict lexical investigation: The abstract ending -ît attached to rōʾš places rēʾšît in a different semantic field.[53] Indeed, one could claim that Humbert's assertion that rēʾšît is a construct is so convincing that Eichrodt is forced to look elsewhere to render Gen 1:1 as an independent sentence.

In addition, all the examples of related words used absolutely but without the article (mērōʾš in Isa 40:21; 41:4, 26; 48:16; miqqedem in Isa 46:10; mēʿôlām in Isa 46:9) are culled from poetic texts, which by nature tend to "omit" the articles for nouns considered definite.[54] Thus, on methodological grounds alone the comparison of poetic texts with Genesis 1 is problematic when used to argue for the absolute function of bĕrēʾšît in Gen 1:1. Indeed, the absence of the article still supports the interpretation of bĕrēʾšît as a construct.

On another front, Ridderbos claims that the term's use in Prov 8:22 (which Humbert concedes implies absolute beginning) and Sir 15:14 is enough to prove absolute temporal significance.[55] The former instance, however, is in construct and obviously has relative meaning: YHWH qānānî rēʾšît darkô. As for the Sirach text, it is probable that 15:14a is to be taken as a temporally dependent clause.[56] Moreover, the term is evidently an awkward quotation of Gen 1:1 (ʾĕlōhîm mibbĕrēʾšît), given the double preposition, which treats bĕrēʾšît as a terminus technicus, or as Di Lella puts it, "a stock phrase that is taken as a single noun."[57] Although Ridderbos grants Humbert's claim that Isa 46:10 has relative meaning, he claims that it is still very much possible that Gen 1:1 has absolute meaning.[58] But Ridderbos cannot prove that it is lexicographically probable, especially when his two examples are questionable. Once again, it is worth pointing out that all the instances commonly cited to support an absolute meaning for bĕrēʾšît without the article are drawn from poetic texts, whose grammatical and stylistic rules differ from those of prose, ȧnd thus cannot be used as strict parallels with the prose text of Gen 1:1-31.[59]

Two other major linguistic refutations against rendering Gen 1:1 as a dependent clause have been recently attempted. In his thorough review of the literature, Hasel shows that the construct rendering does not hinge on the fact that rēʾšît lacks an article, as many early proponents of reading the construct state have claimed.[60] In order to show that rēʾšît in Gen 1:1 is in an absolute state, Hasel (borrowing from Young[61]) relies on the Masoretic accentuation, specifically with the disjunctive accent ṭiphāh under the first word. The force of this argument, however, is undercut by the fact that disjunctive accents are used elsewhere in obvious construct situations of bĕrēʾšît (Jer 26:1; 27:1; 49:34 [with the rĕbîăʿ] and Jer 28:1 [with the pašṭāʾ]).[62]

Waltke makes similar arguments, but ultimately relies on the continuity of early translations, an undoubtedly weighty argument against the construct rendering.[63] However, the force of such argumentation is severely weakened by the fact that the LXX tends to miss the subtle grammatical construction in other instances of a noun in construct with a verb. One clear case is that of Hos 1:2 (tĕḥillat dibber YHWH bĕhôšēaʿ wayyōʾmer YHWH ʾel hôšēaʿ), which most modern translators render as "When Yahweh first spoke through Hosea, Yahweh said to Hosea." The LXX, on the other hand, misses the temporally dependent syntax:

> archē logou kuriou en Osēe kai eipe kurios pros Osēe.
>
> The beginning of the word of the Lord through Hosea.
> And the Lord said to Hosea.

Other examples of misunderstood temporal clauses introduced, for instance, by the temporal particle ʿet include Jer 6:15 (LXX: en kairǭ episkopes; MT: bĕʿēt pĕqadtîm) and 50:31 (LXX 27:31: ho kairos ekdikēseōs sou; MT: ʿēt pĕqadtîkā), in which the finite verb is rendered as a noun in Greek. Clearly, some Greek translators missed this syntactical feature of Hebrew dependent clauses, and this explanation can just as easily be posited for the Greek translation of Gen 1:1.

In addition, even rabbinic texts on occasion misconstrued relative clauses, as in Ps 81:6 and Hos 1:2.[64] Thus the importance often assigned to early translations and treatments of biblical texts is not decisive for interpreting Gen 1:1 as an independent clause, for there are numerous cases both in Greek translation and in rabbinic tradition in which the syntax of biblical Hebrew is missed. As is well known, the possible syntactical construction of Gen 1:1 (clearly evident in Hos 1:2) is a common feature in Akkadian grammar: a noun in construct with a verbal clause without the relative pronoun *ša*.[65] In Hebrew it is less common but nonetheless present (e.g., Lev 14:46; 25:48; 1 Sam 5:9; 25:15; Isa 29:1; Exod 4:13; Jer 2:8; Ps 16:3; 58:9; 81:6).

The Argument from Syntactical Parallels

Both Speiser[66] and Orlinksy[67] employ biblical and extra-bilbical parallels in order to demonstrate that Gen 1:1-3 can be rendered as a "dependent clause-(parenthetical clause)-main clause" construction. The two major parallels cited are Gen 2:4b-7 and *Enuma Elish* lines 1-9.

Gen 1:1	Gen 2:4b
1) *běrē'šît bārā' 'ĕlōhîm 'ēt haššāmayim wě'ēt hā'āreṣ*	*běyôm 'ăśôt YHWH 'ĕlōhîm 'ereṣ wěšāmāyim*

Gen 1:2	Gen 2:5-6
2) *wěhā'āreṣ hāytāh tōhû wābōhû . . .*	*wěkōl śîaḥ haśśādeh ṭerem yihyeh bā'āreṣ . . . wěkol 'ēśeb haśśādeh ṭerem yiṣmāḥ kî . . . wě'ēd ya'ăleh min hā'āreṣ . . . wěhišqāh 'et kol pěnê hā'ădāmāh*

Gen 1:3	Gen 2:7
3) *wayyō'mer 'ĕlōhîm*	*wayyîser YHWH 'ĕlōhîm 'et hā'ādām . . .*

There is much to be said both for and against these parallels. The two texts in Genesis seem to exhibit a similar *general* syntactical outline, if one grants the dependent clause of Gen 1:1. The order of the *waw* + noun + verb marks the parenthetical construction in Gen 2:5-6, a construction identical to Gen 1:2, with the main clause arranged in normal consecutive order (Gen 1:3; 2:7). However, Heidel points out that the parallel is not exact, since the verb aspect is imperfect in Gen 2:5-6 and perfect in Gen 1:2.[68] Yet two reasons can easily account for the use of the imperfect in Gen 2:5-6. The first two instances of the imperfect result from the use of the negative adverb *ṭerem*, which normally takes an imperfect verb but frequently with pluperfect sense (Gen 19:4; 27:33; Num 11:33; see G-K §152r). The last clause (Gen 2:6) uses the imperfect, which is followed by the perfect with *waw*-consecutive to designate iterative action. Indeed, parenthetical constructions of *waw* + noun + verb commonly use the perfect (Jonah 3:3, Zech 3:2-3). Thus, there is little reason against using Gen 2:4b-7 as a syntactical model for Gen 1:1-3, if one simply takes the syntax as a point of comparison. Although Hasel makes much of Westermann's construal of 2:4b-6 as a "Vordersatz" and 2:7 as a "Nachsatz,"[69] the point is merely academic, for Westermann's translation construes 2:5-6 as parenthetical in relation to 2:4b.[70] Despite the fact that he views vv 4b-6 as a "description of the situation,"[71] Westermann elsewhere states that "v. 7 is the main sentence, the statement to which the introduction in v. 4b is directed,"[72] thereby placing 4b on a syntactical level distinct from vv 5-6. Westermann assumes the parenthetical nature of the 2:5-6 without explicitly stating it.

In short, it seems that Gen 1:1-3 and 2:4b-7 do indeed resemble each other syntactically: The dependent clauses introduce *ʾĕlōhîm*; the parenthetical clauses describe the natural condition (the difference being that 1:2 makes a positive statement, whereas 2:5-6 is expressed negatively); and the main clause describes divine action.

The other popular example employed to illustrate the dependent clause of Gen 1:1 is the first nine lines of *Enuma Elish*.

> 1) *enūma eliš la nabû šamāmū*
> 2) *šapliš ammātum šuma la zakrat*
> 3) *Apsûma restu zārušun*
> 4) *Mummu Tiāmat muallidat gimrišun*
> 5) *mêšunu ištēniš iḫiquma*
> 6) *gipāra la kiṣṣuru ṣuṣâ la šeʾû*
> 7) *enūma ilani la šūpū manāma*
> 8) *šuma la zukkuru šimatu la šima*
> 9) *ibbanuma ilani qerebšun*

Speiser identifies lines 1-2 as a dependent temporal clause, lines 3-8 as parenthetical, and line 9 as the main clause.[73] It is clear, however, that the syntactical picture is more complex. Lines 1-7 are all subordinate to line 8, since, with the exception of line 5, all lines contain statives or verbal adjectives (line 3 being nominal), whereas line 9 has a finite verb. From syntax alone, lines 1, 2, 7, and 8 appear to function syntactically on the same level, since lines 1 and 7 are prefaced with the temporal conjunction *enūma* with the following lines (2 and 8) parallel to 1 and 7. In addition, each line contains the negative particle *la*. As such, line 6 could be included as a compound dependent temporal clause. However, the conjunctive particle *ma* at the end of line 5 indicates subordination to line 6. Consequently, lines 1-2 and 7-8 comprise a series of syntactically separate, temporally dependent clauses expressing the "not-yetness" of both the universe and divine world. Lines 3-5, on the other hand, describe the primeval world of Apsu and Tiamat with positive statements. Of note is the fact that lines 3-5 are bracketed by the common particle *ma*. The particle's first instance in line 3 clearly emphasizes the subject Apsu. Line 4 is parallel to line 3 with the mention of Tiamat predicated with the participial form of *alādum*. Thus, lines 3 and 4 are non-finite verbal sentences, yet line 5 contains the preterite form of *ḫâqu* with the coordinating particle *ma*, implying logical subordination to the following clause. The kind of subordination is easily discerned. Line 5 is related causally to line 6: The waters' state of commingling precludes the emergence of land. A working translation of the opening of the epic *Enuma Elish* is as follows:

1) When the heavens above had not yet been named,
2) Nor the earth below had not yet been given name,
3) (There was only primordial Apsu, their progenitor,
4) [and] maker Tiamat, who bore them all,
5) Since their waters had intermingled,
6) No pasture land was yet formed, no marshes yet found),
7) When none of the gods had yet appeared,
8) No god had yet been given name, no decrees yet established,
9) The gods were created therein.

In short, lines 1-2 and 7-8 comprise a series of temporal clauses that depict the "non-nameness" or non-existence of creation, whereas lines 3-5 describe the existence of Apsu and Tiamat and the commingling of their waters. The latter group of lines comprises a parenthetical digression of existence inserted into a series of negative dependent clauses, yet rhetorically they explain the phenomenon described in line 6, the absence of land. In comparison with the Genesis texts, the opening of the *Enuma Elish* is clearly more involved, and illustrates the syntactical complexity of a long sentence in Semitic literature, one that can shift from dependent clauses to parenthetical statements and vice versa.

Structural Considerations

Both the comparison of syntactical parallels and the lexical-statistical method lend only probability to rendering Gen 1:1 as a dependent clause. However, perhaps further light can be shed on the syntax of Gen 1:1 by comparing the beginning and ending of the priestly account:

1:1   *bĕrēʾšît bārāʾ ʾĕlōhîm ʾet haššāmayim wĕʾēt hāʾāreṣ*

2:1   *waykullû haššāmayim wĕhāʾāreṣ . . .*
2:2   *waykal ʾĕlōhîm . . . mĕlaʾkĕtô ʾăšer ʿāśāh*

Gen 1:1 and 2:1 are parallel in structure, given the common merismus *haššāmayim/hāʾāreṣ*. In addition, 1:1 is parallel with 2:2 in light of the common syntactical order verb-subject-object. Since these parallels structurally comprise the beginning and ending (2:1-3) of the creation passage and provide an inclusio, one would expect them to balance each other semantically to some degree. Critical to the interpretation of 1:1 is the predicate (*bĕrēʾšît bārāʾ*); hence, the predicate of 2:1 may very well be the key for unlocking the puzzle. The *Pual* of *klh* in two out of the three instances in which it is attested means "be finished" or "be completed" (Ps 72:20; Gen 2:1), identical in meaning to its active form (*Piel*) in 2:2. Semantically a symmetrical counterpoint to the verb would be an adverbial rendering of *bĕrēʾšît* with *bārāʾ*. That is, "to finish creating" has its counterpoint with "to begin creating." No semantic counterpart to 2:1-2 is to be found if 1:1 is to be rendered in the traditional absolute sense. Thus, *waykal ʾĕlōhîm* and *waykullû haššāmayim wĕhāʾāreṣ* of 2:2 and 2:1 are counterbalanced semantically by *bĕrēʾšît bārāʾ ʾĕlōhîm* of 1:1 only when one takes the prepositional phrase in construct to the verb.

In addition, one wonders whether the epanastrophic relationship[74] between the first two words of Gen 1:1 with the common consonants *brʾ* is any clue that the prepositional phrase and the verb were meant to be considered inextricably bound syntactically. Young argues vigorously that such alliteration "would seem to tie up the concept expressed by *bĕrēʾšît* with that of *bārāʾ*," but, surprisingly, with the aim of demonstrating that Gen 1:1 is an independent sentence.[75] Numerous examples show that the verb *brʾ* is not necessarily bound to temporal beginnings, since its use can also refer to future events (e.g., Jer 31:22; Isa 4:5; 41:20). Hence, a more plausible case for semantically explaining the alliterative link between the first two words is by taking *bĕrēʾšît* as adverbial, modifying *bārāʾ*.

Another argument used for reading Gen 1:1 as an independent clause is frequently cast in the following form: "If the author really wanted to express a dependent clause, he would have . . . ." Heidel, for instance, claims the author would have used *bĕyôm* to introduce the first verse, instead of *bĕrē'šît*.[76] But this would not render the meaning: "when God *began* to create . . ." Waltke claims that "Moses could not have used any other construction to denote the first word as in the absolute state, but he could have opted for a different construction to indicate clearly the construct state."[77] Waltke is thinking of 2:4b with its use of the "unambiguous infinitive construct."[78] His argument partly stems from his denial of the documentary hypothesis, and thus is easily undercut, since one can explain the use of the finite verb by P instead of the infinitive as a stylistic preference (see Lev 14:46; 25:48). Furthermore, Waltke's statement is simply not true: The author could have rearranged the word order to erase the syntactical ambiguity, as in the *Mekilta* of Exod 12:40 (see above). The fact that the Masoretes did not point the preposition as definite still bears some, albeit insufficient, evidence for the dependent construction.

All in all, rendering Gen 1:1 as a dependent clause resolves the structural tension one finds in all the early translations of the Hebrew, namely the tension between 1:1 and 1:3, the first formal report of a creative act. As noted with regard to the LXX (Chapter Two), to render Gen 1:1 as an independent sentence automatically establishes a structural tension with the formal creation section beginning with v 3. The double creation theories from the Neo-Platonic to the modern varieties can all be seen as attempts to maintain 1:1 as an independent clause, and consequently, they must resort to positing two kinds of creation: an initial "pre-creative" creation (1:1) and the formal creation beginning with 1:3.

Such a structural tension has led some scholars, beginning with H. Strack and most notably Gunkel,[79] to suggest that 1:1 is to be taken as a summary statement. Indeed, the argument for considering 1:1 as a title, as opposed to taking it as the beginning of the creation report, attempts to reconcile the meaning of "earth," as part of the organized universe in v 1, with "earth" in a chaotic state in v 2.[80]

However, the construal of v 1 as a circumstantial clause implies an initial predicative state in relation to v 2: "When God *began* to create . . . (the earth being a hodge-podge . . .)." Thus, similar to construing v 1 as an independent title, the circumstantial clause rendering points to the objects *haššāmayim wĕ'ēt hā'āreṣ* as the end products that are temporally distinct from the state of *hā'āreṣ* as described in v 2. A similar temporal relationship is found in the following sentence: "When the woman began to rebuild her house, the house being a shambles after the tornado hit, she first repaired the fire-place." The word "house" in the initial circumstantial clause does not refer to a present condition; the woman is not constructing a "shambles," for if she were, then why would she bother?

What Waltke and others seem to overlook is the temporal force of the word *běrēʾšît*, which implies an initial predicative state while at the same time affirming *haššāmayim wěʾēt hāʾāreṣ* as the finished product. Moreover, whether as a title or a circumstantial clause, one must explain the presence of *hāʾāreṣ* in v 2 in its larger context, especially in relation to 1:10. Thus it is useless to set up 1:1 as an independent title in order to render a more consistent semantic field for the term *hāʾāreṣ*. Gunkel, for instance, claims that the phrase "the heaven and the earth" of 1:1 designates the completed, orderly creation; whereas, the term "the earth" alone in 1:2 connotes chaos.[81] Thus whether one takes the first verse as a summary title or a temporal clause, *hāʾāreṣ* will always show two faces in the first two verses.

One must also point out that nowhere else in the Hebrew Bible does such a title, or "introductory resumé," exist that begins with a prepositional phrase. Of course, the P material frequently employs titles, but of a completely different nature, always beginning with the demonstratives *ʾēleh* (e.g., Gen 2:4; 10:1; 11:10; 25:12; 25:19; 36:1; Exod 1:1) or *zeh* (5:1). To render Gen 1:1 as a title would be unprecedented in the pentateuchal material. As Hasel puts it:

> If the writer of Gen. 1 had wanted to say merely [that God was creator of heaven and earth, that is, as a title] he would certainly not have needed to begin his sentence with *běrēʾšît*.[82]

Conclusion

In summary, Gen 1:1-2 structurally makes best sense if considered as a series of clauses dependent upon 1:3, which describes the first creative act. Theologically, does this then imply the "autonomy of the chaotic matter," as Eichrodt and others so characterize the position of those who argue for a dependent clause?[83] Indeed, the case for the absolute, independent clause, coupled with the doctrine of *creatio ex nihilo*, as argued by Eichrodt and others, betrays a particular concern for preserving the character of God's transcendence and autonomy in relation to creation.[84] The language of syntax is utilized in direct correspondence to divine nature: Absolute transcendence requires an absolute clause, while an independent sentence reflects divine autonomy. Therefore, a relative, dependent clause, it is assumed, can only reflect a dependent deity.

Notwithstanding the inappropriate term "autonomy" to characterize the elements listed in 1:2, one need only realize that the autonomy of chaotic matter is a notion arrived at only when one presupposes its logical opposite, *creatio ex nihilo*, which Gen 1:1-3 neither rejects nor endorses. The first two verses simply do not reveal whether God created the list of "elements" in 1:2, and they certainly do not claim a malevolent, autonomous chaos. Furthermore, a circumstantial beginning to cosmogony need not imply a contingent deity.

Genesis 1:2

The syntax of the *waw* + subject + verb and its meaning have already been discussed in terms of the relation between vv 1 and 2 (and 3). Having established the likelihood that Gen 1:1 is a dependent clause, the question arises whether v 2 or v 3 is the main clause. The view that has won most adherents is that of Rashi. Abraham ibn Ezra's (d. 1167) alternative of considering verse 2 as the main clause has won few proponents, most notably Hugo Grotius (1583-1645) and most recently W. Gross.[85] Both Speiser and Orlinsky have claimed that the subject-verb order in v 2 implies *parenthetical* dependency.[86] Heidel, on the other hand, points out that the reversal of the expected verb-subject order can simply be attributed to the emphasis on the subject *hā'āreṣ*, citing Gen 1:5b, 3:1; and Isa 1:2b as examples,[87] which would be possible if 1:1 were independent. Cassuto argues in opposite fashion that the verb-subject order is *required* for 1:2 to be a dependent clause and cites Jer 26:1; 27:1; 28:1; and Hos 1:2 for support.[88] Cassuto's examples, however, can be cited in support of the syntactical dependency of v 3 on v 1. Hosea 1:2, for example (*tĕḥillat dibber YHWH bĕhôšēaʿ wayyō'mer YHWH*), is identical to the syntactical pattern of Gen 1:1, 3 (*bĕrē'šît bārā' 'ĕlōhîm . . . wayyō'mer 'ĕlōhîm*). The question remains, however, as to the syntactical character of v 2. Thus the debate revolves around the views of Rashi and Ibn Ezra.

Gross poses the issue well by asking whether v 2 constitutes the *Hintergrund* or the *Vordergrund* of the sentence.[89] He opts for the latter and argues that parenthetical constructions are by nature syntactically independent and asyndetically introduced,[90] and that Isa 6:1 is a good parallel (prepositional introduction of time + *waw* + verb).[91] However, the example drawn from Isaiah does not resolve the issue, since the verb is "pronounless" (*bišnat môt hammelek ʿuzziyyāhû wā'er'eh 'et 'ădonāy . . .*), in contrast to the clause beginning with the subject in 1:2. Furthermore,

Gross's categorical statement about parenthetical constructions is groundless. A parenthetical construction can be and usually is syntactically dependent on the preceding clause. Indeed, one typical use of the so-called "disjunctive-*waw*" is explanatory or parenthetical, which can "break into the main narrative to supply information relevant or necessary for the narrative."[92] Lambdin gives the examples of 1 Sam 1:9 and Gen 29:16, to which one can add Gen 13:7 and Ruth 4:6-7 (*IBHS* 39.2.3c). Furthermore, this function can be considered as part of the *waw*'s epexegetical use in that the *waw* serves to clarify or specify the sense of the preceding clause (*IBHS* 39.2.4), in this case, *hā'āreṣ* of the first verse. As mentioned above, 1:3 fits nicely as the main clause of v 1, as illustrated by Hos 1:2, and there is no reason not to consider Gen 1:2 as an epexegetical digression on the pre-creative condition of *hā'āreṣ*, which expresses a condition prior to the action described in 1:3, a digression that is essential for understanding both what precedes and follows 1:2.[93] Thus with this use of the *waw* the subject of the clause, *hā'āreṣ*, is naturally stressed.

It has been suggested by Blythin that Gen 1:2 is an addition.[94] Although Blythin overstates his case by regarding v 2 as a case of scribal interpolation or expansion, one cannot deny the explicative nature of v 2 in relation to the *hā'āreṣ* of v 1 in its temporal setting. Indeed, vv 1 and 3 go very well together syntactically. Furthermore, the primordial categories *tĕhôm*, *tōhû wābōhû*, and *rûaḥ 'ĕlōhîm* of v 2 do not figure elsewhere in the creation account. Thus I would not be adverse to considering 1:2 the result of a later stage in the literary development of the priestly cosmogony. However, it is the final form of the text which is paramount for our investigation: Whether a later stage or not, the parenthetical, explicative character of Gen 1:2 is clear.

The Meaning of tōhû wābōhû

Suggestions as to the exact meaning of the phrase *tōhû wābōhû* are varied. As for the etymological approach, attempts have been made to discern Egyptian antecedents. Kilian, for instance, attempts to trace *tōhû* to the Egyptian Chaos god *Heh* and *bōhû* to the chaos gods of nothingness and transience, most particularly *Niau*.[95] J. Ebach, on the other hand, finds a connection between *bōhû* and the Phoenician God *Baau* mentioned by Philo of Byblos, which he views as reflecting the plural of the Egyptian word *b3*.[96] However, no consideration is given to *tōhû*. Etymologically speaking, the easiest and most reasonable hypothesis is that of Görg, who connects the term directly to the Egyptian verbal bases *th3* and *bh3* ("abweichen" and "kopflos fliehen").[97] In conclusion, he offers the translation "haltlos und gestaltlos" in his attempt to reconstruct the "ornamentale Form des Wortpaars."[98] But how does he make the semantic jump from verbal bases that imply aimless *motion* to the notion of formlessness? I suspect it is because Görg senses that the qualities of motion alone do not fit the context of Gen 1:2, since *tōhû wābōhû* evidently describes a condition and not a direction or motion. If that is the case, then Görg's etymological enterprise is a dead end.

One need not, however, take the etymological route, on which countless suggestions have been made. There are enough occurrences of *tōhû* in the Hebrew literature to connote "devastation" of some sort.[99] Westermann helpfully illustrates its use by suggesting three categories: "desert" (Deut 32:10; Job 6:18; 12:24 = Ps 107:40), "devastation" (Isa 24:10; 34:11; 40:23: Jer 4:23), and "nothingness" (1 Sam 12:21; Isa 29:21; 40:17; 41:23; 44:9; 45:19; 49:4; 59:4). I would differ, however, on the last category, since Westermann appears to use the word "nothingness" as an umbrella term that levels out the variety of nuances *tōhû* can have in various contexts: 1 Sam 12:21 connotes "uselessness;" Isa 29:21, "groundless claims;" Isa 45:19, "uninhabitable chaos." As for Gen 1:2, Westermann's suggestion of a "desert waste" conveys too concrete a picture, especially since the waters and *tĕhôm* play a significant role in the precreative condition described in 1:2. Tsumura focuses exclusively on etymology as the key to unlocking the meaning of *tōhû*, and opts for the meaning "desert" or "aridness."[100] However, like Westermann, Tsumura adopts a rendering that does not match the context of the verse.

What is clear is that the term in its broadest sense implies uninhabitability, the opposite of creation, given the clear parallel in Isa 45:19. Sasson correctly observes that the phrase *tōhû wābōhû* is not quite a merismus (e.g., *haššāmayim wĕʾēt hāʾāreṣ*) and is different from a hendiadys (contra Speiser, Westermann, and Wenham), since neither designation takes account of the alliterative quality of the phrase.[101] Rather, it is a *farrago*, "wherein two usually alliterative words combine to give a meaning other than their constituent parts." The common rendering of "unformed and void" conveys too negative a picture that is unwarranted in the positive description of the condition. Sasson suggests the English word "hodgepodge." One could also suggest other farragos such as "mish-mash" or "topsy-turvy." However, the legitimate objection could be raised that such terms are too colloquial for rendering a priestly *terminus technicus*. This may be said of the last two farragos but not of "hodgepodge." Originally "hotchpotch" or "hotchpot," the term designated a particular dish composed of a mixture of various kinds of meats and vegetables, and was used in a more figurative sense as a mixture of heterogeneous ingredients. However, given the word's modern colloquial usage, one can imagine other descriptive phrases such as or "mingled mass" that would effectively capture the alliterative force of *tōhû wābōhû* in combination with the meaning of undifferentiation and formlessness.[102] Indeed, the alliterative quality of the Hebrew term has ensured its survival in modern language via the loanword "tohu-bohu" in French, meaning hubbub.

The Meaning of rûaḥ ʾĕlōhîm:

The debate between "wind" and "spirit" still rages among scholars and the choice of translation has usually revolved around whether Gen 1:2c should be considered a description of pre-creative chaos as in 1:2ab or a reference to divine creative potency.[103] Both the LXX and Targum Onkelos understand *rûaḥ* as "wind." One need only note that the P material elsewhere in the Genesis narrative uses *rûaḥ* in the sense of "wind" in relation to the waters (Gen 8:1). Orlinsky's helpful, albeit one-sided, article easily demonstrates the physical interpretation as the most likely possibility.[104] Many early proponents for a spiritualized meaning of *rûaḥ* invoked the parallel of a world-egg cosmogony,[105] for which there is scarce evidence. Curiously, Orlinsky sidesteps the issue of the meaning of the *nomen rectum*. Thus even with the translation "wind," the question still remains as to whether 1:2c is a description of chaos or of divine creative potency.

The most recent attempt to translate *rûaḥ ʾĕlōhîm* purely on the natural (as opposed to supernatural) level (e.g., "terrible storm") is given by P. J. Smith,[106] whose structural analysis attempts to demonstrate that all of v 2 is a statement concerning chaos. Smith's position depends, though, on his unproven assumption of the independence of Gen 1:1 and that "all three [of the expressions in v 2] are utilized in the description of the original condition of *hāʾāreṣ*," that is, a description of chaos with *rûaḥ ʾĕlōhîm* equivalent to *ḥōšek*.[107] To the contrary, what is described is a condition of pre-creation, of which *hāʾāreṣ*, *ḥōšek*, and *hammayim/tĕhôm* are all constituent parts. Furthermore, the translation "terrible storm" (with *ʾĕlōhîm* as a superlative) infuses v 2 with the sense of horrific chaos, for which there is no evidence (see below). The typical observation of the parallelism between *ḥōšek* and *rûaḥ ʾĕlōhîm* is forged only by the common preposition (*ʿal-pĕnê*).[108] While such parallelism implies some similarity, the appearance of the active participle in 2c (*mĕraḥepet*) underlines the distinctiveness of the expression over and against 2a and 2b by introducing motion prior to the stage of formal creation.

Lexical investigations are also indecisive in establishing the possibility of *ʾĕlōhîm* as a superlative, suggested as early as Spinoza (1670)[109] and argued by J. M. P. Smith (1928).[110] The best work is still that of D. Winton Thomas, who concludes that the term *ʾĕlōhîm* is never unambiguously used as a superlative.[111] His examination of the underlying issue of religious versus secular significance is helpful and exposes the artificiality of the division drawn to support the latter interpretation:

> If, when we say that the divine names in Hebrew are used to express the superlative, we mean that they have no religious significance at all and are merely intensifying epithets, I do not find a single example which decisively supports such a view.[112]

It is likely, then, that *rûaḥ ʾĕlōhîm* carries superlative connotations, but this in no way precludes any religious connotation. This is confirmed by the fact that *ʾĕlōhîm* is a term used consistently throughout the creation passage (35x) to refer to God.

With the translation "wind of God" lexically probable, what then is its function in cosmogony? The ancient Near Eastern material is ambiguous.[113] Elsewhere in pentateuchal literature, Gen 8:1 and Exod 14:21b speak of a wind sent by God to affect the waters and the Red Sea, respectively. The former is clearly priestly material, and thereby offers the closest parallel to Gen 1:2c. In order to cause the waters to "subside" (*škk*) and thereby reverse the effects of the flood, *ʾĕlōhîm* causes a strong *rûaḥ* to sweep (*wayyaʾăbēr*) over *hāʾāreṣ*. Here, *hāʾāreṣ* clearly refers to the earth in its reverted state, since there is no dry land (cf. 8:7, *yĕbōšet*, similar to *yabbāšāh* in Gen 1:10). Indeed, the flood story represents the reversion and reestablishment of creation.[114] Thus it seems that the *rûaḥ ʾĕlōhîm* of Gen 1:2c refers to the creative activity of the deity. As DeRoche points out, the fact that 1:2c is parallel with 1:2b can simply denote simultaneity rather than synonymity.[115] Hence, the unity of 1:2 is characterized by its temporality. That is, 1:2 describes the *pre*-creative condition: "chaos" and God's readiness to create. The fact that *rûaḥ* nowhere else figures in the account of creation also finds its parallel in the flood story. In both passages "the appearance of the *rûaḥ* is annunciatory."[116] One could also add that the role of *rûaḥ ʾĕlōhîm* as acting upon the waters evidently lies behind the appearance of the dry land in Gen 1:9-10, as is clearly assumed in Gen 8:1-5.

In sum, I would favor Blythin's conclusion that v 2c brings "the activity of God into positive relationship with the chaos" and serves as a natural transition to the initial act of creation in v 3 (cf. Ps 33:6).[117] Luyster convincingly demonstrates the theological significance of wind as connoting divine supremacy over both nature and people (Isa 11:15; Exod 14:21-22; 15:8; Ps 18:15; Hos 13:15).[118] In short, the *rûaḥ* of God is the very breath of God (see Exod 15:8, 10). As DeRoche has pointed out, Orlinsky's distinction between the spirit of God and wind sent by God does not reflect biblical categories: "Certainly the *rûaḥ* *ʾĕlōhîm* is not the third person of the Christian Trinity. But neither is it a wind in the meteorological sense."[119]

As for the relationship between the two verses and verse 3, it is clear that the first command (1:3) formally begins the six days of creation (see next section). The likelihood that *rûaḥ* *ʾĕlōhîm* implies more than simply a "god-awful storm," that is, as something part and parcel of natural chaos, does not thereby make 1:2c a part of the first day section; 1:2c is as much a description of the pre-creative condition of the cosmos as 1:2a and 2b. Gen 1:2, with its listing of undifferentiated elements and the *rûaḥ* *ʾĕlōhîm*, describes the state before creation formally begins. Unlike the Greek text, 1:1-2 of the MT serves only as the introduction to the formal account of creation (1:3-31).

Genesis 1:9

English translators have usually rendered the first half of the command in the passive voice: "Let the waters . . . be gathered together" (NRSV). The root *qwh* appears only once elsewhere in the Hebrew Bible, also in the *Niphal*. In Jer 3:17, the term is applied to the nations "in that day." It is one of three verbs (*qrʾ* and *hlk*), the other two of which are active.

> In that time they will call (*yiqrĕʾû*) Jerusalem
>   "the throne of Yahweh,"
> and all the nations will gather themselves (*wĕniqwû*) to it,
>   to the name of the Yahweh in Jerusalem,
> and they will no longer follow (*yēlĕkû*) after the
>   stubbornness of their evil heart.

Given the parallelism with the verbs, the *reciprocal* meaning of the *Niphal* of *qwh* is to be preferred in this context (see *IBHS* 23.4e). Indeed, to render it passively would be to invoke an *actant*, which is nowhere implied in the immediate context. One finds a similar syntactical

situation in a synonym of *qwh*, namely *ʾsp*. In Gen 49:1 the *Niphal* of *ʾsp* is
used to convey reciprocal action:

> *wayyiqrāʾ yaʾăqob ʾel bānāyw wayyōʾmer hēʾāsĕpû*
>
> Then Jacob called his sons and said, "Gather (yourselves) together . . .
> (see *IBHS* 23.4e).

In the Genesis passage, the waters either "gather (themselves)" or "are
gathered" (by God). To decide the exact nuance, one must look at the
larger context and discern whether the waters exhibit any initiative
quality. Genesis 1:20 and 21b attribute active participation to the *mayim*
in the creation of sea creatures. Hence, water is not an inert object in the
creation account. Furthermore, its counterpart, the earth, is clearly given
creative potentiality in 1:11, 12, and 24. However, one must give precedence to the immediate context of 1:9. Logically the key would lie in the
fulfillment of the command: If God does the gathering of the waters, then
the verb in v 9 must be rendered passively.

However, there is no fulfillment report following the "transition"
formula in the MT. Thus, a narrative gap emerges which must be filled in
the reading/listening process. To "fill" the gap, the transition formula
must function as an *execution formula* by presupposing the fulfillment
rather than leading towards it. As for the kind of fulfillment, clues are
present in the context of the previous and subsequent fulfillments. The
immediately preceding fulfillment is reported in 1:7, in which God
creates the firmament (*wayyaʿaś ʾĕlōhîm ʾet hārāqîaʿ*). In addition, all the
following fulfillments (1:16, 17, 21, 22, 25, 27), with the exception of 1:12,
depict *ʾĕlōhîm* as the active subject of the verbs relating to creation (*brʾ*,
ʿsh, ntn, and *brk*). Thus one would expect the narrative gap following 1:9
to read by analogy with most other fulfillment reports: "So God gathered
the waters" (*wayyiqew ʾĕlōhîm hammayim . . .*). Consequently, by implication the *Niphal* form *yiqqaw* should be taken in a strictly passive sense.[120]

The methodical movement of the creation account from command to
transition formula to fulfillment report in most cases in the MT (and in all
cases in the LXX except 1:26-27) encourages such a reading of 1:9. For an
ancient Israelite the narrative gap in the account would not have
presented itself as a problem as it might for the modern exegete, who
must work at translating and interpreting an ancient text. Rather, the
immediate context of the missing fulfillment report simply nuances the
reading of 1:9 in a particular way, namely in preserving God's active role

in the gathering of the waters presupposed by the execution formula at the end of 1:9.

Genesis 1:30

In 1:30 a new botanical term, *yereq*, is introduced in construct with *ʿēśeb*. Lexically, *yereq* is a more general term than *ʿēśeb*, since it can include both *ʿēśeb* and *ʿēṣ* (Exod 10:15). In Gen 1:30 it seems to refer to any green plant.[121] The term is used in conjunction with *ʿēśeb* in order to delineate what is given to the animals for food. Most scholars make a hard and fast distinction between what is given to human beings and what is given to animals in 1:29: seed bearing plants and fruit trees for human beings, green plants for animals.[122] Yet such a demarcation cannot be rigidly maintained, given the wide semantic range of *yereq*. In other words, *ʿēśeb zorēaʿ zeraʿ* (1:29) and *yereq ʿēśeb* (1:30) are not mutually exclusive categories. To human beings are given the plants that can be sown, a subcategory of the plants given to animals. But this is not to claim that no distinction is made in 1:29 between what human beings and animals are entitled to eat. What is meant is that animals are entitled to all plants, out of which sowable plants are especially designated to human beings. At the same time, there is no wedge driven between animals and human beings in terms of their respective vegetarian diets. Fruit trees, on the other hand, are exclusively designated for human consumption.

Many have noted the parallel in Gen 9:1-3 with Gen 1:28-29. Gen 9:3 reassesses the botanical realm's relation to the animal and human realms in the context of a new relation of animals to human beings:

kol remeś ʾăšer hûʾ ḥay lākem yihyeh lĕʾākĕlāh

Every creeping creature that lives you shall have for food.

kĕyereq ʿēśeb nātatî lākem ʾet kōl

As well as the green plants I hereby give to you every one (i.e., creeping creature).

As Dequeker has pointed out, most modern English translations of the verse are inaccurate (NRSV: "Every moving thing that lives shall be food for you; and just as I gave you the green plants, I give you everything"), since they treat 1:3b as elliptical, but in so doing confuse the botanical terminology established in Gen 1:29.[123] This type of translation is assumed by all modern commentaries and goes as far back as Rashi, who, however, recognized the wide semantic range of the construct phrase by stating with regard to Gen 1:29 that every *yereq ʿēśeb* was to be eaten by both animals and human beings.[124]

The preposition *kĕ* can be used elliptically, but always in conjunction with another preposition.[125] One can see, however, how such English translations arose, since the preposition *kĕ* most commonly expresses comparative likeness:[126] "As with the green plants, I give you every one" (namely, every moving creature). Thus, naturally, one would think of the green plants having been given at a previous time to human beings. But this contradicts Gen 1:30, in which the *yeqer ʿēśeb* is explicitly given to the *animals*! A more plausible interpretation that does not violate the botanical categories that P established in Genesis 1 is to take the preposition not as introducing an elliptical clause but as introducing an object similar to the object of the verb *ntn*, namely *ʾet kōl*, which refers to the animals. In other words, the particle *kĕ* denotes identity. This is common in legal material and is usually found under the construction of *kY kX* (e.g., Lev 24:16; see *IBHS* 11.2.9b) but here the direct object marker *ʾet* precludes the preposition from being attached, although the sense is clear: Both the animals (*kōl*) and the *yeqer ʿēśeb* are specifically given to human beings. As Dequeker puts it, "The meaning of verse 3 . . . is that all living beings, *together with their food*, are given to" human beings (italics added).[127]

Although Dequeker correctly translates 9:3 (without grammatical explanation), this in no way supports his central thesis that 9:3 simply repeats the sense of 1:28-29 and that there was never any distinction between the vegetarian diet instituted in Genesis 1 with the granting of meat in Gen 9:1-3. Dequeker sees no semantic difference between the granting of dominion over the animal kingdom in Gen 1:28-29 (*wĕkibšuhā ûrĕdû*) and granting human beings the right to kill animals for food (*yihyeh lĕʾākĕlāh* or *nātatî lākem ʾet kōl*) in 9:3. But clearly the different terminology implies different meaning. Furthermore, the lack of any mention of human entitlement to animals for food in Genesis 1 coupled with a firm delineation of that right in Gen 9:3-5 marks nothing less than a radical change in the relationship between human beings and animals as introduced by the institution of sacrifice (Gen 8:20-21).[128]

Dequeker notes that many of the Greek texts that Westermann cites as parallels to the original vegetarian diet of the Golden Age are ambiguous. However, a Golden Age characterized by vegetarianism was alive and well in other Greek circles, if not in the examples Westermann cites. Although Hesiod's *Work and Days* (109-26) does not explicitly posit a vegetarian diet for the first stage of history,[129] other Greek traditions attest an original vegetarian diet, despite the fact that vegetarianism as an ethical lifestyle was not originally connected to the Golden Age.[130] The Stoic Aratus (*Phaenomena* 131-32) elucidates a particular legend concerning the "Maiden" (*parthenon*) in which he clarifies Hesiod's schematization according to the vegetarian theory, thereby making the Bronze race the first to eat meat (*prōtoi de boōn epasant' arotērōn*).[131] Furthermore, Plato's *Laws* VI (782C) cites an orphic tradition that posits an age of vegetarianism as an ideal condition of the *Urzeit*.[132] In addition, Plato via the Stranger in the *Politicus* (271D-E, 274B-C) describes a primeval state of harmony between human beings and animals that required a vegetarian diet. Empedocles describes the earliest race as abstaining from the *musos . . . megiston*, "greatest pollution," namely the act of eating animals,[133] in an age in which all animals were friendly towards human beings and vice versa.[134] Later classical writers who describe such an age include Ovid (*Metamorphosis* 15.395ff), Vergil (*Georgica* 1.130; 2.537), Plutarch (*De esu carn.* 998B), and Diogenes Laertius (8.20). Thus the tradition of vegetarianism as the first human diet was widespread in Greek circles, the earliest extant reference coming from the mid-fifth century BCE philosopher Empedocles. However, the tradition itself was most certainly earlier.

In summary, it is clear that Gen 9:3 marks a change in human prerogative over the animal and botanical realms: Human beings in 9:3 become entitled to *both* animals and plants as sources of food.

Formal Structure of Genesis 1:1–2:3 in the MT

As with the LXX account of Gen 1:1–2:3, the following outline attempts to highlight the formal features of the text.

Much of what was said about the formal structure of the LXX applies to the MT. However, several differences can immediately be observed. The introduction consisting of the first two verses does not describe a creative event as in the Greek text; rather, it describes the pre-creative condition, thereby serving as nothing more than an introduction to the formal six days of creation. In addition, the concluding verses exhibit a structure different from that of the LXX. Whereas Gen 2:1-2a in the LXX offers a concluding statement with regard to the completion of the created order before the seventh day section (2:2b-3a), the MT incorporates 2:1-2a into the final section, since the statements of completion are located within the context of the seventh day (2:2a). This structural difference between the Greek and Hebrew texts depends on the difference of one word: *tē hektē* ("sixth") in the LXX and *haššĕbîʿi* ("seventh") in the MT. The reason behind this calendrical difference will be discussed in the following chapter.

Several disparities between the two texts lie within the creation section of 1:3-31. One notable difference is the placement of the "transition" formula. In contrast to the LXX, the formula is not consistently bracketed by the command and its fulfillment in the MT. It has been noted in Chapter Two that Coats's description of the formula as an "execution formula" is more apt for the LXX than for its inconsistent use in the MT, since the MT employs the formula in only fifty percent of the cases as a transition between command and fulfillment (1:11, 15, 24). Cases of dissimilarity appear in three instances.

1. In 1:7, the formula appears after the fulfillment of the command, immediately preceding the divine naming.

2. The formula follows the divine command of v 9, but there is no report of the fulfillment to follow the formula in v 10. Rather, divine naming immediately follows the formula.

3. Within the fifth day section, the formula is nowhere to be found. Instead, fulfillment immediately follows the command in vv 20-21.

The placement of the formula at the end of v 30, as well as its absence at the end of v 26, is also anomalous, as in the LXX. It has been shown with regard to the LXX that the formula's absence at the end of v 26 sets the creation of human beings apart from the other acts of creation, with the exception of the creation of light in v 3 (see Chapter Two). Such a rationale, however, is lost in the MT, given the formula's frequently inconsistent usage elsewhere.

Commentators who see the MT as a corrupt text by virtue of the inconsistent use ("misplacement") of the transition formula fail to note the diverse ways in which the formula can be employed in other contexts. However, before delineating its range of function within the Hebrew creation text, it would be helpful first to discern the formula's function outside of the passage.

The Formula wayhî kēn in Biblical Literature

The formula *wayhî kēn* and its more typical variant, the particle *kēn* with the verb *ʿśh*, occur elsewhere in the Hebrew Bible. The semantic matrix in which the particle *kēn* appears occurs more frequently with verbs of action, most typically with *ʿśh*, than with *hyh*. As for cases of the former, it is typical that a divine command is given and human addressees fulfill it. For instance, in Exod 7:6, Yahweh gives a command to Moses that Moses then fulfills:

wayyaʿaś mošeh wĕʾahăron kaʾăšer ṣiwwāh YHWH ʾotām kēn ʿāśû

The end position of the particle *kēn* corresponds to the adverbial clause: "according to what Yahweh had commanded them." Semantically the particle refers to the content of the command.

The particle *kēn* with *hyh* is of a somewhat different breed. Instead of fulfillment by human action, the act referred to is syntactically impersonal. Instances of this usage outside Genesis 1 are relatively few. In Num 9:15, there is a description of the day in which the cloud covered (*ksh*) the tabernacle. Immediately following this is the phrase: *kēn yihyeh tāmîd*, "and it was continually so," which is again followed by a description of the pattern, but this time cast in the imperfect with iterative force. Here, the particle *kēn* points both backward to the one-day description and forward to the iterative description: It renders the one-day description in v 15 as paradigmatic in relation to what is described in v 16. Rather than a command, a pattern is described.

In a different vein, Gideon barters with God in Judg 6:36-40 by setting conditions that would prove God's credibility in delivering Israel from the Midianites and Amalekites. After Gideon's description of the test, one finds the phrase *wayhî kēn*. Here, the formula assumes the fulfillment of Gideon's request by God, since what follows is not a description of the fulfillment but Gideon's confirmation of the fulfillment. Hence, the formula has subsumed the fulfillment, as it were, by presupposing it as actualized exactly as specified in Gideon's request. The particle *kēn* points backward to the request. But Gideon is not finished; he sets further conditions that God fulfills (*wayya'aś 'ĕlōhîm kēn*). Here, the impersonal formula *wayhî kēn* is synonymous with the active phrase *wayya'aś 'ĕlōhîm kēn*. What follows is a description of the fulfillment that corresponds to Gideon's request. Thus the phrase acts as a formal bridge between Gideon's request and divine fulfillment.

The phrase *wayhî lô kēn* in 2 Kgs 7:20 refers to the fulfillment of a prophecy of Elisha. The phrase is prefaced with a recital of the prophecy in its situational context (vv 18-19) and is immediately followed by a description of its fulfillment, namely in a reference to the violent means by which the prophecy is fulfilled. Again, the formula's transitional force is evident: The phrase both confirms the prophecy (7:19b) as having been fulfilled and points to the particular way in which it was fulfilled (7:20b). Hence, an essential part in effecting a transition from word to event is the formula's word-confirming role, clearly illustrated in the movement from prophecy to fulfillment.

Finally, the formula *wayhî kēn* in 2 Kgs 15:12 refers to a divine promise addressed to Jehu, expressed parenthetically after the historical survey of Zechariah's reign. The subject of the formula refers to the divine prophecy (*dĕbar YHWH*) that Jehu's dynasty will last to the fourth generation; the fulfillment points back to a description of Shallum's usurpation of the throne (v 10). Again, the formula exhibits its confirming role, while also pointing (back) to the particular way in which it was fulfilled.

In short, the formula's situational context usually includes three elements: A) the paradigmatic event, prophecy, or command; B) the transition formula; and C) the description which brings A into realization. In all these cases, the particle *kēn* in B refers both to the content in A and its fulfillment in C, although in one case C is presupposed rather than stated. With regard to the last example cited above, C can precede A, given the parenthetical position of A and B. In sum, this formulaic phrase is by nature transitional: It moves from the general to the actual, from word to event, from paradigm to its instanciation.

The Formula in Genesis 1 of the MT

The formula has a more variegated function in Genesis 1 than in the passages outside it. As already noted, its most common function as a transition marker occurs in vv 11, 15, and 24. However, v 7 is particularly anomalous, since it follows the fulfillment rather than the command.

This position is unique, leading many scholars, following the LXX, to suggest that it is a misplacement due to corruption.[135] However, its function as determined by its placement does make sense, contrary to those who see its anomalous placements as signs of textual corruption in the MT. Clearly, it is not transitional in the sense that it points to verse 8, in which God names the firmament "heaven." Rather, the formula's confirming role comes to the fore as its *exclusive* function. This is made clear when one examines the structure of the movement from command to fulfillment.

I.	Command for a firmament	6
	A. Declarative formula: *wayyōʾmer ʾĕlōhîm*	
	B. Citation of command	
	1. Existence (*hyh*) of a firmament	6a
	2. Spatial location	
	3. Function: division	6b
II.	Fulfillment	7
	A. Indicative formula: *wayyaʿaś ʾĕlōhîm ʾet*	
	B. Result	
	1. Construction (*ʿśh*) of the firmament	7aα
	2. Divine act: division	7aß
	3. Specific spatial location	
III.	Formula *wayhî kēn*	7b

The major change in the transition from command to fulfillment is that the report of the fulfillment is more detailed and specific than the command. The structural and linguistic changes are as follows:

1. The impersonal emergence of a firmament described in the command is replaced by God's creation of the firmament. The firmament does not come into existence on its own, as the divine speech would imply and as is the case with the creation of light in v 3b. "And God made . . ." is the result of a structural conflation of 1) God as the subject of speech in the declarative formula and 2) the firmament as the subject in the command. In other words, not only does the indicative formula (*wayyaʿaś*) of the creative act replace the previous declarative formula (*wayyōʾmer*), it also changes the mode of creation: from an inferred impersonal creation to divine construction.

2. The firmament, previously indefinite, becomes definite by the attachment of the definite article.

3. The function of division becomes more specific. Instead of "between waters and waters," the waters are located in the vertical

dimensions of "under" and "above" relative to the firmament. In addition, v 7 further specifies the spatial location of the firmament as expressed in the command.

The fact that the specifications in the command and in the fulfillment do not match is significant and yields a major clue for understanding the role of the transition marker *wayhî kēn* in the MT. Its unique position can only make sense in virtue of the formula's *confirming* function, since its function cannot be construed as transitionary. Indeed, its placement after the fulfillment highlights the fulfillment in a special way. Instead of the word confirmed in transition, the actual deed is corroborated. Indeed, in light of the differences noted above between the command and the fulfillment, the fulfillment is stressed over and against the command. That is to say, the description of *God* constructing the firmament and dividing the waters receives greater emphasis than the command, in which the firmament is the subject. Thus the formula's role here is best described as confirming the fulfillment.

The second use of the formula comes in v 9, in which the phrase follows the command as one would expect. However, the fulfillment is absent. As noted in Num 9:16 and Gen 1:30, the fulfillment need not be stated, but merely assumed by the formula. However, since v 9 is the only command in the creation account that lacks a fulfillment statement, this particular section, which describes the movement of the waters for the sake of the dry land's appearance, seems truncated. At any rate, the fulfillment is assumed to be executed.

Another clue to the formula's wide range of function in the MT version of Genesis 1 is revealed by its absence in v 20. The command that the waters are to produce (or "cause to swarm"[136]) swarms of sea creatures is immediately followed by the report that God creates them.

I.	Command	20
	A. Waters to produce sea creatures	20a
	B. Winged creatures to fly	20b
II.	Fulfillment: *wayyibrāʾ ʾĕlōhîm*	21
	A. Sea monsters	21a
	B. Sea creatures	21bα
	C. Winged creatures	21bß

Here, the formula is absent perhaps because the command itself is not meant to be highlighted or even confirmed. Instead, the God-creating fulfillment, as in v 7, immediately follows. Neither the command nor the fulfillment receives confirmation. As in v 7, one might expect the formula to follow v 21, thereby stressing the fulfillment. However, its placement after the fulfillment might have been considered superfluous, given the detail and greater length of the reported fulfillment. Consequently, the formula's absence may not be of critical significance here, since its role may very well have been assumed by the fulfillment itself. At any rate, the abrupt movement from command to fulfillment highlights God's creative action over and against that of the waters.

In short, given the inconsistent placement of the formula, one particular aspect of the formula's function comes to the fore, namely that of emphasizing what directly precedes it. This seems particularly relevant in v 7 where the reported fulfillment rather than a command precedes the formula. Another aspect is its assumption of the execution of the command in v 9, wherein its role is not so much one of emphasizing the command as presuming its execution.

The Formula in Ancient Near Eastern Literature

The diverse structural context in which the formula functions is also reflected throughout much of ancient Near Eastern literature, a fact that no one has considered in connection with its use in Genesis 1. Beginning with Sumerian literature, a similar formula is most commonly but not always used in divine discourse. One model example is from the so-called "Sumerian Epic of Paradise" or "Enki and Ninhursag." After a description of Dilmun, a pure land in perfect harmony with nature, Ninsikilla, Dilmun's tutelary deity, complains to Enki that the land lacks sweet water and crop-bearing fields.[137] Though Enki's response is missing from the text, he apparently promises Ninsikilla an abundance of water to be brought out by the sun-god Utu. Lines 53-64 describe Utu's performance, ending with the line:

i-bí-éš ᵈUtu u₄-NE-a ḫur ḫé-na-nam-ma[138]

Kramer translates it: "Now by Utu, on this day, it has become just that."[139] Langdon translates the last phrase "verily, it was so."[140] Jacobsen translates it: "Thus, it verily became."[141] In any case, the function of *ḫur ḫé.na.nam.ma* is clearly due to its placement: It confirms Utu's fulfillment of Enki's promise. Its placement is analogous to that of the formula in Gen 1:7 in the MT, in which the *formula follows and thereby confirms the fulfillment*. Both in the Sumerian material and in Gen 1:7 the formula's placement after the fulfillment makes semantic sense.

The Sumerian historical epic (or admonitory history[142]) "The Curse of Agade" provides a clear transitional use of the formula. Near the end

of the epic the gods utter two curses (lines 210-221 and 225-271), the end
of which is line 272.

i-ne-éš ^dUtu u4-dè-e-a ur5 ḫé-en-na-nam-ma-àm[143]

Cooper translates it: "And with the rising of the sun, so it was!"[144] What
follows is the fulfillment of the curse, which describes verbatim the catas-
trophes depicted in the last segment of the curse (lines 264-271). The
repetition of only part of the curse in the fulfillment report is clearly
meant as an abbreviation for the fulfillment of the entire curse.

A similar example is found in the "Myth of Inanna and Bilulu,"[145] in
which Inanna utters a ten-line curse (lines 110-119) that is immediately
followed by the following line (120):

ì-bí-šè ^dUtu u4-ne [ur5] ḫé-en-na-n[am][146]

The verse introduces the curse's fulfillment, which matches the curse line
by line (121-130). The translation offered by Jacobsen ("And immediately, on that day and (under that) sun, it truly became so")[147] recognizes
the transitional function of the formula.

Another instructive and more unusual example is given in the myth
Lugal ud melambi nirgal (or *Lugal-e*). Four times the formula is used in an
etiological context. For example, in lines 180-81 during the battle between
Ninurta and Azag is the following description:

ì-ne-éš u4-da a-šà-ga ùh-~gi6
me-da úr-an-na he!-me-da-gim sú-a-šè
ur5 ḫé-en-na-nam-ma-àm[148]

Van Dijk translates these two lines as follows:

À ce moment, à ce jour, les champs devinrent cendres noires, pour toute
l'étendue de l'horizon, rougeâtre comme le pourpre, il en était ainsi![149]

But *u4-da* (Akkadian *ūmum* in the bilingual texts) frequently designates
present time, "today," as it clearly does in other related passages of the
myth (see below). Thus, Jacobsen's translation is more appropriate, since
it clearly shows the etiological character of the passage:

And till today black cinders are in the fields, and ever heaven's base
becomes to the observer like red wool—thus verily it is.[150]

Here, the formula (ur5 ḫé.en.na.nam.ma.am) confirms the reality of the contemporary state of affairs reflecting the ancient battle. It functions to stress the connection between the present and the past.

Later in lines 433-5, Ninurta passes sentence, thereby determining the "fate" of a particular stone, as translated by Jacobsen:

> I am lord! Stone be called
>> by the name of your hollow
>> that is hollowed out in you!
> Now, at the sentence passed by Ninurta,
> today, when the 'plant' stone has been cut
>> a hollow is to be drilled in the stone.
>> Thus verily it became (ur5 ḫé-en-na-nam-ma).[151]

Van Dijk also translates the passage with etiological nuance:

> Ce jour (et à jamais), dès que la pierre-plante l'aura touchée, ce sera de la cornaline percée: ainsi il en sera!

Here, the formula affirms both the efficacy of the sentence and its etiological resonance with the present. Lines 462 (ur5 ḫé-en-na-nam) and 512 (ur5 ḫé-na-nam-ma) also contain the formula in etiological contexts.

In sum, Jacobsen remarks concerning this formula:

> This line is one of the stereotypes of Sumerian literature occurring in slightly varied form as introduction and/or close of sections relating that a divine "determining of fate" took effect.[152]

The versatility of the formula's function is due to its placement: either as introducing the fufillment of the decreed fate (i.e., "transitional") or as confirming the fulfillment by appearing at the "close of sections" that report the fulfillment. Such versatility is also reflected in the MT's use of the formula wayhî kēn in Genesis 1.

The Akkadian equivalent to the Sumerian formula ur5 ḫé.na.nam or ur5 ḫé.en.na.nam is usually the phrase šî lu kīam. Its use in bilingual texts such as Lugal-e and elsewhere reflects the same structural usage as in the Sumerian epics examined above.

In Ugaritic literature the adverbial particle km occasionally functions in a similar manner to that of kēn in the Hebrew formula. One such instance is found in the Keret epic (CTA 15.iii.23-25):

> bn.krt.km hm.tdr
> ap.bnt.ḥry kmhm.

> The sons of Keret were (born) just as they had been promised
> Indeed, the daughters of *ḥry* were also (born) thusly.

Here, *km* in line 23 evidently refers back to the promise made by El (CTA 15.ii.21-28) for bearing seven/eight sons, including *yṣb*. The reference to El is clear, contrary to Gordon's and Gibson's suggestion that it is Athirat who is referred to by *tdr*.[153] Nowhere in the epic is Athirat ever mentioned as having made a vow or promise; rather, Keret is the one who makes a vow invoking the *ʾaṯrt. ṣrm* (CTA 14.iv.197-206). Thus *tdr* must be taken as a Gp 3mp form: *tuddaru*.[154] In line 25, reference is made elliptically to El's promise of daughters born to *ḥry* (CTA 15.iii.5-16). In both cases the particle *km* follows the fulfillment of each promise, thereby confirming the fulfillment as a realization of El's word to Keret.

On a more tentative note, the particle *kn* also appears to function in a manner similar to its Hebrew cognate *kēn*. CTA 12.ii.53-55 makes an oblique reference to Baal's death as having been foreordained:

> *bᶜdn ᶜdnm. kn. npl. bᶜl [. . .]*
> *km ṯr. wtkms. hd. p [. . .]*
>
> At the exact appointment of time, thus Baal fell . . .
> as a bull. Indeed, Hadad lay prostrate . . .

Here, *kn* functions to reinforce the providentiality of Baal's demise by the "devourers" (*ʾaklm*).[155] Unfortunately, column 2 of the tablet is so badly damaged that evidence for this is hard to come by. The only possible reference to an announcement of Baal's demise lies in lines 45-46:

> *sbᶜ. šnt.ʾil. mlʾa [. . .]*
> *wtmn nqpnt. ᶜd [. . .]*
>
> In seven years the god filled . . .
> in eight cycles (of years), until . . .

The damaged portion of the text that comes after the preposition *ᶜd* could very well have contained the announcement to which the *kn* in line 54 refers. If correct, the particle *kn* would serve as a transitional adverbial particle, thereby introducing the fulfillment of the announcement.

In sum, a survey of ancient Near Eastern literature readily shows the variegated function of the "transition" formula. With regard to Genesis 1 of the MT, most striking is the fact that the formula can meaningfully appear *after the fulfillment* of a speech or curse, contrary to those who take the view that such irregular placement of the formula in the MT is due to textual corruption.[156] To the contrary, the formula in the MT, as in ancient Near Eastern literature, can function just as easily as the confirmation of a fulfillment in narrative as it can function transitionally.

Thematic Structure

As observed in the previous chapter, the LXX of the Hexaemeron reflects a balanced thematic structure of corresponding creative acts. Scholars have labored hard to describe the structure of the MT in a similar manner. Gunkel traces this particular way of presenting the structure of the Hexaemeron back to K. D. Ilgen in 1798.[157] Gunkel's own account of the structure of the MT is as follows:

1. Light	2. Heaven	3. Sea	4. Land (with plants)
5. Stars	6. Birds	7. Fish	8. Land animals and human beings

It is clear from the start that the alleged point-by-point correspondence of creative acts in two parallel rows does not concur with the formal ordering of the day-sections, since the creation of the sea and land both belong to the third day and that of the fish and birds belong to the fifth day.[158] Gunkel attributed this discrepancy to differing traditions. He attributed the six-day ordering to P and the "Creation report" of eight acts to an earlier tradition.[159] In enumerating the corresponding acts, however, Gunkel did not accurately depict the order in creation. The fish are created before the birds on the fifth day, the order of which Gunkel reversed presumably in order to show their correspondence to heaven and sea, respectively.[160]

More serious, however, is Gunkel's arbitrary division of the acts of creation. Although ten items of creation are mentioned within the six-day scheme (light, heaven, seas, land, vegetation, luminaries, sea creatures, winged creatures, land animals, and human beings), the count of eight creative acts corresponds to the formal structure of the unit:[161]

1. Light	2. Heaven	3. Seas and land	4. Vegetation
5. Luminaries	6. Fish and birds	7. Land animals	8. Human beings

However, the way in which Gunkel divides the creation acts does not correspond to the formal divisions. Human beings and land animals constitute, for instance, separate acts and cannot be lumped together as Gunkel claims. Fish and birds (1:20-23), on the other hand, are described together in one creative act and thus cannot be divided. Moreover, the seas and land are to be taken together (1:9-12) as one creative act. By using the formal division of labor as the criterion by which to separate out the creative acts, Gunkel constructed a thematic structure that lacks clear correspondence. Indeed, Gunkel's particular division of the creative acts was the result of his attempt to tease out of the MT a thematic structure of *correspondence*. What is clear, however, even by Gunkel's tendentious presentation of the thematic structure, is that the divisions of days and labor do not correspond.

Cassuto's description of the Masoretic structure of Gen 1:3-31 is not much of an improvement, since he attempts to harmonize Gunkel's presentation of the thematic structure with the order of days.[162]

1. Light	2. Sea and Heaven	3. Earth (with plants)
4. Luminaries	5. Fish and Fowl	6. Land creatures and human beings

The result is an arbitrary enumeration of six *creation* sections that only partially correspond to the six days. Like that of Gunkel, Cassuto's description of the Masoretic structure misconstrues the order of creation, but in the opposite fashion by reversing "Heaven" and "Sea" under the middle section in order to align them with the "Fish and Fowl" of the fifth day. Furthermore, Cassuto's division of labor is no less arbitrary than Gunkel's schematization.

Another attempt to find a one-to-one correspondence is made by Steck,[163] who suggests that the general division between Days 1-3 and Days 4-6 be divided between "Daseinsbereiche" and "Zugeordnete Wesenheiten."

Himmelsfeste	Gestirne
Meer	Wassertiere
(Luftraum)	Lufttiere
Erde + Pflanzen	Landtiere
	Menschen

Steck departs from the previous attempts by not relating the creation of the winged creatures to the firmament or heaven. Instead, he posits the new category "air space," which is problematic, since there is no mention of this "Daseinsbereich" in the Hebrew text. *Luftraum* is not even alluded to in the passage describing the creation of the seas and the land (1:9-10). Were it to be mentioned in the creation text, it probably would be placed in connection with the creation of the firmament and the vertical division of the waters (1:6-8), but this section precedes the one that depicts the creation of the seas. Thus Steck's attempt to describe the thematic structure reads into the text what is not there.

The latest attempt by a commentator makes a more concerted effort to forge a parallel structure according to day-units:[164]

Day 1 Light	Day 4 Luminaries
Day 2 Sky	Day 5 Birds and Fish
Day 3 Land	Day 6 Animals and Man
(Plants)	(Plants for food)

The outline seems to be coherent at first glance, but breaks down under scrutiny. First, Day 5 and Day 2 only partially correspond, by virtue of the fact that the "Fish" find no parallel. Moreover, no mention is made of the waters, despite the fact that they are commanded to create the sea creatures in Day 5 and congregate in Day 2. The omission is not entirely unjustified for Day 2, since the Hebrew makes clear that the movement of the waters is for the sake of allowing the land to appear. However, the waters play a decisive role in Day 5, and therefore cannot be overlooked in any structural outline. Without the category of water, the "Fish" are left dangling. Thus Wenham's claim that "day 5 [discusses] the birds of heaven"[165] is only half the story.

The variety of suggestions noted above reflects a difficulty in discerning a clear thematic structure in the MT.[166] In fact, there is no precise thematic structure that corresponds to the formal division of labor. This is due in part to the fact that a thematic connection between the sea and winged creatures as products of the waters is lacking; they are treated as separate creations, though formally within one creation section. Hence, the winged creatures, as suggested by most scholars, can be seen as closely associated with the firmament, "heaven." Only if one disregards the formal groupings (marked by [—] in the list below), can one construct a rough correspondence for the MT's Hexaemeron:

Light	Heaven	Water		Earth	
1. Light	2. Heaven	3. Seas ——	4. Land	5. Plants	
6. Luminaries	7. Fish ——	8. Winged Creatures	9. Animals	10. Human beings	

One immediately sees, however, the difficulty of establishing a one-to-one correspondence. One has to posit a chiastic order for the relationship between "2. Heaven" and "3. Seas," on the one hand, and "7. Fish" and "8. Winged Creatures," on the other. This in turn disturbs the classifica-

tion of the creations into categories, as well as separate "1. Light" from
"2. Heaven," thereby forming, possibly, a new category (**Light?**), which
is not a "Daseinsbereich" to use Steck's term.[167] The question of whether
"4. Land" belongs under **Earth** or **Water** remains open, since it is clear in
the Hebrew that the gathering of the waters occurs for the sake of allowing the land to appear (*wĕtērāʾeh*, 1:9). But since formal divisions do not
play a role in the thematic structure of the passage, it is equally plausible
that "4. Land" falls under **Earth**. Moreover, whereas the absence of the
transition formula in the LXX seems to distinguish two creations (namely
light and human beings) from the rest of the creations, such is not the
case in the MT. In addition to the sections describing the creation of light
and human beings, one also finds the creation accounts of the firmament
and the sea and winged creatures lacking the transitional phrase.

In sum, the MT of the Hexaemeron lacks a balanced structural correspondence between creation acts, unlike the LXX. The rough thematic
structure of the MT gives the impression of a structure that has been
partially dismantled.

The Respective Roles of the Earth and the Waters

As in the LXX, the waters and the earth assume active roles in the
process of creation as described in the MT of Genesis 1. This is particularly evident in the divine command. However, outside of this formal
component of the creation text, the earth clearly plays a more pronounced role than that of the waters in the MT. To discern the ways in
which this imbalance emerges, it is necessary to examine first the
structure and rhetoric of the divine command itself.

Structure and the Rhetoric of the Divine Command

A feature that underscores the active nature of the roles the waters
and the earth assume is found in the rhetoric by which God commands
the waters and the earth. A number of commands are expressed utilizing
figura etymologica constructions. These include 1:11 (*tadšēʾ/dešeʾ*), 1:15
(*mĕʾôrot/hāʾîr*), and 1:20 (*yišrĕṣû/šereṣ* and *ʿôp/yĕʿôpēp*),[168] which pertain
to the earth, celestial bodies, and waters (+ winged creatures), respectively. Such constructions in which the predicate is related etymologically to the subject quite often constitute the language of production: The
earth "produces" vegetation, the waters "produce" sea creatures, and
celestial bodies "produce" light. In each of these cases the means of
production is verbally related to the product. The closest parallels, as

cited above, are the respective productive activities of the earth and the waters, the two most active subordinate "agents" involved in creation. It is also not fortuitous that such language is reserved *only* for the divine commands. On the purely aesthetic level, such rhetoric invests divine speech with a verbal artistry and ingenuity not present in the fulfillment reports. On the rhetorical level, the commands exhibit a verbal precision by which the agents (the earth and the waters) are enlisted to exercise the precise means by which to produce their respective products.

Note, for instance, that the fulfillment of the command of v 11 in v 12 begins with *tôṣē' hā'āreṣ deše'* in contrast to the command *tadšē' hā'āreṣ deše'*. The choice of the more generic, all-purpose verb *yṣ'* over and against *dš'* is revealing. There is a certain distinction in God's command to the earth that is lacking in the report of the earth's fulfillment of the divine injunction.

Similarly, while the object and the verb are etymologically related in the command to the waters in 1:20 (*yišrĕṣû* and *šereṣ*), the fulfillment report of v 21 is quite different:

> v 20: *yišrĕṣû hammayim šereṣ nepeš ḥayyāh wĕ'ôp yĕ'ôpēp*
> v 21: *wayyibrā' 'ĕlōhîm 'et hattannînim haggĕdolîm wĕ'ēt kol nepeš haḥayyāh hāromeśet 'ăšer šārĕṣû hammayim . . . wĕ'ēt kol 'ôp*

Along with the change in the creating subject (from *hammayim* to *'ĕlōhîm*), the verbal mode of production is altered (*šrṣ* is replaced by *br'* in 21a), although the original verb is retained in the relative clause in 21b but without the object *šereṣ*. The *šereṣ nepeš ḥayyāh* is replaced by the two classes of sea creatures: *hattannînim* and *kōl nepeš haḥayyāh hāromeśet*. The object of creation in the fulfillment report essentially represents an additional class of sea creatures, the *tannînim*, but neither class is described as "*šereṣ*," as in the command. The terminological shift from command to fulfillment represents a move from the verbal elegance of the command, which focuses on the waters' productive capacity, to the concrete, "hands-on" mechanics of the creative act in which the deity's action comes to the foreground and the waters are relegated to the background.

In sum, the verbal puns in the commands of vv 11, 15, and 20 set in relief the articulate quality of divine speech in contrast to the concrete fulfillment reports. Consequently, the role of God as creative speaker is highlighted not simply by the overall structural repetition of divine speech throughout the account but also by the verbal identification between the product and its mode of production in the commands (in the case of the celestial spheres, the identification is made between them and their function to give light). This verbal correspondence underlines God as *creative* speaker in both senses of the term: God utters speech that both exhibits creative force and is in itself stylistically artistic.

In addition, the verbal similarity also says something about the indirect addressees in the command. In the commands of vv 10 and 20 the verbal correspondence between mode of production and product, in effect, *specifies* precisely the creative powers or means inherent in the earth and the waters. This verbal specification constitutes the rhetoric of creation, which exhibits not only a certain aesthetic eloquence typical of divine speech, but also stresses the active nature of the earth and the waters. When employed within an indirect command, this divine eloquence becomes imbued with rhetorical nuance aimed clearly at enlisting the earth and the waters, the two ancillary actors in the creation account, to exercise their respective powers of production. The verbal artistry of the divine commands in effect highlights the active roles of the earth and the waters and incorporates them into the divine plan of creation.

The Active Role of the Earth

Much of what has been said about the role of the earth as depicted in the LXX applies to the MT. However, unlike the LXX, the earth is first described in its pre-creative state without reference to its creation (1:1-2). Its emergence in 1:9 is dependent upon the movement of the waters' collection into *māqôm ʾeḥād* as depicted in the command. After the divine naming in 1:10, the earth is immediately commanded to exercise its generative powers to produce vegetation (1:11) and subsequently the land animals (1:24).

The Active Role of the Waters

The waters, in contrast, do not equal the creative role of the earth, since the only instance recorded in the MT of the waters' creating anything is in the command given in 1:20, wherein the waters are commanded to produce swarms of sea creatures:

1:20a *wayyōʾmer ʾĕlōhîm **yišrĕṣû** hammayim **šereṣ** nepeš ḥayyāh*

The *figura etymologica* construction of the verb *srs* in v 20 has its "earthly" counterpart in the verbal syntax of 1:11 with the verb *dšʾ*.

1:11aα *wayyōʾmer ʾĕlōhîm **tadšēʾ** hāʾāreṣ **dešeʾ** ʿēśeb*

This marks the only point of similarity between the earth and the waters with regard to their respective generative roles. Yet, unlike the LXX, the MT severs any tie between the aerial creatures and the waters in 1:20.

> 1:20b *wĕʿôp yĕʿôpēp ʿal hāʾāreṣ*

In the MT, the "swarming things" (*šereṣ*) syntactically constitute the only object of the waters' action. The winged creatures, on the other hand, comprise the separate subject of the second half of the verse. As noted in the translation section, the verb *ʿwp* must be considered jussive, whose subject is the *ʿôp*. This is a bit unusual in that 1:20b as part of a command does not designate any particular origin to the winged creatures, be it watery, divine, or impersonal. That is to say, on a purely syntactical level v 20b is the only command statement in which an object of creation assumes the position of the subject of a verb other than *hyh* (like 1:3). "Let the winged creatures fly . . ." would almost seem logically to imply the prior existence of flightless birds, but such an implication is quickly dispelled by the fulfillment report in v 21: *wayyibrāʾ ʾĕlōhîm . . . ʾēt kol ʿôp kānāp lĕmînēhû*. At any rate, what is clear is that the zoological category *ʿôp*, winged creatures, has nothing to do with *hammayim*.

In comparison to the earth's role in creation, the waters' lack of generative power is also confirmed on the structural level. The waters' diminished role is highlighted particularly at those points in the creation account where the formula *wayhî kēn* is absent or anomalously placed.

The omission of the formula in 1:20 thereby eliminates any intervening step between divine command and fulfillment. Instead, one immediately comes to the introduction of the fulfillment report in 1:21a.

> *wayyibrāʾ ʾĕlōhîm ʾet hattannînim haggĕdōlîm . . .*

The abrupt shift from the waters creating creatures to *ʾĕlōhîm* creating (*brʾ*) the *tannînim* and the other sea-creatures has the effect of overshadowing the creative role that the waters were commanded to assume. Divine action (*bārāʾ*) clearly takes precedence over the waters' action (*šārāṣ*) in 1:21.

There is also the peculiar placement of the transition formula at the end of the fulfillment report in 1:7. As noted above, the effect of having the formula follow the fulfillment thereby shifts attention away from the command to the fulfillment.

> 1:6 *wayyōʾmer ʾĕlōhîm yĕhî rāqîaʿ bĕtôk hammāyim wîhî mabdîl . . .*
> 1:7a *wayyaʿaś ʾĕlōhîm ʾet hārāqîaʿ wayyabdēl . . .*

1:7b *wayhî kēn*

By itself the command in v 6 could imply either an impersonally created firmament (*yĕhî rāqîaᶜ*) in the midst of the waters, that is, a creation without direct divine intervention, not unlike the creation of light in v 3, or a firmament resulting from the actions of the water. Yet these possible implications are quickly dispelled by the fulfillment in 7a, which bypasses the intervening step of the transition formula and immediately opens with God as the subject, confirmed by the formula in 7b. Conversely, what is not confirmed, then, is the command in v 6. A firmament appearing impersonally amid the waters could be interpreted as involving some generative participation on the part of the waters. The absence of the transition formula after the command, however, effectively undermines any such speculation.

The absence of the approbation formula in the MT is anomalous in that one would expect it in 1:8aß after the divine naming of the firmament. This absence is anomalous in the overall MT scheme, since all other sections contain this element. While some scholars view this as simply a mistake,[169] it is not hard to discern a rationale. The missing divine approval in v 8 implies that the cosmic state of affairs concerning the waters is not yet complete.[170] As Rashi explains:

lōʾ hāyā nigmār mĕleʾket hammayim ᶜad yōm šĕlîšî.[171]

In other words, the second day cannot be declared good and complete, since "an unfinished action is not in its fullness and goodness."[172] On the third day the horizontal separation of the waters makes possible the appearance of dry land, and only then is the divine approbation given (1:10). Hence, only when the waters are fully divided and contained *both* vertically and horizontally is the approbation granted.[173] In short, the absence of the divine approbation shifts the focus away from the creation of the firmament and the vertical separation of the waters to the emergence of land, as if to show that the only purpose behind the watery divisions was to uncover the land underneath. Approbation is given, thus, only when the land emerges, thereby completing the waters' containment.

The collection of waters on the third day is also anomalous in that the fulfillment report is entirely lacking after 1:9, thereby producing a narrative gap. Consequently, one must infer from the transition marker that the fulfillment is understood as executed. But precisely what kind of fulfillment is understood? As noted in the translation section above, the immediately preceding creation act contains a fulfillment report with God as the subject (1:7). Such a fulfillment that opens with divine action also occurs throughout the creation account in 1:16, 17, 21, 25, and 27. Only in vv 3 and 12 do subjects other than God (ʾôr and hāʾāreṣ, respectively) begin the fulfillment report. The preponderance of divinely initiated fulfillments would lead one to assume or to "read" after the command in 1:9 a fulfillment report that depicts *God* collecting the waters (*wayyiqew* ʾĕlōhîm ʾet hammayim), rather than the waters gathering themselves.

In sum, the waters prove to be an unequal partner in their role in creation when compared to the creative role the earth is given throughout the account. The anomalous placements of the formula *wayhî kēn* in effect focus less on the waters and more on God's creative role.

THE NUMEROLOGICAL STRUCTURE OF
GEN 1:1–2:3 OF THE MT

Cassuto has convincingly demonstrated the heptadic structure of Gen 1:1-2:3 by noting the count of seven (and multiples thereof) with regard to the frequency of key words or phrases in the MT. He was, however, not the first scholar to observe this. By 1862 E. Böhmer was pointing out word counts of multiples of sevens.[174] Indeed, noting particular word counts can be directly traced back to the practice of gematria by rabbinic midrashists, if not earlier.[175] Some of the examples Cassuto cites include ʾĕlōhîm occuring 35 times; the divine approbation (ṭôb), 7 times; ʿereṣ, 21 times; and šāmayim, 21 times (sic![176]).[177] Though some of Cassuto's observations are overstated,[178] the occurrences listed above cannot be accidental.

In addition, particular units also exhibit a numerological orientation, particularly the first and last sections of the creation account. The first section, namely the pre-creative description in 1:1-2, contains a total of 21 words, 7 for 1:1 and 14 for 1:2. Similarly, A. Toeg has pointed out the intricate heptadic structure in the last section, 2:1-3.[179]

2:1	5 words
2:2a	7 words
2:2b	7 words
2:3a	7 words
2:3b	9 words

The "anomalous" sentences 2:1 and 2:3b total 14 words. Hence, sections (1:1-2 and 2:1-3) of the MT's version of the creation account form a numerological envelope.

On a broader scale, there also seems to be a numerological concern with the *total* word count in Gen 1:1–2:3, a point noticed only by C. Schedl.[180] Schedl arrives at a total count of 469 (7 x 67) words in Gen 1:1–2:3 and a count of 364 words for 1:2-28, which corresponds to the number of days in the solar calendar of Jubilees.[181] Although his word count is accurate, Schedl's unit division of 1:2-28 is contrived. The conclusion of creation does not occur in v 28, but rather in v 31. Furthermore, there is no reason to divide v 28 from v 29. However, despite his attempt to divide the text artificially in order to find some calendrical correlate, Schedl has discovered a phenomenon of the MT text that presses the heptadic structure of Gen 1:1–2:3 to its limit. The textual and ideological implications of this structure will be discussed in Chapters Four and Six, respectively.

CONCLUSION

In summary, the MT of Gen 1:1–2:3 exhibits both an inconsistent formal structure and an unclear thematic organization, unlike the LXX. However, a refined numerological structure is clearly evident in the MT. In addition, the waters and the earth are given special emphases by the unique rhetoric of the divine commands. However, due to the inconsistent placement of the formula *wayhî kēn* and other irregular structural arrangements, the waters appear to have a significantly diminished role relative to that of the earth, in contrast to the equally active roles the waters and the earth are given in the LXX.

NOTES

[1] Würthwein, 12.

[2] Mulder, 106.

[3] P. E. Kahle, *The Cairo Geniza* (Oxford: Basil Blackwell, 1959) 75-82.

[4] M. H. Goshen-Gottstein, "Hebrew Biblical Manuscripts," *Biblica* 48 (1967) 285-86.

[5] F. M. Cross, Jr., *The Ancient Library of Qumran and Modern Biblical Studies* (Garden City: Doubleday and Company, 1958) 143; *idem.*, "The History of the Biblical Text," 296-97.

[6] Mulder, 102; D. Barthelemy, "Text, Hebrew, History of," *IDBSV* 879.

[7] See Chapter Four.

[8] E. Tov, "The Text of the Old Testament," in *The World of the Bible*, ed. A. S. Van der Woude (Grand Rapids: William B. Eerdmans Publishing Co., 1986) 167, 184.

[9] Tov, "The Text of the Old Testament," 184.

[10] See concluding chapter.

[11] See below.

[12] The two products of creation have been commonly considered a merismus that constitutes the whole of creation, i.e., the cosmos (C. H. Gordon, *The World of the Old Testament* [Garden City: Doubleday and Company, 1958] 35; A. M. Honeyman, "Merismus in Biblical Hebrew," *JBL* 71 [1952] 16), but no commentator I am aware of has ever offered such a rendering *as a translation*. The difficulty for such a rendering is that the first word of v 2, *hāʾāreṣ*, clearly has some point of semantic continuity with the last word of v 1. Thus its occurrence in v 1 is not simply meant to function as one part of a merismus without independent meaning. Consequently, while the predicate in v 1 seems to refer to the totality of creation, the two elements listed also have independent referential force as separate domains within context of v 2 and elsewhere (1:8, 10, 11, 12, 14, 15, 17, 22, 24, 25, 26, 28, 29, 30). Furthermore, 2:1 seems to imply separate entities.

The term *ʾereṣ* takes on different shades of meaning throughout the creation passage (see N.-E. Andreasen, "The Word 'Earth' in Genesis 1:1," *Origins* 8 [1981] 15-16):

1) Beginning with 1:10, *ʾereṣ* most often refers to dry land.

2) In 1:15-17 the earth is considered part of a larger system in relation to the sun, moon, and the stars, and consequently means more than simply dry ground. In this case *ʾereṣ* includes the seas and the air.

3) The term's context in 1:1 makes *ʾereṣ* part of a totality that encompasses everything except the celestial realm.

4) Finally, its most peculiar nuance is found in 1:2, in which the term designates the earth's pre-creative state.

[13] See below.

[14] See below.

[15] Beginning with Gunkel (*Schöpfung und Chaos in Urzeit und Endzeit* [Göttingen: Vandenhoeck & Ruprecht, 1895] 13-14), most scholars have suggested some sort of connection between the Hebrew word *tĕhôm* and the Babylonian goddess of the primeval ocean of *Enuma Elish*, Tiamat (e.g., B. W. Anderson, *Creation versus Chaos* [Philadelphia: Fortress Press, 1987] 39; B. S. Childs, *Myth and Reality in the Old Testament* [SBT 27; London: SCM Press, 1960] 36; K. Wakeman, *God's Battle with the Monster: A Study in Biblical Imagery* [Leiden: E. J. Brill, 1973] 86-88; and B. Otzen, "The Use of Myth in Genesis," in *Myths in the Old Testament*, ed. B. Otzen, H. Gottlieb, K. Jeppesen [London: SCM Press, 1980] 33). As Gunkel put it:

> The Babylonian name for this chaos monster, Tiamat, finds close correspondence in the technical name for the primeval sea in Hebrew, *tehom*—a name whose constant appearance without the definite article in Hebrew proves that it was once a proper name and was therefore used to designate a mythical figure ("The Influence of Babylonian Mythology upon the Biblical Creation Story," in *Creation in the Old Testament*, ed. B. W. Anderson [Philadelphia: Fortress Press, 1984] 42).

It is impossible, however, to take the Hebrew word as an Akkadian loan word, since one would expect the retention of the feminine morpheme and the appearance of the so-called vowel *sandhi* for the second consonant (tiʾāmtum > tiāmtum > tâmtum) rather than the replacement with a fricative [h] (D. Tsumura, *The Earth and the Waters in Genesis 1 and 2: A Linguistic Investigation* [JSOTSS 83; Sheffield: Sheffield University Press, 1989], 46). Indeed, the Hebrew term is more closely related to the Ugaritic *thm*, which in most cases simply designates "ocean" (Tsumura, 53-54). Moreover, the related Akkadian term *tâmtum* is used frequently even in mythological texts without personified force as in the bilingual version of the "Creation of the World by Marduk" from the Neo-Babylonian period (Tsumura, 79-80).

Hence, *tĕhôm* cannot be viewed as a case of linguistic borrowing from *tiʾamat*. To the contrary, *tĕhôm* simply designates an enormous mass of subterranean water, probably considered the source of all bodies of water. Furthermore, its probable Canaanite origin (from *thm* or *thmt*) in no way gives *tĕhôm* a mythological function in P's cosmogony (e.g., CTA 3.C.22; 4.iv.22; 23.30; see O. Kaiser, *Die mythische Bedeutung des Meeres in Ägypten, Ugarit, und Israel* [BZAW 78; Berlin: Alfred Töpelmann, 1959] 115; J. Day, *God's Conflict with the Dragon and the Sea* [Cambridge: Cambridge University Press, 1985] 50).

[16] See below.

[17] The *Piel* participle *mĕraḥepet* is attested only in Deut 32:11 (ʿal gôzālāyw yĕraḥēp) with the meaning "hover." In the *Qal* stem the verb is found only in Jer 23:9 and refers to the shaking of bones (rāḥĕpû kol ʿaṣmôtay). The related Ugaritic verb *rḥp* is found in KTU 1.18.4.20, 21, 31, 32 and 1.19.1.32, all of which consistently parallel the verb *bṣr* ("to soar"), and denote aerial creatures (eagles? *nšrm*) flying over either Aqhat's or Daniel's house. These attestations from the Aqhat cycle seem to imply movement but not in any particular direction. Rather, the only point of reference is to the object below the flying creatures (ḥbl diym). In KTU 1.18.4.20, 21, 31, and 32, a scene is described that immediately precedes a violent attack upon Aqhat by Yatpan, who has been made "like an eagle" (km nšr and km diy) by Anat. In another text (RS 24.252 in *Ugaritica V*, 551) Anat is likewise portrayed as a flying creature: ʿnt di dit rḥpt [. . .] rm. Here Anat is the bird *par excellence* ("bird of birds"). Ch. Virolleaud offers the translation: "Anat, the most beautiful of the birds that hover (*planent*) above the birds," which he restores as [ʿl ʿṣ]rm, but this makes little sense (*Ugaritica V*, 555). More sensible is assigning the antecedent of the verb as the *singular* participle (rāḥipatu) to Anat herself, as in the case of line 9 (aklt. ʿgl. ʿl. mšt). At any rate, because of the textual problems, this text contributes little to discerning the meaning of *rḥp*. What does seem likely is that the verb denotes general flying movements of aerial creatures, but little more can be said.

The complex preposition ʿal-pĕnê refers to movement over and around something rather than to an arrested condition (J. Sasson, "Time . . . to Begin," in *"Sha'arei Talmon": Studies in the Bible, Qumran, and the Ancient Near East Presented to Shemaryahu Talmon*, ed. M. Fishbane and E. Tov [Winona Lake: Eisenbrauns, 1992] 189). Early critics who claimed that the verb likens rûaḥ to an aerial creature found links to a cosmic-egg cosmogony by taking a possible nuance of the verb and indiscriminately reading into the priestly account of creation a certain mythological tradition that had no attestation elsewhere in the text or in Hebrew literature. Others like E. J. Young argue that the subject of the participle, rûaḥ, must refer to the *living Spirit* of God, since the verb usually refers to flying creatures as in Deut 32:11 and in Ugaritic literature (E. J. Young, "The Interpretation of Genesis 1:2," in E. J. Young, *Studies in Genesis One* [Philadelphia: Presbyterian and Reformed Publishing Company, 1964] 36-37). The Targum Onkelos, however, understood the word as "wind from before YHWH which was *blowing*" (*mĕnaššĕbaʾ*). The issue is whether a verb whose most common meaning refers to flying birds can be more appropriately applied to the movement of wind or to the "hovering" of God's Spirit. If one pushes Young's argument to its logical conclusion, one would have to conclude that *rûaḥ* as spirit assumes ornithological attributes such as wings. Neither God's Spirit nor divine wind fits into such a rigid demarcation of *rḥp*'s semantic range. Indeed, the verb in its *Qal* form has nothing to do with flying creatures (Jer 23:9). Clearly, the most reasonable route is to take the verb *rḥp* in an extended, general sense, as movement in air (cf. Vulgate's *ferebatur*).

[18] The *we*-imperfect/jussive form evidently expresses purpose, since a parallel construction in 1:14-15 has a *weqatal* form for its second and third verbs in the command in order to maintain the jussive force of the first verb. The syntax in v 6 can be classified under the construction of imperative (or jussive) + *we*-imperfect/jussive, indicating result or purpose. 2 Kings 5:8 is a good example. The best description of this syntactical phenomenon is still T. J. Meek's article "Result and Purpose Clauses in Hebrew," *JQR* 46 (1955/6), 40-43. Also of note is the fact that the other instance in which the verb *bdl* is employed in a divine command is clearly meant to be purposeful: 1:14 (*yĕhî mĕʾorot birqîaʿ haššāmayîm lĕhabdîl*).

[19] The participle *mabdîl* is to be rendered as a substantive rather than as a predicate (contra B. K. Waltke and M. O'Connor, *An Introduction to Biblical Hebrew Syntax* [Winona Lake: Eisenbrauns, 1990] 37.7.1b [henceforth designated as *IBHS*]), given the strict parallelism in v 6 and the fact that of all the commands in Genesis 1 *yĕhî* is followed by a noun (vv 3, 6a, 14). Yet the temporal aspect is not to be denied by such a rendering, since progressive action is precisely what is meant here (*IBHS* 37.7.1b; G-K §116r). Indeed, this is precisely the function of the firmament, a function so indigenous to its nature that it appears in the form of almost a second name. V. Hamilton finds the substantive rendering of the participle the best way for underscoring its iterative force (V. P. Hamilton, *Genesis 1-17* [NICOT; Grand Rapids: William B. Eerdmans Publishing Co., 1990] 121).

[20] See below.

[21] Unnoticed by most commentators, the niphal *tērāʾeh* is not the expected shortened jussive form (*tērāʾ*), as one would expect in congruence with the other commands. Rather it is an imperfect with a simple *waw*. Thus, 1:9aß is best rendered with purposeful force (e.g., Judg 9:7, Jer 40:15, and 2 Sam 19:38 [see *IBHS*, 33.4b, 39.2.2; Meek, 40-43]). This is also confirmed by the double command in 1:14, in which the second half of the verse begins with *wĕhāyû*, a *wĕqātal* form, thus, continuing the jussive force of the first verb (*IBHS* 32.2.1d).

[22] Given the structure of this verse, *dešeʾ* evidently stands as the *Oberbegriff* for all plants in the first stage of growth (Paradise, 184). Yet the term does have a more restricted sense in the Hebrew Bible in that *dešeʾ* commonly designates animal fodder especially for wild animals (Job 6:5, Jer 14:5, Joel 2:22). Prov 27:25 states that *dešeʾ* springs up after the harvest of *ḥāṣîr* (Paradise, 202-3, n. 16). "Thus, *dešeʾ* is not a sown crop like wheat but that which springs up naturally as a result of rain" (Paradise, 180), which makes sense in the initial phases of creation when human beings are not yet created. The term's more restrictive meaning of wild animal fodder is evident in

the Greek rendering. However, in the Hebrew the *figura etymologica* construction with the verb necessarily widens the noun's semantic boundaries so as to include all plants in their initial growth (Westermann, 124, but cf. Wenham, who provides a similar rationale yet translates it incorrectly as "grass" [Wenham, 2, 20-21]).

23 The term designates crops that provide food for both animals, especially domestic ones, (Deut 11:15; Jer 12:4; Ps 104:14) and human beings (Gen 3:18; 9:3; Ps 104:14). Thus it includes not only major cereal crops like wheat, barley, and oats, but also peas, beans, lentils, etc. (Paradise, 182).

24 Henri Cazelles claims that the term *mîn* refers to the propagation of living beings with the same characteristics ("*MYN* = espèce, race où ressemblance?" in *Memorial du Cinquantenaire, 1914-1964* [Paris: Bloud et Gay, 1964] 107). Cazelles favors the translation "ressemblance." Similarly, Dillmann translates the term as "kinship," but without seeing it as incompatible with "species-differentiation" (Dillmann, *Genesis*, 171). However, in context the term must also refer to the distinctions between plants, including perhaps the distinctions among species. Indeed, the stress is not only on similarities but also on the diversification of plants and life (Gen 1:21, 24, 25). Elsewhere the term is used in the context of clean and unclean animals (Lev 11:14, 22, 29; Deut 14:13-15, 18) in which the breakdown into animal classes are listed according to species. Westermann makes the case that such distinctions are not scientific since scientific distinctions are "made for [their] own sake"; rather, they are made in their "significance for people" (Westermann, 126). Such a statement is misleading, since clearly the *Oberbegriff dešeʾ* refers to all kinds of plants, not simply those from which human beings receive benefit. Moreover, the variety of classifications of created animals alluded to in 1:21, 24, 25, 26, 28 argues against Westermann's generalization that they are all directly significant to human beings. To the contrary, it appears that *mîn* bears more similarity with modern scientific categories in that the classifications listed in Genesis 1 function to describe the variegated nature of the natural world, not unlike Aristotle's biological classifications (see Chapter Six).

Conversely, one can also argue that no scientific knowledge is completely devoid of human significance, as Westermann implies (Westermann, 126). Though overstated, there is truth in F. M. Cornford's statement: "Science, with its practical impulse, is like magic in attempting direct control over the world" (*From Religion to Philosophy: A Study in the Origins of Western Speculation* [New York: Harper & Row, Publishers, 1957] 158). In short, Westermann sets up an artificial division between ancient "science" and modern science. Such a prejudice is reflected in his viewpoint—shared by many—that the distinction between "plants" and "trees" "is made primarily from the point of view of their meaning for people and for the animals" (Westermann, 126).

25 Or "cause to swarm." The verb *šrṣ* usually has as its subject living animals of various kinds (Gen 9:7, humans; Lev 11:29, land animals; and Ezek 47:9, river creatures) and should be rendered intransitively. For example, in Gen. 9:7 is the command:

wĕʾattem pĕrû ûrĕbû širṣû bāʾāreṣ ûrĕbû bāh

As for you, be fruitful and multiply and **abound** on the earth and multiply in it.

Thus the root meaning of the verb in this case is to "increase in number" or to "exist in great numbers." On the other hand, the passages in Gen 1:20 and 21 as well as in Exod 7:28 and Ps 105:30 have "inanimate" subjects, namely the waters in Genesis 1, the river in Exod 7:28, and the land in Ps 105:30. In each of these cases the verb has an object. The fact that *šrṣ* is attested only in the *Qal* without attestations in the *Hiphil* or *Piel*, allows for a transitive, causative meaning in certain contexts, unlike the *verba copiae* (e.g., *mālēʾ*), which are frequently attested in both the *Qal* (intransitive) and *Piel* (transitive) (cf. G-K §117z, *IBHS* 10.3.1c).

In Exod 7:28 (*wĕšāraṣ hayʾor ṣĕpardĕ⁽îm*) the verb in *Qal* clearly has an object, namely the "frogs." In support of its transitive meaning, the Peshitta uses the *Aphel* form of the verb *rḥs*. The transitive meaning is also confirmed by the LXX (*exereuxetai ho potamos batrachous*) and the Vulgate (*ebulliet fluvius ranas*).

The reference to the land in Ps 105:30 bears a similar construction: *šāraṣ ʾaṣām ṣepardĕ⁽îm*. Evidence for a transitive, causative meaning is consistent from early translations: LXX: *exērpsen hē gē*; Vulgate: *ebullivit terra eorum ranas*. Again, the Peshitta renders the verb *rḥs* in *Aphel*.

In these cases, the verb evidently exhibits a transitive meaning. The ancient translations also confirm the active meaning in Gen 1:20 and 21 (LXX: *exagō*; Vg: *produco*. Even the hyper-literal Greek translation, Aquila, renders the Hebrew verb with transitive meaning:

> *kai eipen ho theos exērpsato ta hudata herpeton . . .*

> And God said, "Let the waters bring forth reptiles . . ."

A transitive rendering is also supported within the MT by the parallel command given to the earth in v 24: *tôṣēʾ hāʾāreṣ nepeš ḥayyāh*. In addition, a gloss in the Targum Neofiti to Gen 7:21 and the Targum Neofiti translation of Lev 11:41 use the verb in its transitive meaning (cf. M. Sokoloff, *A Dictionary of Jewish Palestinian Aramaic of the Byzantine Period* [Ramat-Gan: Bar Ilan University, 1990] 568). In sum, the usual English translation: "to swarm with" or "teem with" is misleading, since it implies merely the state of being crowded or full of something, thereby erasing the transitive force of the Hebrew verb. There is no evidence that the Hebrew verb functions in any fashion similar to the typical English translations.

[26] The verb *yĕ⁽ôpēp*, a *Polel binyan* of the *⁽ûp* is clearly jussive in context. W. S. LaSor's claim that the verb is not jussive ("Notes on Genesis 1:1–2:3," *Gordon Review* 2 [1956] 27) is groundless since the imperfect and jussive forms for the *Polel* are identical in the 3ms form.

[27] The antecedent to the relative particle *ʾăšer* clearly is the *kol nepeš haḥayyāh hārômeśet* but not *hattannînim*, given the object of the verb *šrṣ* in v 20. The *tannînim* are a separate category of sea life, not created in "swarms."

[28] The term *bĕhēmāh* can be used to denote all animals other than human beings (Exod 8:13,14; 9:9,10,22). Here, however, the word belongs to a three-fold division of animals in contradistinction to wild animals (*ḥayyat haśśādeh* [Gen 3:14] or *ḥayyat hāʾāreṣ* [Gen 7:14; 9:10; Ps 50:10]. The term commonly designates cattle (Gen 47:18; Exod 20:10; Lev 19:19).

[29] The term *remeś* can refer to all animals as in Gen 9:3 or sea animals as in Ps 104:25. Elsewhere it is distinguished from winged creatures, domestic, and wild

animals by denoting creatures associated with the ground (*ʾădāmāh*, Hos 2:20; Ezek 38:20). Thus *remeš* includes all low-lying, moving creatures from insects to reptiles.

30 Literally "animal of the land." The term usually designates wild, untamed animals (Gen 9:2, 10). Ps 79:2, 1 Sam 17:46, Ezek 29:5; 32:4; 34:28, and Job 5:22 use the term to denote carnivorous and dangerous animals.

31 The plural rendering is natural because *ʾādām* is clearly used as a collective to refer to people in general in the same way as in the fulfillment report concerning the animals in 1:24-25, which also employs collective nouns. Notice the plural verb in 1:26b.

32 The verb is best taken as an imperfect with a simple *waw*, rather than as a jussive (see 1:9; cf. 1:20b in which the noun precedes the jussive verb). Hence, the construction denotes purpose.

33 The Peschitta includes the "wild animals" under human rule. The MT, however, omits wild animals both in the command and in the fulfillment. Indeed, this category of animal is not included until Gen 9:2-3, when the killing for food is granted. The sense of "over all the land" probably refers to whatever is produced by the soil.

34 The perfect of *ntn* in pronouncements should be translated in the present as a *performative* perfect. This use of the instantaneous perfective represents a situation occurring at the very instance the expression is uttered (*IBHS* 30.5.1e).

35 See below.

36 The imperfect with *waw* consecutive serves as the concluding summary of the narrative (G-K ƒ111k; *IBHS* 33.2.1d).

37 The preposition *lĕ* covers a wide semantic range (*IBHS* 11.2.10e), but one use that makes sense without sounding redundant is its temporal use (*IBHS* 11.2.10c; R. J. Williams, *Hebrew Syntax: An Outline* [2nd ed.; Toronto Press: University of Toronto, 1976] §268). In addition, the verbs *brʾ* and *ʿśh* are synonymous.

38 A. B. Isaiah and B. Sharfman, *The Pentateuch and Rashi's Commentary: A Linear Translation into English*, vol. 1 (Brooklyn: S. S. and R. Publishing Company, 1949) 1-2.

39 A notable exception is J. Skinner, *Genesis* (ICC; New York: Charles Scribner's Sons, 1910) 14.

40 P. Schäfer, "*Bĕrēšît Bārāʾ ʾElōhîm*: Zur Interpretation von Genesis 1,1 in der rabbinischen Literatur," *JSJ* 2 (1971) 163.

41 First discussed by A. Geiger, *Urschrift und Uebersetzungen der Bibel in ihrer Abhängigkeit von der innern Entwicklung des Judenthums* (Breslau: Julius Hainauer, 1857) 344-45, 439.

42 *Mekilta de-Rabbi Ishmael*, vol. 1, trans. J. Z. Lauterbach (Philadelphia: Jewish Publication Society of America, 1976) 111; see xix-xxviii on a discussion of the dating. M. D. Herr places the redaction of the midrash in the fourth century CE ("Mekhilta of R. Ishmael," *EJ*, vol. 11 [Jerusalem: MacMillan Publishing Company, 1971] 1270).

43 H. Beitenhard, *Midrasch Tanhuma B*, vol. 1 (Bern: Peter Lang, 1980) 305.

44 Schäfer, "*Bĕrēšît Bārāʾ ʾElōhîm*," 165-66.

45 See Spurrell, 1.

46 Lasor, 29-31.

47 P. Humbert, "Troise notes sur Genèse 1," *NTT* 56 (1955) 86.

48 Humbert, 87.

49 Humbert, 87.

50 W. Lane, "The Initiation of Creation," *VT* 13 (1963) 67.

51 Lane, 67.

52 W. Eichrodt, "In the Beginning. A Contribution to the Interpretation of the First Word of the Bible," in *Israel's Prophetic Heritage. Essays in Honor of J. Muilenburg*, ed. B. W. Anderson and W. Harrelson (New York: Harper & Row, 1962) 4.

53 See G-K §86l; *IBHS* 5.7d.

54 See *IBHS* 13.7a and D. N. Freedman, *Pottery, Poetry, and Prophecy: Studies in Early Hebrew Poetry* (Winona Lake: Eisenbrauns, 1980) 2-4.

55 N. H. Ridderbos, "Genesis I 1 und 2," *OS* 12 (1958) 217.

56 A. A. Di Lella, *The Hebrew Text of Sirach: A Text-Critical and Historical Study* (London: Mounton and Company, 1966) 120 n. 35, 121.

57 Di Lella, 121.

58 Ridderbos, 218.

59 See W. Gross, "Syntaktische Erscheinungen am Anfang althebräischer Erzählungen: Hintergrund und Vordergrund," *VTS* 32 (1981) 144.

60 G. W. Hasel, "Recent Translations of Genesis 1:1," *BT* 22 (1971) 158; see A. Heidel, *The Babylonian Genesis*, (2nd ed.; Chicago: University Press, 1963) 92.

61 Young, "The Relation of the First Verse of Genesis One to Verses Two and Three," 5.

62 Hamilton notes this as well but disregards it in the text of his commentary (Hamilton, 107 n. 11). Spurrell cites examples in which the *ṭipḥāh* accent is found in words "closely connected in sense with the next following word" (Spurrell, 1 n. 1).

63 B. K. Waltke, "The Creation Account in Genesis 1:1-3, Part III: The Initial Chaos Theory and the Precreation Chaos Theory," *BS* 132 (1975) 223-24.

64 G. Anderson, "The Interpretation of Genesis 1:1 in the Targums," *CBQ* 52 (1990) 22 n. 4; J. Kugel, "Two Introductions to Midrash," *Prooftexts* 3 (1983) 149-50.

65 See *GAG* §166.

66 E. A. Speiser, *Genesis* (AB 1; Garden City: Doubleday & Company, 1964) 12-13.

67 H. Orlinsky, *Notes on the New Translation of the Torah* (Philadelphia: Jewish Publication Society, 1969) 50-51.

68 Heidel, 94.

69 Hasel, 161, n. 53.

70 Westermann, 181.

71 Westermann, 200.

72 Westermann, 203.

73 Speiser, 12.

74 J. Sasson, "Wordplay in the OT," *IDBSV*, 968.

75 Young, "The Relation of the first Verse," 6.

76 Heidel, 95.

77 Waltke, 224.

78 Waltke, 223.

79 Hasel, 164.

80 E.g., Waltke, 219.

81 Gunkel, *Genesis*, 102.

82 Hasel, 154-167.

83 Eichrodt, 10.

84 Eichrodt, 10.

85 Gross, 131-45.

86 Speiser, 12; Orlinsky, *Notes*, 51.

87 Heidel, 93; also Young, "The Interpretation of Genesis 1:2," 30.

88 U. Cassuto, *Commentary on Genesis: Part I, From Adam to Noah: Genesis I–VI* (Jerusalem: Magnes Press, 1961) 19.
89 Gross, 142.
90 Gross, 143.
91 Gross, 145.
92 T. O. Lambdin, *Introduction to Biblical Hebrew* (New York: Charles Scribner's Sons, 1971) 164.
93 See B. Jongeling, "Some Remarks on the Beginning of Genesis I,2," *Folia Orientalia*, 21 (1980) 30-31.
94 I. Blythin, "A Note on Genesis 1:2," *VT* 12 (1962) 120; see also C.A. Simpson, "Genesis," in *The Interpreter's Bible* (New York: Abingdon, 1952) 467; Gunkel, *Genesis*, 103.
95 R. Kilian, "Gen I,2 und die Urgötter von Hermopolis," *VT* 16 (1966), 433-34.
96 J. Ebach, *Weltentstehung und Kulturentwicklung bei Philo von Byblos* (BZWANT 108; Stuttgart: Verlag W. Kohlhammer, 1979) 105-8.
97 M. Görg, "*Tōhû wābōhû*—ein Deutungsvorschlag," *ZAW* 92 (1980) 433-34.
98 Görg, 434.
99 Westermann, 102-03.
100 Tsumura, 41.
101 Sasson, "Time . . . to Begin," 188; Sasson, "Wordplay in the OT," *IDBSV*, 968.
102 "Formless" is precisely what von Rad claims is the meaning of "Tohuwabohu." The fact that von Rad treats the Hebrew phrase as one word implicitly sets its alliterative quality into relief (G. von Rad, *Genesis: A Commentary* [Rev. ed., OTL; Philadelphia: Westminster Press, 1972] 49).
103 Cf. bibliography in M. DeRoche's article "The *rûaḥ ʾĕlōhîm* in Gen 1:2c: Creation of Chaos?" in *Ascribe to the Lord: Biblical and Other Studies in Memory of Peter C. Craigie*, ed. L. Eslinger and G. Taylor (JSOTSS 67; Sheffield: Sheffield University Press, 1990) 305, n. 4; 306, n. 5.
104 H. Orlinsky, "The Plain Meaning of *rûaḥ* in Gen. 1.2," *JQR* 48 (1957/58) 174-82.
105 For example, Dillmann claims:

The fundamental point here is the comparison of the Spirit with a bird, and there might even be in this the glimmering of a distant reference to the world-egg (Dillmann, 59).

106 P. J. Smith, "A Semotactical Approach to the Meaning of the Term *rûaḥ ʾĕlōhîm* in Genesis 1:2," *JNSL* 8 (1980) 99-104.
107 Smith, "A Semotactical Approach," 103-4.
108 See Westermann, 147.
109 B. de Spinoza, *A Theologico-Political Treatise and a Political Treatise*, trans. R. H. M. Elwes (New York: Dover, 1951) 21.
110 J. M. P. Smith, "The Use of the Divine as Superlatives," *AJSL* 45 (1928/29) 212-213.
111 D. W. Thomas, "A Consideration of Some Unusual Ways of Expressing the Superlative in Hebrew," *VT* 3 (1953) 209-24.
112 Thomas, 215.
113 See DeRoche, 307-8.

[114] D. J. A. Clines, *The Theme of the Pentateuch* (JSOTSS 10; Sheffield: Sheffield University Press, 1978) 73-76; S. Niditch, *Chaos to Cosmos: Studies in Biblical Patterns of Creation* (SPSH 6; Chico: Scholars Press, 1985) 22-24; DeRoche, 313.

[115] DeRoche, 315, n. 26.

[116] DeRoche, 315.

[117] Blythin, 121.

[118] R. Luyster, "Cosmogonic Symbolism in the Old Testament," *ZAW* 93 (1981) 1-10.

[119] DeRoche, 317.

[120] See the section on structure.

[121] Paradise, 181, 183-4.

[122] E.g., Westermann, 162; L. Dequeker, "Green Herbage and Trees Bearing Fruit (Gen. 1:28-30; 9:1-3): Vegetarianism or Predominance of Man over the Animals?" *Bijdragen* 38 (1977) 118, 125.

[123] Dequeker, 126.

[124] Isaiah and Sharfman, 16.

[125] Williams, 47-48; see Isa 28:12.

[126] Williams, 46.

[127] Dequeker, 127.

[128] M. A. Katz, "The Problems of Sacrifice in Ancient Cultures," in *The Bible in the Light of Cuneiform Literature*, ed. W. W. Hallo, G. L. Mattingly (Lewiston: Edwin Mellen Press, 1990) 149.

[129] Indeed, Westermann is incorrect on this point (see Westermann, 462).

[130] B. Gatz, *Weltalter, goldene Zeit und sinnerverwandte Vorstellungen* (Spudasmata 16; Hildesheim: Georg Olms, 1967) 165-66.

[131] Cited in *Hesiod: Works and Days*, ed. M. L. West (Oxford: Clarendon, 1978) 188.

[132] Gatz, 167.

[133] H. Diels and W. Kranz, *Die Fragmente der Vorsokratiker*, vol. 1 (Berlin-Charlottenburg: Weidmann, 1951) 362 (henceforth referred to as Diels 31 B 128).

[134] Diels 31 B 130.

[135] E.g., Schmidt, 56; Steck, 41-43; Speiser, 6-7.

[136] See translation above.

[137] S. N. Kramer and J. Maier, *Myths of Enki, the Crafty God* (New York: Oxford University Press, 1989) 24.

[138] S. N. Kramer, *Enki and Ninhursag: A Sumerian "Paradise" Myth* (BASOR SS 1; New Haven: ASOR, 1945) 12.

[139] Kramer and Maier, 24.

[140] S. Langdon, *Sumerian Epic of Paradise, the Flood, and the Fall of Man* (Philadelphia: University Museum Press, 1915) 73.

[141] T. Jacobsen, *The Harps that Once . . . , Sumerian Poetry in Translation* (New Haven: Yale University Press, 1987) 190.

[142] So Jacobsen, *Harps*, 357.

[143] J. Cooper, *The Curse of Agade* (Baltimore: Johns Hopkins University Press, 1983) 63.

[144] Cooper, 63.

[145] T. Jacobsen and S. N. Kramer, "The Myth of Inanna and Bilulu," *JNES* 12 (1954) 160-88.

[146] Jacobsen and Kramer, 176.

[147] Jacobsen and Kramer, 177.

[148] J. Van Dijk, *Lugal Ud Me-lam-bi Nir-gal: Le recit épique et didactique des Travaux de Ninurta, du Deluge et de la Nouvelle Creation*, I (Leiden: E. J. Brill, 1983) 74.

[149] Van Dijk, 74.

[150] Jacobsen, *Harps*, 245.

[151] Jacobsen, *Harps*, 275.

[152] Jacobsen and Kramer, "The Myth of Inanna and Bilulu," 186, n. 74.

[153] C. H. Gordon, *Ugaritic Literature: A Comprehensive Translation of the Poetic and Prose Texts* (Rome: PIB, 1949) 75; J. C. L. Gibson, *Canaanite Myths and Legends* (Edinburgh: T. & T. Clark, 1978) 87.

[154] Cf. J. Aisleitner, *Wörterbuch der Ugaritischen Sprache* (Berlin: Akademie-Verlag, 1963) 203.

[155] See A. S. Kapelrud, "Baʿal and the Devourers" in *Ugaritica VI* (Paris: Mission Archeologique de Ras Shamra, 1969) 319-332.

[156] See Chapter One.

[157] Gunkel cites Ilgen's work (*Die Urkunden des Jerusalemischen Tempelarchivs in ihrer Urgestalt als Beytrag zur Berichtigung der Geschichte der Religion und Politik* [Halle: Hemmerde und Schwetschte, 1798]) in his commentary (Gunkel, *Genesis*, 118).

[158] The arrangement of days placed in order similar to the thematic arrangement would look as follows with only very limited correspondence:

1. Light	2. Heaven	3. Sea and Land
4. Luminaries	5. Fish and Birds	6. Land animals and Human Beings

Cf. discussion by Schmidt, 54-55.

[159] Gunkel, *Genesis*, 118.

[160] Beauchamp has noted this discrepancy in Gunkel's ordering (Beauchamp, 42).

[161] The alternative is to discount the formal divisions altogether in order to discern a corresponding thematic structure, as A. Bertholet has done ("Zum Schöpfungsbericht in Genesis 1," *JBL* 53 [1934] 239):

1. Light	2. Heavenly firmament	3. Sea	4. Dry land	5. Plants
6. Celestial bodies	7. Birds	8. Sea creatures	9. Land animals	10. Human beings

Thus instead of the eight creation sections or formal divisions, Bertholet highlights the ten specific creations as the key to unlocking a clear thematic structure. In so doing, however, Bertholet must still rearrange the order of two acts by placing the creation of the birds (7) prior to that of the sea creatures (8).

[162] Cassuto, 17.

[163] Steck, 211.

[164] Wenham, 7.

[165] Wenham, 7.

[166] Beauchamp notes that the thematic structure in the Masoretic text can only be described as imperfect and general (Beauchamp, 43-44).

[167] Steck, 211.

[168] Of note is the LXX's attempt to replicate such constructions:
v 11: *blastēsatō / botanēn* (cf. v 12: *exenēgken / botanēn*)

v 15: *eis phausin/phainein*
The exception is v 20: *exagageto ta hydata herpeta*, presumably because of the limitations of the Greek translator (but cf. LXX Ps 104:30! [*exērpsen hē gē autōn batrachous*]).

[169] E.g., B. W. Anderson, "A Stylistic Study," 152, n. 13; Steck, 43.

[170] See *Genesis Rabbah* Parashah 4:3 in which Rabbi Yose is asked the question why the second day does not contain the approbation formula. In line 13, he responds:

> *lʾ ngmrh mlʾkt hmym*

The creation of the waters had not yet been completed.

[171] Isaiah and Sharfman, 6.

[172] E. Touitou, "Rashi's Commentary on Genesis 1-6 in the Context of Judeo-Christian Controversy," *HUCA* 61 (1990) 183.

[173] This is suggested also by Dillmann (67).

[174] E. Böhmer, *Das Erste Buch der Thora* (Halle: Buchhandlung des Waisenhauses, 1862) 19.

[175] E.g., Jacob ben Asher (See L. Jacobs, *Jewish Biblical Exegesis* [New York: Behrman House, 1973] 106). Clearly, Pythagorean influence during the Hellenistic period would have led early Jewish commentators to attach significance to certain word counts.

[176] Both U. Cassuto and J. Levenson, who evidently uncritically depended on Cassuto, miscounted. See below.

[177] Cassuto, 14-15.

[178] See J. D. Levenson, *Creation and the Persistence of Evil: The Jewish Drama of Divine Omnipotence* (San Francisco: Harper & Row, Publishers, 1988) 67-68.

[179] A. Toeg, "Genesis 1 and the Sabbath," *BM* 50 (1972) 291.

[180] C. Schedl, *History of the Old Testament: The Ancient Orient and Ancient Biblical History*, vol. 1 (New York: Alba House Press, 1973) 217-18.

[181] Schedl, 216-18.

4

HEBREW RETROVERSION OF THE
LXX OF GENESIS 1:1–2:3

INTRODUCTION

Orlinsky made the following pronouncement regarding the new status that the LXX gained in text-critical studies resulting from the discovery of the Dead Sea scrolls:

> The LXX translations will no longer be blamed for dealing promiscuously with their Hebrew *Vorlagen*; it is their *Vorlagen* that will have to be compared with the preserved MT. This is true not only of anthropomorphisms and other theological matters, but even of minor and non-tendentious items.[1]

In 1910 Skinner noted that at the end of Gen 1:9 the LXX contained a fulfillment report in which the possessive pronoun in the phrase *eis tas synagōgas autōn* "proves at least that [the LXX] rests on a Hebrew original, *hydor* being singular in Greek"[2] and the Hebrew term *mayim* being plural. In addition, one can now cite as proof of Skinner's claim the Qumran fragment 4QGen[k], in which part of the "additional" fulfillment report of the LXX of Gen 1:9 is attested in Hebrew.[3]

This fragment, together with 4QGen[h] (see below), lends support to the possibility that 1) the Greek translation of Gen 1:1–2:3 is closely dependent upon a *Vorlage* different from the MT, and 2) the *Vorlage*'s provenance is not Egyptian, as is the Greek translation, but Palestinian.

Hebrew Reconstruction of the LXX of Gen 1:1–2:3

In Chapter Two the LXX translation was examined with only minimal reference to the Hebrew text. With the LXX as a point of departure, it is now possible to reconstruct a probable Hebrew retroversion of the text, namely its *Vorlage*.

The general procedures for reconstructing the Hebrew *Vorlage* are given by Tov: 1) Isolate the elements in the MT that are also found in the *Vorlage*, 2) isolate the elements in the LXX that could reflect Hebrew readings different from the MT, and 3) identify which Hebrew words the translator had in front of him or had in mind.[4] With regard to the first step, the LXX reflects with very few minor exceptions (see below) all the words of the MT. Consequently, the main textual issue at stake is the nature of the pluses in the LXX: Do they "serve to improve the readability from a linguistic and contextual point of view, clarifying Hebrew or Greek words and explaining their content,"[5] or are they, for instance, entirely redundant or superfluous in light of Greek style and syntax, and thus, genuinely reflect a Hebrew *Vorlage*?[6] Do the pluses found in the LXX reflect genuine Hebrew style and syntax[7] or are they the result of Greek stylistic and syntactical considerations and thus innovations of the translator?

Many reputed innovations attributed to the Greek translation of Genesis 1 by scholars have been judged "harmonizing." Such a verdict, however, is misleading. A case in point is the textual status of the final sentence in the LXX of 1:9, which could easily be seen as an example of structural harmonization on the part of the LXX. However, both Skinner's observation of the Hebraic style underlying the verse and the evidence from Qumran fragment 4QGen[k] point decisively to the attestation of 1:9c in the Hebrew. By extension, any structural "harmonization"[8] in the Greek text can be considered as reflecting its Hebrew *Vorlage*. On the other hand, harmonizations that can be explained purely from syntactic or stylistic reasons reflect the manner of translation. Finally, if common linguistic or textual explanations such as scribal corruption or stylistic considerations are not sufficient for explaining the variants, then one must look for other possible rationales behind the textual variants.

In light of the considerations listed above, the following is tentatively proposed as a reconstruction of the Hebrew text upon which the Greek translator was dependent.

1:1   *běrēʾšît bārāʾ ʾĕlōhîm ʾēt haššāmayim wěʾēt hāʾāreṣ.*

1:2   *wěhāʾāreṣ hāyĕtāh tōhû wābōhû wěḥōšek ʿal pěnê těhôm[9] wěrûaḥ ʾĕlōhîm měraḥepet ʿal pěnê hammayim.*

1:3   *wayyōʾmer ʾĕlōhîm yěhî ʾôr wayhî ʾôr.*

1:4   *wayyarʾ ʾĕlōhîm ʾet hāʾôr kî ṭôb wayyabdēl ʾĕlōhîm bên haʾôr ûbên haḥōšek.*

1:5   *wayyiqrāʾ ʾĕlōhîm lāʾôr yôm wělaḥōšek qārāʾ lāyělāh wayhî ʿereb wayhî bōqer yôm ʾeḥād.[10]*

1:6   *wayyōʾmer ʾĕlōhîm yěhî rāqîaʿ bětôk hammayim wîhî mabdîl bên mayim lāmāyim[11] wayhî kēn.[12]*

1:7   *wayyaʿaś ʾĕlōhîm ʾet hārāqîaʿ wayyabdēl ʾĕlōhîm[13] bên hammayim ʾăšer mittaḥat lārāqîaʿ ûbên hammayim ʾăšer mēʿal lārāqîaʿ.*

1:8   *wayyiqrāʾ ʾĕlōhîm lārāqîaʿ šāmāyim wayyarʾ ʾĕlōhîm kî ṭôb[14] wayhî ʿereb wayhî bōqer yôm šēnî.*

1:9   *wayyōʾmer ʾĕlōhîm yiqqāwû hammayim mittaḥat haššamayim ʾel miqwēh ʾeḥād[15] wětērāʾeh hayyābāšāh wayhî kēn [16]wayyiqqāwû hammayim mittaḥat haššāmayim ʾel miqwēhem[17] watērāʾ hayyabāšāh.*

1:10   *wayyiqrāʾ ʾĕlōhîm layyabāšāh ʾereṣ ûlĕmiqwēh[18] hammayim qārāʾ yammîm wayyarʾ ʾĕlōhîm kî ṭôb.*

1:11   *wayyōʾmer ʾĕlōhîm tadšēʾ hāʾāreṣ dešeʾ ʿēśeb[19] mazrîaʿ zeraʿ lěmînēhû[20] wěkidmûtô[21] ʿēṣ[22] pěrî ʿośeh pěrî ʾăšer zarʿô bô lěmînēhû ʿal hāʾāreṣ wayhî kēn.*

1:12   *wattōṣēʿ[23] hāʾāreṣ dešeʾ ʿēśeb mazrîaʿ zeraʿ lěmînēhû wěkidmûtô wěʿēṣ pěrî[24] ʿośeh pěrî ʾăšer zarʿô bô lěmînēhû ʿal hāʾāreṣ[25] wayyarʾ ʾĕlōhîm kî ṭôb.*

1:13   *wayhî ʿereb wayhî bōqer yôm šělîšî.*

1:14   *wayyōʾmer ʾĕlōhîm yěhî měʾōrōt birqîaʿ haššāmayim limʾôrōt ʿal hāʾāreṣ[26] lěhabdîl bên hayyôm ûbên hallāyělāh wěhāyû lěʾōtōt ûlěmôʿădîm ûlěyāmîm wěšānîm.[27]*

1:15   *wěhāyû limʾôrōt birqîaʿ haššāmayim lěhāʾîr ʿal hāʾāreṣ wayhî kēn.*

1:16   *wayyaʿaś ʾĕlōhîm ʾet šěnê hamměʾōrōt haggědōlîm ʾet hammāʾôr haggādōl lěmemšelet[28] hayyôm wěʾet hammāʾôr haqqāṭōn lěmemšelet[28] hallaylāh wěʾēt hakkôkābîm.*

1:17   *wayyitēn ʾotām ʾĕlōhîm birqîaʿ haššāmayim lěhāʾîr ʿal hāʾāreṣ.*

1:18   *wělimšôl bayyôm ûballaylāh ûlăhabdîl bên hāʾôr ûbên haḥōšek wayyarʾ ʾĕlōhîm kî ṭôb.*

1:19   *wayhî ʿereb wayhî bōqer yôm rěbîʿî.*

1:20   *wayyōʾmer ʾĕlōhîm yišrěṣû hammayim šereṣ nepeš ḥayyāh wěʿôp yěʿôpěpû[29] ʿal hāʾāreṣ ʿal pěnê rěqîaʿ haššāmayim wayhî kēn.[30]*

1:21   *wayyibrāʾ ʾĕlōhîm ʾet hattannînim haggědōlîm wěʾēt kol nepeš haḥayyāh hārōmeśēt ʾăšer šārěṣû hammayim lěmînēhem[31] wěʾēt kol ʿôp kānāp lěmînēhû. wayyarʾ ʾĕlōhîm kî ṭôb.*

1:22   *waybārek ʾotām ʾĕlōhîm lěʾmōr pěrû ûrěbû ûmilʾû ʾet hammayim bayyammîm wěhāʿôp yireb bāʾāreṣ.*

1:23   *wayhî ʿereb wayhî bōqer yôm ḥămîšî.*

1:24   *wayyōʾmer ʾĕlōhîm tôṣēʾ hāʾāreṣ nepeš ḥayyāh lĕmînāh bĕhēmah wāremeś wĕḥaytô ʾereṣ lĕmînāh wayhî kēn.*

1:25   *wayyaʿaś ʾĕlōhîm ʾet ḥayyat hāʾāreṣ lĕmînāh wĕʾet habbĕhēmāh lĕmînāh wĕʾēt kol remeś hāʾădāmāh lĕmînēhû[32] wayyarʾ ʾĕlōhîm kî ṭôb.*

1:26   *wayyōʾmer ʾĕlōhîm naʿăśeh ʾādām bĕṣalmēnû kidmût[33] wĕyirdû bidgat hayyām ûbĕʿôp haššāmayim ûbabbĕhēmāh ûbĕkol hāʾāreṣ ûbĕkol hāremeś hārōmeś ʿal hāʾāreṣ.*

1:27   *wayyibrāʾ ʾĕlōhîm ʾet hāʾādām bĕṣalmô[34] bĕṣelem ʾĕlōhîm bārāʾ ʾōtô zākār ûnĕqēbāh bārāʾ ʾōtām.*

1:28   *waybārek ʾōtām ʾĕlōhîm lēʾmōr[35] pĕrû ûrĕbû ûmilʾû ʾet hāʾāreṣ wĕkibsuhā ûrĕdû bidgat hayyām ûbĕʿôp haššāmayim ûbabĕhēmāh ûbĕkōl hāʾāreṣ[36] ûbĕkōl ḥayyāh[37] hāromeśet ʿal hāʾāreṣ.*

1:29   *wayyōʾmer ʾĕlōhîm hinnēh nāttatî lākem ʾet kol ʿēśeb zorēaʿ zeraʿ ʾăšer ʿal pĕnê kol hāʾāreṣ wĕʾet kol haʿēṣ ʾăšer bô pĕrî (ʿēṣ)[38] zorēaʿ zāraʿ lākem yihyeh lĕʾoklāh.*

1:30   *ûlĕkol ḥayyat hāʾāreṣ ûlĕkol ʿôp haššāmayim ûlĕkol rômeś[39] ʿal hāʾāreṣ ʾăšer bô nepeš ḥayyāh ʾet[40] kol yereq ʿēśeb lĕʾoklāh wayhî kēn.*

1:31   *wayyarʾ ʾĕlōhîm ʾet kol ʾăšer ʿaśāh wĕhinnēh ṭôb mĕʾōd wayhî ʿereb wayhî bōqer yôm haššiššî.*

2:1   *waykullû haššāmayim wĕhāʾāreṣ wĕkol ṣĕbāʾām.*

2:2   *waykal ʾĕlōhîm bayyôm haššiššî[41] mĕlaʾkĕtô[42] ʾăšer ʿaśāh wayyišbot bayyôm haššĕbîʿî mikkol mĕlaʾkĕtô ʾăšer ʿaśāh.*

2:3   *waybārek ʾĕlōhîm ʾet yôm haššĕbîʿî wayqaddēš ʾōtô kî bô šābat mikkol mĕlaʾkĕtô ʾăšer bārāʾ [43] ʾĕlōhîm laʿăśôt.*

CONCLUSION

The retroverted Hebrew of the LXX reveals at many points the conservative nature of the Greek translation of Gen 1:1–2:3 in comparison to the MT. The possible changes evident in the production of the LXX text involve only slight syntactical changes:

1. Addition of the article in 1:2 and 3.
2. Addition of the conjunction *kai* in 1:11 and 26.
3. Translation of suffixed endings of *min* only when they receive particular stress in the Hebrew text:
   a) In 1:21 the Hebrew suffix *lĕmînēhem* is plural and distributive.
   b) In 1:25 the Hebrew suffix receives antecedent stress from the pronoun *kōl* (Greek: *panta*).
4. Addition of the preposition *eis* (*lĕ* in Hebrew) in a listing of prepositional objects in 1:14.

One mistake was noted in the LXX translation, namely the haplograph in 1:28, as well as a small number of changes aimed at smoothing out the Greek translation. Thus, any harmonizing tendency in the LXX, in contrast to the MT, can be seen only in relation to minor changes that conform to Greek syntactical style. As for a major structural harmonizing *Tendenz*, there is no clear evidence that it can be attributed to the LXX.

TRANSLATION OF THE VORLAGE OF THE LXX

Many of the translation issues involved in the retroverted Hebrew of the LXX have been discussed in the treatment of the MT. However, those issues peculiar to the VorLXX are discussed in the following translation:

1:1   When God began to create the heaven and the earth,

1:2   (the earth, moreover, having been a hodgepodge, with the darkness upon the deep and the divine wind sweeping over the waters),

1:3   God said, "Let there be light." So there was light.

1:4   And God saw that the light was good, and God divided between the light and the darkness.

1:5   God called the light day, and the darkness he called night. There was evening and morning, day one.

1:6   Then God said, "Let there be a firmament in the midst of the waters so that it may be a constant divider between the waters." And it came about as follows:[44]

1:7   God made the firmament, and God divided between the waters that were under the firmament and the waters that were above the firmament.

1:8   God called the firmament heaven. And he saw that it was good. There was evening and then morning, a second day.

1:9   Then God said, "Let the waters under the heavens gather into one collection so that the dry land may appear." And it came about as follows: the waters under the heavens gathered into their collection, with the result[45] that the dry land appeared.

1:10 And God called the dry land earth and the collection[46] of waters he called seas. And God saw that it was good.

1:11 Then God said, "Let the earth cause wild vegetation to sprout: plants bearing seed according to their kinds and according to their likenesses, fruit trees bearing fruit whose seed is inside them according to their kinds upon the earth. And it came about as follows:

1:12 The earth brought forth wild vegetation: plants bearing seed according to their kinds and according to their likenesses and trees bearing fruit according to their kinds whose seed is inside it upon the earth. And God saw that it was good.

1:13   There was evening and then there was morning, a third day.

1:14   God said, "Let there be luminaries in the firmament of the heavens to be illuminators of the earth, for separating between the day and the night and let them be for signs, for seasons, for days, and years.

1:15   And let them be as luminaries in the firmament of the heavens to give light upon the earth." Thus it happened as follows:

1:16   God made two great luminaries: the greater luminary for ruling over the day; and the smaller luminary for ruling over the night; and also the stars.

1:17   And God placed them in the firmament of heaven to give light upon the earth,

1:18   And to rule the day and the night and to divide between the light and the darkness. And God saw that it was good.

1:19   There was evening and then morning, a fourth day.

1:20   God said, "Let the waters produce[47] swarms of living creatures and winged creatures that fly about above the earth up to the surface of the firmament of the heavens." And it happened as follows:

1:21   God created the great sea monsters and every living creature that moves, of which the waters produced swarms, according to their kinds, and every winged creature according to its kind. And God saw that it was good.

1:22   And God blessed them, saying, "Be fruitful and multiply and fill the waters in the seas, and let the winged creatures increase on the earth."

1:23   And it was evening and then morning, a fifth day.

1:24   And God said, "Let the earth bring forth living creatures according to their kinds: domestic animals, crawlers, and wild animals, according to their kinds." And it happened as follows:

1:25   God made the wild animals according to their kinds: domestic animals, and every animal that crawls on the ground according to its kind, and God saw that it was good.

1:26   And God said, "Let us make human beings in our image, according to (our) likeness so that they may rule over the fish of the sea and the winged creatures of the sky and the domestic animals and over all the ground, and over every creature that crawls upon the ground."

1:27   So God created human beings in his image, in the image of God he created them, male and female he created them.

1:28   And God blessed them, saying, "Be fruitful and multiply and fill the earth and subdue it and rule over the fish of the sea and over the winged creatures of the sky and over the domestic animals, and over all the ground and over every creature that crawls upon the ground."

1:29   And God said, "See here! I hereby give to you every plant that bears seed upon the whole land and every tree on which the (tree's)[48] fruit bears seed. You shall have it for food."

1:30   And to every wild land animal, to every winged creature of the sky, to every crawler on the ground in which there is the breath of life [I hereby give] all the vegetative plants for food." And so it was.

1:31   And God saw everything that he had made, and look! it was very good. And there was evening then there was morning, a sixth day.

2:1   Thus the heaven and the earth and all their host were completed.

2:2   On the the sixth day God completed his work that he had done and rested on the seventh day from all his work that he had done.

2:3   And God blessed the seventh day and made it holy because on it he rested from all his work that God had made in creation.

FORMAL STRUCTURE OF THE LXX *Vorlage* OF GEN 1:1-2:3

As in previous discussions of Gen 1:1–2:3, the structure of the passage are first presented as an outline, after which the formal features are discussed.

Outline of the Formal Structure

Beginning and Ending

In contrast to the LXX, which exhibits a structural tension between "pre-creation" (1:1-2) and the first formal creation (1:3-5), the VorLXX, as in the MT, sharply delineates between a description of the pre-creative condition (1:2) and the first act of creation (1:3-5). As for the ending of the passage, 2:1-2a is included in the sixth day section, as in the LXX, thereby concluding the Hexaemeron. The seventh day section does not formally begin until 2:2b, with the declaration of God's resting on the seventh day.

The Use of the Transition Formula wayhî kēn

The formula *wayhî kēn* functions as a transition marker, similar to the way in which *kai egeneto houtōs* functions in the Greek text. Its consistent placement between the command and fulfillment report serves as an intermediate step between word and event, both confirming the divine command and introducing the way in which the command is fulfilled. Like the Greek text, the formula's occurrence in 1:30b after God's granting of food serves to confirm as well as presuppose the enactment of the divine declaration, without, however, introducing the next formal component, namely the divine approbation (1:31).

THEMATIC STRUCTURE

The clear corresponding thematic structure evident in the LXX is replicated in the VorLXX, in which the general domains of the heavens, waters, and earth correspond to the specific created objects of lights, sea and winged creatures, and land animals and human beings, respectively.[49] As in the LXX, the transition formula's conspicuous absence in the first and last creative acts hastens the narratival movement between command and fulfillment. The lack of this intermediate step more tightly binds the fulfillment with the command and formally sets apart the respective creations of light and human beings from the rest of creation as special divine acts.

The particular distinction given to light and human beings within the overall creative sweep could be explained by their respective inextricable relations to the divine. Light, for instance, is intimately connected to God in Ps 104:1b-2a:

hôd wĕhādār lābāšĕtā ʿōteh ʾôr kaśśalmāh

You are clothed with honor and majesty,
Wrapped in light as with a garment.

Given the poetic parallelism, light is considered something of a divine attribute. Indeed, solar imagery was not infrequently used to describe Yahweh, usually in the context of royal theology.⁵⁰ On the other hand, the close connection between human beings and God is explicitly described by the terms *ṣelem* and *děmût* in relation to God. Thus both light and human beings are considered objects of creation on a level apart from all other created things.

THE RHETORIC OF THE DIVINE COMMAND

The commands concerning the earth and the waters in the Hebrew *Vorlage* of the LXX are replete with rhetorical nuance. As already observed in the MT, several commands display an etymological relation between predicate and object. Indeed, this is more the case with the VorLXX:

> 1:11 **tadšēʾ** haʾāreṣ **dešeʾ** . . .
>
> 1:14 yěhî **mě'ōrōt** birqîaʿ haššāmayim **lim'ōrōt** haʾāreṣ
>
> 1:20a **yišrěṣû** hammayim **šereṣ** nepeš ḥayyāh
>
> 1:20b wě'ôp yě'ôpēpû 'al haʾāreṣ

Verse 14 is distinguished by the fact that the command calls for the *creation* of the celestial luminaries for illuminating the earth. All other cases, though, are commands indirectly *addressed* to already existing elements, namely the earth and the waters. Verses 11, 20a, and 20b, as already suggested with respect to the MT, exhibit deliberate rhetorical design aimed at *eliciting* from the earth and the waters the *appropriate* products such as vegetation, swarming sea creatures, and flying winged creatures. The means of production and the product are inextricably united by the etymological affinity between the verb and its object.

To cast the divine commands indirectly as jussives, rather than as direct commands, adds to the rhetorical nuance of the commands. The jussive can function as an exhortation, as offering counsel, granting permission, and in the case of a superior addressing an inferior, as a command.⁵¹ Clearly, the series of jussives function within the context of divine commands, but they also exhibit a nuance that is less intrusive and forward than that of a direct command. In other words, the jussive commands bear an element of exhortation. Thus the use of such indirect commands adds to the rhetoric of divine speech, designed to *enlist* aid from the earth and waters in the cosmogonic process. In short, they are exhorted to perform.

The Waters and the Earth as Equal Agents in Creation

Instances of the waters and the earth as active participants in creation are the following:

Earth

1. *wayyōʾmer ʾĕlōhîm tadšēʾ hāʾāreṣ dešeʾ* . . . (1:11). Commanded to produce vegetation of all sorts, the earth executes the command in the fulfillment report (*wattōṣēʾ hāʾāreṣ dešeʾ* . . .).

2. *wayyōʾmer ʾĕlōhîm tôṣēʾ hāʾāreṣ nepeš ḥayyāh* . . . (1:24). The earth is commanded to produce the land animals. In this case, however, *ʾĕlōhîm* creates them in the fulfillment report (*wayyaʿaś ʾĕlōhîm ʾet ḥayyāt hāʾāreṣ* . . .).

Waters

1. *wayyōʾmer ʾĕlōhîm yiqqawû hammayim* . . . (1:9a). The waters are commanded to gather into a single collection, and they fulfill the command precisely as stated.

2. *wayyōʾmer ʾĕlōhîm yišrĕṣû hammayim* . . . (1:20a). The waters are commanded to produce swarms of sea creatures. The fulfillment report recounts their involvement in production, but *ʾĕlōhîm* is described as creating the sea creatures (*wayyibrāʾ ʾĕlōhîm* . . .).

3. *wĕʿôp [hammayim] yĕʿôpēpû* . . . (1:20b). The waters are commanded to "cause the flyers to fly," that is, to produce winged creatures. However, the waters' participation in the fulfillment is not explicitly stated. On the other hand, it is implied elliptically in parallel fashion with 1:21a:

1:21a	*wayyibrāʾ ʾĕlōhîm* . . . *ʾet kol nepeš haḥayyāh*
	hārōmešet ʾăšer šārĕṣû hammayim lĕmînēhem
1:21b	*wĕʾēt kol ʿôp kānāp [ʾăšer yĕʿôpēpû hammayim] lĕmînēhû*

Thus both God and the waters have a hand in producing the aquatic and aerial creatures.

Conclusion

The earth and the waters are treated as separate agents enlisted by ʾĕlōhîm to create life. In one instance apiece, the earth and the waters act without divine intervention: The waters gather into a collection so that the land can appear (1:9) and the earth produces vegetation (1:12). Elsewhere, divine intervention is depicted in the fulfillment reports: in the creation of the land animals and in the creation of the aquatic and aerial creatures. In both cases, God is clearly the *primary* creator. To God alone is reserved the prerogative of *creating*, since the verbs ʿśh and brʾ are used exclusively to describe divine action. The waters, on the other hand, contribute the distinctive qualities that characterize certain sea animals (šereṣ) and all the winged creatures (ʿôp) as swimmers and flyers, respectively. The waters bestow on these animals precisely what defines them as unique in comparison to other animals.

Similarly, the earth in 1:24 is commanded to "bring forth" the land animals. However, the typical etymological affinity between the verb and object is absent. One wonders whether such a construction would at all have been possible within the purview of the author and/or the limitations of the Hebrew language. At the very least any attempt at continuing the rhetorical craft of the previous divine commands would have involved breaking up the list of animals in 1:24 and identifying each species by some characteristic and matching it with a transitive verb to describe its means of production (e.g., *tarmēš hāʾāreṣ remeś*, with the verb *rmś* in the hiphil jussive, unattested in the biblical Hebrew).

At any rate, a comparison of the approximately equal generative powers of the earth and the waters can be outlined with respect to their syntactical position in the commands and fulfillment reports as subjects.

Earth

1:11	Command: earth	1:24	Command: earth
1:12	Fulfillment: earth	1:25	Fulfillment: God

Waters

1:9a	Command: waters	1:20	Command: waters
1:9b	Fulfillment: waters	1:21	Fulfillment: God and waters

The Textual Comparison between the
VorLXX and the MT

So far in the discussion of the LXX and MT it has been established that the Greek text closely follows a Hebrew *Vorlage* that differs significantly from the MT. These changes are essentially structural with the exception of a few linguistic differences. It will be helpful to review the structural differences between the two versions for the purpose of discerning their textual relationship to each other. As already noted, the respective structures of the MT and the LXX result in differing construals of the role of the waters.

The Role of the Waters

The differences in role the waters assume in the MT and the VorLXX are easily discerned by examining both the structural differences and linguistic differences between the two texts.

Structural differences

1. Many of the structural differences between the MT and the LXX of Genesis 1 are due to the location of the transition marker *waykî kēn*. The formula, for instance, is situated in 1:6b in the VorLXX and in 1:7b in the MT. In the VorLXX, *wayhî kēn* is used transitionally as a bridge between the command in 1:6 and its fulfillment in 1:7, whereas in the MT it is employed as a confirmation of the fulfillment. As already noted, the Masoretic placement of the formula shifts attention away from the command by following, and thereby underscoring, the fulfillment. This shift can be illustrated best by a comparison with the previous creation section:

> Command (1:3a): *wayyōʾmer ʾĕlōhîm yĕhî ʾôr*
> Fulfillment (1:3b): *wayhî ʾôr*

Here, a narrative pattern is established whereby the fulfillment is introduced by *wayhî* that precisely replicates the divine command. The correspondence of the verb *hyh* in both command and fulfillment has led some scholars to count the fulfillment as an instance of the formula.[52] Indeed, it could be interpreted as a conflation of the formula and the fulfillment, but such a conclusion is unnecessary. That 1:3b constitutes the fulfillment is clearly obvious, despite the fact that it is an impersonal fulfillment (*yĕhî* . . .) that is entirely unique in the account.

In any case, the second creation section (1:6-8) in the MT breaks the pattern.

	MT	VorLXX
1:6	*wayyōʾmer ʾĕlōhîm*	*wayyōʾmer ʾĕlōhîm*
	yĕhî rāqîaʿ	*yĕhî rāqîaʿ*
1:7a	*wayyaʿaś ʾĕlōhîm ʾet*	**wayhî kēn**
1:7b	**wayhî kēn**	*wayyaʿaś ʾĕlōhîm ʾet*

Rather than the verb *hyh* introducing the fulfillment as in the creation of light, the verb ʿ*sh* begins the fulfillment report. If 1:7a were to match the command of 1:6 in the same way that 1:3b matches 1:3a (viz., beginning with *wayhî rāqîaʿ*) the fulfillment would imply a firmament created in the midst of the waters without divine intervention, possibly implying initiative action on the part of the *hammayim*. This would also be the case, were the formula to follow immediately after the command:

1:6	*wayyōʾmer ʾĕlōhîm **yĕhî rāqîaʿ***
1:7a	*wayhî kēn*

Read apart from the fulfillment report that follows (*wayyaʿaś ʾĕlōhîm* . . .), the *implied* fulfillment (in context with the previous creation section) would also imply a firmament that appears by itself within the waters (*wayhî rāqîaʿ* . . .), occasioned by the utterance of the divine command (1:6). Indeed, such a notion *can be entertained* in the narratival progression of the VorLXX, since the formula's presence immediately following the command serves as an intermediate step, a narratival pause in the movement from word to event. However, due to the MT's placement of the formula after the fulfillment, the fulfillment report thereby follows immediately upon the heels of the command, and consequently underscores divine action as the only means by which the command is realized.

The formula's placement in the MT (in 1:7b) serves to confirm the fulfillment *as a result of divine action*. The VorLXX evidently saw no contradiction between a command that *possibly* implied the creation of a firmament apart from divine action and a fulfillment report that described divine intervention. This theological flexibility is due to the fact that the formula was employed by the VorLXX as a transitionary step to introduce the fulfillment, whereas the MT employed it only to confirm what preceded it, namely the fulfillment. As a result, the MT effectively precluded any possible conjecture that the *mayim* participated in the formation of the firmament, whereas the issue was moot for the VorLxx.

2. The fulfillment report is missing in 1:9 in the MT.

MT	VorLxx
1:9a *wayyōʾmer ʾĕlōhîm yiqqāwû*	*wayyōʾmer ʾĕlōhîm yiqqāwû*
1:9b *wayhî kēn*	*wayhî kēn*
	wayyiqqāwû hammayim . . .

As mentioned above, when read in context with the fulfillment described in the previous section (*wayyaʿaś ʾĕlōhîm*),[53] the fulfillment report's absence in the MT implies a fulfillment introduced with divine action ("And God divided . . . [*wayyiqew ʾĕlōhîm*]). Furthermore, in light of the previous usage of the formula in 1:7 in the MT, the formula *wayhî kēn* in 1:9 confirms the understood fulfillment. Not only is the gathering of waters not reported in the MT, the absence of the fulfillment report implies a fulfillment realized by direct divine intervention. Not so in the VorLxx: The waters initiate the action recorded in the fulfillment report (*wayyiqqāwû hammayim . . .*).

3. The approbation formula is absent in the MT of 1:8.

MT	VorLxx
1:8 *wayyiqrāʾ ʾĕlōhîm*	*wayyiqrāʾ ʾĕlōhîm*
lārāqîaʿ	*lārāqîaʿ*
	wayyarʾ ʾĕlōhîm kî ṭôb
wayhî ʿereb . . .	*wayhî ʿereb . . .*

As already noted, the absence of the approbation formula in the MT precludes conferring a sense of completion on the section depicting the separation of the waters via the firmament. Instead, focus is shifted to the appearance of the land, only after which approval is given (v 10). The presence of the approbation formula in 1:8 in the VorLxx, on the other hand, marks this section (1:6-8) concerning the *first* separation of the waters as independent from that of vv 9-10.

4. In 1:20-24 the transition formula is nowhere to be found in the MT, in contrast to its typical placement in the VorLxx. The formula's absence, similar to its absence in 1:6, serves to hasten the transition between command and fulfillment. In fact, no formal transition takes place.

MT	VorLxx
1:20 *wayyōʾmer ʾĕlōhîm yišrĕṣû*	*wayyōʾmer ʾĕlōhîm yišrĕṣû*

wayhî kēn

1:21   *wayyibrā² ²ĕlōhîm ²et*   *wayyibrā² ²ĕlōhîm ²et*

This section also concerns the waters. The waters are commanded to cause "swarms" of sea creatures "to swarm," whereas the fulfillment report begins by describing divine creation. In the MT the incongruence is mitigated by a sudden transition to the fulfillment report, thereby dispelling any implication from the command that the waters are to initiate the creative action. The VorLXX, on the other hand, places the formula in its typical location, thereby stressing the efficacy of the command that the waters contribute to the generation of *both* sea and winged creatures.

In short, the structural differences between the two versions are the result of different readings of the role of the waters in the creation process. In the MT the commands in which the waters appear to figure prominently in cosmogony are "deconstructed" through the manipulation of the transition formula in 1:6-7 and 1:20-21 and through the omission of both the approbation formula in 1:8 and the fulfillment report in 1:9.

Linguistic Differences

In Gen 1:20 the command involving the waters is different in the two versions.

MT   VorLXX

1:20b *wĕ²ôp yĕ²ôpēp*   *wĕ²ôp yĕ²ôpēpû*

In the VorLXX, the waters (plural) are commanded to cause the sea creatures to swarm *and* the winged creatures to fly. This double command is severed in the MT, whereby the winged creatures are commanded separately to fly about. The textual difference is explained by the presence of the *waw* at the end of the verb *yĕ²ôpēp* in the VorLXX.

Textual Relationship between the MT and the VorLXX of Genesis 1:1-2:3

Having taken account of the major structural differences between the VorLXX and the MT along with the one linguistic difference discussed above, one can now assess the textual relationship between the two versions. The crucial question in textual criticism is which text would be more likely to have evolved from the other. Most scholars have answered this by observing that the LXX is a far more consistent text than the MT. This is undoubtedly correct. The anomalous placements and omissions of the transition marker and other components in the MT do not appear in the LXX. With regard to the transition formula, D. J. Frame's comments are typical:

> It is probable that the Septuagint does not preserve a more original text, but that it merely completes the process of inserting the interpretive phrase "and it was so," a process that P had performed only imperfectly.[54]

Wellhausen claimed that the LXX is based on a "systematischer Überarbeitung," since "eine so konsequente Conformität [ist] nicht das Princip des ursprünglichen Textes."[55] Westermann agrees and attributes to the LXX a tendency to "schematize."[56] Indeed, as noted earlier, the LXX and, therefore, the VorLXX exhibit a parallel thematic structure, whereas the MT lacks such a corresponding outline. A particularly comprehensive and otherwise helpful treatment of the LXX text of Genesis 1-5 simply assumes the harmonizing tendency of the LXX relative to the MT.[57] Such arguments could conceivably invoke the Greek/Hellenistic concern for textual balance and harmony as the reason behind the LXX's harmonized text.

The simple explanation that the LXX harmonized the MT, however, breaks down at several points.

1. The Qumran fragments 4QGen[k] and 4QGen[h] suggest that the LXX was likely based on a Hebrew *Vorlage* of Palestinian provenance.[58] These fragments confirm Skinner's suspicion that Gen 1:9 in the LXX corresponded to a Hebrew text.[59] Arguments solely from a Greek literary style concerned with structural symmetry, therefore, falter at this very point. Admittedly, the Qumran attestations simply drive the issue back to the Hebrew VorLXX as the possible origin of such harmonizing, but the fact that we are now dealing with a native revision rather than a Hellenistic translation casts a different light on the textual relationship. Arguments from Greek influence on form and style are eliminated from the discussion.

2. If structural harmonization were the overarching *Tendenz* of the VorLXX, our revisionist could have done a more thorough job. One glaring example is the section concerning the creation of human beings (1:26-27). Here, the movement from divine command to creation lacks the transition marker one would expect as in every other case in which the formula appears.

1:26   *wayyōʾmer ʾĕlōhîm naʿăśeh ʾādām* . . .

1:27   *wayyibrāʾ ʾĕlōhîm ʾet hāʾādām* . . .

The formula, however, appears after the divine granting of food in 1:30, whereby it functions not as transitionary but as confirming the divine speech and presupposing its realization. Were structural harmony the overriding aim of the VorLxx, this anomalous placement of *wayhî kēn* would clearly have been "corrected" with an addition at the end of 1:26. Another case in point is the formula's anomalous absence in 1:3 in the VorLxx between command and fulfillment. If the VorLxx had harmonized the MT text, why would it have let these two anomalous instances stand?

In Chapter Two, it was noted that light and human beings were considered in the VorLxx as special acts of creation by virtue of the missing transition formulas in the first and last sections. Would such a subtle underscoring of these two creations within the matrix of a balanced structure be more likely the result of a harmonizing revisionist rather than that of an earlier or authorial text? I think not. Like the LXX, the VorLxx exhibits a finely balanced thematic structure, whereas the MT by comparison displays a breakdown of any thematic outline. The thematic structure of the VorLxx represents a subtle level of thematic abstraction that seems more likely to be indigenous to an earlier stage in the text's construction, possibly even the "original" stage, rather than the result of any particular revision thereof, harmonizing or otherwise.

This likelihood is particularly true with regard to the morphological change of the verb *ʿûp* in 1:20. It is unlikely that the VorLxx would have added the *waw* in order to include the formation of winged creatures within the domain of the waters' powers and thereby establish a corresponding thematic structure in which the middle category "water" neatly subsumes both marine and winged creatures. As noted in the MT, the depiction of the waters' role as separate from the formation of the winged creatures prevents any description of a clear thematic structure.

In order to claim that the VorLxx represents a revision of the text preserved in the MT, one would have to account for the textual differences mentioned above by suggesting the following tendencies at work in the VorLxx's revision: 1) harmonization of the formal components in each creation section except the first and the last, 2) abstract thematic structural concerns, and 3) a concern to increase the role of the waters in 1:20. If, on the other hand, one were to claim that the text preserved in the MT represented a revision of the textual tradition reflected in the VorLxx, one need only posit *one Tendenz* in the MT to account for the differences, namely the tendency to limit the role of the waters in creation. The use of Ockham's razor points to the latter explanation as the most likely.

3. In addition, attributing a structural harmonizing *Tendenz* to the LXX does not allow one to escape from asking why the MT anomalously placed the "transition" formula in several places. Explanations resorting to an "imperfect" usage of the formula offer little explanatory force. The consistent-versus-inconsistent placement of the formula can be layed out as follows in the MT:

Consistent Placement	Inconsistent Placement
1. 1:9-10	1. 1:6-8 (after fulfillment)
2. 1:11-13	2. 1:20-23 (absent)
3. 1:14-19	3. 1:26-28 (absent)
4. 1:24-25	4. 1:29 (after granting of food)

With the consistent placement of the formula equaling the number of instances the formula is used inconsistently or is missing, one can thus speak of the MT's *anomalous* placement of the formula without begging the question as to the relationship between the VorLXX and the MT. Thus such anomalous placements must be accounted for even within the MT itself. The generally accepted explanation that these anomalous placements are due to careless scribal activity can easily be dismissed, since it has been shown that a variety of contexts in ancient Near Eastern literature contain similar formulas that meaningfully appear in "anomalous" positions, frequently after the fulfillment report.

Again, the most reasonable explanation to be given (even without reference to the VorLXX) is that less stress is given to the waters' role in creation than to the earth's role. The fact that the VorLXX happens to correspond to a more structurally consistent "text" lends credence to its priority in relation to the textual tradition preserved in the MT.

4. Had the VorLXX or LXX revised the text preserved by the Masoretes with regard to 1:20, a reasonable explanation must be sought as to why there would be such a concern for expanding the waters' role as an active agent equal to that of *hāʾāreṣ*. One possible conjecture is that the prominence of water in the (Vor)LXX is the result of Greek/Hellenistic cosmogonic thinking. However, it will be demonstrated that in the majority of Greek cosmogonic accounts, water consistently participates *in conjunction* with earth in producing life as, for instance, in the mixed form of mud (*ilus*).[60] Nowhere is this implied in the Genesis account, since the formation of life does not begin until the earth, and the waters are formally separated and are active within their own respective domains, whereas mixture of some sort is a necessary precondition for creation in most Greek cosmogonies. Moreover, prominent in many

Greek mythical and philosophical accounts is the almost exclusive role of earth in the formation of life. The Greek cosmogonies that posit water as the source of *all* creation (Homer, Thales, and Hippon) describe the creative process in such general fashion that they bear little resemblance to the *particular* role the waters are given in the Genesis text. Furthermore, nowhere in Greek literature is water considered the cause for the existence of aerial creatures. The origin of this tradition remains obscure, but it may very well have its roots in the traditions surrounding the Sumerian God Enki (Ea in Babylonian literature) or in the Egyptian god Khnum. At least the likelihood is greater that the link between winged creatures and water is rooted in Sumerian/Semitic or ancient Egyptian traditions than in those of Greek/Hellenistic provenance.

However, perhaps the most persuasive argument against a Hellenistic influenced text is the fact that the LXX can be traced back to a Hebrew *Vorlage* of probable Palestinian provenance. In addition, if one were to argue for the VorLXX as a revision of the MT, the strongest case would be made on harmonizing grounds rather than from any ideological concern to heighten the role of the waters in creation by manipulating the structural arrangement of the text and yielding a revision that *coincidentally* forges a more consistent structure for the VorLXX.

Conversely, an Israelite creation text that underscores the generative activity of the waters could easily be seen as diminishing God's control over the created order and therefore invite revision. In short, of the two texts, the VorLXX could be seen as the harder text from a theological perspective, as will be seen in the following chapter.

The Role of the Heptad

The above discussion on the role of the waters only accounts for one set of textual variations. Another set of discrepancies must be analyzed. As noted earlier, the MT of Gen 1:1–2:3 exhibits a heptadic structure in terms of both the frequency with which certain words occur and the total word count. Such a numerological structure is not as readily evident in the longer text of the VorLXX, though it is not entirely lacking. Intimations of a heptadic structure occur in the word count of the first two verses concerning the precreative state of affairs: 7 words in v 1 and 14 in v 2, as also in the MT. In addition, the three last verses of the account (2:1-3) contain a total word count of 35, with vv 2a, 2b, and 3a each containing a count of seven words. But such is the extent of any numerological orientation for the author of the VorLXX.

As noted earlier, several minuses in the MT in comparison to the VorLXX occur in redundant contexts: *ʾĕlōhîm* in 1:7b and the words *pĕrî* and *ʿal hāʾāreṣ* in 1:12. The latter two minuses can be attributed to the MT's concern to work out a total word count that is a multiple of seven, namely 469 (7 x 67), once the structural differences have been worked out. The total word count for the VorLXX totals 494, and this can be broken down verse by verse to facilitate corroboration. The discrepant word counts between the two Hebrew texts are italicized.

Verses	Masoretic Text	VorLXX
1	7	7
2	14	14
3	6	6
4	12	12
5	13	13
6	*11*	*13*
7	*17*	*16*
8	*10*	*14*
9	*13*	*21*
10	12	12
11	*20*	*22*
12	*18*	*22*
13	6	6
14	*16*	*19*
15	9	9
16	18	18
17	8	8
18	12	12
19	6	6
20	*15*	*17*
21	23	23
22	13	13
23	6	6
24	14	14
25	18	18
26	19	19
27	13	13
28	*22*	*23*
29	27	27
30	21	21
31	15	15
2:1	5	5
2:2	14	14
2:3	16	16
TOTAL	469	595

The difference in total-word numerological orientation between the LXX *Vorlage* and the MT is perhaps significant. However, since any Hebrew retroversion of the LXX can only be made on the grounds of probability, a comparison of the total word count of the MT with the VorLXX can only remain indecisive. One cannot exclude the possibility that the VorLXX had a total word also divisible by seven. However, more decisive for comparative purposes is the word count of key words:

		Masoretic	VorLXX
1.	ʾĕlōhîm	35	36
2.	ʾereṣ	21	24
3.	šāmayim (+ rāqîaʿ and mabdîl)	21	22
4.	ṭôb (or approbation formula)	7	8

The word count of the divine name ʾĕlōhîm differs in both texts because of three textual changes in the MT. The absence of the approbation formula in 1:8 in the MT decreases the word count by one. In addition, the MT contains an extra ʾĕlōhîm in 1:28a, wherein God is described as personally addressing the human beings. These two changes have been noted as intentional. With a total so far of 36, the elimination of the redundant divine name in 1:7 reduces the word count to thirty-five (7 x 5).

The difference in the word count of ʾereṣ can be attributed to three changes, two of which are intentional in the MT. As noted in the Hebrew retroversion of the LXX, the absence of ʿal hāʾāreṣ in 1:12 and limʾōrōt ʿal hāʾāreṣ in 1:14 does not significantly change the meaning of these verses in the MT in comparison to the VorLXX. In fact, they could be considered redundant, since they are repeated or similarly mentioned elsewhere in context. It has been suggested that the absence of the phrase ûbabĕhēmāh ûbĕkol hāʾāreṣ in 1:28 was due to a scribal mistake in the MT. Once this "mistake" became part of the Masoretic tradition, the count for ʾereṣ was 23. It was then easy to eliminate the other two instances as redundant uses of the term.

The terms designating "heaven" (šāmayim, rāqîaʿ, and mabdîl) bring the total in the VorLXX to twenty-one. This may or may not be evidence for a numerological Tendenz. However, since other key terms (e.g., ʾĕlōhîm) do not exhibit such a trend, it is more probable that the count is fortuitous in the LXX. One would suspect this to have been retained in the MT, but one instance of šāmayim was eliminated as a result of the deletion of the entire fulfillment report at the end of 1:9, thereby reducing the count to twenty.[61] Finding it difficult to add another šāmayim or rāqîaʿ to the text, the MT counted mabdîl in 1:6b, due to its function and parallelism in 1:6a, as a referent to šāmayim.[62]

The absence of the approbation formula in 1:8 of the MT is one instance in which both the concern for numerological significance and the *Tendenz* to limit the role of the waters coincide. By eliminating the formula so as to avoid granting the approval to the (incomplete) separation of the waters, the term *ṭôb* was consequently reduced by one count, thereby decreasing its occurrences to seven.

Also of note is the MT's word count for *mayim*, twelve. With *yam*, the total adds to sixteen. In comparison to the other key terms that bear a heptadic count, one could attribute the count of *mayim* to the lack of numerological concern for the waters in contrast to *ʾereṣ*, heaven, *ʾĕlōhîm*, etc. on the part of the MT.[63] In addition, another textual difference between the two texts can also be attributed to the MT's more thorough numerological agenda, namely the designation of the day in 2:2. This frequently noted textual variant has usually been resolved by giving preference to the MT, since it appears to be the more difficult text, whereas the LXX seems to be more accurate by declaring the day in which God completed his work to be the *yôm haššiššî* ("sixth day"). However, plausible reasons can be offered that make sense of the MT's use of *haššĕbîʿî*.[64]

1. From a structural standpoint, the sixth day ends in 1:31, and a description of the seventh day begins in 2:2. In addition, 2:2a and 2b are very much parallel:

> *waykal ʾĕlōhîm bayyôm haššĕbîʿî mĕlaʾkĕtô ʾăšer ʿaśāh*
> *wayyišbōt bayyôm haššĕbîʿî mikkōl mĕlaʾkĕtô ʾăšer ʿaśāh*

2. The usual translation for *waykal ʾĕlōhîm bayyôm haššĕbîʿî* is "And on the seventh day God finished the work that he had done" (NRSV). However, such a rendering conflicts with 1:31 and 2:2b. To avoid a blatant contradiction, the *Piel* form of the verb *klh* could be rendered intransitively in English: "And God *was finished* with his work on (or by) the seventh day," a rendering occasionally implied in the use of the *Piel* (see Ezra 10:17; 1 Chr 27:24; 2 Chr 24:14; 29:17; 31:1), or simply rendered as a pluperfect: "And God had finished his work by the seventh day." Such renderings do not imply work done on the seventh day; rather, the onset of the seventh day marks the end of work. Such a rendering follows semantically, if one is to avoid considering 2:2a as simply a scribal mistake in the MT. It is clear the MT considered the verbs *klh* and *šbt* as semantically co-terminous on the temporal level.

It appears, then, that this textual variation with respect to the particular day contained in 2:2 of the MT can be explained by a concern for numerological consistency in the last section of the creation account. Thus, the MT of 2:2a should not be considered the more difficult text, which the LXX consequently corrected. Rather, the MT included 2:2a in the last section and heightened the numerological significance of the last section of the creation account, as well as equated completion (klh) with rest (šbt) on the *seventh* day.

Conclusion

In summary, the argument that the LXX is simply a harmonizing translation of the text of the MT is found wanting: The reputed harmonistic *Tendenz* of the LXX is not consistent enough to be harmonizing. To the contrary, the structural anomalies of the MT can be better explained by positing a tendency to minimize the role of the waters in creation and a numerological tendency to make the counts of certain key words, if not the total word count of the text, divisible by seven. In light of these concerns, it is plausible to suggest that the LXX preserves a Hebrew *Vorlage* that is prior to the text preserved by the Masoretes.

Having established the textual relationship between these two texts, one can now investigate the possible rationales that would explain the textual differences, particularly with regard to the role of the waters in cosmogony. The next chapter explores the ancient traditions that underlie these differences. As mentioned above, what is of immediate concern is determining whether the Greek cosmogonies influenced the LXX's (or VorLXX's) favorable treatment of the waters in creation.

NOTES

[1] H. Orlinsky, "The Textual Criticism of the Old Testament," in *The Bible and the Ancient Near East*, ed. G. E. Wright (Garden City: Doubleday & Company, 1961) 121.

[2] Skinner, 22, n. 9.

[3] Davila, 9-10.

[4] Tov, *The Text-Critical Use of the Septuagint*, 99.

[5] Tov, *The Text-Critical Use of the Septuagint*, 83.

[6] Tov, *The Text-Critical Use of the Septuagint*, 85.

[7] Tov, *The Text-Critical Use of the Septuagint*, 101.

[8] For our purposes, "harmonization" can be defined as the addition of a sentence or part thereof that contributes to the structural consistency of the passage as a whole.

[9] The Greek includes an article with the prepositional object: *epano tēs abyssou* (Hebrew reconstruction: ʿal pĕnê hattĕhôm). However, the presence of the article is probably due to Greek grammatical style rather than to any Hebrew variant. Note that the parallel colon has the prepositional object containing an article (*epano tou*

hydatos), which matches the MT (*ʿal pĕnê hammayim*). With the exceptions of Isa 6:13 and Ps 106:9, the term *tehom* is never attached to an article in the Hebrew Bible.

¹⁰ The LXX's use of the cardinal number *mia* rather than the ordinal *prōtē* for the Hebrew *ʾeḥād* reflects the LXX's precision with regard to translating the Hebrew.

¹¹ The lack of articles in the Greek before the repeated term *hydatos* reveals the care with which the LXX translates its Hebrew *Vorlage*, identical in this case to the MT (cf. 1:7, in which the LXX reproduces the Hebrew articles in the repeated prepositional phrase *ana meson tou hydatos*).

¹² The additional transition marker in the LXX is most likely attributable to its Hebrew *Vorlage*, given the LXX's strict adherence to many MT equivalents (see above) and the attestation of Qumran fragments supporting the structural consistency of the LXX against the MT (see below).

¹³ The name *ʾĕlōhîm* is attested in the LXX but absent in the MT and can be best attributed to the LXX's *Vorlage*, since its position in the Greek after the verb is indicative of Hebrew syntax and its occurrence is redundant in the context of 1:7a. Its absence in the MT is likely an instance of the MT's *Tendenz* to reduce the word count for the word *ʾĕlōhîm* to a multiple of seven, namely from thirty-six to thirty-five (see below).

¹⁴ The approbation formula present in the LXX but lacking in the MT can be traced to the Masoretic stance against granting premature approval (of completion) to the activity of the waters (see Chapter Two).

¹⁵ The MT has the rendering *māqôm* ("place"), whereas the LXX renders it *synagōgēn*, thus clearly reading the word in question as *miqwēh*. One could maintain that the Greek text simply harmonized 1:9 with 1:10 (*miqwēh hammayim*). However, the prominence of the *figura etymologica* constructions elsewhere in the MT text would argue against an original *māqôm* (see Chapter Three). There have been several attempts at reconciling the LXX with the MT. Some simply take the MT *māqôm* as a misreading of an original *miqwēh* (e.g., Gunkel, 107; Speiser, 6). However, this would require a scribe to misread the letter *he* as a final *mem*, an unlikely graphic confusion. D. N. Freedman proposes that the Hebrew text originally read *miqwêm*, contracted from *miqwêhem* with syncopation of the *he*, thereby rendering the original to mean "one gathering of them" ("Notes on Genesis" *ZAW* 64 [1952] 190-91). However, this does not explain how the LXX read the word as *miqwēh*, thereby disregarding the third plural masculine suffix. Another attempt is made by T. L. Fenton, who argues that *māqôm* was a scribal mistake for an original *miqwîm*, resulting from a "virtual haplography" of the consonants *waw* and *yod* (" 'One Place,' *māqôm ʾeḥād*, in Genesis I 9: Read *miqwîm*, 'Gatherings,'" *VT* 34 [1984] 438-45). Fenton notes a tension between the plural name *yammîm* ("seas") in 1:10 and the singular terms *māqôm* in 1:9 and *miqwēh hammayim* in 1:10. However, Fenton creates more problems than he solves: He cannot account for the addition of the word *ʾeḥād* ("one") after *māqôm* (alias *miqwîm*) in 1:9, and to be logically consistent, he also has to posit an original plural *miqwê hammayim* for the singular *miqwēh hammayim* in 1:10, for which he provides no explanation. What Fenton deems as a "simple solution" involves a rather intricate and convoluted reconstruction of the textual history. Most decisive, however, is his underlying assumption that no Hebrew manuscript would contain the reading *miqwēh ʾeḥād*. This is proven false by 4QGen^h, since it contains the word *miqwēh* for 1:9 (Davila, 8-9). Thus *miqwēh ʾeḥād* is most likely attested in the *Vorlage* of the LXX.

[16] The material from here to the end of the verse (9b) is attested only in the LXX, but is clearly part of its *Vorlage*, given the discrepancy between the subject *hydor* and its suffixed reference *autōn*, which is best explained with reference to a Hebrew *Vorlage* (see above).

[17] The plural, suffixed form of *miqwēh* is reflected in the Greek *synagōgas autōn*, whose antecedent is the singular *hydor* at the beginning of the verse. The Hebrew, of course, attests only to the plural *mayim*. This awkward transition from singular attestation to plural reference in the Greek is best attributed to a close dependence on a Hebrew *Vorlage* (see above). Beginning with 1:10, the Greek translation renders the word *hydor* in the plural. One cannot rule out, however, that the LXX *Vorlage* had a *singular* attestation for *miqwēh* in the fulfillment of the command (1:9c), which the LXX simply misread as a plural (*synagōgai*). Indeed, the singular would likely be the identical form *miqwêhem* (as given in the BHS apparatus), since morphologically *miqwēh* was originally a III-*Yod* noun (See Lambdin, 129-30). This is analogous to the case of *maḥănēh*, which exhibits a separate plural form *maḥănôt* and assumes suffixes on its singular form, which resembles common plural noun forms, such as in Deut 23:15 (*maḥănekā*) and in Am 4:10 (*maḥănêkem*). Another example is *mištēh*, whose form *mištêhem* in Jer 51:39 is probably singular with the plural suffix. Unfortunately, there are not enough attested suffixed forms of *miqwēh* to decide whether *miqwêhem* is to be taken as singular or plural. I suspect in context of the reconstructed Hebrew of Gen 1:9 (*miqwēh ʾeḥād*), the noun is best rendered in the singular (see translation). At any rate, it is no surprise the LXX read it as a plural, since such a rendering makes the transition from *hydor* singular (1:2-9a) to *hydata* plural (1:10-21) in connection with the formation of "seas."

[18] The LXX introduces the new term *systemata* to refer to *miqwēh*. From a syntactical standpoint, the LXX produced a plural translation in light of the plural name *yammîm* ("seas"), without being able to reproduce the collective force behind the singular *miqwēh*. For the meaning of the Greek term, see translation in Chapter Two.

[19] The LXX makes a construct chain out of *dešeʾ ʿeśeb* (*botanēn chortou*), but this does not reflect any variation between the Hebrew *Vorlage* and the MT.

[20] The LXX does not translate the suffixed pronoun in the Hebrew, as attested in the MT, since *genos* can be used in the technical sense of genus or species in Greek literature.

[21] After *zeraʿ* the LXX contains the phrase *kata genos kai kathʾ homoiotēta*, which is unattested in the MT. The argument that 1:11 in the LXX is a harmonization of 1:12 (as attested in the MT) seems at first glance forceful. However, this does not account for the attestation of the Greek term *homoiotēs*, which appears in both 1:11a and 1:12a without support from the MT. Is it likely the LXX simply added it, and if so, why? The phrase is repeated in 1:12a, but not in 1:12b, although the MT contains identical terms (*lĕmînēhû*). If the LXX was simply harmonizing, why did it not employ *homoiotēs* in all four cases in which *kata genos* occurs unless it was constrained by its *Vorlage*? It seems more likely that the term *homoiotēs* reflected a Hebrew equivalent in the *Vorlage* of the LXX. If so, the equivalent would most likely have been *kidmût*. The Greek translators commonly rendered *kidmût* with similar terms as *homoiōs* (Isa 13:4), *homoiōma* (Isa 40:18; Ezek 1:4, 16, 22, 26) and *homoiōsis* (Gen 1:26; Ps 57:4; Ezek 1:10). Its absence from Gen 1:11 and 12 in the MT could be easily explained by its use in Gen 1:26 and 5:1, 3 as a quality endemic to human beings in relation to *ʾĕlōhîm* (*naʿăśeh ʾādām bĕṣalmēnû kidmûtēnû*). The LXX translation in 1:26 for *kidmût* is *homoiōsis*, a term

synonymous with *homoiotēs*, since both mean "likeness" or "resemblance" (*LS* 1225). Elsewhere, the LXX translates *kidmût* with *eikona* (5:1) and *idea* (5:3). Thus the Greek translator(s) of Genesis felt no rigidity in translating the term any one way. However, it is also plausible that the reason 1:11 does not contain the identical term as in 1:26 is the same reason the term was excluded by the MT in 1:11 and 12, namely to highlight the uniqueness of human beings in virtue of their relationship to God. In short, the appearance of *homoiotēs* in both 1:11 and 1:12 suggests a Hebrew equivalent in the LXX's *Vorlage*. Consequently, there is reason to take the "additions" attested in the LXX in 1:11 as direct renderings of the *Vorlage*.

²² The MT lacks the *waw* conjunctive, whereas the LXX includes it in *kai xylon*. Whether the *waw* was present in the LXX's *Vorlage* is unclear; however, since the absence of the *waw* makes for a harder text stylistically, it is more probable that the *waw* was lacking in the VorLxx.

²³ The different verb from that of its parallel in 1:11 (*dš'*) in the MT is directly attested by the Greek (*blastanō* in 1:11 and *ekpherō* in 1:12).

²⁴ The botanical term *pĕrî* is absent in the MT. It is uncertain whether the word was present in the VorLxx, since its presence is entirely redundant. Possibly its omission in the MT can be attributed to the Masoretic concern for reducing the total word count of the passage (see next section).

²⁵ The prepositional phrase *'al hā'āreṣ*, attested already in 1:11, is repeated in the LXX but absent in the MT. Given its redundant usage in v 12, it is likely that the MT omitted it to reduce the word count of the term *hā'āreṣ* in Gen 1:1-2:3 (see next section).

²⁶ The phrase *lim'ôrōt hā'āreṣ* is absent in the MT. Such a retroversion is based on the fact that the same Greek phrase, *eis phausin*, is used in the following verse for *lim'ôrōt*, as is the case elsewhere in the LXX (Judg 13:13; Ps 73:16). It was probably considered redundant by the Masoretes, hence its omission in the MT. In addition, its omission could be attributed to the MT's concern for manipulating the word count of *hā'āreṣ* (see below).

²⁷ Whether the preposition *lĕ* for the last term in the verse was present in the *Vorlage* of the Greek (*eis eniautous* = *ûlĕšānîm*) cannot be decisively judged. However, it is plausible that the preposition was added by the Greek translators for reasons of syntactical harmony, since *šānîm* is the only prepositional object in the series without its prefixed preposition in the MT.

²⁸ The Greek has *eis archas*, that is, a plural object of the preposition. It is possible the Greek read the Hebrew term as a plural, namely *memšĕlôt*. The usage of the Hebrew term in the plural is not without precedence (see Pss 136:9; 114:2). Indeed, the difference in Hebrew vocalization is not semantically significant. In Ps 114:2 the subject (*yiśrā'el*) is singular.

²⁹ The Greek participial phrase *peteina petomena epi tēs gēs* presupposes a Hebrew equivalent that differs from the MT: the MT employs the finite verb *yĕ'ôpēp* in the imperfect, whose subject is *'ôp*, whereas the LXX would appear to presuppose a participle. There are two possibilities for retroverting the Hebrew of the LXX:

1) Substituting the verbal prefix (*yod*) with a prefixed *mem* thereby renders the imperfect *Polel* verb as a participle (see Isa 14:29 and 30:6: *śārāp mĕ'ôpēp*). Indeed, elsewhere in the creation account, *remeś* is described "etymologically" with participles (1:26, *hāremeś hārōmēś*; 1:30, *romeś*). Such a reconstructed Hebrew variant would render *'op* as the object of the verb *šrṣ* in the first clause of the command.

Semantically, evidence for this outside the creation account comes from Deut 14:19 with reference to the unclean winged creatures:

> *wĕkōl šereṣ hā'ôp ṭāmē' hû' lākem lō' yē'ākēlû*

And all the swarms of winged creatures are unclean for you; they shall not be eaten.

However, in light of the classifications of unclean birds immediately preceding Deut 14:19, this Deuteronomic injunction clearly refers to swarming insects. The problem with this reconstruction for Gen 1:20 is that the priestly account evidently intends to cover *all* winged creatures, including, for instance, birds of prey, which presumably do not "swarm." Moreover, winged creatures that fly to the very reaches of the heavens (*'al pĕnê rĕqîa'*) would not include insects. In addition, such a Hebrew variant requires the textual substitution of a letter (from *yod* to *mem*) and disturbs the chiastic parallelism of the two cola.

2) Adding a *waw* at the end of the finite verb renders the second clause: *wĕ'ôp yĕ'ôpĕpû 'al hā'āreṣ*. Hence, a suitable translation for the command would be: "Let the waters produce swarms of living creatures and produce winged creatures to fly about . . ." (literally, "cause flyers to fly about" in the same way the first clause literally reads "cause swarms of living creatures to swarm"). In support of this retro-version is the fact that the LXX uses the generic verb *exagō* to apply to both the *herpeta* and *peteina*. This was evidently required by the fact that the Greek language lacks a transitive verb meaning "cause to fly" (cf. *petomai, hiptamai, aphiptamai, exiptamai, ekpetomai*). Thus the LXX translator had to subsume the transitive sense of the second Hebrew verb under the first verb (*exagō*) with a participial modifier. Hebrew, on the other hand, employs the *Polel* of the verb *'ûp* both intransitively and transitively. As for the latter usage, Ezek 32:10 has:

> *bĕ'ôpĕpî ḥarbî 'al pĕnēhem wĕhārĕdû lirgā'îm*

When I wield my sword before them, they shall tremble every moment.

Here, the verb *'ûp* is cast in the form of an infinitive construct, meaning literally "to cause to fly about." Indeed, the *Polel* like the *Piel*, frequently carries transitive meaning, and thus it is no surprise to find a transitive usage in the *Polel* for the verb *'ûp*. With such a reconstruction of the VorLXX, the retroverted verse exhibits typical chiastic form with respect to verb-object order:

> *yišrĕṣû hammayim šereṣ . . . we'op yĕ'ôpĕpû 'al hā'āreṣ*

Consequently, the simple dropping of the *waw* suffixed ending in effect severs the waters' generative relationship to the winged creatures as well as "detransitivizes" the contextual meaning of the verb.

[30] The transition formula is lacking in the MT.

[31] The biological classification is read as plural by the LXX. Indeed, the Masoretic spelling is most likely defective. In addition, here is one of only two instances (see also 1:25) in which the LXX translates the suffixed ending, most probably due to the Hebrew's use of the plural. Like English, directly translating a singular suffix ending in Greek in light of a collective antecedent is awkward. Hence, the LXX translates the last *lĕmînēhû* with a plural suffix in v 25.

³² See preceding note. The LXX chose only to translate the suffixed ending of the last *lĕmîn*, probably because of the inclusive force of the pronoun *panta* (Hebrew, *kōl*) for the last category of animals (*ta herpeta*).

³³ The LXX adds the conjunction *kai* before *homoiōsin*, but lacks the possessive pronoun (Hebrew: *kidmûtēnû*). Instead, the LXX uses the emphatic form of the posses- sive pronoun (*hemeteran*) to modify only *eikona*. Though a judgment call, it would seem plausible that the addition of the conjunction is a Greek innovation done for stylistic reasons (as is also attested in the Samaritan Pentateuch), but the lack of the second possessive pronoun is an instance of inconsistency that is more likely rooted in the *Vorlage*, as opposed to the MT.

³⁴ This word is not attested in the Greek, but it can best be explained by supposing that the Greek translator overlooked it as a haplograph or a case of *homoioteleuton*. As Z. Frankel describes it, "Das Auge irrte über das erste *kat eikona* zum dem zweiten hinüber" (*Vorstudien zu der Septuaginta* [Leipzig: Wilhelm Vogel, 1841] 69). The words are almost identical (*bṣlmw* and *bṣlm*) and thus provide an ideal condition for causing a scribal mistake (compare the *kĕtîb* and *qĕrê* of Judg 20:13 and 2 Sam 18:20). J. Cook, on the other hand, sees it as a harmonizing *Tendenz* of the LXX and refers to Gen 5:2 (Cook, "The Exegesis of the Greek Genesis," 107). But such an argument is ground- less, since only the synonym *dĕmût* is used in 5:2.

³⁵ Instead of the MT's *wayyōʾmer lāhem ʾĕlōhîm* to introduce the second clause, the LXX has the participle *legōn*, which parallels 1:22 (Hebrew: *lēʾmōr*). This would lead one to conclude that the LXX has harmonized the openings of the two blessings and/or found the finite Hebrew construction unnecessarily redundant. However, it is clear in the MT that the *lēʾmōr* of 1:22 and the *wayyōʾmer lāhem* connote two different things. The former is a generic, object-less opening of a divine declaration; the latter is a personal, divine address. Of note is also the fact that the MT cites *ʾĕlōhîm* a second time, stressing direct divine address to human beings. The difference in formulations points to the difference in creations: the sea and aerial creatures, on the one hand, and human beings, on the other. Thus it is equally plausible that the different intro- ductions of divine speech is attributable to a change in the MT to highlight the onto- logical separation between animal life and human beings. Curiously, Westermann also supports the Greek reading here, claiming that "the way in which the first two sentences in 1:28 are linked is stylistically improbable with P and syntactically harsh," since the narrative sequence of the imperfect consecutive cannot be under- stood as a continuation of *wybrk* (Westermann, 79). However, Westermann overlooks the prospect that the narrative sequence (*waw* + prefixed conjugation) is epexegetical (See *IBHS* 33.22a), with the second sentence giving content or explanation to the divine act of blessing.

³⁶ Absent in the MT is the phrase *ûbabbĕhēmāh ûbĕkol hāʾāreṣ* (LXX: *kai pantōn tōn ktēnōn kai pasēs tēs gēs*). Its inclusion in the LXX brings the blessing in 1:28 in parallel with the command given in 1:26, which would argue against its authenticity. However, one can just as easily propose that the MT omitted it, due to a scribal slip of the hand, since the first two letters *waw* and *bet* at the beginning of the omitted material are identical to the following word in the MT. Furthermore, the third letters *bet* and *kap* can be graphically confused.

MT:	*wbʿwp hšmym*	*wbkl ḥyh*
LXX *Vorlage:*	*wbʿwp hšmym wbbhmh*	*wbkl hʾrṣ wbkl ḥyh*

It appears this is a simple case of *homoioarchton*. In addition, one cannot explain why human rule over the domestic animals (*bĕhēmāh*) would be excluded from the fulfillment report of the command. Thus the appearance of this phrase in the LXX and its absence in the MT are plausibly due to a Masoretic scribal mistake, rather than any expansionistic tendency on the part of the Greek translator. As a result, the phrase is most probably present in the LXX's *Vorlage*.

37 The generic zoological term *ḥayyāh* does not match the *ḥāremeś* in the command of v 26 in the MT; however, their respective participial qualifiers make the terms semantically identical. Thus *ḥayyāh* is translated identically by the LXX, and there is no reason to see any variation between the LXX *Vorlage* and the MT here.

38 The MT uses the noun *ʿēṣ* as a *nomen rectum* of *pĕrî*, which the LXX translated together as *karpos*. A literal translation was evidently too wooden for the Greek translator, given the fact that the verb *echō* was employed in the relative clause (*ho echei en heautō karpon spermatos sporimou*), which is only understood in the MT (and the LXX's *Vorlage*).

39 The LXX translation *panti herpeto to herponti* is most likely reflective of a Hebrew phrase identical to that of the MT, namely *lĕkol rōmeś*, rather than a reconstructed *lĕkol remeś hāromeś*, which is nowhere found in the MT (cf. MT: 1:26b). It is understandable that the LXX would not have translated the Hebrew participle with only a Greek participle, since *herpeton* can also refer to a *particular class* of animals that *herponton* ("creeps").

40 The LXX adds the conjunction *kai*, which reconstructed in the Hebrew would be *wĕʾet* (cf. MT, 1:29 [*wĕʾet kol hāʿēṣ*]). Its presence can be explained as a Greek concern for syntactical harmony within the listing of animals. Thus the *waw* was quite probably absent in the *Vorlage* of the LXX.

41 Because of the evidence from the LXX, the SP, and the Peschitta, it is most probable that the Hebrew *Vorlage* of the LXX had *haššiššî* instead of the MT's *haššĕbîʿî*. Such a view is preferable to the proposal that the LXX is a Greek harmonization of the "harder reading" of the MT (see following section).

42 The LXX translates *mĕlaʾkĕtô* in the plural throughout 2:2-3, making explicit the collective force behind the singular Hebrew noun.

43 The LXX employs the verb *archomai* (Hebrew *hāḥal?*), which is at odds with the MT's *bārāʾ*. Indeed, the task of translating *bārāʾ ʾĕlōhîm laʿăśôt* in any language is daunting, and the Greek rendering may very well represent the translator's valiant but unsuccessful attempt. However, it is more probable that an exegetical point is at stake. Note, for instance, that *archomai* of 2:3 forms an inclusio with 1:1 (see Chapter Two and J. Cook, "The Exegesis of the Greek Genesis," 108-10).

44 The formula *wayhî kēn* acts as a transition formula in 1:6, given its more common placement between divine command and fulfillment. Due to the formula's placement, the English translation of this formula must differ from the translation of the formula at the end of 1:7 in the MT.

45 Rendering the second clause in the command as a telic or purpose clause has already been discussed (Chapter Three). It is only logical contextually that the second clause in the fulfillment report be rendered as a result clause, which can be formed by means of a simple consecutive sequence (Williams, *Hebrew Syntax* §525; *IBHS* 38.3a). As Meek has pointed out, the so-called "*waw* conversive" rather than the *waw* conjunctive expresses result (Meek, 40-43).

46 The term *miqwēh*, if taken singularly in vv 9 and 10, is meant to be taken collectively (no pun intended). The term *miqwēh ʾeḥād* evidently refers to a singular system of restricted bodies of water (*yammîm*).

47 See the note on translation of 1:20 in the MT and the note on the Hebrew retroversion in this section. A more literal translation would be: "Let the waters cause swarms of living creatures to swarm and cause the winged creatures to fly . . ."

48 See the note on the Hebrew retroversion.

49 See Chapter Two.

50 M. S. Smith, "The Near Eastern Background of Solar Language for Yahweh," *JBL* 109 (1990) 29-39.

51 See discussion in *IBHS* 34.3.

52 E.g., Schmidt, 58; Wenham, 6.

53 Contra Cook, "Genesis I in the Septuagint as Example of the Problem," 31-32.

54 D. J. Frame, "Creation by the Word" (Unpublished Dissertation: Drew University [Ann Arbor: University Microfilms] 1969) 187.

55 J. Wellhausen, *Die Composition des Hexateuchs und der Historischen Bücher des Alten Testaments* (2nd ed.; Berlin: Georg Reimer, 1889) 187.

56 Westerman, 79.

57 Alexandre, 45, 151.

58 See the discussion of these fragments in Davila, 8-11.

59 Skinner, 22.

60 See Chapter Five.

61 Both Cassuto (Cassuto, 14) and Levenson (Levenson, 67) claim that the word count for "heaven" (*šāmayim* and *rāqîaʿ*) is actually 21 in the MT. This, however, is simply not true. One must also add *mabdîl*.

62 See note on translation of the MT for 1:6 in Chapter Three.

63 The significance of the word count of *mayim* in the MT is explored in Chapter Six.

64 One such attempt is by O. Loretz (*Schöpfung und Mythos: Mensch und Welt nach den Anfangskapiteln der Genesis* [Stuttgart: Katholisches Bibelwerk, 1968], 63) who takes the verb in a figurative sense: God "finishes" creation on the seventh day not through any further act of creation but through rest.

5

The Role of Water in Ancient and Classical Cosmogonies

Introduction

In the foregoing discussion it has been established that the structural variants between the VorLxx and the MT of Genesis 1 point to different roles assigned to water in the creation account. These dissimilar roles reflect in part certain ancient traditions. In the following discussion, these traditions will be examined with regard to their treatments of the role of water in cosmogony and to their possible influence on the different perspectives one finds in the VorLxx and MT of Genesis 1. Four ancient cultural centers in the Mediterranean world and the Near East provide good candidates for such an examination: Greece, Mesopotamia, Egypt, and Canaan.

The Role of Water in the Greek Cosmogonies

It could be argued that the prominent role assigned to the waters in the LXX (and/or its Hebrew *Vorlage*) of Genesis 1 is the direct result of Greek/Hellenistic influence. However, a survey of the major mythological and philosophical accounts from the eighth to the third century BCE demonstrates that the Greek accounts are in little agreement as to the function of water in cosmogony.

146   STRUCTURE, ROLE, AND IDEOLOGY IN GENESIS 1:1–2:3

Mythological Texts: Hesiod and Homer

The *Theogony* of Hesiod is usually dated to the last third of the eighth century BCE, possibly predating the Homeric epics.¹ Thus the work represents the earliest complete cosmogonic/theogonic work within the extant mythological Greek corpus, though the genre of theogony undoubtedly had a long history before Hesiod.² The subject of the *Theogony* is the origin and genealogy of the gods, including the events that led to the establishment of Zeus as king.³ This catalogue of gods contains approximately three hundred names, only some of which designate gods who were worshiped in the Greek cult or played signifi-cant roles in mythology. Hence the work is more a history of the gods than a cosmogony. What is explicitly cosmogonic comprises only a small portion of the poem, namely lines 116-32. In this passage, the gods constitute the essence of cosmic phenomena.

Water does not assume an initial place in this genealogical procession of the gods:

> ētoi men protista Chaos genet'· autar epeita Gai' eurysternos, pantōn hedos asphales
> aiei athanaton hoi echousi karē niphoentos Olympou, Tartara t' ēeroenta mychǭ
> chthonos euruodeies, ēd' Eros, hos kallistos en athanatoisi theoisi⁴

> First came Chaos; then, after him, broad-breasted Earth (*Gaia*), an immov-able, eternal dwelling-place for all the immortal gods who rule Olympus' snowy peaks. Next came Tartarus of the dark mist in a recess of the broad-pathed earth (*chthonos*); Then Love (*Eros*), the most beautiful among the immortal gods.⁵

For Hesiod, Chaos marks the beginning of the created order. This cosmological term can be rendered as "gaping void"⁶ or "chasm."⁷ It appears to designate the region either between Heaven and Earth⁸ or between Earth and Tartarus.⁹ In any case, this primordial entity has nothing to do with water (despite a much later Stoic allegorization [see below]). Rather, Chaos is the primeval chasm filled with darkness, since from it arise Erebos and Nyx (line 123). Only later does Earth engender the sea (Pontos [lines 126-7, 129-132]):

> Gaia de toi prōton men egeinato ison heōutę̄ Ouranon asteroenth', hina min peri panta kalyptoi,

> geinato d' ourea makra . . . Nympheōn . . . ede kai atrygeton pelagos teken oidmati thuion, Ponton, ater philotētos epimerou·

> Earth bore first of all one equal to herself, starry Heaven, so that he should cover her all about,

Earth bore the long Mountains . . . the Nymphs . . . and also the unharvested sea (*Pontos*) with its furious swell, without delightful union.[10]

The sea, as an open sheet of water (*pelagos*), is described as "unharvested" or "barren" (*atrygetos*), a common adjective used by Hesiod (*Theogony* 696) and Homer to designate the sea:

para thin' halos atrygetoio[11]

Along the banks of the barren sea.

The precise nuance of the term *atrygetos*, however, is uncertain, since it could also mean "impossible to dry out" or "undraining."[12] Regardless of meaning, the sea is considered a child solely of Earth, and its generative powers are readily apparent (line 105-7):

*kleiete d' athanatōn hieron genos aien eonton, hoi Gēs t' exegenonto kai Ouranou asteroentos Nyktos te dnopheres, **hous th' halmyros etrephe Pontos**.*

Celebrate the holy race of immortals who are forever, those who were born of Earth and starry Heaven, and gloomy Night, *and those whom the briny Pontos fostered.*

What Pontos or the sea fosters are divine beings. No mention is made of the creation of mortal life, human or otherwise. In short, sea water is considered a derivative of Earth alone, a creation of the Earth produced without intercourse (line 132). By contrast, Earth bears in union with Heaven "deep-swirling Oceanus" (*Okeanon bathydinēn* [lines 132-33]), along with eighteen other gods and goddesses, including Tethys and the youngest, Kronos. Like Pontos, Oceanus is not depicted by Hesiod as primeval, but as a child among many from the parentage of Earth and Heaven. In Homeric literature, Oceanus is the river surrounding the earth at its very rim and the source of all rivers (see *Iliad* 16.200; 21.195-97).[13] In contrast to Hesiod, Homer describes Oceanus as the "father of the gods" (*theōn genesis* [*Iliad* 14.201, 246, 302]) and Tethys, the mother, as the one who rears Hera, wife of Zeus. Hesiod, however, portrays them as children of Heaven and Earth. In addition, Hesiod appears to maintain a rigid distinction between Oceanus and Pontos in terms of pedigree, perhaps reflecting the distinction between fresh and sea water.

An instance in which Sea (Pontos) is treated merely as an inanimate substance is in the etiological story of Aphrodite (lines 188-200): Once Kronos throws the castrated genitals of Heaven into the "surging sea" (*polyklysto eni ponto*, line 188), *aphros ap' athanatou chroos ōrnyto· tǭ d' eni kourē ethrephthe.*

About them (the waves) grew a white foam from the immortal flesh, and in it a girl formed.

tēn d' Aphroditēn kikleskousi theoi te kai aneres, hounek en aphrǭ threphthē.

Gods and men call her Aphrodite, because she was formed in foam.

ēde philommeidea, hoti medeōn exephaanthē
and "genial," because she appeared out of genitals.[14]

Here, the sea contributes little to the genesis of Aphrodite. All credit is due to the "immortal flesh" of Kronos's genitals. Later, however, Hesiod tells of Sea's own progeny (233-39):

Pontos (sea) fathered Nereus, reliable and true, the eldest of his children.

Again, he fathered great Thaumas and noble Phorcys in union with Earth, and Ceto of the lovely cheeks, and Eurybia.

All of Pontos's children live in the sea, namely, three sons and three daughters (233-39). Nereus is the sea god known as the "Old Man of the Sea." Nereus and Doris, a daughter of Oceanus, together produce fifty daughters, the Nereids or sea-nymphs, who are in one way or another associated with the sea.

Oceanus, on the other hand, produces two daughters: Doris, "lovely-haired daughter of Oceanus, the perfect river" (240) and Electra, "a daughter of deep-flowing Oceanus" (*Okeanoio bathyrreitao thygatra* [265-66]). In union with Oceanus, Tethys bears the "swirling Rivers" (*Potamous teke dinēentas* [337]), which number twenty-five. She also bears the "Holy family of Nymphs" (*kouraōn hieron genos* [346]), forty-one total. In addition, in lines 364-68 she is described as giving birth to:

three thousand graceful-ankled Oceanids; widely scattered they haunt the earth and the depths of the waters everywhere alike, shining goddess-children.

And there are as many again of the Rivers that flow with splashing sounds, sons of Oceanus that lady Tethys bore.

Here, Oceanus is credited with fathering the innumerable female Ocean-nymphs, including Styx, the river of the underworld, and the innumerable male "Rivers." Thus Oceanus is the great river from whose subterranean connections issue forth all other rivers.[15]

In summary, neither Oceanus nor Pontos in Hesiod's work constitutes the origin of all things. Although both assume high positions

relative to many other gods, Hesiod does not place them at the primordial beginning. Homer, on the other hand, makes Oceanus and Tethys
the originators of all the gods, resembling the roles that Tiamat and Apsu
are given in the Babylonian theogony *Enuma Elish*. Like Pontos the sea,
Oceanus is a son of Earth and Heaven. Both Homer and Hesiod agree
that these divine beings produce divine creatures appropriate to their
nature: Pontos produces divine beings tied to sea water, while Oceanus
begets river beings. Only the later descendants of these two gods include
occasional mortal, albeit legendary, creatures (e.g., the "Old Women"
and Medusa [270ff.]) in the *Theogony*. In short, Hesiod, in contrast to
Homer, places Earth in the role of primary generator.[16] The two deities
associated with water are derived from earth. In addition, they have little
role in the creation of mortal life.

Orphic Fragments

Much early Greek cosmogonic poetry is attributed to Orpheus.
Orpheus, if he existed at all, is usually considered to have lived no later
than the sixth century BCE.[17] Writings attributed to him existed in three
principal versions, according to the Neo-Platonist Damascius (fifth/sixth
century CE).[18] This is signficant in that the three present differing
theogonies. The version *Rhapsodiae*, or "epic lays," places Chronos (Time)
as the first principle. The version quoted by Eudemus makes Night the
first principle. The third version, produced no earlier than the third
century BCE by Hieronymus and Hellanicus,[19] begins with water:

> *hydor ēn, phēsin, ex archēs kai hylē ex hēs epagē hē gē, duo tautas archas hypotithe-
> menos prōton, hydor kai gēn,*[20]

> Originally there was water, (Orpheus) says, and mud (or matter [*hylē*]), from
> which the earth solidified. He posits these two as first elements, water and
> earth.

These two elements or principles (*archai*) together engender a divine
creature whose name is Chronos or "ageless time" (*Chronos agēraos*). The
element or principle of water rises to even greater prominence in
Athenagoras' description of Orphic theogony:

> The gods, so they say, did not exist from the beginning; rather each of them
> was born just as we are born. And this is agreed by them all, Homer saying:
> "And Oceanus, the father of the gods, and mother Tethys."[21]

Athenagoras then explains:

> For water was according to him the origin of everything, and from the water mud (*ilys*) formed, and from a pair of them a living creature was generated, a serpent with an extra head growing upon it of a lion.[22]

Clearly Athenagoras employed contemporary (2nd century CE) philosophical language to describe Orpheus's cosmogonic views. Consequently, it is even questionable whether an early tradition existed at all that attributed to Orpheus a Homeric view concerning the watery origin of the cosmos.[23] Of note also is Athenagoras's interpretation that water in conjunction with earth produces life.

Acusilaus

Hesiod's cosmogonic views were was not without their advocate in the person of Acusilaus of Argos (sixth century BCE). Instead of positing Oceanus as the primeval entity in creation, Acusilaus postulated Chaos:

> Hesiod claims that Chaos came into being first . . . and after Chaos these two came into being: Earth and Eros. Thus Acusilaus agrees with Hesiod.[24]

For Acusilaus, Chaos, rather than water, was the first principle (*tē protē archē*) with Earth next in line.[25]

Pherecydes

Thales, considered by Aristotle as the first philosopher, is cited with Pherecydes by Achilles Statius (2nd or 3rd century CE) in *Isagoge* as identifying the waters with Chaos:

> Thales of Miletus and Pherecydes of Syros suppose that water was the source of everything, and Pherecydes calls it Chaos.[26]

The statement, however, is inaccurate. Pherecydes of Syros (7th or 6th century BCE) was the author of a particular cosmogonic myth that described Zas (Zeus) celebrating his wedding with Chthonie. Three days after the marriage, Zas makes a beautiful robe on which he embroiders Earth, Ogenos (Oceanus), and the palace of Ogenos.[27] Zas then addresses Chthonie:

> Because I desire that your marriage (with me) occur, I honor you with this (gift).

This account, the author notes, describes the origin of the first unveiling ceremony, when the bride exchanged her wedding veil for her husband's wedding gift. Unfortunately the papyrus breaks off before Chthonie replies after receiving Zeus's gift.

In this creation allegory, Zeus is considered the original creator by whom the Earth and Oceanus are fashioned. Diogenes Laertius claims to quote Pherecydes:

> Zas, Chronos, and Chthonie always existed; but Chthonie's name became "Earth," because Zas gives her Earth as a (wedding) present.[28]

Pherecydes's cosmogonic myth says more about Earth than about Oceanus; therefore, Achilles's conclusions as to the close connection between Pherecydes and Thales are unfounded and may represent a later Stoicizing tradition that identified water with Chaos, beginning around 300 BCE (see below).[29]

Thales of Miletus

The famous astronomer and mathematician of Miletus is traditionally viewed as the founder of philosophy.[30] Thales was most known for his theory concerning water. According to Aristotle:

> Some say that (the earth) rests on water. This is the most ancient explanation we have received, which is said to be the account of Thales of Miletus: that it stays where it is because it floats like wood (*menousan hōsper xylon*) or something similar.[31]

More importantly, however, was the thesis that water constituted the origin of all things, thereby making Thales, according to Aristotle, the first philsopher of nature:

> Most of the early philosophers thought that the first principles in the form of matter were the only principles of everything. The source of all existing things—that from which first of all they come into being and into which they finally perish, the substance remaining but changing in its qualities—this, they say, is the element (*stoicheion*) and first principle (*archē*) of existing things.[32]

With this overview of the basic tenet in early philosophy, Aristotle describes Thales' place:

> Thales, the originator of this sort of philosophy, says that (the principle) was water.[33]

Aristotle goes on to conjecture the reasons behind Thales' thesis, namely that Thales observed that the nourishment of all things is moist, that seeds have a "moist nature" (*physin hygran*).[34] Aristotle saw as a precursor to Thales' thought the mythological depiction of Oceanus and Tethys, the "parents of creation" (*tēs geneseōs pateras*).[35] Others, however, saw traces of Egyptian mythology (Proclus and Simplicius).[36] Burnet takes issue with Aristotle (and Guthrie[37]) by suggesting that Thales' thesis is based on the fact that water can easily change its states, that is, into air under heat and solid under cold.[38] As evidence, he cites one of Thales' successors, Anaximenes, who viewed air as vapor and stones as solid water (cf. below). Indeed, the phenomenon of evaporation and solidification was most probably common knowledge perhaps as far back as Thales' time.[39] It is entirely possible that both features of water, namely its "moist," fertile nature[40] and its capacity to change states, were behind Thales' reasoning, of which unfortunately there is no direct textual evidence.

It is doubtful that Thales employed the technical vocabulary Aristotle employed to describe his thought, most particularly such terms as *stoicheion* ("element"), *ousia* ("substance"), and *hypokeimenon* ("substratum").[41] However, it is possible that Thales used the term *archē*, since it was evidently in common use during Thales' time,[42] but not necessarily in the technical sense that Aristotle used it.

Anaximander

Anaximander is usually considered the next participant in the philosophical debate over cosmogony. Instead of identifying one of the elements to account for the universe's origin, he posited the "infinite" (*apeiron*).[43] Anaximander described this "first principle" as eternal and ageless (*aidion . . . kai agērō*).[44] Furthermore, Anaximander evidently considered the "infinite" alive.[45]

According to Anaximander, the process of the formation of the world-order is one of differentiation or separation:

> The opposites, which are present in the one, are separated out, Anaximander says.[46]

These opposites can be identified specifically:

> *enantiotētes de eisi thermon, psychron, xēron, hygron, kai ta alla.*[47]

The opposites are the hot, the cold, the dry, the moist, and the rest. The four elements (earth, air, fire, and water) emerge from the interplay of the opposites within the infinite.

As for water, Anaximander credits moisture with the origin of land animals:

> Anaximander held that the first animals arose in moisture, being enclosed in spiny "barks" (*phloiois*) but as they grew older they emerged onto the drier land (*xēroteron*) and there, the "bark" having broken away, survived for a short while.[48]

Anaximander was first philosopher to address specifically the origin of life by stating that life arose from moist places on the earth. Moisture (*hygros*) clearly refers to mud or moist earth, as shown by Anaximander's use of the comparative adjective from *xēros*. From Censorinus is a similar description of Anaximander's thought concerning the sea:

> Anaximander of Miletus held that there arose from warm water and earth (*ex aqua terraque calefactis*) animals that were either fish or fish-like. Inside these, human beings were formed, remaining there like fetuses until puberty. At this time they broke open, and men and women already able to get food for themselves emerged.[49]

Plutarch gives a similar description:

> The first human beings arose inside fish (*en ichthysin*), and that having been nurtured like dog-fish, and having become able to fend for themselves sufficiently, they emerged and took to the land.[50]

In fact, Anaximander, like Thales, saw the earth as having a moist origin:

> They (some philosophers) say that at first the whole region about the earth was moist (*hygron*). But as the sun dried it out, the water that evaporated gave rise to winds the solstices of sun and moon, while what was left became the sea. Thus they think that the sea is now drying up and diminishing, and the end will come when it will all be dried up.[51]

In short, Anaximander considered moisture, presumably in the form of mud, in conjunction with the sun as the source of dry land and life. Indeed, Anaximander appears to have denounced Thales' claim that the earth was supported by water; rather, it was air by which the earth was suspended:

Anaximander seems to say that the earth remains where it is both because it is supported by air and because of its equilibrium and "indifference."[52]

Anaximenes

Anaximenes (mid-sixth century BCE) modified Anaximander's *apeiron* significantly by qualifying it as "air" (*aera*).[53] For Anaximenes, everything was derived from air and is the result of varying degrees of dilation and compression.[54] Anaximenes considered water simply as one of the derived elements.

Xenophanes

By mid-sixth century BCE, rain was correctly attributed to the cycle of evaporation. This theory was most carefully worked out by Xenophanes:

> Xenophanes says that atmospheric changes are due primarily to the warmth of the sun. For when moisture is evaporated from the sea the sweet part of it, which is distinguished by its lightness, forms a mist and becomes a cloud; and this falls as rain when contraction takes place and winds scatter it.[55]

A quote attributed to Xenophanes by Aetius describes the crucial importance of the sea in the process:

> The sea is the source of water and the source of wind. For there would be no winds to blow outwards from the clouds were it not for the great sea, nor rivers nor showers of rain from heaven, but the great Pontus (sea) is the begetter of clouds, winds and rivers.[56]

Xenophanes viewed the sea as the *indirect* source for the winds: There would be no wind without the clouds, and without the sea, no clouds.

Xenophanes also observed the generative powers of water in conjunction with those of earth:

> *gē kai hydor pant' esth' hosa ginontai ēde phuontai.*[57]
> All things that come into being and grow are earth and water.

> *pantes gar gaiēs te kai hydatos ekgenomestha.*[58]
> For we are all born of earth and water.

The inclusion of earth as a generative element for Xenophanes apparently gave him the reputation of being the only philosopher to stress the primacy of earth in cosmogony. From Aristotle is the following remark.

> *tēn men gar gēn oudeis edoxasen einai archēn, ei mē Zenophanes ho Kolophonios.*[59]

No one claimed that the earth was the first principle except Xenophanes of Colophon.[60]

The earth as the origin of life was a prominent theme in Plato and Aristotle, both of whom admitted that earth was rightly called mother.[61] However, Xenophanes attributed the origin of life to the combination of earth and water.

Heraclitus

Around 500 BCE, Heraclitus produced a book that turned the cosmogonic theories of Thales and Anaximenes on their heads:

This world-order, the same for all, neither god nor human made, always was and is and will be everlasting fire, kindling by measure and extinguishing by measure.[62]

In place of Anaximenes' air as the basis and origin of the cosmos was fire:

The changes of fire: first sea, and of sea half is earth and half fiery waterspout. . . . Earth is dissolved into sea, and is measured out in the same proportion as before it became earth.[63]

According to Heraclitus, the transformation of sea into earth was balanced by an equal and opposite process of earth transformed into sea, with the equilibrium of the whole preserved by these changes in fire. Diogenes Laertius describes the changes Heraclitus claimed that resulted in the elements: On a "downward path" fire condenses to become water, and water condenses to become earth. In the opposite direction earth rarefies to become water, and water, in turn, rarefies into "exhalations" that are akin to fire.[64]

Because of fire's inherent quality of perpetual motion Heraclitus postulated fire as the basis of creation.[65] In effect, Heraclitus' cosmogony denied water any signifcant generative role, although water's fluid property occasionally served as an apt metaphor for the fluid nature of the cosmos.[66]

Melissus of Samos

Similar to Parmenides, Melissus of Samos (mid-fifth century BCE) claimed the impossibility of anything's coming into existence out of nothing. Melissus classified reality as having no beginning or end.[67] In addition, he criticized the notion that reality was composed of separate elements, including earth, air, fire, and water. Rather there was only the eternal, infinite One (*hen*).[68]

Empedocles

The philosopher who fancied himself as a god exiled among mortals, Empedocles (mid-fifth century BCE), developed the classical formulation of the "four elements":

> *tessara gar pantōn rizōmata prōton akoue· Zeus argēs Herē te pheresbios ēde Aidōneus Nestis th', hē dakruois teggei krounōma Broteion.*[69]

> Hear first the four roots of all things: bright Zeus, life-bearing Hera, Aidoneus, and Nestis, who moistens the mortal spring by shedding tears.

Elsewhere, Empedocles listed the four elements as fire, earth, air, and water (see below). How they corresponded exactly to the gods mentioned above was the topic of some debate among the ancient commentators. Aetius suggested that Zeus and Hera were Fire and Air (ether), respectively, since they reigned in the heavens, and that Aidoneus, god of the underworld, was to be identified with earth.[70] Evidently the divine names were of little importance to Empedocles, since elsewhere he called fire Hephaestus[71] and named the four elements according to their natural names:

> *pos hydatos gaiēs te kai aitheros ēeliou te kirnamenōn eide te genoiato chroia te thnētōn toss' hosa nyn gegaasi synarmosthent' Aphroditei*[72]

> How from the mixture of Water, Earth, Ether, and Sun there came into being the forms and colors of mortal things in such numbers as now exist fitted together by Aphrodite. . . .

At any rate, of note in the "divine" listing above is Hera's (earth's) description as life-bearing. In contrast, water (Nestis, probably a local water-goddess, otherwise unknown[73]) was relegated by Empedocles to simply providing for the springs of the earth. Common to all the elements, however, was their internal homogeneity[74] and uncreated nature:

> *agenēta: stoicheia. par' Empedoklei*[75]

Empedocles viewed the formation of the elements as a centrifugal process of separation determined by relative weight. Being the heaviest, earth formed at the center, where it solidified by the force of rotation; water formed above the earth; and the lighter elements, air and fire, moved out to the periphery.[76] The concentric spheres of earth at the center, which were surrounded by spheres of water, air, and fire, evidently became the classic description of the spatial rank of the elements among Greek philosophers, including Plato, Aristotle (with the addition of ether) and the Stoics.[77]

The notions of "coming into existence" and "passing away," Empedocles claimed, describes the mingling (*mixis*) and separation (*diallaxis*) of these elements.[78] The order of this process, according to Empedocles, began with ether (*aithera*), next fire (*pyr*), and then earth (*gē*). Then:

> From the earth, having contracted (*perisphiggomenēs*) drastically because of the force of the rotation, water gushed forth.[79]

Elsewhere, Empedocles described the sea as the *gēs hidrota* ("the sweat of the earth").[80] Evidently, the "wet" did contribute to the formation of life, but its role was minor compared to that of the earth:

> At first undifferentiated forms of earth arose, having a portion both of water and warmth.[81]

Life resulted from the mixing of the four elements in conjunction with Love, as opposed to Strife.[82]

As for the genesis of particular life forms, Empedocles claimed that species separated into groups according to the predominant element present in their composition: Water creatures contain mostly the element of water, those composed mostly of fire fly upward in the air, and the heaviest sink to earth.[83] Thus flying creatures and water creatures had little connection for Empedocles (as opposed to Genesis 1 of the [Vor]LXX). In addition, Aristotle cites Empedocles as holding a nonsensical view towards the origin of water creatures:

> Empedocles is mistaken in saying that for the most part the creatures containing heat or fire live in the water, thereby escaping the excess of heat that lies in their nature. . . . In general it is absurd to suppose it possible that water animals should originate on dry land and transfer to the water: Most of them even lack feet. Yet in describing their original structure he says that they began on dry land and migrated to the water.[84]

According to Aristotle, Empedocles appears to deny any role to water with respect to even the generation of water animals.

Hippon of Samos

Hippon of Samos (mid-fifth century BCE) brought water back to its primary cosmogonic position. Because of this, Aristotle criticized him for the *euteleian autou tēs dianoias*, "worthlessness of his thought."[85] Hippon went so far as to say that water even generated fire[86] and the life-principle or soul.[87] As Aristotle observed:

> Some of the less exact thinkers like Hippon have declared the soul to be water. This belief seems to arise from the fact that the seed of all things is moist.[88]

Thus Hippon's reasoning was evidently biological, similar to Hippolytus' observation:

> *kai gar to sperma einai to phainomenon hemin ex hygrou, ex ou phesi psychēn ginesthai.*[89]
>
> For also sperm appears to us to come from moisture, from which, he says, the soul comes into being.

Hippon's (and Thales') thesis on the primacy of water in the production of life, however, was not taken up by later thinkers.

Anaxagoras

Anaxagoras of Clazomenae (mid-fifth century BCE) was the first to do away with the limited number of basic elements. He asserted that all things were in all things:

> In everything there is a portion of everything, except mind; but some things contain mind also.[90]

In order to support such a claim, Anaxagoras introduced the category of smallness:

> All things were together (*chrēmata*), infinte in number and in smallness. For the Small was also infinite.[91]

Or as Lucretius disparagingly describes:

> [Anaxagoras] asserts that in everything there is a hidden mixture of everything, but that one thing is apparent whose particles are the most numerous and most conspicuous and are placed nearest to the surface.[92]

Thus air, water, and earth were for Anaxagoras merely three among an infinte number of elements. Yet Anaxagoras considered Air (*aēr*) and Ether (*aithēr*) the most important of the elements in the great mixture.[93] With regard to the other elements, he claimed:

> The dense and moist and cold and dark gathered where now is earth, and the rare and the hot and dry went outwards to the furthest part of the Ether.[94]

Then:

> From these, while they are separating off, earth solidifies; for from the clouds, water is separated off, and from the water, earth, and from the earth, stones are solidifed by the cold; and these move outwards more than water.[95]

In short, water appears to play a significant role in Anaxagoras' cosmogony, since Anaxagoras considered earth to be derived from water in the process of separation and solidification. Animal life, however, originated somewhere in the process in combination with moisture, heat, and earth:

> *Zōia gignesthai ex hygrou kai thermou kai geōdous,*[96]

According to Irenaeus, Anaxagoras claimed that animal life was created by the fall of "seed" from heaven to earth, and afterwards by reproduction.[97]

Archelaus

A pupil of Anaxagoras, Archelaus gives a similar cosmogonic account of the earth:

> Archelaus claimed there were two causes of generation: heat and cold. Also living things were produced from mud (*ilys*). . . . Water is melted by heat and produces on the one hand earth in so far as by the action of fire it sinks and coheres, whereas, on the other hand, it generates air in so far as it overflows around about. . . . Living things, he claims, are formed from the heat of the earth and mud equivalent to milk as a sort of nourishment. And in this way were humans also produced.[98]

Thus Archelaus also saw water's changing state as the basis for the genesis of earth and air. Life, however, came from moist earth or mud.

Diogenes of Apollonia

Diogenes of Apollonia (latter half of the fifth century BCE), a younger contemporary of Anaxagoras, reunited what Anaxagoras had split asunder, namely matter and Mind. He began by claiming that everything in the cosmos was reducible to one:

> It seems to me, in summary, that all existing things are created by the alter-ation of the same thing, and are the same thing. This is obvious. For if the things now existing in this universe (earth and water and air and fire and all the other things which are seen to exist in this world), if any one of these things were different in its own nature . . . in no way could things mix with one another . . . nor could any plant grow out of the earth, nor any animal or any thing come into being, unless it were so compounded to be the same.[99]

While claiming that the distribution of the elements could only be attributed to Intelligence (*noēsis*),[100] Diogenes identified air as the One substance:

> And it seems to me that that which has Intelligence is that which is called air by human beings; and further, that by this, all things are guided, and that it rules everything.[101]

Air was thus considered by Diogenes as the life-force and the very basis of all phenomena, embodying both matter and mind. Furthermore, Diogenes used biological principles to illustrate the life-giving force of air by asserting that air constituted semen by being in blood in the form of "foam" (*aphron*).[102] Water, therefore, was excluded from any position of primacy in the generation of life.

The Atomists

The four elements lost their significance with the Atomists Leucippus (of Abdera?) and Democritus of Abdera, both active near the end of the fifth century BCE. They championed the view that indivisible, indestructible, and infinitely numerable atoms constituted the cosmos.[103] As for the origin of life, Democritus restates the traditional view that human beings were created from mud and dirt:

> Democritus of Abdera held that human beings were first created from water and dirt.[104]

Thus the atomists denied water, as well as the other elements, any primordial role in the cosmogonic process except in relation to the formation of human beings, and only then in conjunction with earth in the form of mud.

Plato

The most extensive cosmogony present in Plato's works is found in the *Timaeus*. Unfortunately, the work is wrought with logical ambiguities, having given ancient interpreters a wealth of interpretational problems that still have not been satisfactorily resolved.[105]

Briefly, Timaeus, who is described as a distinguished philosopher and astronomer,[106] describes the work of God (*theos*) in fashioning the cosmos. Timaeus likens God to a craftsman (*dēmiourgos*) who uses an incorporeal model to create an object.[107] The model from which the Demiurge constructs the visible universe is by nature eternal,[108] since it lies in the realm of Ideas or Forms. Likewise, the material that the Divine Craftsman uses is in some sense primeval. Plato refers to the precursors of the four elements as existing formless before creation.[109] As for the initial stage of the cosmogony, Plato describes divine action upon the state of disorder:

> When [God] took over all that was visible, seeing that it was not in a state of rest but in a state of discordant and disorderly motion, he brought it into order out of disorder, deeming that the former state is in all ways better than the latter.[110]

More specifically, the Demiurge acts as follows:

> All these things were in a state of disorder, when God implanted in them symmetry both in relation to themselves and in their relations to one another, to the extent that it was possible for them to be in harmony and in proportion.[111]

Symmetry (*symmetria*), harmony or conformability (*analogon*), and order (*taxis*) characterize the cosmogonic process. All these qualities find their intersection in the notion of *kalon*, meaning good, beautiful, or desirable.[112] In short, the universe is invested with the fullest possible measure of goodness and rationality in accordance with the Forms.

The creative acts of the Demiurge are aimed at establishing order and structure amid disorder by employing the Forms as models to copy. The elements, including that of water, are considered mere transient copies of the elemental Forms. Thus, water appears to have no special place apart from the other elements in the cosmogonic process.

Aristotle

Aristotle does not directly contribute to the discussion of cosmogony and the role of water therein because he considered the world as ungenerated and indestructible.[113] However, an important feature of Aristotle's cosmogony is the *active* nature of the elements:

> Imperishable things are imitated by those things that are involved in change, such as earth and fire; for the latter also are always active, since they have their motion independently and in themselves.[114]

Elsewhere, Aristotle grants the elements the quality of spontaneous action.[115] Thus, Aristotle's view of the universe was far from a mechanistic one of inert elements.[116]

Aristotle classifies the elements as each having two qualities: Fire is hot and dry; water is cold and wet; earth is cold and dry; and air is hot and fluid.[117] Underlying them all is *hylē*, the "underlying subject" (*hypokeimenon*).[118] For Aristotle, air can become water by substituting heat (via condensation[119]) for cold, and fire can become air by substituting wetness for dryness. The condensation of air into water can occur above as well as below the earth.[120]

Contrary to Thales and Hippon, Aristotle did not consider the sea as the source of all water. Rather all rivers flowed into the sea: The sea was the goal (*teleutē*) of all water rather than its *archē*.[121] Indeed, Aristotle criticized Plato in the *Phaedo* (111C) for positing a source of water located at the center of the earth called Tartarus,[122] a theory reminiscent of the mythological conception of Oceanus. For Aristotle, of all the elements, water was distinctive in that it was the only element to be easily contained.[123] In addition, water held the earth together[124] and *in conjunction with the earth* provided food for plants.[125]

Aristotle's empirical approach undercut many previous philosophical tenets, while expanding on others. Aristotle's views stressed the ordered, teleological nature of the self-moving cosmos within the framework of its wondrously differentiated nature, while conceding to God only the remote function of a prime mover. As for water, Aristotle's empirical perspective downplayed its role in cosmology, yet ascribed to all the elements a measure of animation.

Zeno

Zeno (335-262 BCE) is considered the founder of a philosophical movement that reclaimed the cosmos as a purely physical system. Zeno theorized that the universe was composed of "matter" (*hylē*) and "substance" (*ousia*), corresponding to passive (*to poioun*) and active (*to paschon*) principles respectively.[126] The active is variously identified as cause, God, reason, *pneuma* (breath or life-principle), or *logos*.[127] In contrast to Plato and Aristotle, incorporeality was an impossibility in Zeno's system.[128] Within this dynamic materiality of the cosmos, Zeno and the Stoic movement gave water a critical role in the formation of the cosmos.

In order to advance his cosmogony, Zeno evidently sought support from earlier cosmogonic works, most particularly Hesiod's *Theogony* (lines 116-20). In his allegorization of the *Theogony*, Zeno linked the term *Chaos* with the verb *cheō*:

> Nam Zeno Citieus sic interpretatur, aquam **Chaos** appellatam **apo tou cheesthai**.[129]

> Zenon of Citium understands it [Hesiod's *Theogony* 116] in such a way that *Chaos*, from *cheesthai*, denotes water.

The verb *cheō* in the passive sense (with reduplication of the epsilon in the root) means "to dissolve" or "become liquid." Consequently, Zeno's etymological *tour de force* appears to place water at the head of the cosmogonic order. However, this conclusion is significantly modified in light of the overall claims of Stoic cosmogony.

The Stoics, beginning with Zeno, did not place water as the *archē* of the cosmos;[130] instead they chose another element to assume the initial position, namely fire. Fire represented the active aspect of *archē*, the self-moving creative force (see Heraclitus, above).[131] Fire as a creative force was fundamental in Stoicism, equated with the essence of nature or God.[132]

> They say that the elementary stuff of things is fire, as Heraclitus did, and that its principles are matter and God, like Plato.[133]

That God is equated with a corporeal, creating, fiery force for the Stoics is confirmed by Eusebius:

> According to the Stoics who say that the fiery and hot substance was the "governor" (the principle part of the soul) of the cosmos and that the God was corporeal and was the Demiurge itself being none other than the energy of fire. . . .[134]

As for the nature of this fire:

According to their view nature is a craftsmanlike fire (*pyr technikon*), pro-
ceeding methodically to creation, which means breath, fiery and creative.[135]

The cosmos, then, in its active aspect is an artist, creating itself, as it were.
For Zeno, the universe was not a static object but a changing construction; the term "nature" referred to the dynamic force that brought the
cosmos into being and directed all of its processes.[136] The fiery *archē* did
not come directly from the objects in the universe, rather it provided the
base from which the four elements were created. Thus this primordial
fire must be distinguished from the element fire. Indeed, Zeno's fire was
nothing less than divine.[137]

The cosmogonic process beginning with fire was illustrated devel-
opmentally in the familiar processes of condensation and rarefaction.

> The cosmos comes into being when its substance is converted from fire
> through air into moisture, then the coarser part of the moisture is condensed
> as earth, while the lighter part turns into air, and as this becomes more
> rarefied, fire is generated. Then out of these elements plants and animals
> and all the other kinds of things are formed by mixture.[138]

Elsewhere, Diogenes Laertius places God in the role of fire in his
description of Zeno's cosmogony:

> In the beginning, being by himself, [God] transformed the whole of the
> substance through air into water. . . . Then he created first the four elements:
> fire, water, air, and earth.[139]

God, the divine fire, the active principle of matter, initiates the process of
generation whereby the formation of the elements proceeds via purely
physical means. Water is evidently the residue of the total moisture by
which substance is transformed into the other three elements:

> Periodically the orderly arrangement of the universe from the substance
> must be such as this: whenever there occurs a change from fire through air
> to water, a part settles down and earth is formed, [and] of the rest some
> remains as water. From that which is vaporized, air is formed, while from
> some of the air, fire is kindled. Mixture occurs through the transition of the
> elements (*stoicheia*) into each other, when a body in its entirety spreads
> through another in its whole extent.[140]

D. E. Hahm suggests that for the Stoics water was of crucial importance
in the cosmogonic process in that of all the elements only water could be
perceived by a hypothetical observer.[141] Yet like earth, water was consid-

ered a *passive* substance, in contrast to fire and air.[142] In sum, Zeno and the later Stoics considered water critical in the production and mainte-nance of the cosmos, for from this medium the elements were produced. However, fire, along with air, maintained the ultimate position of primacy in the cosmogony.

But why is water given any place within the cosmogonic process in the Stoic system? Its role appears to be biological:

> As the seed is contained in the semen, so also [God], being the seminal formula (*spermatikos logos*) of the cosmos, remained behind as such in the moisture, adapting matter to himself for the creation of subsequent things. Then he gave birth first to the four elements: fire, water, air, earth.[143]

Water is compared to semen, the vehicle of productivity. As Hahm points out, "the account bristles with biological terms."[144] Indeed, this was no mere analogy. Zeno defined human semen as a compound substance: *pneuma meth' hygrou*.[145] The wet was considered the vehicle for the actual reproductive force embodied in *sperma*, *pneuma*, or soul.[146] Elsehwere, Zeno states that fire is

> like a seed, possessing the *logoi* of all things and the cause of things, past, present, and future.[147]

Thus this divine productive force or fire is present in all moisture. Here, cosmogony is biology. Consequently, it is no surprise that Zeno and the later Stoics viewed the cosmos as a living being.

The analogy between microcosm and macrocosm was employed frequently among the Stoics. The cosmos was not simply *like* a living creature, it was one.[148] Like a human being, it was pervaded with *pneuma*, *psychē*, and *nous*. As noted above, this active principle consti-tuted its own generating force. For Zeno, water served as the vehicle or medium by which creation took place.

Conclusions

In the mythological literature of Homer, Hesiod, and Orpheus (?), water figures in various ways. In Hesiod's *Theogony*, Oceanus and Sea are water gods who generate, either by sexual union or independently, divine beings appropriate to their nature, namely the fresh water and the sea, respectively. Homer places Oceanus and Tethys as the primal parents of all the gods, similar to the primal roles of Apsu and Tiamat in the Babylonian theogony *Enuma Elish*. Water's function, thus, has a universally general role in theogony. Hesiod, on the other hand, depicts

Oceanus and Pontos as gods derived from Earth. Of crucial importance, however, is the fact that water is nowhere explicitly cited in the formation of physical life in either Hesiod or Homer.

Beginning with Anaximander, there is a wide consensus among the Pre-Socratic philosophers that moisture plays an essential role in the genesis of life. It is likely that this notion can be traced back to Thales. However, more often than not, the origin of life was conceived of as a joint product of the wet and the dry, of water and earth.[149] In this respect, Anaximander was followed closely by Xenophanes and Archelaus. In addition, Anaximander, Anaxagoras, and Archelaus introduced a third player in the cosmogonic process, namely heat. Accordingly, the sun played a decisive role in the production of living things from moisture.

Diodorus Siculus' introduction to his *bibliothekē historikē* gives an anonymous cosmogonic account that could very well have been typical of philosophical accounts of the sixth or fifth centuries BCE.

> According to their account, when in the beginning the universe was being formed, both heaven and earth were indistinguishable in appearance, since their elements were intermingled. Then, when their bodies separated from one another, the universe took on in all its parts the ordered form in which it is now seen. The air set up a continual motion, and the fiery element in it gathered into the highest regions. . . . That which was like mud and thick and contained a mixture of moisture sank because of its weight to a place.[150]

Diodorus then describes the process by which life begins:

> As the sun's fire shone upon the land, it first became hardened. Then, since its surface was seething with heat, some moist portions swelled up in many places, and fermentations arose there enclosed in delicate membranes (*hymesi*) . . . . While the moisture was thus being impregnated with life by the heat, the creatures were directly nourished at night from the mist which descended out of the surrounding atmosphere, and solidified in the daytime by the burning heat. Finally, when the embryos had reached their full growth, and when the membranes were well heated and broken open, all kinds of animals were produced.

Next, diversification of the species occurs:

> Those that had received the most warmth set off to the higher regions, having become winged, and those that retained an earthy consistency came to be numbered in the class of crawling animals and other land animals, while those whose composition shared in the most of the moisture gathered into the region most compatible to them, receiving the name of water animals.

Of note is Diodorus' claim that the creation of birds is inextricably linked with heat (and consequently air). Once the earth becomes drier, the process of cosmogony stops and reproduction begins:

> And when the earth solidified further by the action of the sun's fire and the winds, it was no longer able to generate any of the larger animals; rather, each kind of living creature was now created by breeding with one another.

Thus the gradual emergence of dry land under the action of the sun was accompanied by the formation of living things within the moist element. Diodorus' account has much in common with the cosmogonic theories of Anaximander, Empedocles, Anaxagoras, and Xenophanes. Indeed, the "membranes" (*hymēn*) in his account assume a similar role to that of the "barks" of Anaximander.[151]

In short, underlying many of the cosmogonic theories is the notion that water and earth *together* constitute the basis for life. This notion is implied by the frequent use of the term *hygros* (moisture). With the possible exception of Thales and Hippon, rarely is water in and of itself considered the basis of life. If Aristotle is correct, Thales based his theory upon observations of plant growth.[152] In addition, much if not most of Greek mythology depicts the creation of human beings as coming from the earth.[153] Lucretius (94-55 BCE), who drew most of his cosmological theories from the Greek atomists, pays tribute to the earth as the creator of all things:

> In the beginning the earth brought forth grasses after their kinds and luxuriant greenery. . . . Thereafter, it created the generations of mortal creatures, arising in many kinds and in many ways by different processes. For animals cannot have fallen from the sky, nor can creatures of the land have come out of the salt pools. Therefore, it remains that the earth merits the name of "mother" which she possesses, since from the earth all things have been created.[154]

Indeed, Lucretius claims that the earth alone is the generator of life. As noted above, Archelaus gave similar status to the earth, even depicting the earth as oozing milk for the nourishment of all animal life. Thus, the generation of animals from the earth is prominent in much of Greek philosophy. Plato describes Socrates posing the following question:

> But then, Stranger, how did animals come into existence? How were they begotten of one another?[155]

In response, Plato places in the mouth of the Stranger the traditional view that all animals were "earth-born" (*gēgenēs*). The term and its cognates were widely used in Greek mythology to depict the origin of human beings.[156]

Consequently, both in mythology and early Greek philosophy, what constitutes the basis of life was not water *per se*, but water in conjunction with earth (and heat). Indeed, of the four elements, the earth appears to play the more significant role in the generation of life in Greek thought, despite water's occasional prominent place in the process. All in all, *it is a distortion to claim that Greek thought regarded water alone as the basis of life*. It is hard to imagine the *general* creative powers that Thales and Hippon assigned to the waters as having had a direct influence on the LXX or VorLXX of Genesis 1, in which the waters, separated from the earth, are commanded to create only *specific* animals, namely sea and aerial creatures.

In addition, nowhere in the texts discussed above is there any specific mention of the creation of aerial creatures by water or the sea. However, snippets of traditions are present here and there in the Greek cosmogonic corpus. Lucretius had perhaps relied on earlier tradition when he recounted the origin of winged creatures.

> *principio genus alituum variaeque volueres ova relinquebant exclusae tempore verno, folliculos ut nunc teretis aestate cicadae lincunt sponte sua victum vitamque petentes. tum tibi terra dedit primum mortalia saecla.*[157]

> First, the race of winged things and the different birds issued from their eggs, having hatched in the springtime, even as now in summer when the cicadas by their own accord leave their filmy husks, to see life and the living. Then first, look you, the earth gave forth the generations of mortal creatures.

For the atomist Lucretius, the earth had the exclusive role in generating the winged creatures.

It has been suggested that Gen 1:20 of the LXX, in which the waters are commanded to "bring forth" both aquatic and winged creatures, can be traced back to a Greek tradition attested in Plato's *The Sophist* (220B).[158] In this work, the Eleatic stranger converses with the young Theaetetus about easy subjects for the purpose of establishing the correct methodology before meeting Socrates' challenge to define the sophist. The stranger first chooses to define an angler (*aspalieutēs*).[159] In so doing, he categorizes two types of animal hunting (*zōothērikos*): land-animal hunting (*pezothērikos*) and water-animal hunting (*enygrothērikos*).[160] The latter pursuit has as its object "swimming creatures" (*neustikoi zōoi*) or creatures able to "swim." This category is then immediately broken down into two classes: one class (*phylon*) is winged (*ptēnon*) and the other lives in the water (*enydros*).[161] The hunting of the former is called *ornitheutike* ("fowling") and that of the latter is called *halieutikē* ("fishing"). The critical term that links birds and fish is *neustikos*: both birds and fish are observed to "propel" themselves by the use of fins or wings.[162] The term's verbal base *neō* (*LS* 1172) can be related to the Latin verb *nare*, which describes either the action of swimming or flying.[163]

In addition, Aristotle uses the term *enydros*, used by the Stranger in *The Sophist* strictly for fish, to refer to birds.[164] However, Aristotle uses the term to refer to particular birds that live by rivers and marshes, namely the "shearwater and the plunger" (*aithuia kai kolymbis*).[165] Many have, of course, webbed feet.[166] Indeed, for Aristotle, the category "swimmers" (*neustika*) does not include birds (*ornithes*), which are considered land animals (*chersaia*),[167] although some birds can swim, such as those of the web-footed variety (*steganopodes tōn ornithōn*).[168] Furthermore, Aristotle finds much dissimilarity between birds and fish:

> *ptenon de monon ouden estin hōsper neustikon monon ichthys.*[169]

No animal is merely able to fly, as the fish is merely able to swim. Nevertheless, Aristotle concedes some similarity between them, most notably the similarity between wings and fins:

> *homoiōs d' echousin hoi ornithes tropon tina tois ichthysin. tois men gar ornisin ano hai pteryges eisi, tois de pterygia duo en tō pranei. . . .*[170]
>
> Birds in a way resemble fish, for birds have their wings in the upper part of their bodies, fishes have two fins in their fore-part. . . .

Aelian also finds some similarities between fish and birds, but only in that some members of both species exhibit similarities:

> *petontai de hotan deisōsi kai exallontai tēs thalattēs hai te teuthides kai hoi hierakes hoi thalattioi kai hē chelidon hē pelagia. kai hai men teuthides epi mekiston attousi tois pterygiois,*[171]
>
> Squids, flying gurnards, and flying-fish when scared fly and leap out of the sea. Squids leap furthest with the aid of their fins and rise high and are borne along together in flocks like birds.

With regard to the genesis of birds, Aristotle makes no mention. In his discussion of the generation of birds, he finds it sufficient to begin simply with the egg.[172]

All in all, nowhere do Plato, Aristotle, and Aelian make reference to birds and fish having a common genesis. Rather, there is only the recognition of some common characteristics borne out by specific types of birds and fish. Thus *The Sophist* is unique in that it clearly depicts a link between birds and fish described in terms of their respective means of movement. But no hint is made of their respective origins. Rather only their similar behavior provides the grounds for comparison. If any Greek tradition of a common genesis for birds and fishes existed, it must not have been widespread.

THE COSMOGONIC ACCOUNT OF PHILO OF BYBLOS

Another ancient cosmogony in which water appears to play a prominent role is the one attributed to Philo of Byblos. Philo produced in the late first or early second century CE an account of Phoenician traditions entitled the *Phoenician History*.[173] Porphyry records that Philo of Byblos translated the work from a certain Phoenician named Sanchuniathon into eight volumes.[174] Eusebius, on the other hand, claims that Philo presented Sanchuniathon's work in nine books.[175] From the latter half of the nineteenth century to the present, scholars have vigorously debated the authenticity of Philo's work, attested only in fragments recorded by Eusebius.[176]

One piece of evidence supporting the authenticity of Philo's source comes from the likelihood that the reputed author's name Sanchuniathon is derived from the Semitic personal name *Sknytn*, "(the god) Skn has given," which is attested in inscriptions found at Hadrumetum, a Phoenician colony, with other names compounded with the theophorous element *skn*.[177] Thus the name Sanchuniathon may very well have belonged to a native Phoenician. In addition, Ugaritic mythological texts have been cited by many as decisive proof of Sanchuniathon's reliability.[178] However, those who cite such evidence give widely diverging dates for this elusive figure. Indeed, suggestions for the dating of Sanchuniathon's cosmogony have ranged from the second millennium BCE to the Hellenistic period.[179]

Other scholars have questioned Sanchuniathon's existence or antiquity, most notably J. Barr, H. W. Attridge, and R. A. Oden, Jr.[180] Some have pointed out that a correspondence between Ugaritic texts and the

Phoenician History is not sufficient evidence to prove that Philo utilized an ancient Phoenician source. Moreover, even if Philo did use such a source, it does not necessarily follow that it would date from remote antiquity.[181]

In addition, Philo's account lacks any structure corresponding to that of other ancient Semitic narratives.[182] Attridge and Oden point out that the rational presentation of Philo's account as well as its euhemeristic analysis of mythology (the gods conceived as deified mortals) indicate at the earliest a Hellenistic dating.[183] Most decisive for a late dating is the work's attention to the history of culture and human progress, a great interest among Hellenistic thinkers.[184] Attridge and Oden conclude that,

> if Philo did use a source, its author, Sanchuniathon, was a man much like Philo himself, a patriotic local ethnographer of the Hellenistic or Roman periods, who . . . composed a harmonized and rationalistic account of Phoenician myth and legend. . . . Although it is thus doubtful that the *Phoenician History* is based upon a written source antedating the Hellenistic period, the work remains a valuable witness to Canaanite mythology and to the ways in which that ancient religious tradition was perceived and interpreted in the first centuries of our era.[185]

In the context of their overall analysis, Attridge's and Oden's last statement seems to be more a concession than a conclusion. Given the fact that the extant fragments of Philo's work bear the definitive marks of Greek philosophical cosmogonies, it is questionable whether any elements are at all attributable to ancient Near Eastern myth.

The Fragments

Evidence of Philo's work is found primarily in Eusebius' first book of the *Praeparatio evangelica*. It is here that Philo's cosmogony is recorded:

> *Tēn tōn holōn archēn hypotithetai aera zophōdē kai pneumatōdē ē pnoen aeros zophōdous, kai chaos tholeron, erebōdes. tauta de einai apeira kai dia polyn aiŏna mē echein peras.*[186]
>
> [Sanchuniathon] posits as the source of the universe a dark and windy gas, or a stream of dark gas, and turbid, gloomy chaos. These things were infinite and for ages were without limit.[187]

Philo's description of primordial material resembles Anaximander's notion of infinity (*apeiron*) and Anaximenes' qualification of it as air.[188] Instead of Zeno's supposition that Hesiod's chaos consisted of water,[189] gas (*aēr*) is used in Philo's description as an element alongside chaos. In an Orphic cosmogony the related term *aither* is found in conjunction with *chaos*, and both are considered products of Chronos out of which the divine egg is formed.[190] As for *aēr* and *chaos*, Philo records Sanchuniathon as saying:

> *Hote de phēsin ērasthē to pneuma tōn idiōn archōn kai egeneto sygkrasis, hē plokē ekeine eklēthē pothos. hautē dʾ archē ktiseōs hapantōn.*[191]
>
> He says, "When the wind lusted after its own sources and a mixture came into being, that combination was called Desire. This was the beginning of the creation of all things."

The first statement is confusing: What exactly are the wind's sources (*idiōn archōn*)? Indeed, the relationship between gas, wind, and chaos is obscure. The elements *pneuma* and *aēr* are most probably synonymous terms in the text: Wind is simply air or gas in movement. Hence, presumably, the statement describes the union between *aēr/pneuma* and *chaos*.[192] On the other hand, J. Ebach suggests that the section implies self-generation, that wind alone begets creation.[193] However, pure self-generation would preclude any "mixture" (*sygkrasis*) from taking place. The verb from *eramai* clearly refers to sexual love. Hence, the description either alludes to a primordial incestuous relationship[194] or simply depicts the action of the mixing process not unlike Empedocles' description of the actions of Love (*philotes*) and the mixing of the elements.[195] However, unlike Empedocles, Desire (*pothos*) is considered the result rather than the force behind the union. At any rate, crucial is the process of combination and mixing (*plokē, sygkrasis*). As for the resultant creation,

> *auto de ouk eginōske tēn hautou ktisin, kai ek tēs autēs symplokēs tou pneumatos egeneto Mōt. touto tines phasin ilyn, hoi de hydatōdous mixeōs sēpsin. kai ek tautēs egeneto pasa spora ktiseos kai genesis tōn holōn.*[196]
>
> But it was not aware of its own creation. From the same combination of the wind, Mot came into existence. Some say that this is mud; others, that it is a putrefaction of the moist mixture. From this substance came every seed of creation and the genesis of the universe.

The wind is described as unaware of the creative process it has set in motion by mixing with its sources. Indeed, the statement underscores the mechanical nature of the process. "Mixture" (*symplokē*) can be rendered as "intercourse,"[197] but given the naturalistic tenor of the passage, the term is more likely synonymous with *sygkrasis*.[198]

As for the identity of Mot, various explanations have been offered without any resulting consensus.[199] One possibility suggested is that the name alludes to the Canaanite deity Mot (*mt*), the lord of the underworld in the Baal epic.[200] However, there are linguistic problems with this identification[201] as well as the more glaring problem of how the Ugaritic deity of death could constitute the primordial *Urstoff* of the cosmos. At any rate, Philo took the name *Mōt* to refer to "mud." The term *ilys*, as noted earlier, is used extensively in Diodorus Siculus' rational cosmogonic account, which has its roots in the earlier systems of Anaximander, Xenophanes, and Anaxagoras, all of whom posit some sort of mixture as an initial cosmogonic state.[202] This commonality also applies to Philo's description *hoi sepsin hydatodous mixeos*, which evidently refers to a mixture of watery and earthy substances. Aristotle refers to both *ilys* and *sepsis* in his account of the production of certain fishes:

> *hosa de mēt' ōotokei mēte zōotokei, panta gignetai ta men ek tēs iluos ta d' ek tēs ammou kai tēs epipolazouses sēpseōs.*[203]
>
> Those that are neither oviparous nor viviparous are all formed either out of mud or out of sand and the putrefrying matter on the surface.

Philo's description is clearly in line with the scientific language of Greek/Hellenistic philosophy. The function of Mot as the *Urschlamm* directly resembles Greek cosmogonic thinking rather than ancient Near Eastern mythology.[204] As for the creatures produced:

> *En de tina zōa ouk echonta aisthēsin, ex hōn egeneto zōa noera, kai eklēthē zophasēmin, tout' estin ouranou katoptai. kai aneplasthē homoiōs ōou schēmati, kai exelampse Mōt hēlios te kai selēnē asteres te kai astra megala.*
>
> There were some living creatures without sensation, from which came intelligent creatures and they were called "Zophasemin," i.e., "heavenly observers." They were formed roughly in the shape of an egg. Mot shone forth, with sun and moon, stars and great constellations."

The Zophasemin clearly refer to the intelligent creatures (*zōa noera*), since they, rather than the "creatures without sensation" (celestial bodies?), have the capacity to see. The syntactical subject to *aneplasthē* is ambiguous, but it is most probably the Zophasemin.[205] The egg (*ōon*) is widely attested in Orphic cosmogonies[206] and in Aristophanes' *Ornithes* in the birth of Love (693-5), in addition to its use by Athenagoras and Diodorus Siculus (i.27.5).[207]

Next, Philo, as recorded by Eusebius, says of Sanchuniathon and the Phoenicians:

Such was their cosmogony, which openly introduces atheism (*atheotēta*). Next let us see how he says that the generation of animals took place. He says: "And when the air became luminous, there arose, due to the heating of both the sea and the land (*dia pyrōsin kai tēs thalassēs kai tēs gēs*), winds and clouds and very great downpours and floods from the celestial waters. These were separated out and removed from their proper place through heating by the sun (*dia tēn tou hēlious pyrōsin*). When they all intermingled once again and collided in the air, then peals of thunder and flashes of lightning were produced. At the crash of the thunder the intelligent creatures previous mentioned awoke (*egrēgorēsen*). They were alarmed at the noise, and male and female creatures began to stir on both land and sea."

The actions once again are described in terms of mixing and separation and are attributed to the heating of the sun. Again, one finds striking similarities with the cosmogonic account of Diodorus Siculus (1.7.3-4), which describes the sun's heating of the watery mixture in the formation of life. However, a major difference is that Philo views the process merely as an event that awakens the already created animals. Several scholars have interpreted the violent description of the collision as an allusion to an earlier myth depicting a battle between the storm god and a water monster as in the *Enuma Elish* (Tablet IV. 13-VI. 10) and the Baal epic (*CTA* 2).[208] However, this is sheer conjecture, given the fact that the event is described in purely naturalistic terms typical of Greek philosophical cosmogonies.[209] Indeed, the phrase *antikrys atheotēta eisagousa* ("introducing atheism openly") has an apologetic ring to it, intended to lend credibility to the ancient figure Taautos, Philo's ultimate source.[210]

Conclusion

Ebach perceptively notes that the Philonic cosmogony is not so much a "Weltschöpfung" as it is a "Weltentstehung."[211] The account is undoubtedly replete with Greek philosophical principles and concepts.[212] However, such concepts cannot fully account for all the features in the narrative: e.g., the awakening of the intelligent creatures, the "lustful" actions of the wind, and the title *Mōt*.[213] On the other hand, these disjunctures do not directly correspond to any extant ancient Near Eastern cosmogonic myths. For the purposes of reconstructing an ancient Phoenician cosmogony, Philo's work fails from every methodological standpoint. The work is far too entrenched in Greek naturalistic philosophy to reveal any clear mythological antecedents, if indeed there are any to reconstruct.[214]

As for discerning the role of water in Philo's cosmogony, water is alluded to only in connection with the mysterious figure Mot, who bears the alternative designation *ilys* ("mud"), according to some Hellenistic opinions, or *sēpsis* ("putrefaction"), according to others. Clearly, Philo's "survey" of opinions is fraught with Greek natural philosophy; hence, it is impossible to discern any clear ancient Near Eastern, specifically Phoenician, antecedents. In any case, with respect to Genesis 1, Mot as a muddy, slimy mixture is a far cry from the role that the VorLxx assigns to the separated waters of the seas. As with most Greek cosmogonic systems, it is difficult to establish a connection between the Philonic cosmogony and the *Vorlage* of the Lxx with respect to the generative role of water.

THE GENERATIVE ROLE OF WATER IN ANCIENT NEAR EASTERN LITERATURE

Ancient Near Eastern traditions concerning the wide-ranging procreative powers of water are extensive. In this section the ways in which water functions generatively in Sumerian, Akkadian, Ugaritic, and Egyptian cosmogonic literature are examined with particular attention to the association of water with aerial creatures.

Sumerian and Akkadian Literature

Water is most concretely symbolized in Sumerian mythology by Enki, the god of the watery abyss, one of the four creating deities.[215] Enki (or Ea in Akkadian literature) is frequently portrayed in cylinder seals with two streams issuing from his shoulders and/or holding a vase from which water is poured, symbolizing blessing.[216] In addition, Enki is considered by Sumerian mythographers as the god of wisdom, since he is depicted as the organizer of the universe and keeper of the *me*, the authoritative, universal decrees.[217]

In the myth Kramer entitles "Enki and Inanna: The Organization of the Earth and its Cultural Processes" (or "Enki and the World Order"[218]), Enki's watery abode extends up to heaven:

Line 10: [*é-z*] *u-maḫ abzu-ta si-ga dim-gal-an-ki-a*[219]

Your noble [house] is founded in the Apsu, the great "mast" (or temple) of heaven and earth.[220]

A similar structure is evident in lines 166-67:

> urì-gal abzu-ta si-ga an-dùl-le-eš ag-a
> gizzu-bi ki-šár-ra lá-a uku-e ní-[t]e-en-te[221]

The standard that reaches [?] out from the Apsu that has been made into a canopy, whose shade stretches over the entire earth, refreshing [its] people.[222]

In the "Hymn to the *E-engur-ra* of Eridu" Enki's temple is described in line 2 as "fashioned together with heaven and earth, terrace of heaven and earth."[223] Similarly, in a temple hymn praising Enki, the ziggurat of Enki's Apsu is described as stretching toward the sky.[224]

> Line 18: u_6-nir èš-maḫ an-né^2 ús-sa-x-za

The unlimited height of Enki's watery abode is all the more remarkable in that the myth concerning the creation of human beings ("Enki and Ninmah") describes *E-engur* (lit. "house watery deep") as "a well into which waters seeped, a place the inside of which no god whatever was laying eyes on."[225]

> Line 13: ^{d}en-ki-ke$_4$ engur-bùru a-sur-ra ki dingir-na-me šà-bi u_6 nu-um-me[226]

Thus Enki's domain of reign is as high as it is deep. It is not limited to the sea and its depths, but extends to the upper regions, due to Enki's control over the "waters above," which appear as clouds and rain ("Enki and the World Order," lines 308-09):[227]

> im-a!-a-an-na-ka gù ba-an-dé
> IN-DIRIG-dirig-ga-gi[n$_x$] bí-in-ús
> He called the rain, the water of the heaven,
> He caused them to come along . . . as floating clouds.[228]

Enki's extensive realm, thus, includes the domain of the aerial creatures.

In the myth "Enki and the World Order" Enki stocks his house as well as the lagoons and water marshes of southern Sumer with fish and birds (lines 97-99, 274-281).[229] Enki then erects a holy shrine in the sea and appoints the sea-goddess Nanse in charge of it. She is described in lines 417-20 as:

the noble *nin/en*, at whose feet the holy u_5-bird stands, is now the customs inspector of the sea. Good fish, tasty birds, she grants her father Enlil in Nippur.[230]

Both birds and fish are directly related to Nanse, since she provides them to Enlil. Similarly, Van Buren points to several clay reliefs from Ur that portray a goddess (Nina?) who is sitting on a large bird, holding a vase out of which water gushes.[231]

In the myth of Enki's travel to Nippur, Enki's city of Eridu is described as "the mazelike mountain" that "floats upon the waters" and in which "birds brood, the *suhur*-fish frolics, . . . the *gud*-fish swings his tail. . . ."[232] In the sixth *kirugu* of the myth entitled "Enki and His Word: A Chant to the Rider of the Waves," fish and birds are linked together with Enki (line 159):

> *mu-ku₆-mušen-zu en-na mu-pàd-da-šè*
> [Master of the Absu] for the sake of your fish and birds, as many as have
> been called a name.[233]

In the ninth *kirugu* Enki is called both fisher and fowler (lines 182-83).[234]

The close connection between Enki and the fish and birds is also illustrated in cylinder seals belonging to the time of Bur-Sin of the third dynasty of Ur (Louvre, AO. 3727; Constantinople, I.O.M. 4269, 9870, 6641).[235] They typically portray Enki as seated and holding a vase from which two streams flow out. Above him is frequently depicted a large bird with wide-spread wings. On a tablet from Kara-Euyuk, Van Buren identifies the sitting figure holding a cup as Ea (Akkadian for Enki). The basis for the identification is the presence of a "big fish which swims up close to his knee."[236] In addition, there is a bird perched on the figure's knee. On a Syro-Cappadocian cylinder sea (Louvre AO. 1864), Van Buren identifies Ea with a nude hero who holds a vase of surging water, above which two immense fishes and a bird hover around each side of his head.[237] On a similar cylinder seal in the Louvre (AO 1866) is depicted a bird perched on one of the streams.[238]

In the creation prologue of "The Disputation between the Bird and the Fish" Enki brings life-giving waters together in the form of the Tigris and Euphrates and sets up cities on the land. He then stocks "the [swamps] and water holes, lagoons with fish and birds" (line 14).[239] Further evidence of Enki's close relationship with fish and birds may also include the controversial "Cylinder of Adda" (B.M. 89115), in which Enki's figure (identified by the two fish-filled rivers streaming from his shoulders) also appears to be touching or holding a bird of prey. The relationship portrayed between the bird and Enki has been the focus of much debate.[240] I would suggest that this enigmatic illustration concerning Enki can plausibly be seen in connection with the epic "Lulgalbanda and the Thunderbird."

line 28: u_4-ba-giri$_x$(KA)-zal ^{gis}hu-rí-in-^{d}en-ki-ke$_4$
line 29: hur-sag-^{na_4}igi-gùnu-^{d}inanna-ka[241]

In those days did Enki's noble 'eagle tree,' poised like a storm cloud atop the carnelian foothills. . . .[242]

This tree is, in fact, the home of Imdugud, the Thunderbird. Thus Enki's association with Imdugud's home may very well point to a tradition in which the bird of prey was regarded as a special creation of Enki.

In short, Enki's procreative powers comprise an integral part of his character. It is worth noting that the Sumerian language does not differentiate between semen and water (*a*),[243] as does Akkadian with *nīlu* (semen) and *mû* (water). Enki represents the power of fertility.[244] It is also worth noting that Enki's mother Nammu or Namma, the primeval waters, bears the epithet *ama-tu-an-ki*, "the mother who gave birth to heaven and earth."[245]

Enki's particular procreative role must have been widely assumed in Akkadian literature, given the numerous instances of bilingual texts that translated Sumerian mythological texts into vernacular Akkadian. Moreover, there are separate instances in Akkadian literature in which Enki's procreativity is highlighted. For instance, in the Old Babylonian epic *Atra-hasis*, Ea (Enki) instructs Atrahasis to build a boat and says to him:

a-na-ku ul-li-iš u-ša-az-na-a-na-ak-ku
hi-iş-bi iş-şu-ri bu-du-ri nu-ni

I will rain down upon you here an abundance of birds, a profusion of fish.[246]

This is paralleled in Gilgamesh XI in which Utnapishtim recounts the flood story, whose lines 43 and 44 are unfortunately fragmentary:

[eli k]a-a-šu-nu u-ša-az-na-nak-ku-nu-nu-ši nu-uh-šam-ma . . . issuri pu-zu-ur
nûni^{pl}-ma[247]

[Upon y]ou he will rain down plenty . . . of birds, a treasure (?) of fish.

These two passages are particularly noteworthy since they both cast Enki as the water god who provides, in addition to fish, birds from the waters above. That birds are closely associated with water is also evident from the (Sumerian) Cylinder A of Gudea (v.9): "bird-men made *tigid*-vases, let sparkling waters flow and flow." Jacobsen suggests that this is a representation of the rain clouds as flying winged creatures pouring down water from vases they hold in their hands.[248]

Sumerian mythological accounts in which Enki does not play a role also conjoin birds with fish. In the Hymn to Enlil, the fish of the waters and birds of heaven are listed together with the sea, which is described as having progenitive powers.[249] In the myth of "Emesh and Enten," Enlil creates the cultural being Enten to whom he assigns specific duties:

> The birds of the heaven, in the wide earth he had them set up their nests.
> The fish of the sea, in the swampland he had them lay their eggs.[250]

In addition, Enlil, taking on the function of Enki, is described in a hymn:

> Your glow brings in the deep the fish to maturity.
> You let the birds in heaven, the fish in the deep,
>   eat their fill.[251]

These two instances, as well as the passage concerning the sea goddess Nanse, show that deities associated with the water were frequently depicted in Sumerian mythology as having a creative association not only with fish but also with birds.

In Akkadian literature, specifically Old Babylonian and Standard Babylonian literature, Enki assumes the name of Ea and acts predictably, as is evident in *Atra-hasis* and the epic of *Gilgamesh*, mentioned above. Ea is "the Lord of intelligence, the wise one who dwells in the Apsu" in the myth *Anzu* (Tablet 1, line 100).[252] A telling line in the tablet hints at Ea's relationship to the bird-monster Anzu:

> *mìndema A.MEŠ šá n[i-li . . .]*
> *KÙ.MEŠ A.MEŠ DINGIR.MEŠ šu-ut a[p-si-i . . .]*
> *i-ri-šu-ma er-ṣe-tu₄ šu-ú [d-du-ul-tu₄]*[253]

> Of course, the waters flo[od . . .]
> The holy waters of the gods of A[psu . . .]
> and the very wide Earth conceived him.

Unfortunately the text is fragmentary, but what is apparent is that the waters of the Apsu figure in some way in conjunction with the earth in creating Anzu.[254] Such a connection could very well point back to a tradition in which the creative activity of Ea had a role in the bird-monster's origin. This would lend further support to interpreting the

Cylinder of Adda as depicting a creative link between Enki and Imdugud, assuming that Imdugud and Anzu correspond. At any rate, the extension of Ea's powers to include authority over and some creative investment in aerial creatures is clearly evident. Furthermore, Ea's (Enki's) creative ventures are consistently seen as thoroughly positive acts in Sumerian and Akkadian literature.

Egyptian Literature

The figure Nun represents the "primeval waste of waters" in much of Egyptian cosmogony.[255] Nun was the deity of the primeval ocean or power of chaos[256] and was given the common epithet "father of the gods" (it nṯr.w). One way in which Nun's relationship to the other gods was expressed is evident in Ptah's name Tatenen (t3-ṯnn) in the so-called "Memphite theology." The name literally means "the land rising [out of the primeval ocean]."[257] Precisely which land emerges from Nun is variously identified: Memphis, Heliopolis, Hermopolis, and Thebes, all competing temple cities with their rival cosmogonies.[258] In the first part of "The Book of the Cow of Heaven," the creator-god Atum (Re) declares his origin from Nun:

> Then Re said to Nun: "O eldest god in whom I came into being, and ancestor gods, look, humanity, which issued from my Eye, is plotting against me."[259]

For the most part Nun or Nwn wr ("Nun, the eldest one,"[260]) was considered more or less a static entity out of which emerged the creating gods, not unlike perhaps Oceanus in Greek mythology. As early as the Coffin Texts, the name was associated with the verb nny, denoting inactivity or inertness.[261] Moreover, Nun was often pictured as a stagnant primeval ocean that the air churned in order to bring about the appearance of the "hillcock."[262] As Kaiser notes:

> Trotz der Benennung des Nun als "Vater der Götter" darf man ihn nicht als das eigentlich schöpferische Prinzip der Welt betrachten.[263]

In order to create, Ptah (as Ptah-Nun) had to "seize the powers latent in the primeval material and incorporate them into his own being."[264] In short, Nun functioned only in a generally creative sense in that the primordial god was considered the ultimate theogonic source. As Tobin puts it, Nun was not so much a primary substance but a "mythic symbol of the abstract reality of the full potential of being."[265] Nun was the "milieu within which creation unfolds."[266] Concrete life forms such as animals and human beings were never derived from Nun, but rather from the creation gods who emerged out of Nun.[267] As Brandon observes:

> Either the original creator or creators dwell in Nun, apparently in an inert and unconscious manner, and from which they at length emerge to begin the work of creation, or Nun itself possesses the potentiality of producing creative emanations from itself.[268]

With respect to the latter, one can cite the cosmogony of Hermopolis in which four divine pairs, male and female, of gods constitute primeval matter, Nun being primary.[269] Of note is the stress placed on the actions of the wind that initiate the creative process.[270]

Egyptian, like Sumerian, cosmogonies generally lacked any conflict motif;[271] thus, Egyptian mythology by and large treated water as positive with the exception of the deluge accounts.[272] Water, as personified by Nun, exhibited a generally creative potency in Egyptian mythology that may in part constitute the background behind Gen 1:2[273] and even Gen 1:9[274] (in either the Greek or Hebrew versions).

Another Egyptian deity particularly associated with the creation of the birds and fishes was the ram-god Khnum. He is described in Egyptian wisdom literature as a potter who fashions life.[275] The most detailed description of Khnum's creative prowess comes from the Roman period in the "Great Hymn to Khnum" of the Esna temple.[276] From the potter's wheel,

> He has fashioned gods and men,
> He has formed flocks and herds,
> He made birds as well as fishes,
> He created bulls, engendered cows.[277]

In addition, he is associated with Nun:

> God of the potter's wheel,
> Who settled the land by his handiwork;
> Who joins in secret,
> Who builds soundly,
> Who nourishes the nestlings by the breath of his mouth;
> Who drenches this land with Nun,
> While round sea and great ocean surround him.[278]

In private graves of the fourth and fifth dynasties, inscriptions described Khnum as reigning over the "house of Life" (ḥnty pr ʿnḥ).[279] It appears, then, that Khnum's predominant role was that of a craftsman who created living creatures, most particularly human beings.[280] However, at least in one letter from the Twentieth Dynasty, Khnum is referred to as having "fashioned the great and august Ogdoad," and thus was considered equal to the primeval god Nun.[281] Moreover, in the so-called Famine Stela, Khnum is identified with Nun.[282] His connection to water was most clearly established for the cities of Elephantine, Hypselis, Esna, and Antinoe, in which the deity was thought to rule the first cataract region by controlling the inundations of the Nile (Hapy).[283]

Khnum's connection with the creation of the fish and the birds in the hymn cited above is striking, although it is mentioned within the context of Khnum's *universal* creative sweep, which encompasses everything from human beings to plants. However, the creation of the fish and birds was not the exclusive prerogative of the deity Khnum. In the Great Hymn to Amun, Amun is described as the one "who made the fish to live in the rivers, and the birds in the sky."[284] Similarly, the Nile is described as "the lord of fish and rich in birds."[285] In short, water is often described in Egyptian cosmogonies as having a creative link not only with aquatic creatures such as fish, but also with birds. Such cosmogonic traditions along with the Sumerian and Akkadian attestations of the water god Enki (Ea) provide the clearest mythological antecedents behind Gen 1:20 of the VorLXX.

In surveying recent studies of Egyptian cosmogony, one cannot help note the increasing attention in scholarship given to the close parallels between the priestly account of Genesis 1 and the Egyptian cosmogonies.[286] Concomitant with this development is an increasing appreciation of the philosophical characteristics of Egyptian cosmogonies, most especially noted by James P. Allen.[287] Allen observes, for example, that the so-called "Memphite Theology" from pharaoh Shabaka (c. 715-701 BCE) of the 25th Dynasty is "governed by intellectual principles."[288] How such descriptions of Egyptian cosmogonies shed light on the genre and tenor of Gen 1:1-2:3 of the VorLXX will be discussed in the following chapter.

Ugaritic Literature

Unfortunately, with the exception of the mythological text CTA 23, there are no clear theogonic or cosmogonic Ugaritic texts available at present. Thus any examination of the procreative powers of water in

Ugaritic religion can only be tentative. When one reflects on the role of "water" in Ugaritic literature, one immediately thinks of the figure *Yam* in the Baal epic (CTA 1 and 2). However, no progenitive powers are ever assigned to him and the context of his struggle against Baal nowhere involves references to cosmic creation.[289] He is frequently described by the following epithets: *tnn* ("dragon") or *ltn* ("Leviathan"), *btn ʿqltn* ("twisting serpent") or *btn brḥ* ("slippery serpent"), and *šlyt d šbʿt rʾašm* ("tyrant with seven heads") (CTA 3.iiiD.37-39; CTA 5.i.1-3, 28-30). Yam's character is essentially negative and only by his defeat at the hands of Baal (and/or Anat [cf. CTA 3.iiiD.35-36; PRU II, no. 3 [VI MF]) is construction of Baal's palace made possible (see CTA 4.vi.1-6). Thus, the character of Yam in Ugaritic mythological texts is not relevant for any investigation of the procreative nature of water.

One can find a positive and procreative side to water in the mythological character of Athirat, El's consort. Indeed, she is often called *rbt ʾaṯrt ym* ("dame Athirat of the sea," CTA 4.i.14-15, 22; ii.28-29; iii.27,28,29,38) and *qnyt ʾilm* ("creatress of the gods," CTA 4.i.23; iii.26,30; iv.32). As a character in the mythological narratives, she primarily assumes a positive role. She pleads on behalf of Anat and Baal that El grant permission for the construction of Baal's palace (CTA 4.iv.40-v.81). Her role is more ambiguous in the epic concerning Baal and Mot, in which she insists that her son Athtar assume Baal's vacant throne (CTA 6.i.54-55), despite El's negative evaluation of Athtar's physical prowess (CTA 6.i.49-52). Though Athtar figures rather insignificantly in the plot, his epithet is reminiscent of Enki (Ea) when his mother declares: *bl nmlk ydʿ ylḥn* ("Yes, let us make him king who has knowledge [and] intelligence," CTA 6.i.48). At any rate, Athtar proves inadequate for the job of occupying Baal's throne and is consequently relegated to the "earth of El, all of it" (*bʾarṣ ʾil klh*, CTA 6.i.65). He is apparently defeated with Athirat's other sons by Baal upon Baal's return (CTA 6.v.1). Thus mother Athirat indirectly plays a negative role, but this is the only discernible instance in the Ugaritic corpus.

The most significant text, however, is theogonic (CTA 23): Athirat is one of two wives of El who bear Shachar and Shalim and the children of the sea (*bn ym*, CTA 23.53-59), children who devour both the "birds of the heavens" (*ʿṣr šmm*) and the "fish of the sea" (*dg dym* [62-63]). This in itself is significant: Both heaven and sea are included in the domain of the *bn ym*. Indeed, it is the very mouths of these "sea-children" which span the area between the sea and the heavens (CTA 23 61b-62):

št špt l'ars
špt lšmm

It is of interest to note that whereas "one lip" is stretched to the earth as the other reaches the heavens, the animals mentioned for sustenance do not include land animals. The imagery may be merely merismic in order to stress the far-reaching expanse of their mouths. Nonetheless, it is significant that such sea children are described as having an appetite for both birds and fish.

Conclusion

In sum, one can point to a widespread ancient Near Eastern tradition reaching as far back as the Sumerian and early Egyptian mythographers in which water plays a positive role in the formation of not only water creatures but also aerial creatures. Such a tradition casts a generally positive light upon the role of water in creation, in contrast to other traditions that highlight the negative, resistant role water often assumes in mythological texts (E.g., *Tiamat* in *Enuma Elish*, *Yam* in Ugaritic literature). The ancient Near Eastern god Enki or Ea relates to the role of the waters in Genesis 1 of the VorLxx in two possible ways: 1) Enki, lord of the waters, is generally cast in a positive light, and hardly ever as an evil chaotic force; and 2) Enki's creative link to birds provides a possible background behind the command in Gen 1:20 of the VorLxx. One can also add the Egyptian deities Khnum and Hapy as possible candidates for such influence on the Genesis text.

The close connection between the winged creatures and water is well illustrated in Ps 104:12.

ʿălêhem ʿôp haššāmayim yiškôn
Upon (the streams) dwell the winged creatures of heaven.

All in all, one discerns a widely attested tradition in the ancient Near East, from Mesopotamia to Egypt, with regard to the positive cosmogonic role of water and its association with both aquatic and aerial creatures. Such is not consistently the case in Greek cosmogonic literature. Thus ancient Near Eastern cosmogonic traditions, rather than those of Greek/Hellenistic provenance, seem to provide the most adequate traditio-historical background to the prominent role the waters are given in the VorLxx.

THE NEGATIVE ROLE OF THE WATERS IN
BIBLICAL LITERATURE

It has been widely recognized that water in ancient Near Eastern mythology often assumes a negative role. For instance, Tiamat and Apsu in the Babylonian theogony *Enuma Elish* represent primeval forces that must be overthrown by the next generation of gods before Marduk can create the world.[290] It is not fortuitous that these two primordial figures denote sea and fresh water, respectively.[291] Similarly, Ugaritic literature treats the sea or sea serpents as the arch-rivals of Baal and Anat (Baal vs. Yam or Judge Nahar: CTA 2.iv; Baal vs. Tannin: PRU II, No. 2; Anat vs. Yam, Nahar, Tannin, and Shaliyyat: CTA 3.iii.34-38; Baal vs. Lotan and Shaliyyat: CTA 5.i.1-3, 27-30).[292] In the most extensive account of a *Chaoskampf* in Ugaritic literature, Yam's defeat by Baal (CTA 2.iv) provides the occasion for the construction of Baal's palace (*CTA* 3,4).[293] Throughout these accounts, water or sea is depicted as a source of conflict with the protagonist god(s). Frequently, *mayim* or *yam* in the Hebrew Bible seems to presuppose this role of conflict in varying degrees. Examples are many, but for the purposes of illustration a few will suffice.

Water as an Impotent Cosmic Force

Ps 104:6-7, 9 depicts the waters as fleeing before God.

> v 6   těhôm kallěbûš kissîtô ʿal hārîm yaʿamědû mayim
> v 7   min gaʿărătěkā yěnûsûn min qôl raʿamkā yěḥāpēzûn
> v 9   gěbûl śamtâ bal yaʿăbōrûn bal yěšûbûn lěkassôt hāʾāreṣ

> You covered [the earth] with the deep as with a garment,
> the waters stood above the mountains.
>
> At your rebuke,[294] they fled, at the sound of your thunder
> they took to flight.
>
> You set a boundary so that they would not pass,
> so that they might not again cover the earth.

Though the waters present no source of conflict in the passage, they are nonetheless depicted as intimidated by God and permanently confined. In a recent article, Dion claims that Psalm 104 is dependent upon ancient Near Eastern storm-god mythology, while

at the same time, the drastic reduction of allusions to fighting shows how far
the biblical writers could go towards rubbing off features they felt theologically obsolete.[295]

Without any explicit reference to a battle, the waters in Psalm 104 are
rendered impotent; they no longer figure as *mayim* after v 9. Instead, they
are only alluded to in the creation of streams (*hamšallēaḥ maʿyānîm
bannĕḥalîm*). Similar depictions are evident in Ps 77:17, 20.

> *rāʾûkā mayim ʾĕlōhîm rāʾûkā mayim yāḥîlû ʾap yirgĕzû tĕhōmōt*
> *bayyām darkekā ûšebîlĕkā bĕmayim rabbîm*

> When the waters saw you, O God, when the waters saw you, they were
> afraid; indeed, the deeps trembled.
> Your way was through the sea, your path, through many waters.

Within the context of the Red Sea episode, the waters are frightened by
the very sight of God. The phrase *mayim rabbîm* frequently, though not
always, denotes an inimical cosmic force (2 Sam 22:17; Ezek 1:24; 43:2; Ps
18:16; 32:6). May describes the *mayim rabbîm* as "chaotic, disorderly,
insurgent elements which must be controlled."[296] However, the efficacy
of such connotations in Ps 77 is effectively erased in v 20, in which God is
portrayed as making a path through the sea.

Hab 3:8-15 connects the chaotic force represented by the *mayim
rabbîm* with a military campaign:

> v 8   *hăbinhārîm ḥārāh YHWH ʾim bannĕhārîm ʾapekā ʾim bayyām ʿebrātekā kî
>   tirkab ʿal sûseykā markĕborteykā yešûʿāh*
> v 15 *dāraktā bayyām suseykā ḥōmēr mayim rabbîm*

> Was your wrath against rivers, O Yahweh,
> Or your rage against the rivers,
> Or your rage against the sea,
> When you drove your horses, your chariots to victory?
> You tread the sea with your horses, churning the many waters.

While many cosmic elements are affected by God's wrath (*hāʾāreṣ*, vv 9,
12; *hārîm*, v 10; *šemeš, yārēaḥ*, v 11), water is singled out to bear the brunt
of divine rage. The waters' impotence is signaled by the verb *dārak* in v
15, suggesting a picture of defeat under the horses' hooves.

Another form of divine action against the waters is depicted in Isa
50:2b.

hăqāṣôr qāṣĕrāh yādî mippĕdût weʾim ʾên bî kōaḥ lehaṣṣil
hēn bĕgaʿ ʿărātî ʾaḥărîb yām ʾāśîm nĕhārôt midbār
tibeʾaš dĕgātām mēʾēn mayim wĕtāmōt baṣāmāʾ

Is my hand shortened, that it cannot redeem
  or have I no power to deliver?
Indeed, by my rebuke I dry up the sea,
I make the rivers a desert;
Their fish stink because there is no water;
  they die on the thirsty ground.

In this series of rhetorical questions (50:1-2a), the efficacy of divine power is described by specific reference to God's power over the sea (*yam*), which brings about the sea's complete dissolution. The waters' resulting impotence could not be more radically stated.

Personification

In more explicitly mythological passages, water is associated with a particular creature, as in Job 26:12.

bekĕḥō rāgaʿ hayyām ûbitbûnātô māḥaṣ rāhab

By his power he stilled the sea;
By his understanding he struck Rahab.

Or in Ezek 32:2 with reference to Egypt:

kĕpîr gôyîm nidmêtā wĕʾatāh kattannîm bayyammîm wattāgah bĕnaḥarôteykā
wattidlaḥ mayim bĕragleykā wattirpōs nahărôtām

You consider yourself as a lion among the nations, but you are really like a sea serpent in the seas; you thrash about in your streams, trouble the waters with your feet, and foul their streams.

The description in Ezekiel is a rhetorical "set-up," since by identifying Egypt as a sea serpent, contrary to Egypt's own self-conception, Ezekiel can then describe Egypt's destruction in graphic fashion in vv 3-6: The serpent is hauled onto an open field and devoured by animals, its flesh and blood dispersed among the mountains and valleys.

Elsewhere in biblical literature this serpent is known as "Leviathan," as in Ps 74:13-14.

ʾattāh pôrārtā bĕʿāzzĕkā yām sibbartā rāʾšê tannînîm ʿal hammāyim
ʾattāh riṣṣaṣtā rāʾšê liwyātān tittĕnennû maʾăkāl lĕʿām lĕṣîyîm

You divided the sea by your might; you broke the heads of the
sea serpents in the waters.

You crushed the heads of Leviathan; you gave him as food for
the creatures of the wilderness.

One can also cite Isa 27:1, which describes Leviathan as the *tannin ʾăšer
bayyam*. Its association with the sea is clearly evident in the ironic word
play in Job 3:8

> *yiqqĕbuhû ʾōrĕrê yôm hāʿătîdîm ʿōrēr liwyātān*
>
> Let it be damned by those who curse the day,
> Those who are ready to rouse Leviathan.

The apparatus of the *BHS* suggests amending *yôm* to *yām*, which seems
logical, given the parallelism between *yām* and *liwyātān*. Indeed, Fishbane
cites an Aramaic inscription from Nippur that sets both in parallelism.[297]
Fishbane suggests, however, on textual grounds that *yôm* should be
retained, concluding that it is a magical wordplay. In either case, a
connection is made between the sea (*yām*) and Leviathan.

Lastly, Isa 51:9b-10 connects the defeat of the sea-serpent Rahab with
the drying up of the Red Sea:

> *hălôʾ att hîʾ hammaḥṣebet rahab mĕhôlelet tannin*
> *hălôʾ att hîʾ hammăḥărebet yām mê tĕhôm rabbāh*
> *haśśāmāh maʿămaqqê yām derek laʿăbōr gĕʾûlîm*
>
> Was it not you who cut Rahab into pieces,
>   who pierced the dragon,
> Was it not you who dried up the sea,
>   the waters of the great deep,
> Who made the depths of the sea a way for the
>   redeemed to cross over?

In all the above cases, water is depicted as a negative cosmic force,
frequently personified as the mythological figures of Leviathan and
Rahab, but elsewhere treated simply as a locus of power that is no match
for divine power. The waters' fate is described in various degrees of
destruction, from impotence to complete evaporation.

Containment

To a lesser degree, water is invested with a certain locus of negative
power in passages that refer to its containment. Ps 104:9 has already been

mentioned in connection with the waters' fleeing from divine rebuke. Another passage is Jer 5:22.

haʾôtî lōʾ tîrāʾû nĕʾum YHWH ʾim mippānay lōʾ tāḥîlû ʾăšer śamtî ḥôl gĕbûl layyām haq ʿôlām wĕlōʾ yaʿabrenhû wayyitgāʿăšû wĕlōʾ yûkālû wĕhāmû gallāyw wĕlōʾ yaʿabrunhû

Do you not fear me? says Yahweh;
Do you not tremble before me?
I placed sand as a boundary for the sea,
A perpetual barrier so that it cannot pass.
Though the waves toss, they cannot prevail,
Though they roar, they cannot pass over it.

A less detailed description is given in Prov 8:29.

bĕsûmô layyām ḥuqqô ûmayim lōʾ yāʿabrû pîw bĕḥûqô môsĕdê ʾāreṣ

When he assigned to the sea its limit, so that the waters might not transgress his command,

A more unusual description is found in Ps 33:7.

kōnēs kannēd mê hayyām nōtēn bĕʾōṣārôt tĕhōmōt

He gathers in a bottle[298] the waters of the sea,
He puts the deeps in storehouses.

The Waters as Metaphor for Social Threat

There are several passages in which the waters denote social threat or danger. Isaiah 17:12-13 casts the waters in the form of a simile in describing the threatening foreign nations.

hôy hāmôn ʿammîm rabbîm kahămôt yammîm yehĕmayûn ûšĕʾôn lĕʾummîm kišʾôn mayim kabîrîm yiššāʾûn
lĕʾummîm kišʾôn mayim rabbîm yiššāʾûn wĕgāʿar bô wĕnās mimmerḥāq

Ah, the roar of many peoples are like the roaring of the seas,
The roar of nations are like the roaring of mighty waters,

The nations roar like the roaring of many waters,
But he will rebuke them, and they will flee far away.

In this passage the "many peoples" are identified with the "many waters."[299] The nations are treated in the same way (17:13b) as the waters in Ps 104:7: By divine rebuke they are rendered impotent.

In many cases the waters represent personal enemies in the Psalms and elsewhere. One example is Ps 18:17-18 (= 2 Sam 22:17-18):

> *yišlaḥ mimmārôm yiqqāḥēnî yamšēnî mimmayim rabbîm*
> *yaṣṣîlēnî mēʾōybî ʿāz ûmiśśōnʾay kî ʾāmēṣû mimmennî*
>
> He reached down from on high, he took me;
> He drew me out of many waters;
> He delivered me from my strong enemy and from those who hate me,
>   for they were too mighty for me.

The psalmist's enemies are set in parallel with the *mayim rabbîm*. Similarly, Psalm 69 is replete with water imagery in its description of personal distress.

> v 2   *hôšîʿēnî ʾĕlōhîm kî bāʾû mayim ʿad nāpeš*
> v 3   *tabaʿtî bîwēn mĕṣulāh wĕʾên māʿŏmād*
>   *bāʾtî bĕmāʿămaqqê mayim wĕsibōlet šĕṭāpātĕnî*
>
> Save me, O God, for the waters have come to (my) throat.
> I have sunk into deep mire, and there is no foothold;
> I have come into deep waters and the flood sweeps me.

Elsewhere, the psalmist points to personal enemies as the cause of his distress.

> v 15   *haṣṣîlēnî miṭṭîṭ wĕʾal ʾētbāʿāh ʾinnāṣĕlāh*
>   *miśśōnĕʾay ûmimmaʿămaqqê māyim*
>
> Deliver me from mire so that I will not sink,
> Let me be saved from my enemies and from the deep waters.

Verses 20-30 describe in graphic detail the wrongs committed against the psalmist, matched only by his fervent desire for retribution. In more ambiguous contexts, the waters are given a role that seems to imply general distress without concrete reference, such as in Job 22:11, Lam 3:54, Ps 32:6, and Cant 8:7.

The metaphor of waters as denoting distress need not always be considered antithetical to God's purpose. In Jer 47:2, the overwhelming waters are compared to an attacking army, presumably from Egypt.

> *hinnēh mayim ʿōlîm miṣṣāpôn wĕḥāû lĕnaḥal šôṭēp*
> *wĕyištĕpû ʿereṣ ûmĕlôʾāh ʿîr wĕyōšĕbê bāh*
> *wĕzāʿāqû hāʾādām wĕhêlil kōl yōšēb hāʾāreṣ*
>
> See, waters are rising from the north, becoming an overflowing torrent.

They shall overflow the land, filling it, including city and its inhabitants.
The people will cry out and all the inhabitants of the land will wail.

Immediately following v 1, Jeremiah describes an attacking army (47:3). In contrast to Isa 17:2, the waters in Jeremiah 47 are used to describe *Yahweh's* attack against the Philistines (47:4). One can also cite the Jeremianic oracles against Babylon (50:42; 51:42; 55-56), in which the metaphor of the waters is employed to express impending destruction via divine agency. Of note is also Isaiah's description of Ephraim's doom in 28:2.[300]

> *hinnēh hāzāq wĕ°ammiṣ la°dōnāy kĕzerem bārād śaʿar qāṭeb*
> *kĕzerem mayim kabbîrîm šōṭĕpîm hinnîaḥ lā°āreṣ bĕyād*
>
> See, the Lord has one who is mighty and strong;
> Like a storm of hail, a destroying tempest,
> Like a storm of overflowing waters;
> With his hand he will hurl to the ground.

Similarly, in Isa 8:7-8 the "king of Assyria," whom Yahweh is "bringing up" (*maʿăleh*), is likened to the waters of the river (*mê hannāhār*). Machinist discerns an indirect link in Isaiah's description of the Assyrian king to Neo-Assyrian texts in which the *abūbu* ("flood") is identified as a weapon of the king or is directly compared to him.[301] Ezek 1:24 uses the metaphor in a theophonic context. Ezekiel describes the "living creatures" (*haḥayyāh*) in the following manner:

> *wā°ešmaʿ °et qôl kanpêhem kĕqôl mayim rabbîm kĕqôl šadday bĕlektām qôl hămullāh*
> *kĕqôl maḥăneh*
>
> I heard the sound of their wings like the sound of many waters, like the sound of *šadday*, when they moved. The sound of tumult was like the sound of an army.

Here, the sound of the *mayim rabbîm* is paralleled with that of an army. The inclusion of waters in theophonic contexts is not infrequent, as for instance in Jer 10:13 (51:16):

> *lĕqôl titô*[302] *hămôn mayim baššāmayim wayyăʿaleh*
> *nĕśi°îm miqṣēh hā°āreṣ birāqîm lammāṭār ʿāśāh*
> *wayyôṣē° rûaḥ mē°ōṣĕrōtāyw*
>
> At the sound of his uttering, there is a tumult of waters in the heavens,
> And he makes a mist rise from the ends of the earth.
> He makes lightnings for the rain,
> And he brings out the wind from his storehouses.

One can also cite Ps 18:12 and its approximate duplicate in 2 Sam 22:12 as further examples of theophonic descriptions that incorporate the metaphor of the threatening waters.

Conclusion

The passages discussed above illustrate a widespread tradition in which the waters are regarded as symbolizing antagonistic or threatening forces. Indeed, biblical tradition often presupposes a conflict, albeit one-sided, between this particular force of nature and Yahweh, while in other instances water imagery is used to describe Yahweh's fearsome power in theophany. In the former case Yahweh is described as rendering the waters impotent in varying degrees.

This negative side of the waters as depicted in ancient Near Eastern and biblical literature provides a contrasting comparison with the role of the waters in the VorLXX of Genesis 1. In the VorLXX the waters play a consistently positive role in the creative process. The waters move on their own accord without divine intervention to form seas (*yammîm*) and thereby contribute to the formation of land as well as an innumerable variety of living entities, both sea and air bound, all at the behest of God. However, given the widespread negative appraisal of the waters found in the texts listed above, the waters' role in the priestly creation account of the VorLXX strikes one as highly anomalous in comparison to the more mythological treatments of water. In light of the texts discussed above, one could conceivably interpret the waters' powerful and positive role in the VorLXX as in effect a concession of God's power over creation to the forces of nature. In other words, given the waters' traditional inimical character, any depiction of the waters' acting independently and generating life would not reflect a God who is in complete control of the cosmos. In light of such an interpretation, the text of Genesis 1 in the MT can be seen as reflecting a revision that in effect limits the role of the waters in cosmogony. That is to say, the waters' role in the creative process is textually suppressed in the MT. The ideological implications behind this dismantling of the waters' powerful role in cosmogony will be explored more fully in the following chapter.

NOTES

[1] Hesiod, *Theogony and Works and Days*, trans. M. L. West (Oxford: Oxford University Press, 1988) vii-viii.

[2] West, M. L. *Hesiod Theogony* (Oxford: Clarendon Press, 1966) 14-15.

[3] West, *Hesiod Theogony*, x.

[4] Hesiod *Theogony* 116-20.

[5] With some alterations, the translation is based on J. M. Robinson, *An Introduction to Early Greek Philosophy: The Chief Fragments and Ancient Testimony with Connecting Commentary* (Boston: Houghton Mifflin Company, 1968) 4.

[6] H. J. Rose, *A Handbook of Greek Mythology Including its Extension to Rome* (New York: E. P. Dutton & Co., 1959) 19.

[7] West, *Hesiod Theogony*, 192.

[8] So F. M. Cornford, *The Unwritten Philsophy and other Essays* (Cambridge: University Press, 1952) 98-99; Robinson, *An Introduction*, 5.

[9] West, *Hesiod Theogony*, 192-93.

[10] This and subsequent translations of Hesiod are based on West's translations (Hesiod, *Theogony and Works and Days*, 8).

[11] *Iliad* 1.316.

[12] West, *Hesiod Theogony*, 199.

[13] A. Cotterell, *A Dictionary of World Mythology* (Oxford: Oxford University Prss, 1986) 172; West, *Hesiod Theogony*, 201.

[14] West's translation is especially appropriate, since it reproduces the Greek pun with an English equivalent (*Theogony and Works and Days*, 9).

[15] See A. F. von Pauly, *Paulys Real-Encyclopädie der Classischer Altertumswissenschaft*, vol. 17, ed., G. Wissowa (Stuttgart: J. B. Metzlersche Verlagsbuchhandlung, 1937) 2308-20.

[16] See Aristotle *Metaphysica* 1.989a10:

> *panta gar einai phasi gēn, phēsi de kai Hesiodos tēn gēn prōtēn genesthai tōn sōmatōn· houtōs archaian kai dēmotikēn symbebēken einai tēn hypolēpsin.*

> "Everything is earth" (so many people say). Indeed, Hesiod too says that earth was the first of the corporeal things to be generated, so ancient and popular is the conception.

(Unless otherwise noted, all translations from the Greek and Latin philosophical texts are based upon, but not limited to, the translations from the LCL series. Those cited from Diels and Kranz are based upon K. Freeman's translations in *The Pre-Socratic Philosophers: A Companion to Diels Fragmente der Vorsokratiker* [Oxford: Basil Blackwell, 1949]).

[17] Freeman, 1.

[18] Freeman, 5.

[19] See discussion in M. L. West, *The Orphic Poems* (Oxford: Clarendon Press, 1983) 176-190.

[20] Damascius 123 (Diels 1 B 13); O. Kern, *Orphicorum Fragmenta* (Berlin: Weidmann, 1922) 130-31 (Fr. 54).

[21] Athenagoras *Pro Christianis* 18 p. 20, 12 (Kern, 137 [fr. 57]).

[22] Athenagoras *Pro Christianis* 18 p. 20, 12 (Kern, 137 [fr. 57]).

23 See G. S. Kirk and J. E. Raven, *The Presocratic Philosophers: A Critical History with a Selection of Texts* (Cambridge: Cambridge University Press, 1983) 13-15.

24 Plato *Symposium* 178B (Diels 9 B 2).

25 Damascius *De princ.* 124 (Diels 9 A 1).

26 Achilles Statius *Isagoge* 3 (Diels 7 B 1a).

27 Grenfell-Hunt Greek Papyr. Ser. ii n. 11 p. 23 (Diels 7 B 2).

28 Diogenes Laertius i. 119 (Diels 7 B 1).

29 West, *The Orphic Poems*, 183.

30 Aristotle *Metaphysica* 983b6. But cf. Robinson, *An Introduction to Early Greek Philosophy*, 293.

31 Aristotle *De caelo* 294a28.

32 Aristotle *Metaphysica* 983b7.

33 Aristotle *Metaphysica* 983b21.

34 Aristotle *Metaphysica* 983b27.

35 Aristotle *Metaphysica* 983b32.

36 Diels 11 A 11, 20, respectively.

37 W. K. C. Guthrie, *A History of Greek Philosophy*, vol. 1 (Cambridge: University Press, 1962) 61-62.

38 J. Burnet, *Greek Philosophy, Part 1: Thales to Plato* (London: MacMillan Publishing Company, 1914) 21.

39 See Herodotus 2.25:

> [The sun] draws water to itself, and having so drawn it, expels it away to the inland regions, and the winds catch it and scatter and dissolve it.

> Cf. Anaximenes, a successor of Thales, below (e.g., Hippolytus *Ref* 1.6.4 [Diels 12 A 11]).

40 Cf. Anaximander's stress on moisture (below): Aetius v. 19. 4 (Diels 12 A 30).

41 Guthrie, *A History of Philosophy*, 1, 56.

42 Guthrie, *A History of Philosophy*, 1, 57.

43 Simplicius *Physica* 24, 13 (Diels 12 A 9).

44 Hippolytus *Ref.* i.6.1 (Diels 12 A 11).

45 Cf., Aristotle *Physica* 203b6 (Diels 12 A 15); Guthrie, *A History of Philosophy*, 1, 87-89.

46 Aristotle *Physica* 187a20 (Diels 12 A 9).

47 Simplicius *Physica* 150, 24 (Diels 12 A 9).

48 Aetius v. 19. 4 (Diels 12 A 30).

49 Censorinus *De die nat.* iv. 7 (Diels 12 A 30).

50 Plutarch *Symp.* viii. 8 (Diels 12 A 30).

51 Aristotle *Meterologica* 353b6 (Diels 12 A 27).

52 Simplicius *De caelo* 532, 14 (cited from Robinson, *An Introduction to Early Greek Philosophy*, 30).

53 Simplicius *Physica* 24, 26 (Diels 13 A 5).

54 See also Hippolytus *Ref.* i. 7. 2-3 (Diels 13 A 7) and Plutarch *De prim. frig.* 7 (Diels 13 B 1).

55 Aetius iii. 4. 4 (Diels 21 A 46).

56 Aetius iii. 4. 4 (Diels 21 B 30).

57 Simplicius *Physica* 188, 32 (Diels 21 B 29).

58 Sextus Empiricus *Adversus Math.* x. 314 (Diels 21 B 33).

59 Olympiodorus *De arte sacra lapidis philos.* 24 p. 82, 21 (Diels 21 A 36).

60 Cf. *Metaphysica* 989a7-13, in which Aristotle states that no philosopher ever posited earth as the *archē.*

> For some [early philosophers] name fire [as the primary element], others water, and others air. But why do they not suggest earth too, as many claim? For they say "everything is earth." Furthermore, Hesiod says that earth was the first of the corporeal things to be generated.

61 Plato *Timeaus* 23D-E; *Politicus* 271A-C, 274A; Aristotle *De generatione animalium* 716A 15-17. Aristotle states:

> This is why in cosmology too the nature of the earth is spoken as female and is called "mother," while heaven and the sun and everything else of that kind is given the title of "generator," and "father."

See discussion in D. E. Hahm, *The Origins of Stoic Cosmology* (Columbus: Ohio State University Press, 1977) 85, n. 18.

62 Clement *Stromata* v. 105 (Diels 22 B 30).

63 Clement *Stromata* v. 105 (Diels 22 B 31).

64 Diogenes Laertius ix 9 (Diels 22 A 1).

65 Robinson, *An Introduction to Early Greek Philosophy*, 90.

66 See Plato *Cratylus* 402A (Diels 22 A 6); Arius Didymus in Eusebius *PE* xv. 20 (Diels 22 B 12).

67 Simplicius *Physica* 29, 22 (Diels 30 B 3); 111, 18 (Diels 30 B 7).

68 Simplicius *De caelo* 558, 19 (Diels 30 B 8).

69 Aetius i. 3. 20 (Diels 31 B 6).

70 Aetius i. 3. 20 (Diels 31 A 33).

71 Simplicius *Physica* 300, 19 (Diels 31 B 96); 32. 3 (Diels 31 B 98).

72 Simplicius *De caelo* 529, 28 (Diels 31 B 71).

73 Freeman, 181.

74 See Simplicius *Physica* 160, 26 (Diels 31 B 22):

> For all these things: bright Sun and Earth and Heaven and Sea, are united with their own parts: all those (parts) which have been sundered from them and exist in mortal limbs. Similarly all those things which are more suitable for mixture are made like one another and united in affection by Aphrodite. But those things that differ most from one another in origin and mixture and the forms in which they are moulded are completely unaccustomed to combine, and are very baneful because of the commands of hate, in that Strife has wrought their origin.

75 Hesychius of Alexandria (*Lexicographus*) I 312, 3 (Diels 31 B 7).

76 Robinson, *An Introduction to Early Greek Philosophy*, 163.

77 F. H. Sandbach, *Aristotle and the Stoics* (CPSSV 10; Cambridge: Cambridge Philological Society, 1985) 43.

78 Plutarch *Adv. Coloten* 11, p. 1113 A (Diels 31 B 9); 10, p. 1111 F (Diels 31 B 8).

79 Aetius ii. 6. 3 (Diels 31 A 49).

80 Aristotle *Meterologica* 356a24 (Diels 31 B 55).

81 Simplicius *Physica* 381, 29 (Diels 31 B 62).

82 Simplicius *Physica* 1124, 9 (Diels 31 B 20). See also *Physica* 32, 3 (Diels 31 B 98):

> And Earth, having been finally anchored in the perfect harbors of Cypris (the goddess of Love), joined with these in about equal proportions: with Hephaestus, with moisture, and with all-shining Ether, either a little more (of Earth) to their less or a little less to their more. And from these came blood and the forms of other flesh.

Elsewhere, Empedocles uses the analogy of human limbs (*guia*) to describe the harmonious unity of the cosmos formed by Love (Simplicius *De caelo* 529, 1 and *Physica* 32,13 [Diels 31 B 35]). However, when Strife has its way, the cosmic limbs become severed (Simplicius *Physica* 1124, 9 [Diels 31 B 20]; *De caelo* 587, 19 [Diels 31 B 58]), resulting in a separation of the elements:

> For when the whole is separated into the elements by Strife, fire is aggregated into one, and so with each of the other elements (Aristotle *Metaphysica* 985a25 [Diels 31 A 37]).

83 Aetius v 19, 5 (Diels 31 A 72). Cf. Philo, *De gigantibus* ii.7:

> For the universe must be completely animated, and each of its primary elementary divisions contains the forms of life which are akin and suited to it.

84 Aristotle *De respiratione* 477b1-7.
85 Aristotle *Metaphysica* 984a3 (Diels 38 A 7).
86 Hippolytus *Ref.* i. 16 (Diels 38 A 3).
87 Aetius iv 3, 9 (Diels 38 A 10).
88 Aristotle *De anima* 405b1 (Diels 31 A 4).
89 Hippolytus *Ref.* i. 16 (Diels 38 A 3).
90 Simplicius *Physica* 164, 22 (Diels 59 B 11).
91 Simplicius *Physica* 155, 23 (Diels 59 B 1).
92 Lucretius *De rerum natura* i. 876-79.
93 Simplicius *Physica* 155, 23 (Diels 59 B 1, 12-16); 155, 30 (Diels 59 B 2).
94 Simplicius *Physica* 179, 3 (Diels 59 B 15).
95 Simplicius *Physica* 179, 6 (Diels 59 B 16).
96 Diogenes Laertius ii. 9 (Diels 59 A 1, 9).
97 Irenaeus ii. 14. 2 (Diels 59 A 113).
98 Diogenes Laertius ii. 16-17.
99 Simplicius *Physica* 151, 28 (Diels 64 B 2).
100 Simplicius *Physica* 151, 28 (Diels 64 B 3).
101 Simplicius *Physica* 151, 28 (Diels 64 B 5).
102 Clemens *Paedagogus* i. 6, 48 (Diels 64 A 24); Simplicius *Physica* 153, 13 (Diels 64 B 6).
103 Simplicius *De caelo* 242, 18 (Diels 67 A 14); Aetius i. 16.2 (Diels 68 A 48).
104 Censorinus 4. 9 (Diels 68 A 139).
105 Cf. W. K. C. Guthrie, *A History of Greek Philosophy*, vol. V (Cambridge: Cambridge University Press, 1978) 241-42. Indeed, Timaeus himself admits that inquiries into cosmogony will always be inconsistent and inexact, to which Socrates enthusiastically agrees (29C-D)! Furthermore, Timaeus claims that the "casual and random" aspect of language is what gives rise to the logical tensions (34B-C; see T. M.

Robinson, "Understanding the *Timaeus*," in *Proceedings of the Boston Area Colloquium in Ancient Philosophy*, vol. 2, ed. J. J. Cleary (Lanham: University Press of America) 117.

[106] Plato *Timaeus* 20A and 27A.

[107] Plato *Timaeus* 28A.

[108] Plato *Timaeus* 29A.

[109] Plato *Timaeus* 48B.

[110] Plato *Timaeus* 30A.

[111] Cf. also *Timaeus* 69C.

[112] Robinson, "Understanding the *Timaeus*," 105.

[113] Aristotle *De caelo* 279b4-283b22.

[114] Aristotle *Metaphysica* 1050b28-30. Cf. Aristotle *De generatione et corruptione* 337a1-7.

[115] A. E. Taylor, *Aristotle* (New York: Dover Press, 1955) 63.

[116] J. Owens, "The Teleology of Nature in Aristotle," in *Aristotle: The Collected Papers of Joseph Owens*, ed. J. R. Catan (Albany: State University of New York Press, 1981) 142.

[117] Aristotle *De generatione et corruptione* 390b2-6.

[118] Aristotle *De generatione et corruptione* 329a28-35; *Physica* 191a15-25.

[119] Aristotle *Meterologica* 349b15-27.

[120] Aristotle *Meterologica* 349b24-27.

[121] H. Cherniss, *Aristotle's Criticism of Presocratic Philosophy* (Baltimore: Johns Hopkins Press, 1935) 136; Aristotle *Meterologica* 356a.

[122] Aristotle *Meterologica* 355b33-356a2.

[123] Aristotle *De generatione et corruptione* 335a1.

[124] Aristotle *Metaphysica* 335a2-4.

[125] Aristotle *De generatione et corruptione* 335a2-14.

[126] H. A. K. Hunt, *A Physical Interpretation of the Universe: The Doctrines of Zeno the Stoic* (Carlton, Australia: Melbourne University Press, 1976) 17-25.

[127] G. E. R. Lloyd, *Greek Science after Aristotle* (New York: W. W. Norton Co., 1973) 27.

[128] Lloyd, *Greek Science after Aristotle*, 28.

[129] Valerius Probus, *Comm. in Verg. Bucol.* vi 31, p. 344 (*Stoicorum Veterum Fragmenta* [ed. I. von Arnim; Leipzig: Teubner, 1905-24] 1.103 [hereafter referred to as *SVF*]).

[130] See Seneca *Naturales questiones* iii, 13:

> Thales thinks [water] was the first element, and all things arose from it. We Stoics are also of this opinion or close to it. For we say that it is fire which takes possession of the universe and changes all things into itself; it becomes feeble, fades, and sinks, and when fire is extinguished nothing is left in nature except moisture, in which lies concealed the hope of the universe.

[131] Hunt, 47.

[132] Hunt, 47.

[133] Aristocles *Apud Eusebium praep. evang. XV* p. 816d (*SVF* 1.98).

[134] Eusebius *PE* III 9,9 (*SVF* 2.1032). See Hunt, 50.

[135] Diogenes Laertius vii. 156 (*SVF* 1.171). See also Clement of Alexandria *Al. Stromat.* V 14 p. 709 Pott. (*SVF* 2.1134). See Hunt, 47.

136   Sandbach, *Aristotle and the Stoics*, 38.

137   Augustine *Adv. acad.* ii 17.38 (*SVF* 1.157).

138   Diogenes Laertius vii. 142. See Hunt, 51.

139   Diogenes Laertius vii. 136. See Hunt, 51.

140   Stobaeus *Ecl.* i. 17. 3 p. 152, 19 (*SVF* 1.102). See Hunt, 52-53.

141   D. E. Hahm, *The Origins of Stoic Cosmology* (Columbus: Ohio State University Press, 1977) 57, 83, n. 2.

142   Lloyd, *Greek Science after Aristotle*, 28.

143   Diogenes Laertius vii. 136. See Hunt, 37.

144   Hahm, 60.

145   *SVF* 1.128; 2.742 See discussion Hahm, 68-69.

146   Hahm, 68.

147   Aristocles *Apud Eusebium praep. evang.* XV p. 816d. (*SVF* 1.98).

148   Lloyd, *Greek Science after Aristotle*, 29.

149   C. H. Kahn, *Anaximander and the Origins of Greek Cosmology* (New York: Columbia University Press, 1960) 110-11.

150   Diodorus Siculus i. 7. Translation based on C. H. Oldfather, *Diodorus of Sicily* (LCL, Greek authors; London: William Heinemann, 1933).

151   Kahn, 110.

152   Aristotle *Metaphysica* 983b27-28.

153   The myth of Deucalion in Ovid's *Metamorphosis* (i. 381-437) is a good example. The earth, in conjunction with the moisture from the flood and the heat of the sun, spontaneously produces all animal life (434-37). According to Apollodorus, Prometheus fashions humans out of earth and water. In Plato's *Menexenus* (237D), Socrates praises Athens with the following preface:

> At the time when the whole earth was sending up and bringing to birth creatures of every kind, both animals and plants, our own land was innocent and barren of wild beasts, but chose for herself and gave birth to humans.

154   Lucretius *De rerum natura* v. 783-84, 791-96.

155   Plato *Politicus* 271A.

156   E.g., the story of Cadmus, the founder of Thebes. See discussion in W. K. C. Guthrie, *In the Beginning* (Ithaca: Cornell University Press, 1957) 21-25. Also of note is Aristotle's reference to the common belief that the earth was considered the generator of all things (*Metaphysica* 989a8-10).

157   Lucretius *De rerum natura* v. 801-5.

158   Robbins, 32, n. 3.

159   Plato *The Sophist* 218E.

160   Plato *The Sophist* 220A.

161   Plato *The Sophist* 220B.

162   Plato *The Sophist* 220B.

163   See Augustine *De Genesi ad litteram libri duodecim* 3.6.8.

164   Aristotle *Historia animalium* 559a21.

165   Aristotle *Historia animalium* 487a23.

166   Aristotle *De partibus animalium* 694b2-4.

167   Aristotle *Historia animalium* 487b15-23.

168   Aristotle *De incessu animalium* 714a8-9.

[169]   Aristotle *Historia animalium* 487b22.
[170]   Aristotle *De incessu animalium* 714b3-5.
[171]   Aelian *On the Characteristics of Animals* 9.52.
[172]   Aristotle *De generatione animalium* 749a10ff, 749b.
[173]   The time of Philo's literary career is recorded in the medieval dictionary *Suda*, which indicates that he was born sometime during the reign of Nero and lived at least into the reign of Hadrian.
[174]   Porphyry *De abstinentia* 2.56.
[175]   Eusebius *PE* 1.9.23.
[176]   For a brief survey, see H. W. Attridge and R. A. Oden, Jr., *Philo of Byblos: The Phoenician History: Introduction, Critical Text, Translation, Notes* (CBQMS 9; Washington: The Catholic Biblical Association of America, 1981) 1-9; J. Barr, "Philo of Byblos and his 'Phoenician History,'" *BJRL* 57 (1974) 18-21.
[177]   W. F. Albright, *Archaeology and the Religion of Israel* (Baltimore: Johns Hopkins University Press, 1942) 70; F. L. Benz, *Personal Names in the Phoenician and Punic Inscriptions* (Studia Pohl 9; Rome: Biblical Institute Press, 1972) 365-66.
[178]   W. F. Albright, *Archaeology and the Religion of Israel*, 70-71; O. Eissfeldt, "Religionsdokument und Religionspoesie, Religionstheorie und Religionshistorie: Ras Schamra und Sanchunjaton, Philo Byblius und Eusebius von Cäsarea," in *Kleine Schriften* 2 (Tübingen: J. C. B. Mohr [Paul Siebeck], 1963) 135; "Zur Frage nach dem Alter der phönizischen Geschichte des Sanchunjaton," in *Kleine Schriften* 2, 128; P. Walcot is particularly confident of Philo's authenticity:

> It is surely reasonable to conclude that Philo did actually translate from Phoenician into Greek a text like those we know from Ugarit. . . . (*Hesiod and the Near East* [Cardiff: University of Wales Press, 1966] 18).

[179]   Eissfeldt argues for a second millennium BCE date ("Zur Frage," 129 n. 4); Albright suggests a dating of 700-500 BCE (*Archaeology and the Religion of Israel*, 70); M. L. West settles on a Persian or Hellenistic dating, though "the myths he related may, of course, have been much older"(*Hesiod Theogony*, 26); A. I. Baumgarten suggests a dating for the cosmogony between 100 BCE to 200 CE (*The* Phoenician History *of Philo of Byblos: A Commentary* [Leiden: E. J. Brill] 128, 130-31).
[180]   J. Barr, 17-68; Attridge and Oden, *Philo of Byblos*, 6-9.
[181]   Attridge and Oden, *Philo of Byblos*, 6.
[182]   Attridge and Oden, *Philo of Byblos*, 6-7.
[183]   Attridge and Oden, *Philo of Byblos*, 7-8.
[184]   Attridge and Oden, *Philo of Byblos*, 8.
[185]   Attridge and Oden, *Philo of Byblos*, 9.
[186]   Eusebius *PE* 1.10.1.
[187]   The following translations are based on Attridge and Oden, *Philo of Byblos*, beginning on p. 37.
[188]   See the section on Greek philosophy above.
[189]   See the section on Stoic philosophy above.
[190]   Damascius *De principiis* 123 (Diels 1 B 12).
[191]   Eusebius *PE* 1.10.1.
[192]   Attridge and Oden, *Philo of Byblos*, 76, n. 25.
[193]   As J. Ebach puts it:

Die eigene *archai*, die der Wind liebt, sind seine Substanz, jedenfalls kann nicht an 'Anfänge' gedacht werden im Sinne eines anderen Stoffes, von dem er abstamte. Die zugrundeliegende Vorstellung ist die der Selbstbegattung (*Weltentstehung und Kulturentwicklung bei Philo von Byblos* [BZWANT 108; Stuttgart: W. Kohlhammer, 1979] 24).

[194]   So Attridge and Oden, *Philo of Byblos*, 76, n. 25.

[195]   See the section on Empedocles (e.g., Diels 31 B 20, 31).

[196]   Eusebius *PE* 1.10.1.

[197]   Aristotle *Historia animalium* 540b21.

[198]   So Attridge and Oden, *Philo of Byblos*, 76, n. 28. Note the discussion on translation.

[199]   See discussion by Attridge and Oden, *Philo of Byblos*, 76-77, n. 29.

[200]   This is evidently what Cross has in mind when he notes that the Phoenician traditions preserved by "Sakkunyaton" share much in common with the Ba'al texts (Cross, *Canaanite Myth and Hebrew Epic*, 113). See *CTA* 5.ii.15 and 4.viii.12 with Cross's translation (*Canaanite Myth and Hebrew Epic*, 117) and Coogan's translation (M. D. Coogan, *Stories from Ancient Canaan* [Philadelphia: Westminster Press, 1978] 106). Baumgarten also sees a connection but concedes that "*Mot* of the cosmogony has none of the functions of his Ugaritic equivalent" and that "putrefaction and mud as the material of spontaneous generation were alternative Greek theories" (Baumgarten, 112-13).

[201]   Ebach points out that usually the Semitic *tāw* corresponds to the Greek *theta*, while the Greek *tau* relates to the Semitic *ṭet* (Ebach, 41).

[202]   See the section on Greek cosmogony and philosophy.

[203]   Aristotle *Historia animalium* 569a28.

[204]   So also Ebach, 45-46. In comparison to the wealth of Greek similarities, Baumgarten's evidence for Babylonian and Egyptian antecedents is peripheral (Baumgarten, 113).

[205]   So Baumgarten, who also identifies Mot with the Zophasemin (Baumgarten, 115).

[206]   See Kirk and Raven, 23-28.

[207]   See discussion in Attridge and Odin, *Philo of Byblos*, 77-78 n. 35.

[208]   See discussion in Attridge and Oden, *Philo of Byblos*, 78, n. 38.

[209]   Baumgarten considers this passage a piece of "'scientific' meterology" that cannot be traced to ancient Near Eastern antecedents (Baumgarten, 119).

[210]   See Eusebius *PE* 1.9.23-29.

[211]   Ebach, 29.

[212]   So also Barr, who points out that the concepts in Philo's work are "Greek rather than Semitic" (Barr, 46).

[213]   So Baumgarten, 96.

[214]   Ebach observes that Philo's source marks "eine Zwischenstufe zwischen Mythologie und Naturphilosophie" (*Weltenstehung*, 79). Similarly, Baumgarten concludes that Philo's cosmogony is a product of a Phoenician tradition "brought up to date and into harmony with the best science of the day--Greek science" (Baumgarten, 123). However, it is entirely unclear what can be reconstructed as Phoenician tradition.

[215] S. N. Kramer and J. Maier, *Myths of Enki, the Crafty God* (New York: Oxford University Press, 1989) 2.

[216] E. D. van Buren, *The Flowing Vase and the God with Streams* (Berlin: Hans Schoetz, 1933) 1.

[217] Cf. the myths "Enki and Inanna, The Organization of the Earth and Its Cultural Processes," (Kramer and Maier, *Myths of Enki*, 39-56) and "Inanna and Enki: The Transfer of the Arts of Civilization from Eridu to Erech" (57-68). See also the "Hymn to Enki with a Prayer for Ur-Ninurta" (91):

> O Enki, you gathered all the *me* that are, you fixed them at the Abzu,

and "Fragment of a Hymn to Enki" (Kramer and Maier, *Myths of Enki*, 92):

> *En*, craft at deciding for the gods, their controller below and above who holds the staff, decrees their fates, makes the Annuna stand by, who by himself gave the *me* of the whole world force, you whose orders make whatever is right flower, who makes the *me* of heaven and earth study.

[218] C. A. Benito, "'Enki and Ninmah' and 'Enki and the World Order'" (Unpublished Diss.: University of Pennsylvania [Ann Arbor: University Microfilms, 1969]) 77.

[219] For the transcription see Benito, "'Enki and Ninmah'," 77.

[220] Kramer and Maier, *Myths of Enki*, 39 and 216, n. 8.

[221] Benito, 94.

[222] Kramer and Maier, *Myths of Enki*, 218, n. 56.

[223] Kramer and Maier, *Myths of Enki*, 94.

[224] A. W. Sjoberg and E. Bergmann, *The Collection of the Sumerian Temple Hymns* (Locust Valley: J. J. Augustin, 1969) 17.

[225] Translation by T. Jacobsen, *The Harps that Once . . . , Sumerian Poetry in Translation* (New Haven: Yale University Press, 1987) 154. Transcription by Benito, 22.

[226] Benito, 22. Benito translates: "Enki, in the deep *Engur* where water flows, into whose midst no god can see" (Benito, 35).

[227] Kramer and Maier, *Myths of Enki*, 50. Transcription by Benito, 101.

[228] Translation by Benito, 129.

[229] Kramer and Maier, *Myths of Enki*, 43, 48.

[230] Kramer and Maier, *Myths of Enki*, 55, 221, n. 125. The Sumerian reads:

> line 417: ^{d}*nanše-nin-en-e u$_5$*(!)-*kù-ga gìr-ni-šè ba-šub*
> line 418: *enku-ab-ba-ka ḫé-em*
> line 419: *ku$_6$-níg-dug nig-ku$_7$-ku$_7$*
> line 420: *a-a-ni-*^{d}*en-líl-ra nibru*^{ki} *-šè s[u]ḫu-mu-na-ra-bu-i*
> (Benito, 110).

[231] Van Buren, 75. Cf. 79 concerning the cylinder seal.

[232] Kramer and Maier, *Myths of Enki*, 72.

[233] Kramer and Maier, *Myths of Enki*, 80, 230.

[234] Kramer and Maier, *Myths of Enki*, 82, 231. Lines 182 and 183 read:

> *ú-KU-engur-ra ù-mu-un nu-um-te*
> *mušen-du-kur-ùr-ra ù-mu-un nu-um-te*

[235] Van Buren, 77.

236   Van Buren, 121.

237   Van Buren, 137.

238   Van Buren, 137.

239   Kramer and Maier, *Myths of Enki*, 87, 235, n. 31.

240   See H. Frankfort, *Cylinder Seals: A Documentary Essay on the Art and Religion of the Ancient Near East* (London: Macmillan Publishing Company, 1939) Plate XIXa, cf. 107. He assumes a negative connection between Enki and Imdugud: "The bird was shown in the hands of Ea . . . to indicate that the capture and conviction of the enemy had preceded the god's liberation" (134). Frankfort misidentifies the liberated god as Ea's son Marduk, rather than the sun-god Utu or Samas. Van Buren sees Enki's extended right hand as a sign of exhortation (Van Buren, 27), adding that "Ea, surrounded by his streams, appears to hasten forward to aid with his counsels and propitious spells, just as he did when Marduk went forth against Tiamat" (Van Buren, 29). Van Buren sees the scene as depicting the myth of the Anzu-bird and identifies the rising god as Adad (Van Buren, 29). Kramer and Maier essentially agree, though they identify the rising god as Ninurta, based on *UET* 6, no. 2 ("Ninurta's Pride and Punishment" [Kramer and Maier, *Myths of Enki*, 122]). A different interpretation is offered by P. Amiet. Skeptical of previous attempts to identify a *particular* myth depicted in the cylinder, Amiet suggests the bird is a descending eagle representing a "hostile force" in the context of a great epiphany of nature in early spring (P. Amiet, "The Mythological Repertory in Cylinder Seals of the Agade Period [c. 2335-2155]," in *Ancient Art in Seals*, ed. E. Porada (Princeton: Princeton University Press, 1980] 45). Jacobsen identifies the bird with Imdugud, the thunderbird, which signifies the "clouds rising from the waters" (T. Jacobsen, *Treasures of Darkness* [New Haven: Yale University Press, 1976] 94, 111).

241   C. Wilcke, *Das Lugalbandaepos* (Wiesbaden: Otto Harrassowitz, 1969) 92.

242   Jacobsen, *Harps*, 323. The lines are misidentified as lines 30 and 29.

243   A. Diemel, *Sumerisch-Akkadisches Glossar* (Rome: Verlag des Päpstl. Bibelinstituts, 1934) 1.

244   Jacobsen, *Treasures*, 111.

245   S. N. Kramer, *Sumerian Mythology* (New York: Harper and Row Publishers, 1961) 114, n. 41.

246   W. G. Lambert and A. R. Millard, *Atra-Hasis: The Babylonian Story of the Flood* (Oxford: Clarendon Press, 1969) 88-89.

247   R. C. Thompson, *The Epic of Gilgamesh: Text, Transliteration and Notes* (Oxford: Clarendon Press, 1930) 61.

248   Jacobsen, *Harps*, 393, n. 24.

249   A. Falkenstein, *Sumerische Götterlieder* (Heidelberg: Carl Winter, 1959) 17, 23.

250   Kramer, *Sumerian Mythology*, 49-50.

251   Jacobsen, *Treasures of Darkness*, 99.

252   W. W. Hallo. and W. L. Moran, "The First Tablet of the SB Recension of the Anzu Myth," *JCS* 31 (1979) 86.

253   Hallo and Moran, "The First Tablet," 80.

254   Hallo and Moran take the verb from *erû* to include both the waters and the Earth as subjects, although the verb itself is singular ("The First Tablet," 80). Dalley suggests a separate verb lost at the end of the first line: "Surely water of the spate [begot Anzu]" (*Myths from Mesopotamia* (Oxford: Oxford University Press, 1989) 206.

In either case, it is clear that both the waters and the earth contributed to Anzu's creation.

255 S. G. F. Brandon, *Creation Legends of the Ancient Near East* (London: Hodder and Stoughton, 1963) 16.

256 S. Morenz, *Egyptian Religion*, trans. A. E. Keep (Ithaca: Cornell University Press, 1973) 171.

257 M. S. Holmberg, *The God Ptah* (Lund: CWK Gleerup, 1946); V. A. Tobin, *Theological Principles of Egyptian Religion* (AUSTR 59; New York: Peter Lang, 1989); Morenz, 172; see *ANET* 4.

258 Brandon, 14-26.

259 Translation by M. Lichtheim, *Ancient Egyptian Literature, Vol. II: The New Kingdom* (Berkeley: University of California, 1976) 198. See *ANET* 11.

260 J. Bergman, "Ancient Egyptian Theogony in a Greek Magical Papyrus," in *Studies in Egyptian Religion* (ed. M. H. van Voss, E. J. Sharpe, R. J. Z. Werblowsky; Leiden: E. J. Brill, 1982) 34.

261 O. Kaiser, *Die mythische Bedeutung des Meeres*, 12; R. Kilian, "Gen. I 2 und die Urgötter," 421; J. P. Allen, *Genesis in Egypt: The Philosophy of Ancient Egyptian Creation Accounts* (YES 2; New Haven: Yale University Press, 1988) 4.

262 Morenz, 176. Of note is Morenz's designation of the Hermopolis cosmogony as evolutionary and scientific as opposed to creative and theological (Morenz, 176-84).

263 Kaiser, 12.

264 Morenz, 172.

265 Tobin, 60.

266 Allen, *Genesis in Egypt*, 13.

267 E.g., the so-called *Instruction for King Meri-ka-re* (Brandon, 56-57).

268 Brandon, 63.

269 See discussion in Morenz, 174-77; Kilian, 421-23; Kaiser, 15-17; Tobin, 61-62.

270 Kaiser, 17, 116-18.

271 That is not to say that Egyptian literature did not have its inimical water monsters. See line 131 of the *Instruction to King Merikare* (ninth/tenth Dynasty?):

> He made sky and earth for their sake,
> He subdued the water monster (*snk n mw*),
> He made breath for their noses to live.
> (Translation by Lichtheim, *AEL*, vol. I, 106)

(See J. K. Hoffmeier, "Some Thoughts on Genesis 1 and 2 and Egyptian Cosmology," *JANES* 13 [1983] 39-49). In addition, Kaiser mentions Proverb 11:13 from the Hearst Papyrus (28th Dynasty), in which reference is made to the sea's threatening nature.

> So wie Seth das Meer besprochen hat,
> So bespricht Seth auch dich,
> Du Krankheit der Asiaten.
> (Kaiser, 37)

Kaiser attributes this infrequent negative view of the sea in Egyptian mythology to Ugaritic influence (Kaiser, 36-38).

272 In the Eighteenth Dynasty version of the *Book of the Dead*, Atum makes the following threat:

I shall destroy all that I have made, and this land will return to Nun, into the floodwaters, as (in) its first state (*ANET* 9).

Brandon also mentions an inscription from the time of Pharaoh Osorkon III that refers to Nun's covering the land (Brandon, 16). See *ANET* 10-11.

[273] See K. Sethe, who sees Amun's creative activity stirring the waters as a parallel to the *rûaḥ ʾĕlōhîm* in Gen 1:2 (*Amun und die Acht Urgötter von Hermopolis* [APAW 4; Berlin: Verlag der Akademie der Wissenschaften, 1929] 77).

[274] See the Theban creation account in *ANET* 8.

[275] Lichtheim, *AEL*, 2, 154.

[276] For translation see M. Lichtheim, *Ancient Egyptian Literature, Vol. III: The Late Period* (Berkeley: University of California, 1980) 110, 111-15.

[277] Lichtheim, *AEL*, 2, 112.

[278] Lichtheim, *AEL*, 2, 112.

[279] B. L. Begelsbacher-Fischer, *Untersuchungen zur Götterwelt des Alten Reiches im Spiegel der Privategräber der IV. und V. Dynastie* (OBO 37; Freiburg: Universitätsverlag, 1981) 42.

[280] See C. Gordon ("Khnum and El," *SH* 28 [1982] 203-14), who discerns parallels between the creation of *ʾādām* in Gen 2 and Khnum's modeling of human beings from clay. See also Morenz, 161, 183-84. See texts: Two Hymns to the Sun-God (Lichtheim, *AEL*, 2, 87); "Three Tales of Wonder" (Lichtheim, *AEL*, 1, 220-21); "The Admonitions of Ipuwer" (Lichtheim, *AEL*, 1, 151, 154); "Stela of Sehetep-Ib-Re" (Lichtheim, *AEL*, 1, 128); "The Instruction of Amenemope," chapter 9 (Lichtheim, *AEL*, 2, 154); "The Two Brothers" (Lichtheim, *AEL*, 2, 207); "Statue Inscription of Djedkhonsefankh" (Lichtheim, *AEL*, 3, 15).

[281] LRL No. 15. Translation by E. F. Wente, *Letters from Ancient Egypt* (WAW 1; Atlanta: Scholars Press, 1990) 197.

[282] See discussion in Kaiser, 29.

[283] Lichtheim, *AEL*, 1, 109. Cf. the "Famine Stela" (96-100). Also of note is Hapy's connection with both fish and birds, as evident in an inscription from the Middle Kingdom:

> Friend of Geb, lord of Nepri,
> Promoter of the arts of Ptah.
> Lord of the fishes,
> He makes fowl stream south,
> No bird falling down from heat.
> Maker of barley, creator of emmer,
> He lets the temples celebrate.
> . . .
> Birds will not come down to deserts.
>
> (Lichtheim, *AEL*, 1, 206, 208)

[284] See discussion in J. D. Currid, "An Examination of the Egyptian Background of the Genesis Cosmogony," *BZ* 35 (1991) 13.

[285] Currid, 13.

[286] E.g., Hoffmeier, 39-49; Currid, 3-17.

[287] In addition to the work cited above is his more recent work *Religion and Philosophy in Ancient Egypt* (YES 3; New Haven: Yale University Press, 1989).

[288] Allen, *Genesis in Egypt*, 46. Lichtheim, drawing from the conclusions of H. Junker (*Die Götterlehre von Memphis* [APAW 23; Berlin: Verlag der Akademie der Wissenschaften, 1-77] 1940), considers the Shabaka stone a "theological treatise" because of its "inner unity and cohesion" (*AEL*, 1, 51).

[289] J. Day makes the tentative claim that the Canaanites "may have associated the creation of the world with Baal's victory over the dragon and the sea" (Day, 17). However, as P. E. Dion has pointed out:

> There is no positive evidence that those episodes had more to do with creation than CTA 2 iv; as Day himself admits (pp. 17-19), El is more likely creator than Baal.

(P. E. Dion, "YHWH as Storm-god and Sun-god: The Double Legacy of Egypt and Canaan as Reflected in Psalm 104," *ZAW* 103 [1991] 54, n. 41.)

[290] Translations and discussion include *ANET* 60-72, 501-503; Heidel, *The Babylonian Genesis*; Jacobsen, *The Treasures*, 167-191; J. V. O'Brien and W. Major, *In the Beginning: Creation Myths from Ancient Mesopotamia, Israel and Greece* (ASR 11; Chico: Scholars Press, 1982) 9-32; Dalley, 228-77.

[291] Jacobsen, *The Treasures*, 168.

[292] See discussion of these texts in J. Day, 13-16.

[293] For translation and discussion, see H. L. Ginsberg, *ANET* 129-127; A. Caquot, M. Sznycer, and A. Herdner, *Textes Ougaritiques, Tome-I: Mythes et Legends* (LAPO 7; Paris: Editions du Cerf, 1974) 121-221; J. C. L. Gibson, *Canaanite Myths and Legends* (Edinburgh: T. and T. Clark, 1978) 2-8, 37-45; M. D. Coogan, *Stories from Ancient Canaan*, 96-106.

[294] G. May suggests that the verb *gʿr* be translated "roar" rather than "rebuke," in the context of the storm-god conflict with the sea dragon ("Some Cosmic Connotations of *Mayim Rabbîm*, 'Many Waters,'" *JBL* 74 (1955) 17, n. 32).

[295] Dion, 55.

[296] May, "Some Cosmic Connotations of *Mayim Rabbîm*," 10. In correspondence, J. Strong has demonstrated to me May's tendency to overstate his case, since May presupposes that every use of the motif in Ezekiel points to the background of a cosmic battle.

[297] M. Fishbane, "Jeremiah iv 23-26 and Job iii 3-13: A Recovered Use of the Creation Pattern," *VT* 21 (1971) 160.

[298] The parallelism suggests that *nēd* be amended to *nōd* from *nōʾd* (KB 584).

[299] May, "Some Cosmic Connotations of *Mayim Rabbîm*," 10.

[300] For a historical interpretation, see J. H. Hayes and S. A. Irvine, *Isaiah, the Eighth-Century Prophet: His Times and His Preaching* (Nashville: Abingdon, 1987) 323.

[301] P. Machinist, "Assyria and Its Image in the First Isaiah," *JAOS* 103 (1983) 727.

[302] The textual emendation suggested in the *BHS* transposes the first two words to *lětitô qôl*. However, good sense can be made in the present order.

6

Structure and Ideology of the VorLXX and the MT of Gen 1:1–2:3

Introduction

Having established the respective formal and thematic structures of the VorLXX and the MT of Gen 1:1–2:3 as well as the formative traditions that lie behind the differing roles the waters assume in the texts, one can now begin to examine the ideological implications of the creation texts. In the first chapter, ideology was generally defined as the structure of values reflected in a particular text. Lotman and Uspensky point out that ideology is essentially a cultural enterprise:

> The fundamental task of culture is in structurally organizing the world around man. Culture is the generator of structuredness, and in this way it creates a social sphere around man which, like the biosphere, makes life possible.[1]

A formulated cosmogony is an explicit indicator of the way in which the physical/social world may be structured by a particular culture. A cosmogony, then, is as prescriptive as it is descriptive of the natural and social order. Consequently, two questions related to the ideological examination of cosmogony need to be posed for the VorLXX and the MT: 1) How is the cosmic/social world structured? and 2) Why is it structured in this way?

STRUCTURE AND IDEOLOGY IN THE VorLXX OF GEN 1:1–2:3

As noted above, particular in cosmogonic texts, structure and ideology are inextricably tied together. From a methdological standpoint, then, the structure of such texts must be carefully examined before one can make any claims about the social values inherent in the prescribed structure.

Structure in the VorLXX of Gen 1:1–2:3 and the Priestly Work

To recapitulate, the structure of the VorLXX, like that of the LXX, is marked by symmetry and balance, as evident in the text's generally consistent use of such structural components as the divine command, the transition formula, the fulfillment report, and the approbation formula. Such structural balance thereby treats the earth and the waters as co-equals in the creative process: Both are exhorted to create (that is, with jussive commands confirmed by the transition marker) and are depicted as active in varying degrees in the fulfillment reports. Their respective functions and domains are depicted as entirely separate: The earth's domain is separate from that of the waters, and the earth's "creations" (plants and land animals) are indigenous to that domain. Similarly, the domain of the (lower) waters includes both water and the atmosphere or the *Diesseits* of the heavens (1:7 and 1:20).

Both the earth and the waters function as separate but equally active agents in collaboration with *ʾĕlōhîm* in the construction of the cosmos. This structured balance of activity is broken by the revisionist activity evident in the text preserved by the Masoretes.

Given the priority of the VorLXX of Gen 1:1–2:3, it is likely that the VorLXX more accurately preserves P's cosmogony than the MT, *at least in terms of the balanced structure it exhibits*. Thus in dealing with exegetical matters related to priestly work as a whole, such as P's literary structure or communicative intent, it is best to select the cosmogonic text of the VorLXX rather than the text of the MT for study. In order to gain a clearer picture of the implied social structure undergirding the cosmogony in the VorLXX, one must take into account the way in which the priestly writer has presented his structured social world within the priestly literary corpus.

In his positive analysis of structure in social theory, Callinicos makes the general observation that "structures figure ineliminably in the explanation of social events."[2] At the most general level, a social structure consists of inter-related subjects and agents and a structure that provides a framework for action.[3] By such criteria, the priestly cosmogonic account qualifies as depicting in some sense a social structure: God assumes the role as the "total" subject, the earth and the waters are depicted as agents and occasionally subjects in the process of creation, and the remaining objects of creation are commanded to be agents in the maintenance of order, all within a rigorously consistent structure.

Furthermore, the structure of Gen 1:1–2:3 (in either the VorLXX or MT) closely parallels other sections in the priestly literary corpus that presuppose structured social relations. J. Blenkinsopp has observed recurrent formulaic expressions in P that indicate "a) the successful completion of a work, and b) the execution of a command given directly or indirectly by God."[4] The usage of these formulaic expressions, Blenkinsopp notes, points to P's demarcation of three prominent points in the narrative: the creation of the world (the conclusion formula in Gen 2:1, 2), the construction of the sanctuary (the conclusion formula in Ex 39:32; 40:33), and the establishment of the sanctuary in the land with the land's division between the tribes (the conclusion formula in Josh 19:51).[5]

In an attempt to discern even closer parallels, Kearney has noted that P's instructions concerning the construction of the sanctuary in Exodus 25-31 occur in seven divine speeches,[6] each correlating with a day of creation in Gen 1:1–2:3. Indeed, a comparison between creation and the construction of the sanctuary goes back as early as Jewish midrash.[7] However, in few instances is such correspondence explicitly evident in the text. Kearney, for example, finds in the fourth speech to Moses (Exod 30:22-33), in which God gives instruction for the manufacture and use of anointing oil, a correlation with the fourth day of creation. He finds the connection in Psalm 89, which proclaims God's anointing of David (v 21), whose "throne shall be like the sun before me, like the moon which remains forever" (v 37). As Levenson has pointed out, many of Kearney's alleged correlations are overstated.[8]

The best material, however, for a structural comparison appears to be between the account describing the construction of the sanctuary (Exodus 35-40) and the priestly cosmogony. As Janowski observes, the erection of the sanctuary at Sinai represents the high point and goal of the priestly historiography.[9]

Exodus 35-40 opens with Moses' declaring to the congregation of Israel (ʿădat bĕnê yiśrāʾēl) the divine commandment to observe the sabbath (35:2). Exod 35:1-19 serves as a summary of the previous seven divine speeches in Exod 25-31, in which the bĕnê yiśrāʾēl are commanded with jussives, with the exception of the first command (qĕḥû, v 5).

The fulfillment of the seven commands of Exodus 25-31 as summarized in 35:1-19 begins in 35:20: The ʾēdāh ("congregation") departs and returns with the necessary material, thereby fulfilling the command in 25:1-7. The priestly writer, however, makes it clear that those who return consist only of those whose "spirit moved them" (nādĕbāh rûḥô ʾōtô, 35:21). Similarly, the craftsman Bezalel, son of Uri, who is to supervise the construction along with his assistant Oholiab, is endowed with the spirit of God (rûaḥ ʾĕlōhîm, 35:30, see 31:2). Thus, Bezalel and Oholiab are "endowed with the ability to give instructions to others, which is a divinely bestowed gift."[10]

Once the necessary material is brought, the construction of the tabernacle is described in Exod 36:8–39:31. Throughout the elaborate description, the verb ʿśh predominates for the most part, with Bezalel as its subject. However, 36:8 (kol ḥăkam lēb) and 39:1-30 interchange singular and plural forms of the verb, the latter presumably referring to bĕnê yiśrāʾēl of 39:32. Interspersed throughout the fulfillment report, most notably in chapter 39, is the clause kāʾăšer ṣiwwāh YHWH ʾet mōšeh ("just as YHWH had commanded Moses"), which is placed after the fulfillment sections and functions to connect the process of construction with the previous divine commands, thereby confirming the fulfillment. The clause occurs seven times in the MT, whereas the LXX has it occurring ten times (Exodus 36 to 39:11). In either case, the connection between divine word and human fulfillment is tightened by this formula, similar to the way in which the transition formula operates in Genesis 1.

The conclusion of fulfillment in Exod 39:32 mirrors the conclusion in Gen 2:1-2.[11]

> wattēkel kol ʿăbodāt miškan ʾōhel môʿēd
>
> So all the work on the tabernacle of the tent of meeting was completed.

Exod 39:32b and 42 provide the final fulfillment-confirming formulae (wayyaʿăśû . . . kāʾăšer [or kĕkōl ʾăšer] ṣiwwāh YHWH ʾet mōšeh kēn ʾāśû). Cast similarly to the final approbation formula in Gen 1:31, Exod 39:43 depicts Moses in a role similar to that of ʾĕlōhîm in the final inspection:

> wayyarʾ mōšeh ʾet kol hammĕlāʾkāh wĕhinnēh ʿaśû ʾōtāh kāʾăšer ṣiwwāh YHWH kēn ʿaśû waybārek ʾotām mōšeh
>
> And Moses saw all the work and, indeed, they had done it just as Yahweh had commanded, so they had done it. And Moses blessed them.

Instead of declaring the creation as *ṭôb* (as in Gen 1:31),[12] Moses blesses the workers, the people of Israel. Moses' blessing parallels God's blessing of the seventh day in Gen 2:3.[13]

The structural elements of Exodus 40, which describes the erection of the tabernacle, also echo the priestly cosmogony. Verses 1-15 contain a lengthy divine command issued to Moses, followed by a bona fide transition formula (40:16):

> *wayyaʿaś mōšeh kĕkōl ʾăšer ṣiwwāh YHWH ʾōtô kēn ʿāśāh*

> And Moses did according to everything that Yahweh commanded him; so he did (as follows).

One can easily discern the double duty of the particle *kēn*. In its immediate context, it clearly refers to the phrase *kĕkōl . . . ʾōtô*, which in turn points to the divine speech in 40:1-15. On the other hand, the fact that Moses follows the divine instructions step by step indicates the transitional function of *kēn ʿāśāh* in its wider context and thereby points to the fulfillment in 40:17-33. However, not all the instructions are carried out by Moses in chapter 40. The instructions outlining the anointing of the tabernacle and the priests in vv 9-15 remain unfulfilled until Leviticus 8. Thus the statement of conclusion in 40:33b, which parallels Gen 2:2,[14] seems premature:

> *waykal mōšeh ʾet hammĕlāʾkāh*

> Thus Moses finished the work.

Yet the sentence fully intends to conclude the section, for the following material describes the habitation of Yahweh's *kābôd*.

Another important feature of the fulfillment report is the frequent occurrence of the execution formula *kāʾăšer ṣiwwāh YHWH ʾet mōšeh* in Exod 40:17-33. The formula confirms every step in the process as fulfilled in exact accordance with the divine instructions. The phrase occurs seven times in the MT, but only five times in the LXX. In any case, the overall structure of Exodus 40 most closely resembles the general structure of Gen 1:1–2:1, except that the divine commands and the fulfillments appear in separate sections and that anything resembling an approbation formula is absent. Instead, approval appears to be implicitly conveyed by the entry of the divine *kābôd*.

In short, the account concerning the construction and erection of the tabernacle exhibits structural features that strongly resemble those used in the creation account of Gen 1:1–2:3. As Levenson points out:

> The function of these correspondences is to underscore the depiction of the sanctuary as a world, that is, an ordered, supportive, and obedient environment, and the depiction of the world as a sanctuary, that is, a place in which the reign of God is visible and unchallenged, and his holiness is palpable, unthreatened, and pervasive.[15]

Levenson focuses specifically on the finished products, namely the cosmos and the tabernacle, in his comparison. However, another valid point of comparison is the *process* by which the construction is described. Indeed, the formulaic structures are employed precisely to illustrate the orderly and methodical process of construction; hence, any comparative examination that focuses exclusively on the similarities of the *finished* products (the cosmos and the tabernacle) is too narrow.

One way of comparing the account of the construction of the cosmos with that of the sanctuary is to examine the varying levels of creative agency expressed in both accounts. In P's cosmogony, the hierarchy of creative activity evident in Gen 1:1–2:3 of the VorLXX can be described in descending order:

1. God: commander and creator
2. Earth and waters: collaborative creative agents
3. Products:
   a) light, celestial luminaries, vegetation, firmament, etc.
   b) animals and human beings

The earth and the waters are considered second only to God in creative agency, since they themselves are not depicted as created in Genesis 1 and are portrayed as active contributors to the creative process. The rest of creation is clearly considered the product in P's cosmogony. However, even the *created* order remains a *creating* order: Animals and human beings are commanded to procreate, and the other objects of creation, though devoid of life (*nepeš*), maintain certain established functions.

The situation is more complex in Exod 35–40. Yahweh remains clearly at the head of the hierarchy of construction by issuing specific commands to Moses; however, the deity is never directly involved in the actual creation. That role is given to the *běnê yiśrāʾēl*, Bezalel, and Oholiab.[16] In varying degrees, these three agents take on the roles of fulfilling the commands. Bezalel, endowed with the *rûaḥ ʾělōhîm*, assumes in part a divine role as creative agent: His most common task is to "make" (*ʿśh*). Similarly, the *běnê yiśrāʾēl*, specifically those of a "generous heart" (*nědîb libbô*, 35:5), are involved in the process, though clearly under the supervision of Bezalel.

The *běnê yiśrā'ēl* are described in complementary fashion: Their hearts are "stirred" or are willing (*nědîb libbô*, 35:5; *nědîb lēb*, 35:22), their "spirit incites them" (*nāděbāh rûḥô 'ōtô*, 35:21), and they are able (*ḥăkām lēb*, 35:10; 36:1,8; *hakmat lēb běyādeyhā*; 35:25). The women are singled out as ones especially able to spin thread (35:25-26) and therefore are most suitable in providing fine linen for the tabernacle. Thus the *běnê yiśrā'ēl* represent the willing and able work force in the construction program. Together with Bezalel and Oholiab, they are the "creators" of the tabernacle. Moses, too, as the deliverer of instructions assumes a "divine" role, especially as the one who "sees" the completed work and blesses the workers (39:43). The tabernacle and its components are clearly the objects of the construction process. A relationship of hierarchy can be drawn up as follows:

1. Yahweh: commander
2. Moses: deliverer of commands, inspector, blesser
3. Bezalel: creator (*'śh*), supervisor
4. *běnê yiśrā'ēl*: collaborative creative agents
5. Products: the tabernacle and its furnishings

Bezalel (with Oholiab) and the *běnê yiśrā'ēl* are clearly cast in the role of co-creators, with the *běnê yiśrā'ēl* placed in a subordinate role under Bezalel. Consequently, the roles of God, Moses, and Bezalel can be grouped together, since all are given divine attributes and together represent the composite role assumed by *'ělōhîm* in Gen 1:1–2:3. The role of the *běnê yiśrā'ēl*, on the other hand, most closely resembles the roles that the earth and the waters are assigned in cosmogony: They contribute actively in the creative process, yet clearly in a subordinate position.

In conclusion, a comparison with the priestly account of the construction of the tabernacle sets in relief the social dimension inherent in VorLxx of Genesis 1. As P's description of the construction of the tabernacle in Exodus is inherently a social process whereby a social hierarchy ranging from God and Moses to the *běnê yiśrā'ēl* is employed as the means for creating the final product, so it is also with the priestly cosmogony.

This social dimension of the priestly cosmogony is most evident in the respective roles of the earth and the waters in relation to God. The earth and the waters are treated as active creators in Genesis 1 and work in collaboration with God. Hence, each bears a social function in relation to *'ělōhîm*. Like the *běnê yiśrā'ēl*, the waters' and the earth's respective contributions in the process are made in the context of service. It has been noted earlier that the etymological eloquence characteristic of the divine commands addressed to the waters and the earth have the effect of underscoring their respective abilities in the formation of products suitable for the divine creative scheme.[17] Similarly, the Exodus account describes Bezalel and the *běnê yiśrāʾēl* as fully capable of constructing the furnishings suitable for the tabernacle. As M. Welker has recently pointed out with respect to the creation account:

> The creature's own activity is not only the result and consequence of God's action; it goes along with God's action, and at times it is practically interchangeable with God's action.[18]

This sense of creaturely cooperation and connectedness with the creator is particularly true of the earth and the waters. The equal treatment given to both agents is descriptive of a social process whose result depends upon a communal effort between *ʾĕlōhîm* and the elements. God is not set *over and against* the created order; rather God is portrayed as acting fundamentally *with* the created and creating order.

In summary, a comparison of the priestly cosmogony in Genesis 1 (as preserved in the VorLXX) and the account of the sanctuary's construction in Exodus 35-40 reveal structural similarities that are utilized to describe the inherently social process of creating. In addition, the active roles played out within the respective accounts as, for example, the *běnê yiśrāʾēl*, on the one hand, and the earth and the waters, on the other, also find some correspondence. Furthermore, both Gen 1:1–2:3 and Exodus 35-40 describe the realization of the respective end products, the cosmos and the tabernacle, as a methodical process in which any resistance or opposition is entirely absent.

The Ideology and Rational Tenor of P's Cosmogony in the VorLXX

The structure of Gen 1:2–2:3 in the VorLXX is cast with symmetrical precision, both formally and thematically. This structural consistency is matched by a rational tenor with which the text outlines the cosmogonic process as an orderly unity. The elements of creation either participate or are produced in perfect harmony with the divine commands; there is no hint of opposition in the created order. A good point of comparison is the treatment of the *tannînim* in Gen 1:21 and *tnn* in the Ugaritic text *CTA* 3.iiiD. 34-39, in which the latter is considered the mythological opponent of Baal and Anat:

What enemy rises against Baal?
What foe against the rider on the clouds?
Did I not destroy El's beloved Yam?
Did I not bring to an end Nahar the great god?
Was not the dragon (*tnn*) captured (and) vanquished?
I destroyed the slithering serpent,
the tyrant with seven heads.[19]

By sheer contrast, Gen 1:21 relegates the *tannînim haggedōlîm* with the other sea-creatures in the same creative moment. Their curious absence in the divine command (v 20) also points to a matter-of-fact regard to their creation. The same can be said of the treatment of *tĕhôm* in 1:2. Even if a linguistic connection between *tĕhôm* and Tiamat were granted, which is unlikely, *tĕhôm* is so remote in function that "any possible relationship is blurred beyond recognition."[20]

It has been widely considered that the priestly account of creation represents a demythologized cosmogony. It is the conclusion of this subsection that Genesis 1, as presented in the VorLxx, exhibits certain tendencies that qualify its account as a rationally oriented and empirically based treatise on creation as opposed to an intuitive, mythopoeic account.

B. W. Anderson, in his popular introduction to the Old Testament, describes the priestly cosmogony in the following way:

> The majestic cadences of Priestly prose, which verge on poetry, evoke a sense of wonder before the mystery and marvel of the creation. . . . Anyone who is looking for a scientific account of the origin of the world can find plenty of discrepancies in the Priestly story. . . . The Priestly account is not a treatise on scientific origins. Here the poetry of faith speaks of something which lies behind or beyond human experience and scientific inquiry.[21]

For Anderson, P's cosmogony is thoroughly "mythopoeic":

> As Gunkel observed in his monumental study, there are traces of the mythopoeic language of creation in this story, even though there is no *Chaoskampf*. . . . In the mythopoeic portrayal, chaos is not destroyed but is only placed within bounds. . . . The cosmos is not eternal and self-perpetuating, as Greek philosophers maintained; it is sustained in being by the Creator. . . . Mythopoeic language cannot be converted into scientific language any more than poetry can be reduced to prose. . . . Mythopoeic language provides a different approach to reality via the faculty of poetic intuition or imagination.[22]

The term "mythopoeic" is invoked by Anderson and others to classify a poetic form of ancient Near Eastern literature and isolate it from the language and conceptions of modern science. Clearly, modern science and priestly cosmogony cannot be reconciled in either content or form. However, Anderson's description wants to do more than simply acknowledge the irreconcilable differences between ancient and modern conceptions of the cosmos.

As cited above, Anderson drives a wedge between poetry or that which is "verging on poetry" and prose, as if poetic form automatically casts poetic literature into an isolated and unique world of meaning. First, from a purely formal standpoint P's account is not poetic, at least not in the way that prophetic texts are poetic. Indeed, the priestly prose account of the construction of the tabernacle (Exodus 35-40) is similar in language to Genesis 1. Secondly, Bakhtin's indictment against the Russian Formalists regarding the nature of meaningful discourse reveals that Anderson's formalistic distinction between poetry and prose entails an artificial separation of form and content. Granted, poetry and "scientific language" have different formal features, and one cannot formally be converted into the other, as Anderson correctly implies. However, it does not necessarily follow that mythopoeic language, by virtue of its form, however defined, conveys an entirely "different approach to reality" that thereby plays no part in the social meaning generated by, for instance, practical language.[23] In other words, poetic language is not made up of unique linguistic forms employed to unique representational ends.

The fact that P's cosmogony is not a product of *modern* science does not thereby make P's treatment purely intuitive or imaginative, as Anderson characterizes Genesis 1. Furthermore, Anderson's false characterization of the "Greek philosophers" (clearly, he is thinking only of Aristotelean cosmology) contributes to the misconception that P's cosmogony is "mythopoeic." To the contrary, one can readily observe certain features of Genesis 1 (of the VorLXX) that would count against such a characterization.

Unity and Generalization

Guthrie notes that a characteristic mark of early Greek philosophy is its tendency towards generalization.[24] Similarly, Sambursky regards simplicity as the foremost characteristic of early science, which he credits the Greeks as discovering. After discussing Thales, Sambursky states:

We have here before us an application of the scientific principle that a maximum of phenomena should be explained by a minimum of hypotheses. It may be regarded as a criterion of the simplicity of a theory if it succeeds in asserting the largest possible number of facts from the smallest number of assumptions. Every step in that direction can be taken as a scientific progress.[25]

In other words, the early Greek philosophical enterprise was characterized by a concern to generalize and simplify the understanding of the processes by which the natural world with its innumerably diverse phenomena came into being.

Such an observation does not thereby qualify the Genesis 1 text as early scientific literature. Clearly, unlike the Pre-Socratic philosophers, there is no single universal natural substance underlying the cosmos according to P. However, one can see Anderson's sharp demarcation between Greek philosophy and P's cosmogony begin to break down when one notes that generalization and unity typical of early Greek philosophical cosmogonies are also traits characteristic of Genesis 1. The tendency towards generalization is characteristic of the priestly cosmogonic process, namely in the concentrated movement from divine word to creative act, with ʾĕlōhîm serving as the ultimate archē or source of all creative activity. Every product of creation is embedded in this well-honed matrix of movement from command to fulfillment.

In addition, there is a unity of movement from the general to the particular in the cosmogonic sweep.[26] On the one hand, light is created on the first day, thereby providing the fundamental differentiation of light from darkness (Gen 1:3-4). On the other hand, God creates the celestial luminaries that separate day and night (Gen 1:14-18). Similarly, the waters on the second day-section collect themselves into seas, thereby allowing the land to appear. On the fifth day, the waters help produce the particular animals of both the sea and air, which are then commanded to procreate.

The earth produces two classes of vegetation on the third day and helps form three varieties of land animals on the sixth. The divine speech in 1:28-30 revels in the sheer diversity of living forms. Hence a general movement towards increasing complexity is discernible in the process, as well as a movement from constituent bases (light, water, and green earth) to the particular "social" forms they help produce and sustain. Both human beings and land animals, for instance, are entirely dependent upon the vegetation that the earth produces on the third day. The relationship between general light and particular lights is not explicitly stated, but it is of interest to note that 1) the particular lights are given the same function as that of light in general (vv 4 and 18), and 2) two of these particular lights are to fulfill the social function of ruling (*mšl*) and to ensure the regularity of "appointed times."

All in all, in the VorLxx of Gen 1:1–2:3, generalization and simplicity characterize P's cosmogony through 1) its balanced structure in the interplay between word and event, 2) its highly structured thematic movement,[27] and 3) the movement from the general to the particular in content. These characteristics set the priestly cosmogony of Genesis 1 in sharp contrast to the cosmogonies of the ancient Near East.

Stability and Regularity

The structural balance of Genesis 1 stresses the stability and regularity of creation. Stability and regularity are also the hallmarks of the cosmogony of Plato's *Timaeus*[28] and Aristotle's cosmological descriptions of the natural world.[29] For the Pre-Socratics, cosmic stability was cast in terms of the irreducibility of one substance or the dynamic equilibrium of several elements. For P, stability is described in terms of the structured process by which creation is established, coupled with a lack of conflict or tension in P's description.

The perpetual regularity of cyclical time is depicted by Aristotle in the eternal circular motion of the celestial spheres.[30] For Plato, the movement of the celestial bodies initiates and maintains time.[31] In Genesis 1 the alternation between night and day consistently looms in the background of every creative event, as well as provides the text's overall form. In addition, stress is placed upon the regularity of the celestial bodies in terms of the larger cycles of seasons and years (1:14). For P, Plato, and Aristotle, clockwork is the art of cosmological maintenance.

God and the Elements

The VorLxx presents the priestly account as a structured complex of creations in which each creative act functions as an indispensable part of the cosmos. P's creation is a system of self-sustaining yet interdependent parts, and this interdependence is most evident in terms of the living, creative qualities attributed to the earth and the waters. The waters, for instance, allow the earth to emerge. Both the earth and the waters are instrumental in producing living creatures that are related to each other hierarchically.

Similarly, in early Greek philosophy the cosmological substances are often, to use the technical term, *hylozoistic*.[32] They have a life of their own, as it were, since they are capable of movement and are endowed with generative power. Though one may see indirect mythological roots, the attribution of life to the elements or to the cosmos as a whole in Greek philosophical thought depicts the orderly and dynamic nature of the cosmos.

Like many of the Greek philosophical cosmogonies, there are no inert substances in the priestly cosmogony. Earth, water, and light are active agents in function (light and the celestial luminaries), if not in creative action (earth and the waters).[33] They are interdependent agents whose active potentials are actualized at the behest of God's commands. Is such a conceptualization best explained as a mythological remnant of a "demythologized" account of creation? To the contrary, the hylozoistic qualities of these agents are inextricably tied to the rational tenor of the account, which describes the dynamic, "social" nature of the cosmos. These agents in no way represent a threat to God's sovereignty over the creative process; rather, only cooperation and harmony characterize their respective roles. In common with the Greek philosophical treatment of cosmic origins, one could say that light, earth, and water are treated as active elements.[34]

Empirical Cosmogony: Differentiation and Continuity

Genesis 1 and Aristotle share a common empirical approach to nature, namely to present systematically the observable variety of natural phenomena in terms of differentiated categories and species.[35] Such an approach is evident in P's frequent use of the technical term *mîn*, denoting species or genus.[36] The priestly writer clearly recognized the differentiated zoological and botanical classes in nature. Indeed, such empirical knowledge was a mark of wisdom in ancient Israel.[37]

On a broader level, Genesis 1 presents a *scala naturae*, ranging from plants to human beings, with the latter at the apex of this structured evolutionary-like movement. Human beings remain separate from the rest of the created life-forms in that they are not distinguished by kind (*lĕmînēhû*), that is, by types classifed under mutually common characteristics; instead, human beings are set apart by their shared characteristic with the divine (*bĕṣelem ʾĕlōhîm*, 1:27). In both the VorLXX and MT the creation of human beings is considered the pinnacle of the created order within a continuum of created life forms. In short, the priestly account presents the created order in terms of diversity and continuity. As S.

Talmon observes, the account in Genesis 1 "reads altogether like an ancient treatise which conceives of the universe as one comprehensive whole, made up in orderly fashion of clearly defined categories."[38] An appreciation of the natural world's differentiation within a unified whole is the key to both Aristotle's empirical treatises on biology and zoology and P's depiction of nature. In short, contrary to Anderson's view, Genesis 1 exhibits a rational scheme based on empirical observation and deep reflection.[39]

Genre and Intent

The rational tenor of the priestly cosmogonic account, as reflected in the VorLXX, sheds new light on the continuing discussion of the alleged mythological dimensions (or what Anderson calls "traces"[40]) of Gen 1:1–2:3. The issues were already formulated in the debate between Gunkel and Wellhausen over the exegetical status of P's cosmogony. Gunkel's foundational work *Schöpfung und Chaos in Urzeit und Endzeit* (1895) investigated the mythological material contained in the priestly creation account, traditional material that P himself probably did not even understand or was aware of. Gunkel set his approach against that of Wellhausen by ascribing to him the view that P's work was simply a free innovation.[41] Gunkel, for example, objected to Wellhausen's claim that the sabbath was a priestly invention, since the notion of God's resting had to go back to ancient mythological traditions.[42] Also Gunkel considered the term *tĕhôm* of Gen 1:2 as equivalent to the Babylonian goddess Tiamat of the *Enuma Elish*.[43] In short, Gunkel saw in Genesis 1 "eine Reihe nachklingender mythologischer Züge."[44]

Wellhausen, on the other hand, had little interest in tracing the mythological antecedents of P's cosmogony, since from an exegetical standpoint they were irrelevant if they resided outside the consciousness of the author.[45] Such an approach as Gunkel's was useful only for antiquarian reasons. Gunkel, however, viewed such reasons as more than antiquarian,[46] contending that the "History of Religion" approach formed an essential part of the exegetical enterprise.[47] Indeed, Gunkel accused Wellhausen in effect of not being historical enough.[48] Wellhausen's indictment that Gunkel's enterprise was an antiquarian exercise was met by Gunkel's characterization of the Wellhausen school as adhering to the principle *quod non est in actis, non est in mundo*, a sort of "out of sight, out of mind" mentality.[49] Hence Gunkel classified Genesis 1 with the genre of a "faded myth."[50] Wellhausen, on the other hand, claimed that the author of Genesis 1 meant "to give a cosmogonic theory."[51]

> He seeks to deduce things as they are from each other: he asks how they are likely to have issued at first from the primal matter, and the world he has before his eyes in doing this is not a mythical world but the present and ordinary one.[52]

M. Brett perceptively notes that Wellhausen and Gunkel had different exegetical goals: Within the common discipline of historical criticism, Wellhausen focused on authorial intention, while Gunkel sought the underlying traditions behind the text.[53] With regard to authorial intent, Brett observes that most modern treatments of Genesis 1 tend to equivocate between the two enterprises, which he labels motive and communicative intention.[54] According to Brett, motives concern themselves with *why* something is said; communicative intention concerns itself with *what* the author says.[55] Elsewhere, Brett seems to say that what makes a particular literary product unique can only be investigated under the quest for communicative intention,[56] whereas the motive "penetrates below the explicit layer" of intention.[57] The search for motive operates on the level of generality, as for example with regard to mythic function.[58] I would add that Brett's distinction can also be seen in terms of conscious and unconscious purposes: Communicative intention designates what is solely conscious and deliberate; motive, because of its more general application, can operate either on the conscious or unconscious level.

Brett's distinction is helpful, but it does not particularly pertain to Gunkel's enterprise, since Gunkel himself admitted that the wealth of mythological antecedents lay outside the purview of P; therefore, such antecedents could not even be considered motives. A more helpful distinction is offered in Bakhtin's emphasis on the socially determined meaning in discourse, the context of social interaction between author and addressee. In such a context, both communicative intent and motive are considered part and parcel of the social context of the author; whereas Gunkel's program of tracing the mythological antecedents of certain words and concepts treated P's use of them as if they were never spoken at all. In other words, Bakhtin would focus attention upon the individual speaker and particular audience, that is, upon the social context, rather than upon the "chimera of 'the words themselves.'"[59] Similar to Bakhtin, Wellhausen considered the latter irrelevant for interpreting the text.

Later exegetes, however, have continued making such connections along the mythological vein. In his claim that the term *těhôm* is "a remnant of the time long past when the term did denote a mythical personality,"[60] J. Day, like Gunkel, assumes that this is not part of P's *communicative* arsenal.

On the other hand, many exegetes advocate conscious demythologization on the part of the priestly writer. Saggs claims that Genesis 1 contains a polemical reaction against Babylonian ideas, rather than a demythologization of earlier Israelite concepts.[61] Similarly, Hyers observes that Genesis 1 is an outright polemic that "decisively rejected polytheism and its complex mythological accounting of relationships between the various nature deities which such pantheons required."[62] Kapelrud claims that "the author of Genesis 1 was capable of reading out of the rather wild mythological narrative in the *Enuma Elish* certain basic events, possibly one might dare say principles."[63] Kapelrud contends that P's creation story reflects the importance of the sabbath for the exiles as a distinguishing mark of a religious group.[64] In contrast, Lambert highlights only the "mythical ancestry" of Genesis 1, that is, P's direct adaptations of the mythological cosmogonies.[65]

All of these suggestions examine P's account in terms of motive rather than communicative intention. Indeed, much of the scholarly debate concerning the issue of P's relationship to ancient Near Eastern mythology operates on this level. Whether P consciously adapted or reacted against ancient Near Eastern mythological cosmogonies is an issue that probes the motives that underlie the creation account. Such probes can, provisionally at least, be considered secondary when investigating P's particular communicative intention.

For example, if one states that P's creation account is a polemical tract against the polytheistic cosmogonies of the Mesopotamian world, as Hyers and others assume, one could ask why this is not more explicit in the priestly cosmogony. Indeed, unlike, for instance, Deutero-Isaiah, the tone of P's cosmogony does not betray any hint of polemical attack against the Mesopotamian pantheon, as if P had his own copy of *ANET* as a source book that he set out to refute. Rather, P's cosmogony stands aloof from the whole issue. Moreover, identifying a polemical motive, which may indeed be present at some vague level of motive behind P's cosmogony, is woefully insufficient in accounting for the cohesive unity and rational tenor of the text.

On the level of communicative intention, Westermann suggests that P's cosmogony functions as a universalistic overture to Israel's covenantal history.[66] Brett makes the disappointingly vague proposal that P's communicative intention is historiographic.[67] Both in Brett's and Westermann's case, P's cosmogony is treated exclusively on the level of literary intention. Such claims are, of course, legitimate, since P's cosmogony clearly relates to the larger priestly schematization of Israelite history. However, such conclusions are limited to describing only the overall literary context of P's communicative intention without addressing "what P is trying to say" with respect to cosmogony itself.

Given the rational tenor and balanced structure of Genesis 1, the priestly cosmogony is, to say the least, unlike any cosmogonic myth of the ancient Near East. Indeed, in comparison with Greek philosophical treatises, it resembles most closely Plato's *Timaeus*, in which God is cast as the Demiurge who artistically constructs the cosmos from primordial matter, weaving symmetry, structure, and stability into the very fabric of the cosmos.[68] Yet P's empirical approach also has affinities with Diodorus Siculus' cosmogony and Aristotle's empirically based treatises, a watershed in the development of Greek intellectual thought. Finally, P's generalizing *Tendenz* to account for the diversity of the natural world within a *scala naturae* and a particular structure places Gen 1:1-2:3 solidly within the arena of intellectual, even philosophical thought. One cannot deny the level of intellectual sophistication that sets the tone of this cosmogonic account.[69]

Coats suggests that the genre of P's cosmogonic account is a "report," claiming that P's cosmogony "shares with [the genre of] history the intention to record without developing the points of tension characteristic for a plot."[70] Thus Coats correctly observes that Gen 1:1-2:3 is not a story, but rather a chronologically sequenced account. However, the title of "report" takes into account neither the cohesive unity and consistent structure of the text nor the particular qualities that make P's cosmogony a product of rational reflection. Coats's genetic label identifies only the most basic literary level of the unit. Indeed, Coats himself seems to want to say more from a genetic standpoint than what the label itself implies: The Genesis account sets out doctrine (so also Schmidt[71] and von Rad[72]) and is "teaching in the form of history."[73]

In short, "report" is much too vague a label to identify meaningfully any particular body of ancient literature that is characterized by rational thinking based on empirical observation. Despite his pedagogical stress, Coats opts for the lowest common denominator: The report "communicates events for the sake of communication."[74] More descriptive would have been the claim that Gen 1:1-2:3 communicates events for the sake of *teaching,* which Coats himself acknowledges. Coats's genetic title fails to account for the qualities that the priestly text exhibits in consonance with other ancient texts. A more descriptive genetic designation for Gen 1:1–2:3 is that of "treatise."

It must be noted at this point that similar conclusions have been reached with regard to some Egyptian cosmogonies, especially the so-called "Memphite Theology."[75] As noted earlier, Junker suggested that the account is a treatise (*Lehre*), given its empirical sensitivity and cohesion.[76] Agreeing with Junker, Lichtheim calls the inscription a "theological treatise."[77] Similarly, Allen characterizes several Egyptian cosmogonic texts as philosophical:

> Though primarily funerary or "religious" in purpose, [many cosmogonic texts] amount to a sourcebook of ancient Egyptian physics. This is because they deal with, or at least reflect, the Egyptian understanding of what the universe is like, how it works, and how it came to be. . . . None of the Egyptian sources is the record of scientific or philosophical speculation for its own sake. All serve some practical end, whether the worship of God or the attempt to secure a successful afterlife for the dead. Yet there is at base a fundamental sameness between the Egyptian record and our own more familiar [scientific] tradition. Like later philosophers and scientists, the Egyptian thinkers must have speculated, discussed, and passed on their concepts to subsequent generations.[78]

Allen's rationales are admittedly general and his use of the terms "scientific" and "philosophical" overstate his case, but clearly what he claims for Egyptian cosmology as a product of empirical speculation applies equally to the priestly cosmogony.

Positively, the conclusion that Gen 1:1–2:3 is a theological/empirical treatise can be supported by the observation that P's cosmogonic account shares some commonalities with Greek and Egyptian philosophical inquiries into the origins of the cosmos. Criticisms against such a classification (as well as against Coats's genetic identification) all come from discerning trajectory links to subsequent priestly narratives, but this is to jump too quickly to the larger literary context in which the cosmogony functions rather than letting it stand on its own.[79]

With the genetic designation of treatise, one can now investigate the "structure of values" or ideology of form present in the VorLxx. The positive and collaborative roles the elements are given by P in the creation account convey a sense of total harmony with respect to the created cosmos. Since there is no hint of dissonance in the process of P's cosmogony, one can juxtapose this text with that of Psalm 104, which seemingly portrays an orderly and harmonious world that appears to be created without flaw, except for one telling note of dissonance in v 35:

Let sinners be consumed from the earth, so that the wicked be no more.

V. S. Parrish points out that this verse precludes the conceptual world of the psalmist from being ideal.[80] The presence of sinners is the one blemish that mars a near perfect world; hence the psalmist calls upon God for their liquidation.

However, one must add to Parrish's sensitive rhetorical analysis the observation that the storm-god images in v 3,[81] the intimidation and confinement of the waters in vv 7 and 9, and the threat of cessation of life in v 29 and of devastation in v 32 all contribute to the psalm's description of divine action and to the rhetoric of the psalm as a whole. Verse 35 must be seen as part of a larger rhetorical framework in which the psalmist describes a world whose establishment is realized in violent images. God is portrayed as a divine warrior who neutralizes any potential threat to the created order, hence, the psalmist's desire that God do the same to sinners as he has treated the waters (v 7) and as he can do to the earth (v 32) and all of life (v 29). The stress upon God's might matches the social threat the psalmist perceives within his world view.

By contrast, the VorLxx of Gen 1:1–2:3 neither gives any hint of such threat nor, consequently, cloaks God in storm-god imagery. God's task to create is undertaken methodically via corresponding exhortations and fulfillments, in which God may or may not directly intervene in action. The jussive commands in Genesis 1 connote a sense of collaboration among the agents, especially the earth and the waters, the two most active "elements" in the creative process. Indeed, the approbation formulas express approval not only of God's handiwork but also of the "handiwork" of the active elements, earth and water. As pointed out above, a comparison with the priestly construction of the tabernacle in Exodus 35-40 underscores the social nature of P's cosmogony as a collaborative program, a program in which everything works harmoniously like clockwork.

The rational tenor and lack of any detectable hint of conflict or threat in the VorLxx all point to an ideal world in which God rules absolutely, yet also in collaboration with the divinely created order. God rules *with* creation not *over and against* creation. Nothing is to be overcome or defended. Instead, a sense of trust characterizes the establishment of the created order, a trust that allows for and enables the process of differentiation. The conceptual world of the VorLxx, as representative of P, is preeminently one of harmonious collaboration. P is convinced that only such a "social" ordering can result in perfect (*ṭôb*) work and order. It will be recalled in Exodus 36 that after the work force is set for constructing the tabernacle, the first command to the *bĕnê yiśrā'ēl*, namely to bring the necessary raw materials (Exod 35:4-5), yields better than expected results (36:5-6)! Such is the unwavering trust of the priestly writer in his conceptual, if not utopian, world (see below).

To probe any deeper into the Vor₍ₗₓₓ₎ would begin to investigate possible motives, as Brett calls them, behind the text. At this point, the level of uncertainty increases. A few suggestions, however, can at least be entertained. Given the absolute lack of tension within the text, one can conclude that P perceives or at least envisions a perfectly ordered world in which threat and evil are nonexistent. This perfect order is enhanced by the cohesive structure and rational tenor of the text. The text's rational perspective envisions a social world in which satisfying work (*'śh* and *br'*) and leisure (*šbt*) go hand in hand. Aristotle contended that leisure (*scholē*) was the beginning of wisdom, the mother of philosophy.[82] Ben Sirach makes the similar remark in 38:24:

> The wisdom of the scribe depends on the opportunity of leisure; and he who has little business may become wise.

It is indeed a truism that leisure is the basis of culture, and one wonders whether the divine institution of the sabbath rest in Gen 2:2-3 is not unrelated to cultural development in P.[83]

At any rate, the social matrix inferred from the priestly cosmogony seems to be rooted in a world, whether actual or envisioned, of an economic and culturally stable environment. However, whether this treatise seeks simply to legitimize existing social structures is an open question. In his ideological study of the doxological psalms, Brueggemann claims a *legitimizing* function for most of the creation psalms (e.g., 147 and 148):

> In this glad doxology of creation, there are no abrasive scandals, no dissonant voices, no disobedient choir members in the great cosmic choir, no problems, no wrongs, no evil, no injustice. All is "very good" (Gen 1:31), which I submit is an uncritical cover-up of the real world in which Israel's awkward, identity-giving history has happened.[84]

In short, Brueggemann contends that such psalms are directly tied to royal liturgy, which "legitimates a social order that cannot be criticized or changed."[85] By implication, "creation theology is allied with the king,

with the royal liturgy, and therefore with reasons of state."[86] Brueggemann also categorizes Gen 1:1–2:4a as a "liturgical text."[87]

Does P's cosmogony present an ideological posture that seeks simply
to legitimate the social order of the status quo? In the aim of discerning
the ideological motives of the text, Bakhtin warns against neglecting the
formal structure and the subtle nuances of a piece of literature, as well as
jumping to simplistic ideological conclusions.[88]

The rational tenor and consistent structure of the VorLxx suggest a
certain intellectual sophistication that would presuppose a stable and
affluent social matrix. In addition, the structured roles of ʾĕlōhîm, hāʾāreṣ,
hammayim, and hammāʾôr reveal a complex matrix of differentiated social
relations in which the created order is composed of creative agents working in collaboration with the creator. P's created order tolerates neither
inert substances nor forces that could potentially threaten the created
order. God's role in the cosmogonic process does not exhibit any hint of a
divine warrior or absolute despot. Rather the deity exhorts, delegates,
collaborates, and finally approves of the created order. God extends the
privilege and responsibility of royal rule both to human beings in general
(rdh)[89] and to the sun and moon (mšl), as well as creates in collaboration
with the earth and the waters.

Thus P's depiction of cosmogony imagines a social order in which
there is no rigid demarcation in praxis between creator and creature.
Although ʾĕlōhîm remains the exclusive decreer (nothing of the created
order is given the facility of speech), a harmony of collaboration between
creator and the created order characterizes the process of fulfillment.
Such a social structure certainly does not seek to depict a rigid hierarchy
in which power is wielded indiscriminately for the purposes of preserving the status quo and/or suppressing rebellious forces. However,
neither does the complex of social relations depicted in P's cosmogony
convey a particularly liberating message, since the social hierarchy works
only by obedience. What is clear, however, is that to be limited to only
these two alternatives, endorsement of the status quo and the liberation
of the oppressed is simplistic at best.

A more fruitful alternative from an ideological perspective is to
regard P's cosmogonic social world, as preserved in the VorLxx, as
utopian, that is, literally of "no place,"[90] since the text presents such a
thoroughly harmonious world, a world in which threat and obstacle are
nowhere acknowledged.[91] As Ricoeur observes about contemporary
utopias:

> In utopia . . . everything is compatible with everything else. There is no
> conflict between goals. All goals are compatible; none has any opposing
> counterpart. Thus, utopia represents the dissolution of obstacles.[92]

The priestly cosmogony exhibits precisely such a "dissolution of
obstacles": ʾĕlōhîm is no divine warrior and no part of the created order
poses any resistance to the divine plan. In fact, all parts work in active
collaboration with the Diety in the production and maintenance of the
cosmos. Conversely, social forces are never conceived otherwise than as
being in conflict, except in utopias.[93]

A utopia is "defined by its claim to shatter the existing order."[94] Yet
there is an intractable naive side to many utopias, as Ricoeur notes in his
discussion of Mannheim:

> [They are] based on a trust in the power of thought as an educative, infor-
> mative process. The utopia is in conflict with an existing order, but in the
> name of an idea. . . . In a sense we may say that the university proceeds from
> this utopia, because the notion is that we may change reality by better
> knowledge, by higher education, and so on. This form is utopian to the
> extent that it denies, and sometimes very naively, the real sources of power
> in property, money, violence, and all kinds of nonintellectual forces. It
> overemphasizes the power of intelligence to form and to shape.[95]

This is what Mannheim calls the liberal-humanitarian utopia.[96] Similarly,
with respect to Saint-Simon, "the kernel of the utopia is the power of
knowledge."[97] Given the text's rational orientation towards a perfectly
harmonious primordial world, Gen 1:1–2:3 conveys a sense of naiveté
that would seem to dull any rhetorical edge towards transforming the
existing social order. In comparison to Psalm 104, for example, in which
dark and turgid social forces are acknowledged, Gen 1:1–2:3 conveys an
impression of innocence. Its rhetorical and transformative appeal lies
solely in its rational presentation.

In addition, utopias commonly require the elimination of social hierarchy in areas such as gender roles: "For utopias sexuality is not so much
an issue about procreation, pleasure, or the stability of institutions as
about hierarchy."[98] In Gen 1:27, no hierarchy is introduced in the
creation of males and females; both share equally in the *imago dei*. This
deinstitutionalization of social relationships is also evident in the role of
ʾĕlōhîm in relation to the created order. Despite the creator/creature separation, God works in collaboration with the created order and provides
for its sustenance. God, thus, embodies the ideal ruler:

The utopia has two alternatives: to be ruled by good rulers—either ascetic or ethical—or to be ruled by no rulers. All utopias oscillate between these two poles.[99]

P's "naive" approach to cosmogony, however, need not be a hindrance in appreciating the priestly cosmogonic order and its transformative power. Such utopian visions in the world of antiquity were often descriptions of a primeval Golden Age, a period in which evil and conflict were non-existent. Examples most notably come from the classical world, although, instances of this form of historiography go back as far as Sumerian culture.[100] That P intends his cosmogony to be a description of a pure and perfect age is also confirmed in its larger historiographic context: Gen 1:1–2:3 is sharply demarcated in the priestly material as a particular period in history distinct from all subsequent history. The literary demarcation occurs in Gen 6:11-12 with a depiction of the cosmos completely at odds with the newly created order of Gen 1:1–2:3. The ontological status of creation as "very good" has now changed to very "corrupt" and full of "violence" (ḥāmās, 6:11). The demarcation is highlighted by a variation of the divine approbation formula of P's cosmogony in 6:12:

wayyar² ²ĕlōhîm ²et hā²āreṣ wehinnēh nišḥātāh

And God saw the earth and indeed it was corrupt.

Structurally, the sentence matches the final approbation formula of Gen 1:31. This, then, is P's authorial demarcation. As a result, the relationship between human beings and animals is irrevocably altered in Gen 9:3.

As a utopia, the cosmogonic age (the first seven days) is a period of "history" to which one cannot return. The world of this primordial age knows no evil, no recalcitrant forces, nothing to disturb the balance of the created order. As a utopia, the ideological motive behind the VorLxx of Gen 1:1–2:3 is disclosed in the intent to describe an ideal world that conceptually shatters the existing world order, while recognizing perhaps the practical unfeasability of this ideal world's realizability by virtue of its remoteness from human history. Yet precisely because of its remoteness from the vicissitudes of human history, this conceptual world holds an irresistible power, inviting the reader/listener to ponder what once was.

Social Interest and Ideology

The preceding sections have attempted to answer the first question of the ideological examination of the cosmogony as preserved in VorLXX of Gen 1:1–2:3, namely how the world was (and thus is to be) organized, as well as set the stage for examining the underlying ideological motives. The priestly cosmogony views the created order as a harmonious process of differentiation and incorporation of powers. The differentiated forces or elements are held together by an incorporation of collaborative elements. In effect, P's rational cosmogony (as preserved in the VorLXX) exudes a sense of unabashed confidence and optimism in the cooperative interdependence of the cosmological/social order that once was.

The question still remains, however, as to the social interests underlying such a cosmogony. To ask the question brings one into the field of study known as the "sociology of knowledge," which attempts to identify relationships between "changing structures of thought and changing historical circumstances."[101] Here, again, it is extremely difficult to make specific claims, simply in virtue of the fact that one's knowledge of the social history of ancient Israel is sparse and that any modern reconstruction thereof is inevitably laden with assumptions. Hence, one can only suggest possible social scenarios. Indeed, the following observations are to be considered only suggestive.

Widely taken for granted has been P's exilic origin or final redaction in Babylonia.[102] However, such a supposition is far from clear for Gen 1:1–2:3, since the cosmogony nowhere specifically addresses itself, polemically or otherwise, to Babylonian conceptions of cosmogony. Indeed, in terms of P's mythological antecedents, it was observed that P's cosmogony may bear as much Egyptian as Mesopotamian influence.[103] Indeed, the most that can be said is that the mythological background of P's cosmogony is generally ancient Near Eastern. Yet mythological background aside, an exilic or more likely an early post-exilic background for P is plausible.[104] By working with this assumption, one can tentatively suggest possible social interests behind P's cosmogony.

The social situation of any text or, in Bakhtin's terminology, "utterance," minimally includes the author and his/her audience. As discourse, P's cosmogony must be considered a word on target, addressed to a particular community. This must be made clear from the outset in any discussion of P's ideological interests, since the innumerable studies of P's cosmogony that concentrate exclusively on issues of mythological background and polemics in effect treat the priestly text almost *as if* it were directly addressed to the Babylonian intelligentsia, rather than to an Israelite audience. That is not to say that the priestly cosmogony is not on some general level a response to the ancient Near Eastern polytheistic systems; however, the fact that the treatise is directed towards an Israelite audience in a particular socio-historical context sets in relief more immediate ideological interests. To state the obvious, P's audience is internal, comprised of Israelites, whether exiled or (re)settled in Palestine.

As for the author in question, the intellectual sophistication and deep reflection evident in the priestly cosmogonic treatise is likely reflective of a highly educational, if not aristocratic, background. Indeed, the Judean exiles, predominantly upper class, were granted a liberal measure of economic and social freedom in Babylon.[105] Unlike the Assyrian practice of dispersing Israelite exiles in an attempt to liquidate them ethnically and politically, the Babylonian conquerors settled the Judean exiles into compact groups, wherein Israelite ethnic and religious identity flourished amid some inevitable assimilation to Babylonian culture.

If one is to assume a dialectical relationship between P's conceptual world and the existing social order it addressed, P's cosmogonic vision of a harmonious social order most likely addressed a social situation in which some conflict had emerged, yet within which there was indication of the potential for recreating, or, at the very least, improving upon the social situation. As Mannheim points out, any liberal utopia arises out of a disagreement with the existing order, yet it does not serve as a blueprint for action (e.g., revolution) but rather as a "measuring rod," by means of which the existing social order is theoretically evaluated.[106] The priestly vision of internal solidarity and inter-dependence between creator and created order, on the one hand, and of harmonious balance between the active elements in the created order, on the other, serves as a measuring rod by which the level of cultural cohesion and social harmony within a differentiated hierarchy is critically assessed.

As a utopian ideal, then, P's cosmogony functions more as a critical posture than as a specific call to action. P's intellectual, even detached, outlook betrays a positive acceptance of prevailing culture in general, even perhaps of foreign culture; P's cosmogony is far from expressing subjugation of any particular part of the created order. Instead, P finds a positive place and role for each and every differentiated segment in the created order. Nothing must be subdued or forced into its productive or functional position. Thus stable cohesion and harmonious balance are crucial social standards valued by P.

The optimistic confidence that characterizes P's vision of the created order would function, it seems, particularly well within a community whose cultural/religious goals (as P perceives them!) were not yet entirely established and in which no particular segment required ideological vindication at the expense of another. For P a cohesiveness characterized by collaboration in which all segments of the cosmic/social order are incorporated according to their respective abilities pervades his cosmogonic vision.

For a community struggling at some level to restore its cultural identity or realize a particular cultural/religious goal, P's utopian vision is particularly apt. By appearance alone, P's idealistic vision seems to cohere with the (naive) optimism of a community that is beginning to institute a particular cultural program and has not yet encountered significant opposition from within or experienced the disillusionment of frustrated goals. Yet this aura of optimism surrounding P's cosmogony could very well be strategic for the priestly program. A utopian depiction of cosmogony could effectively establish the "naturalness" or even "innocence" of a group's own social needs and perceptions, namely the need for a fully differentiated hierarchy in which each segment knows its place and perfectly obeys and performs its duty towards a common cultural goal such as, for instance, in the construction of the temple (see Exod 35-40).

Viewed from an ideological perspective, P's cosmogony offers a cosmic prolegomenon for the realization of a clearly differentiated community, for the inauguration of a new age in the cultural history of the exilic/post-exilic community, as well as a utopian ideal by which anything less than perfect cooperation and order can be critically assessed. As discourse, P's cosmogonic vision is programmatic, though not particularly pragmatic: The cosmogony constructs a complex of social, interdependent relationships that function in perfect order without resistance, similar to the way in which P depicts the construction of the tabernacle in Exodus 35-40. In addition, P's cosmogony paints a vision of a new order by intellectually appealing to an ideal original order. As a treatise, its rhetorical appeal for social change is derived from its power to impart wisdom, not unlike the modern liberal utopian mentality discussed above.

P's "reasonable optimism" matches in some ways that of Second Isaiah but is expressed in an entirely different manner.[107] While Second Isaiah employs highly emotive mythical imagery for the purpose of reestablishing the exilic community in its native land,[108] P presents a cosmogonic program for the community's cultural restoration. Indeed, the methodical manner with which P describes cosmogony comes close to matching the meticulous care of Ezekiel 40-48 in describing the architecture of the temple and roles of the priests within it.[109] However, in the visionary restoration program of Ezekiel social roles are even further defined, with the boundaries between the holy and the common sharply delineated.[110] Indeed, the so-called restoration program of Ezekiel shows clear signs of struggle over the issues of conflict and control.

In contrast, the priestly cosmogony[111] abstains from explicitly dealing with such issues, and thus, quite possibly, represents an earlier attempt at cultural formation before opposing social forces became so pronounced as to require a textual program of *explicit* ideological vindication, as in Ezekiel 40-48. The hardening of social boundaries, such as between the common and the holy (*ḥōl* and *qōdeš* [Ezek 42:20]) and between the Israelite and the foreigner (*nēkār*), is not reflected in any explicit or implicit way in the priestly account of creation. Rather, the creative work of *ʾĕlōhîm* is one of incorporation and collaboration resulting in the universal goodness (*ṭôb*) of creation. That is not to say that the priestly writer did not recognize or acknowledge social opposition in relation to his ideological goals.[112] Indeed, the reasonable optimism that characterizes the priestly account was most likely strategic from a rhetorical standpoint. Yet given the underlying supposition that everything is good and can work well together, the priestly writer did not give up hope for an inclusive effort in the formation of what he considered indispensable for the post-exilic community's cultural identity.

P's overarching social interest, thus, is the cultural formation or restoration of his community, concretely embodied, quite possibly, in the restoration of the second temple. The optimistic quality with which P describes the cosmogonic process indicates a hopeful attitude in the realization of such a cultural objective, a goal that has not yet been frustrated by internal opposition. The fact that friction and strife are not acknowledged within P's cosmogonic order in effect relegates opposition and conflict to a realm outside P's constructed social system.[113] A hierarchy characterized by internal cohesion and cooperation, qualities essential for the maintenance of a differentiated community, acts as a safeguard against outside conflict.

Given the ideological conflicts between the established Zadokite priesthood and the disenfranchised Levites in the early second temple period,[114] the priestly cosmogony could have served as a prolegomenon for establishing the Zadokite restoration program quite soon after the exile.[115] In contrast, the ideological shift evident in the MT of Genesis 1 fully acknowledges social threat within the social system and offers a radically different solution to the problem of conflict from that of the utopian vision depicted in the VorLxx.

STRUCTURE AND IDEOLOGY IN THE MT OF GEN 1:1–2:3

Textual transmission is essentially a "reproductive" enterprise: A new text is constructed that allegedly claims to have accurately reproduced an earlier or original text. Hence, the dynamics of textual transmission are analogous to the phenomenon of reported speech or the "politics of quotation."[116] Deliberate textual changes resulting from transmission inevitably raise the issue of how and why meaning is governed a certain way, that is, how much of the base text's meaning is conveyed (or permitted to be conveyed) by another text, how much of the text's meaning is suppressed or altered, what social situation is being addressed, and who presides over such changes.

This section hopes to offer some suggestions that would account for the textual changes evident in the MT within the "politics of textual reproduction." The ideological reasons behind the MT's revision of the VorLxx begin to come into focus in specific textual variations. These textual changes can be classified under two general headings: the role of the waters and the heptadic structure of the MT.

The Role of the Waters

The MT's rearrangment and omission of certain structural components in Genesis 1 as well as the linguistic alteration in Gen 1:20[117] are by necessity subtle textual changes, lest the reviser break the formulaic design and rational tenor of the creation treatise. But, taken together, such textual changes preserved in the MT amount to nothing less than a suppression of the waters' role in creation. As noted earlier, a strong precedent is evident throughout much biblical and ancient Near Eastern literature that depicts the waters as a force inimical to a particular deity, be it Yahweh, Baal, or Marduk. Such depictions contrast sharply with the positive and collaborative roles the waters are given in the VorLxx.

The reviser who produced the text now preserved in the MT found it peculiar, at best, that the VorLxx depicted the waters as initiating action on their own (1:9c) and actively producing both sea and aerial creatures (1:20). From the reviser's perspective, *hammayim* denoted an inimical force that could only be dealt with in terms of confinement or destruction. In the eyes of the reviser, the *mayim* in Genesis 1 represented nothing less than the *mayim rabbîm*. Such an understanding thereby required a subtle textual dismantling of the waters' creative powers and positive character, thereby making *ʾĕlōhîm* more prominent in the creative process.

J. Cook argues in his most recent study of the LXX of Genesis 1—a rejection of his earlier study[118]—that the MT's manipulation of the transition formula ("ending formula for the Wortbericht") was designed to counter the "possible doctrine concerning the generative power of Chaos," or to "avoid the possible deduction that water was able to generate parts of creation by itself."[119] Though essentially correct, Cook fails to identify the larger issues at stake. In his claim that in the MT "God was seen as the sole creator of the universe,"[120] Cook simply draws the wrong conclusion. In the MT, *hāʾāreṣ* retains its full creative role as an active agent working in collaboration with *ʾĕlōhîm*, and thus was not evidently considered problematic by the reviser. Thus God as the independent or "sole creator of the universe" was not the primary issue for the reviser. God could freely work with active agents in the cosmogonic process, agents that the reviser considered capable of making positive contributions. In other words, divine acts of collaboration in and of themselves were not considered by the reviser as limitations upon divine sovereignty over creation.

The *mayim*, however, did not qualify for the reviser as a positive collaborative power like the earth. Rather the waters denoted a force that required neutralization and confinement. Thus the reviser reduced the waters to inert matter in Gen 1:7 and 9 and confined them to "one place" (*māqôm* instead of *miqwēh* [cf. Ps 104:8!]). Only a vestige of the waters' creative potency remains in 1:20b in the MT, a potency confined exclusively to the waters' domain, namely in the formation of small sea-creatures. Total neutralization of the waters was not the aim of the reviser, rather restraint and confinement.

The reviser's reading (or more accurately misreading) of the VorLXX seems to depend on two assumptions: 1) the waters represent an inimical, cosmic force, and 2) their active role in the cosmogonic process could in effect give the chaotic waters free reign in the cosmos at the expense of God's control over creation. Thus there appears to be a distrust of the waters' role, a hermeneutic of suspicion, as it were, operative in the reviser's reading of the VorLXX and indicating his concern to protect creation from diabolical forces such as the *mayim rabbîm*. To achieve such protection, God must consequently be set *over and against* this particular aspect of the creation, that is, in the position of absolute despot, in order to neutralize the water.

One can see the reviser grappling with the larger issues of power and conflict, issues that the VorLXX leaves unaddressed in any explicit manner. At root is the reviser's somewhat dualistic view of the cosmos, a dualism that preempts the structure of the divine/agent collaboration one finds in the VorLXX. As a result, the reviser thereby introduces the mythological conception of water, the "dark side" of the waters, into an otherwise rational cosmogony. By restricting the role of the waters, the reviser must paradoxically introduce the "reality" of conflict into the priestly cosmogony in order to contain it. As a result, the priestly cosmogony is brought "up to date," as it were, by weaving the dimension of conflict, endemic to historical and contemporary experience, into the very fabric of creation. In other words, the reviser has on the literary level introduced a dose of realism into P's utopian cosmogony. The Golden Age of perfection and immunity from threat is tarnished at the hands of the reviser. God's sovereignty over creation is translated in terms of power over and against creation.

It may be noted in passing that a dynamic similar to that between the MT and the VorLXX can be discerned among modern scholars who have exegeted Gen 1:1–2:3, namely those who read mythological allusions into the role of the waters, especially in their pre-cosmic state as *těhôm*, and others who find an unbridgeable chasm between P's depiction and the mythological cosmogonies. May is representative of the former position when he states,

> There is a suggestion of a cosmic dualism, for there continues throughout history the kind of conflict which is posited at creation when Yahweh's wind blew over the watery abyss, or at the time when, in the distant past, Yahweh slew the dragon Leviathan or Rahab.[121]

In comparison, Hamilton's view is much less dramatic and comes close to describing the tenor of the VorLXX: "The *deep* of Gen. 1 is not personified, and in no way is it viewed as some turbulent, antagonistic force."[122] A middle position is represented by Day's comment with regard to *těhôm*: "God's *control* of the waters [in Gen 1:2] is simply a job of work."[123] The continuing scholarly debate over the role and background of the waters in P's cosmogony bears the ancient precedent one finds in the ideological clash between the VorLXX and the MT.

By introducing the new elements of conflict and control into P's cosmogony, the reviser effectively shatters P's utopian ideal by bringing its cosmogony down to earth, as it were. Whereas P (as reflected in the VorLxx) only indirectly addressed the issue of social conflict by denying it any negative efficacy within the conceived order, the reviser's solution to the problem of social conflict is an expressed "ideology of dominance."

No longer is there the confident and optimistic ideal of cooperation by incorporation as the way to ensure the restoration of a new community. To the contrary, the reviser's text explicitly acknowledges the "reality" of threatening forces that must be subdued in order that the structure of the cosmos be maintained or restored. Threatening forces are depicted as an internal and immediate threat to the cosmos, a threat that requires a divine or imperial response of suppression.

In short, the different conception of the role of the waters between the VorLxx and the MT represents nothing less than an ideological struggle over the significance of the *mayim*. The innocently benign *mayim* of the VorLxx is invested by the reviser with an antagonistic connotation that, consequently, requires subjugation. On the socio-historical plane, clear indication in post-exilic literature of such negative associations with the water occurs in apocalyptic literature. Within the biblical literature, a prominent example is Daniel 7:2b.

> *waʾărû ʾarbaʾ rûḥê šĕmayyāʾ mĕgîḥān lĕyammāʾ rabbāʾ*
>
> The four winds of heaven stirred up the great sea.

As J. Collins and others have recognized, the *yammāʾ rabbāʾ* "recalls the many waters (*mayim rabbîm*) of the Psalms."[124] In addition, the dramatic vision of the wind and the waters, contend Hartman and Di Lella, echoes the primordial scene of Gen 1:2.[125] The four beasts that emerge from the sea are clearly characters derived from the biblical mythological figures Leviathan and Rahab,[126] whose roots can be traced back to Ugaritic mythology. Drawing from ancient Near Eastern and biblical mythical treatments of the waters, the author of Daniel paints a picture of terrifying chaos.[127] By association the author in effect "remythologizes" Gen 1:2 by reading *tĕhôm* and *hammayim* as inimical forces.

Another example of a mythologizing reading of the waters in Genesis comes from 1 *Enoch* 69:18.

> By that oath, the sea was created; and he put down for it a foundation of sand which cannot be transgressed at a time of its anger, from the beginning of creation; and forever![128]

In this passage, the waters of creation require containment, due to their proclivity towards anger. Similarly, 2 *Enoch* 28 (both J and A) describes the creation process as requiring confinement of the waters "with a yoke."[129] Manuscript J describes God addressing the waters:

> Behold, I give you an eternal boundary. And you will break through from your own waters.[130]

Finally, explicit mythological associations with the waters or the sea are clearly given in Revelation. Clearly echoing Dan 7:2, Rev 13:1 describes a beast rising out of the sea. In Rev 17:1 the figure of the "great whore" is seated "on many waters" (*epi hydatōn pollōn*), which are interpreted as symbolizing the "peoples and multitudes and nations and languages" (Rev 17:15). Lastly, in Rev 21:1b the renewal of the cosmos is described:

> For the first heaven and the first earth had passed away, and the sea was no more.

It appears, thus, that the resurgence of mythological associations with the waters, specifically the association of the waters with the negative forces of chaos, became a hallmark of much apocalyptic literature, beginning at least by the late pre-Maccabean period in Israelite history.[131] Reinvesting the waters with such mythical connotations could very well have been the editorial response of a reviser who was entrenched in the ideological goals of the apocalypticists, whose literary works marked a resurgence in the use of mythical motifs.[132] At the very least, one can say that the early apocalypticists had "nuanced" *mayim* so thoroughly that the reviser could only "read" the term with negative connotations. As a result, the "innocent" role of the waters in the VorLXX of Genesis 1 became in the hands of the reviser a locus of discord.

If one posits a *direct* association between the reviser and the ideological interests of the early apocalypticists, the "textual" suppression of the chaotic forces embodied by the *mayim* (*rabbîm*) could reflect an interest in the radical transformation of Israel's social environment. However, any direct social connection can only be conjectured. In any case, the reviser's conceptual world presupposes a social world in which force, divine or otherwise, is the appropriate means for maintaining or changing social order.

At what point historically did such a revision of Genesis 1:1–2:3 occur can only remain an open question. One can speculate that if scribal editing of the Masoretic text of the Pentateuch was flourishing as late as the early Maccabean period,[133] such revision was roughly contemporaneous to the production and/or editing of the Book of Daniel. Given the similar mythical treatments of water in the respective works, one could presume some common ideological goals.

Of note is a particular party of scribes referred to as the Hasidim in 1 Macc 7:12-13, whose allegiance to the Maccabees was initially strong but ultimately disintegrated during the reign of either Jonathan or Simon.[134] With varying degrees of confidence most scholars posit a historical connection between this group and those martyred on the sabbath by Antiochus's soldiers, as described in 1 Macc 2:29-38.[135] The extent to which this party of scribes contributed to apocalyptic works has been extensively debated.[136] Though prolific in the production of apocalyptic works, the Hasidim, according to Collins, were not specifically responsible for the Book of Daniel, which espouses a pacifistic view.[137] The textual evidence is much too slim for Tcherikover to identify the Hasidim as the "chief scribes and authoritative interpreters of the regulations and commandments of the Torah."[138] However, one wonders whether in their role as scribes, the members of the Hasidim party or some other scribal group (the *maśkîlîm* in Daniel?[139]) that employed apocalyptic symbols and categories of thought were responsible for the scribal revisions one finds in the MT of Gen 1:1–2:3.

Historical reconstructions aside, it is clear at least that the role of the *mayim* in creation had become the arena in which different ideological contentions and perceptions were brought to bear. These differences were textually embodied in the struggle over the status of the *mayim* in creation. Whereas the cosmogony of P (as preserved in the VorLXX) sought in its optimistic social perception to preserve and further hierarchical social structures to their idealistic limits, the slight textual emendation evident in the MT of Gen 1:1–2:3 was the work of scribes advocating through their use of apocalyptic motifs social change.[140] The result transformed the *mayim*'s innocent role in cosmogony to one of opposition that required the divine imposition of confinement.

Heptadic Structure of the MT

Another set of textual changes can be accounted for by the reviser's concern to provide a thoroughly heptadic structure for the cosmogonic text, hence, the omission of redundant words and phrases to achieve heptadic counts. One could easily attribute this carefully refined structure simply to aesthetic or stylistic concerns and leave it at that.

However, the point of contact with the reviser's ideological treatment of the waters is established from the fact that the total word count of *mayim*, in contrast to *ʾĕlōhîm*, *hāʾāreṣ*, and *šāmayim* (plus *mabdîl* and *rāqîaʿ*) is indivisible by seven.

Furthermore, the count of seven is not without its own ideological significance. It is widely recognized that the number seven in the Hebrew Bible as well as in much of ancient Near Eastern literature is a particularly sacred number.[141] In the priestly literature seven clearly connotes completeness and perfection. The seventh day of creation is marked off as separate and holy (*qdš*, 2:3), as the time in which God ceased from creative activity. The symbolic meaning of the number seven perhaps can be traced back to the Sumerian-Akkadian lexical equation "7 = *kiššatu*," meaning whole or totality.[142]

As already noted, non-discriminative word counts (as opposed to counts of particular words) in Gen 1:1-2 and 2:1-3 are already present in the VorLXX. This stylistic device underscores the pre-creative and final sections. That there is such a count in the final section is no surprise, since this section reports on the post-hexaemeral situation. However, a clear heptadic structure at the very outset in the description of the pre-creative stage is unexpected and gives a teleological slant to the introduction, whereby the pre-creative state of affairs points to its completion. In addition, the use of a heptadic structure in the VorLXX establishes a numerological inclusio.

The text of the MT, on the other hand, effectively undercuts the unique significance of the inclusio by using the literary device both to highlight certain key words that figure significantly within the body of the creation account and to establish a total heptadic word count in 1:1–2:3. References to heaven, the earth, and God are all attested in such multiple counts. As a result, these "elements" are invested with the teleological status of completion or perfection. In other words, although creation is not entirely completed until the in-breaking of the seventh day (2:2), the particular parts of the created order are, as it were, bent towards completion within the creative process.

Not so, however, with *mayim*: The waters, whose creative role is equal to that of the earth in the VorLXX, remain without such designation. In effect, *hammayim* is designated to remain in a state of "perfectionlessness" or incompleteness. The word's numerological incompatibility with the created order accords well with the reviser's intent to neutralize the role of the waters evident in the VorLXX. The waters bear no such teleological quality as do other crucial parts in the priestly cosmogony.

One wonders whether the waters' lack of such teleological status is tacit recognition of the waters' subversive or chaotic side. That is, the numerological incompatibility of the waters relative to the other "elements" could be another subtle way of acknowledging the waters' nature to remain irreversibly rebellious or "restless." The fact that *hammayim* does not numerologically fit within a creative order moving towards completion sets in relief the waters' ambivalent nature in relation to the other cosmogonic elements. This "restless" quality requires, thus, confinement and restraint (1:9). Only with the reins tightly drawn can the waters be allowed to contribute to the creative process (1:20b).

The correspondence between the suppression of the role of the waters and the heptadic structure in the MT betrays an ideological program that possibly conjoins an interest in the significance of the sabbath with the desire for radical change. Again, from the slim extant textual evidence describing the history of the late pre-Maccabean period, the Hasidim's reputedly strict adherence to the sabbath (1 Macc 2:29-38) would cohere well with the textual revisions noted in Gen 1:1–2:3.[143] Admittedly, such a claim is purely speculative. However, these two "patterns" of textual revision reflect, directly or indirectly, a correspondence between traditional priestly concerns, such as the observance of the sabbath, and a concern for social change. In any case, the corresponding textual revisions of the priestly cosmogony betray a potent blend of traditional and radical social interests not uncommon with any group that looks forward towards a new social order through the lens of established tradition.

NOTES

[1] Y. Lotman and B. Uspensky, "On the Semiotic Mechanism of Culture," *New Literary History* 9 (1978) 213.

[2] A. Callinicos, *Making History: Agency, Structure and Change in Social History* (Ithaca: Cornell University Press, 1988) 236.

[3] See Callinicos's rationale for the positive function of structure in social theory in his discussion of subjects, agents, and structure (Callinicos, 1-95, 235-37).

[4] J. Blenkinsopp, "The Structure of P," *CBQ* 38 (1976) 283.

[5] Blenkinsopp, 276, 278.

[6] P. J. Kearney, "Creation and Liturgy: The P Redaction of Ex 25-30," *ZAW* 89 (1977) 375.

[7] In the Midrash Pesiqta of R. Kahana (8f), the desert sanctuary is inextricably tied to creation:

Before the sanctuary was erected, the world shook; [but] from the moment the sanctuary was erected, the world became firmly established.

(The passage was translated from P. Schäfer, "Tempel and Schöpfung. Zur Interpretation einiger Heiligtums-traditionen in der rabbinischen Literatur," *Kairos* 16 [1974] 132.)

[8] J. D. Levenson, *Creation and the Persistence of Evil: The Jewish Drama of Divine Omnipotence* (San Francisco: Harper & Row, Publishers, 1988) 83.

[9] B. Janowski, "Tempel und Schöpfung. Schöpfungstheologische Aspekte der priesterschriftlichen Heiligtumskonzeption," in *Schöpfung und Neuschöpfung* (JBTh 5; Neukirchen-Vluyn: Neukirchener Verlag, 1990) 68.

[10] N. M. Sarna, *Exodus* (JPSTCS; Philadelphia: Jewish Publication Society, 1991) 224.

[11] See Blenkensopp, 276, 281; Levenson, 85.

[12] Sarna, 156.

[13] Blenkensopp, 280; Levenson, 86.

[14] Sarna, 156.

[15] Levenson, 86.

[16] Cf. Psalm 115:16

The heavens are Yahweh's heavens
But the earth he has given to human beings.

[17] See Chapter Four.

[18] M. Welker, "What is Creation? Rereading Genesis 1 and 2," *Theology Today* 48 (1991) 64.

[19] The translation is based with minor alteration on J. C. L. Gibson's translation (*Canaanite Myths and Legends* [Edinburgh: T. & T. Clark, 1978] 50).

[20] Hamilton, 111.

[21] B. W. Anderson, *Understanding the Old Testament* (4th ed.; Englewood Cliffs: Prentice-Hall, 1986) 456.

[22] B. W. Anderson, "Introduction: Mythopoeic and Theological Dimensions of Biblical Creation Faith," in *Creation in the Old Testament*, ed. B. W. Anderson (IRT 6; Philadelphia: Fortress Press, 1984) 15-18.

[23] See Chapter One.

[24] Guthrie, *A History of Greek Philosophy*, 1, 36.

[25] S. Sambursky, *The Physical World of the Greeks*, trans. M. Dagut (New York: MacMillan Publishing Company, 1956) 6.

[26] This is also pointed out by Welker, 66.

[27] See Chapters Two and Four, which illustrate the thematic structure of the LXX and VorLXX, respectively.

[28] See Plato *Timaeus* 30A, 69C. See also R. D. Mohr "Plato's Theology Reconsidered: What the Demiurge Does," in *Essays in Ancient Greek Philosophy, III: Plato* (ed. J. P. Anton and A. Preuss; New York: State University of New York Press, 1989) 294.

[29] E.g., Aristotle *De generatione et corruptione* 336a15-337a34); see H. Tredennick's discussion in his introduction to *Aristotle: The Metaphysics*, Books I-IX (LCL, Greek authors, 271; London: William Heinemann, 1933) xxix-xxx.

[30] E.g., Aristotle *Metaphysica* 1072a26-1072b14; *De caelo* 285a29-30; *De generatione et corruptione* 336a15-337a34.

31   Plato *Timaeus* 38C-D.

32   See discussion in D. Furley, "The Cosmological Crisis in Classical Antiquity," in *Proceedings of the Boston Area Colloquium in Ancient Philosophy*, II, ed. J. J. Cleary (Lanham: University Press of America, 1987) 15; Guthrie, *A History of Greek Philosophy*, 1, 62-67.

33   Such a view sharply disagrees with Y. Kaufmann's position:

> To be sure, the biblical God fashions some of his creatures out of matter already at hand. But this matter is not alive, charged with divine forces; it *neither opposes nor participates* in creation (italics added; *The Religion of Israel: From Its Beginnngs to the Babylonian Exile* [trans. M. Greenberg, New York: Schocken, 1972] 68).

To the contrary, Genesis 1, especially in the VorLxx, depicts what Kaufmann labels "matter" (in the form of water and earth) as positively participating in creation.

34   Wellhausen adopts this term to describe the cosmogonic process (Wellhausen, *Prolegomena*, 297).

35   E.g., Aristotle *Historia animalium* 588b4-13. See discussions in G. E. R. Lloyd, *Aristotle: The Growth and Structure of His Thought* (Cambridge: University Press, 1968) 89-90; Guthrie, *A History of Philosophy*, 6, 258-63.

36   See textual note in Chapter Three.

37   See 1 Kings 5:9-14, in which Solomon's wisdom is characterized in part by his knowledge of botany and zoology. Cf. Aristotle *De partibus animalium* 645a and Lloyd, *Aristotle*, 70-72.

38   S. Talmon, "The Biblical Understanding of Creation and the Human Commitment," *Ex Auditu* 3 (1987) 115.

39   See a similar conclusion reached by J. H. Hayes, *Introduction to the Bible* (Philadelphia: Westminster Press, 1971) 240-41.

40   Anderson, "Introduction," 15.

41   Gunkel states: "Genesis 1 ist nicht eine freie Construction des Verfassers," (*Schöpfung und Chaos in Urzeit und Endzeit* [Göttingen: Vandenhoeck & Ruprecht, 1895] 4). M. G. Brett notes the discrepancy between Gunkel's quote ("freie Construction") and Wellhausen's claim that Genesis 1 is a "systematische Construction" (from Wellhausen's third edition of the *Prolegomena*, 317), not a free composition (Brett, "Motives and Intentions," 1, n. 1). Gunkel, however, is not misreading Wellhausen, as Brett suggests, but contrasting Wellhausen's treatment of Genesis 2-3 with the systematic tenor of the priestly cosmogony (Gunkel, 5).

42   Gunkel, 14.

43   Gunkel, 7. Gunkel points to the absence of the article as a sign that the term was "uralt."

44   Gunkel, 14.

45   See discussion in Brett, "Motives and Intentions in Gen 1," 3, n. 5. See also W. McKane's discussion in *Studies in the Patriarchal Narratives* (Edinburgh: Handsel Press, 1979) 225-29. One could say that Kaufmann stands somewhat in the Wellhausian exegetical tradition when he comments on the notion of *tohu wabohu*:

> The notion of a pre-existent stuff thus lurks in the background of biblical cosmologies as a vestigial idea which has no meaningful role in the accounts themselves (Kaufmann, 68).

[46] McKane, 226.

[47] H. Gunkel, "The 'Historical Movement' in the Study of Religion," *ET* 38 (1926/27) 533-34.

[48] See R. A. Oden, Jr., *The Bible Without Theology: The Theological Tradition and Alternatives to It* (San Francisco: Harper & Row, Publishers, 1987) 33-34.

[49] Gunkel, "The 'Historical Movement'," 534.

[50] Gunkel, *Schöpfung und Chaos*, 28.

[51] Wellhausen, *Prolegomena*, 298.

[52] Wellhausen, *Prolegomena*, 298.

[53] Brett, 4.

[54] Brett, 5-9.

[55] Brett, 5.

[56] In discussing Westermann's analysis of the "original function" of Genesis 1, Brett remarks that "[The level of communicative intention] is precisely what makes the one set of stories different to the other" (Brett, 8).

[57] Brett, 8.

[58] See Brett's discussion of Westermann and Lohfink (Brett, 8-9, 13).

[59] See discussion in Clark and Holquist, *Mikhail Bakhtin*, 213-14.

[60] Day, *God's Conflict with the Dragon and the Sea*, 50.

[61] H. W. F. Saggs, *The Encounter with the Divine in Mesopotamia and Israel*, (London: Althone Press, 1978) 52-53.

[62] C. Hyers, *The Meaning of Creation: Genesis and Modern Science* (Atlanta: John Knox Press, 1984) 52.

[63] A. S. Kapelrud, "The Mythological Features in Genesis Chapter 1 and the Author's Intentions," *VT* 24 (1974) 181.

[64] Kapelrud, 185.

[65] W. G. Lambert, "Old Testament Mythology in its Ancient Near Eastern Context," in *Congress Volume: Jerusalem 1986*, ed. J. A. Emerton (VTS 40; Leiden: E. J. Brill, 1988) 124-43.

[66] Westermann, 93.

[67] Brett, 15-16.

[68] E.g., Plato *Timaeus* 30A, 69C.

[69] In discussing the function of P's cosmogony, Westermann spends a great amount of attention demonstrating that ancient cosmogonic accounts in general are not the "result of intellectual inquiry" (Westermann, 21):

> The importance of the intellectual inquiry about the origins should not be disputed; but it is something which has been added later.

Yet Westermann does not then reckon with this "added" element, which so thoroughly characterizes P's cosmogony.

[70] Coats, 10, 47.

[71] Schmidt, 180-81.

[72] von Rad, 47-48.

[73] Coats, 47.

[74] Coats, 47.

[75] See discussion in Chapter Five.

[76] Junker, *Die Götterlehre von Memphis*, 70-77. See also *idem.*, *Die Geisteshaltung der Ägypter in der Frühzeit* (OAW 237, 1; Wein: Hermann Böhlaus NFG, 1961) 24, 140.

77 Lichtheim, *AEL*, 1, 51.

78 Allen, *Genesis in Egypt*, 56.

79 Brett, "Motives and Intentions," 14-15. E. Zenger, for example, finds in Gen 1:28-30 "vielschichtigen Spannunsmomente" in the context of the flood story and Exod 1:7 (*Gottes Bogen in den Wolken* [SBS 112; Stuttgart: Katholisches Bibelwerk, 1983] 56) See also D. J. A. Clines, *What Does Eve Do to Help? and Other Readerly Questions to the Old Testament* (JSOTSS 94; Sheffield; Sheffield Academic Press, 1990) 41-45. In order to highlight the (implicit) andocentric values of P's cosmogony, Clines necessarily looks towards the larger literary context, such as Lev 27:2-8 and Genesis 2-3 (Clines, 45). By letting the larger literary context determine and constitute the meaning of Genesis 1 "in itself," Clines overlooks the clear literary demarcation of P's cosmogony from subsequent material (2:4a). With the sharp literary demarcation evident in Gen 2:4a, the priestly writer requests the reader/listener to consider Gen 1:1-2:3 as distinct vis-à-vis all that follows.

80 V. S. Parrish, "The Rhetoric of Creation: Psalm 104 as a Subversive Text," (forthcoming).

81 For a recent discussion of the storm-god imagery of Psalm 104, see Dion, 48-58.

82 Aristotle *Metaphysica* 981b16.

83 Welker, for instance, describes the day of rest as "the cradle of all cognitive and normative culture" (Welker, 62).

84 W. Brueggemann, *Israel's Praise: Doxology against Idolatry and Ideology* (Philadelphia: Fortress Press, 1988) 106.

85 Bruggemann, *Israel's Praise*, 108.

86 Brueggemann, *Israel's Praise*, 101.

87 Brueggemann, *Israel's Praise*, 11. Curiously, Brueggemann does not describe Gen 1:1-2:3 in this way, given his analysis of the creation psalms. See also "The Kerygma of the Priestly Writers," in *The Vitality of Old Testament Traditions*, ed. W. Brueggemann and H. W. Wolff (Atlanta: John Knox Press, 1975) 103-4.

88 See Chapter One.

89 By citing Egyptian examples, W. H. Schmidt suggests that the language of Gen 1:26-28 is rooted in royal tradition (Schmidt, 139):

> Was sonst nur dem König zugesprochen wird, is hier auf alle Menschen übertragen.

Such a democratizing transformation underscores P's radical social world view (see also H. Wildberger, "Das Abbild Gottes," *TZ* 21 [1965], 495-97). Van Seters relates a recently published Neo-Babylonian text to Gen 1:26-28, claiming that "it becomes virtually conclusive that the Priestly Writer has democratized the myth of the creation of the king in order to apply it to mankind in general" ("The Creation of Man and the Creation of the King," *ZAW* 101 [1989] 341).

90 J. Ferguson, *Utopias of the Classical World* (AGRL; Ithaca: Cornell University Press, 1975) 7.

91 See P. Ricoeur's discussion of Mannheim's and Saint-Simon's treatments on utopia in *Lectures on Ideology and Utopia*, ed. G. H. Taylor (New York: Columbia University Press, 1986) 272-73, 285, 298-300.

92 Ricoeur, 296.

93 See discussion in Clark and Holquist, 220.

94 Ricoeur, 285.

95 Ricoeur, 285.

96 K. Mannheim, *Ideology and Utopia: An Introduction to the Sociology of Knowledge*, trans. L. Wirth and E. Shils (New York: Harcourt, Brace and World, 1936) 219.

97 Ricoeur, 288.

98 Ricoeur, *Lectures on Ideology and Utopia*, 299.

99 Ricoeur, 299.

100 E.g., Enki and Ninhursag (*ANET* 38). For classical examples, see discussion in Chapter Three. In his work *Utopias of the Classical World*, Ferguson has collected and analyzed classical utopian conceptions, most particularly of the philosophical variety.

101 D. McLellan, *Ideology* (CST; Minneapolis: University of Minnesota Press, 1986) 43.

102 But cf. J. G. Vink, "The Date and Origin of the Priestly Code in the Old Testament," *OS* 15 (1969) 1-144; Kaufmann, 175-200; A. Hurvitz, "The Evidence of Language in Dating the Priestly Code," *RB* 81 (1974) 24-55; *idem.*, *A Linguistic Study of the Relationship between the Priestly Source and the Book of Ezekiel* (Cahiers de la Revue Biblique 20; Paris: Gabalda, 1982); and most recently J. Hughes, *Secrets of the Times: Myth and History in Biblical Chronology* (JSOTSS 66; Sheffield: Sheffield Academic Press, 1990) 51-54.

103 See Chapter Five.

104 For an exilic dating, see, for instance, A. S. Kapelrud, "The Date of the Priestly Codex (P)," *ASTI* 3 (1964) 58-64 and K. Elliger, "Sinn und Ursprung der priesterlichen Geschichtserzählung," *ZTK* 49 (1952) 121-43. For an early post-exilic dating, see Hughes, *The Secrets of the Times*, 39-40, 51-52. I am sympathetic with Hughes's suggestion that the chronological system in P reveals a symmetrical schema in which there is a 480-year period from the exodus to the foundation of the first temple and an equal period from the foundation of the first temple to that of the second temple (Hughes, 51). In addition, the inordinate amount of attention given to the construction of the tabernacle in Exodus 25-40 could very well reflect or anticipate the historical opportunity for the initial construction of second temple. Although the question as to whether the material in Gen 1:1-2:3 can be dated as late must presently remain open, the structural similarities between Gen 1:1-2:3 and Exodus 35-40 noted above might suggest some historical correspondence.

105 As for those directly related to the cult, the Zadokites were evidently the priestly class most affected by the exile, whose imprint upon the priestly layer of the Pentateuch is unmistakable (See P. Hanson, *The Dawn of Apocalyptic* [2nd ed.; Philadelphia: Fortress Press, 1979] 223-28).

Recent general discussions of the conditions of the Judean exiles in Babylonia include B. Oded, "Judah and the Exile" in *Israelite and Judaean History*, ed. J. H. Hayes and J. M. Miller (London: SCM, 1977) 480-86; J. M. Miller and J. H. Hayes, *A History of Ancient Israel and Judah* (Philadelphia: Westminster Press, 1986) 431-35; S. Herrmann, *A History of Israel in Old Testament Times*, trans. J. Bowden (2nd ed.; Philadelphia: Fortress Press, 1981) 292-94; J. A. Soggin, *A History of Ancient Israel*, trans. J. Bowden (Philadelphia: Westminster Press, 1984) 253-55; J. D. Purvis, "Exile and Return: From the Babylonian Destruction to the Reconstruction of the Jewish State," in *Ancient Israel: A Short History from Abraham to the Roman Destruction of the Temple*, ed. H. Shanks (Washington, D.C.: Biblical Archaeological Society, 1988) 154-61.

106 Mannheim, 219.

107 See Hanson's discussion of Second Isaiah in *The Dawn of Apocalyptic*, 24-25.

108 See most particularly Isa 51:9-11.

109 See discussion in Hanson, 71-74. The similar programmatic, methodical styles of the narratives of Gen 1:1-2:3 and Ezek 40-48 likely indicate that the priestly writer(s) or tradition bearers of P were Zadokite (see Hanson's sociological survey, 220-62). Hanson claims, admittedly crudely, that Ezekiel 40-48 is the work of pragmatic realists (71-72, n. 44). However, such a categorization cannot apply to Gen 1:1-2:3, which bears the marks of utopian thinking.

110 E.g., Ezek 44:6, 23; 42:14; 43:7.

111 One can also include the account of the construction of the tabernacle in Exodus 35-40.

112 See, e.g., Numbers 16. P acknowledges and addresses ideological conflict in his account of the wilderness experience, the "liminal" area between release from Egypt and settlement in Canaan.

113 See n. 111 above.

114 Hanson, 223-62.

115 This early restoration program is perhaps more concretely embodied in the account of the building of the tabernacle (Exodus 35-40).

116 See discussion in Clark and Holquist, 236-37.

117 See Chapter Four.

118 J. Cook, "Genesis I in the Septuagint as Example of the Problem: Text and Tradition," *JNSL* 10 (1982) 25-36. Here, Cook argues vigorously for the harmonizing tendency of the LXX!

119 J. Cook, "The Exegesis of the Greek Genesis," in *VI Congress of the International Organization for Septuagint and Cognate Studies, Jerusalem 1986*, ed. C. Cox (SCS 23; Atlanta: Scholars Press, 1987) 102, 105.

120 Cook, "The Exegesis of the Greek Genesis," 106.

121 May, "Some Cosmic Connotations of *Mayim Rabbim*," 11-12.

122 Hamilton, 111.

123 Day, 52 (italics added).

124 J. J. Collins, *The Apocalyptic Vision of the Book of Daniel* (HSM 16; Missoula: Scholars Press, 1972) 99.

125 L. F. Hartman and A. A. Di Lella, *The Book of Daniel* (AB 23; Garden City: Doubleday & Company, 1978) 211.

126 See also *1 Enoch* 60:7; *2 Enoch* 6:52.

127 J. J. Collins, *The Apocalyptic Imagination* (New York: Crossroad, 1987) 80-81.

128 Translation from E. Isaac, "1 (Ethiopic Apocalypse of) Enoch," in *OTP*, 1. 48.

129 See F. I. Andersen's translation, "2 (Slavonic Apocalypse of) Enoch," in *OTP*, 1. 146-47.

130 See also *4 Ezra* 4:17. However, of note is 6:48, in which the waters are commanded to "bring forth living creatures, birds, and fishes," a statement that echoes the role of the waters found in the LXX (and VorLXX), even though the waters are described pejoratively as "dumb and lifeless."

131 The so-called "Isaianic Apocalypse" of Isaiah 24-27 is too difficult to date with any certainty.

132 See Hanson, 26.

133 See Conclusion: The Historical Relationship.

134 See E. Schürer, *The History of the Jewish People in the Age of Jesus Christ (175 B.C.– A. D. 135)*, vol. 1, ed. G. Vermes, F. Millar, M. Black (Edinburgh: T. & T. Clark, 1973)

143, 145-46, 157, n. 6; *idem.*, *The History of the Jewish People in the Age of Jesus Christ (175 B.C.–A. D. 134)*, vol. 2, ed. G. Vermes, F. Millar, M. Black (Edinburgh: T. and T. Clark, 1979) 474; Collins, *The Apocalyptic Vision of the Book of Daniel*, 203-4; *idem.*, *The Apocalyptic Imagination*, 62.

[135]   Cf. Collins's cautionary evaluation in *The Apocalyptic Vision of the Book of Daniel*, 201.

[136]   See G. W. E. Nickelsburg's review of the literature in "Social Aspects of Palestinian Jewish Apocalypticism," in *Apocalypticism in the Mediterranean World and the Near East*, ed. D. Hellholm (Tübingen: J. C. B. Mohr [Paul Siebeck], 1983) 641-45. A particularly critical work that severs all conection between the Hasidim and the producers of apocalyptic literature is J. Kampen, *The Hasideans and the Origen of Pharisaism: A Study in 1 and 2 Maccabees* (SCS 24; Atlanta: Scholars, 1988) 23-33.

[137]   Collins, *The Apocalyptic Vision of the Book of Daniel*, 202-5.

[138]   V. Tcherikover, *Hellenistic Civilization and the Jews* (Philadelphia: Jewish Publication Society, 1959) 197, see also 125-26.

[139]   See J. Collin's discussion in "Daniel and His Social World" in *Interpreting the Prophets*, ed. J. L. Mays and P. J. Achtemeier (Philadelphia: Fortress Press, 1987) 251-57 (reprinted from *Interpretation* 39, 2 [1985] 133-40).

[140]   Presuming, of course, some connection between the scribal reviser and the apocalypticists of the mid-second century BCE.

[141]   M. H. Pope, "Seven, Seventh, Seventy," *IDB*, 4. 294-95.

[142]   B. E. Schafer, "Sabbath," *IDBSV*, 760.

[143]   See the discussion on scribes and their conflict with the priests in Schürer, 2. 322-35.

7

CONCLUSION: THE HISTORICAL
RELATIONSHIP

Despite appearances, this study is essentially a textual investigation, for its thesis is concerned with the textual relationship between the *Vorlage* of the LXX and the MT of Gen 1:1-2:3. However, a new approach has been introduced into the textual investigation in order to discern the "more difficult reading." Employed in this study is a particular kind of ideological criticism that recognizes the subtle structural and verbal nuances of texts and the ideological interests and values that shaped them.

Utilizing such an approach recognizes that seemingly minor textual differences between textual versions may uncover entirely different intentions and motives. Such is not claimed, of course, for every variant arising from textual transmission. However, against the criticism that the investigation conducted here is a case of pedantically reading too much into the text, I can only point to the highly structured text of P's cosmogony. No other text is so densely structured in the Hebrew Bible; every word seems to bear the mark of extensive reflection. And why should it not be for a text that deals with nothing less than the very origins of the cosmos? Von Rad's observations are particularly appropriate:

> Nothing is here by chance; everything must be considered carefully, deliberately, and precisely. . . . The [exegetical] exposition must pains-

takingly free this compact and rather esoteric doctrine sentence by sentence, indeed, word by word. These sentences cannot be easily overinterpreted theologically! Today's reader, preoccupied with the problem of faith and knowledge, must be careful not to read such tensions into the text.[1]

The investigation conducted in this study has attempted to demonstrate a textual relationship that in effect counters much of recent scholarship. I have attempted to demonstrate that the LXX reflects a Hebrew *Vorlage* that predates the text preserved in the MT by noting significant changes in structure, the roles of the "characters" within the respective structures, and ultimately the ideology that underlies both texts. In text-critical terminology, I have tried to show that the VorLXX of Gen 1:1–2:3 is in fact the *lectio difficilior* with respect to the role of the waters in cosmogony, a role that can easily be read theologically as a threat to the created order. Having established a relative dating, the final task at hand is to take up the issue of the historical relationship between the two texts.

If one assumes that the text of the VorLXX in Gen 1:1-2:3 is identical with original P material, *at least in terms of the consistent formal structure it exhibits,* a date in the latter half of the sixth century BCE, assuming a late exilic or early post-exilic connection, seems reasonable. The first indication of a considerably different text comes from the MT, which can be traced back with confidence to no earlier than some time in the second century BCE.[2] The LXX translation of the Pentateuch, or at least of Genesis, can be pushed back to the mid-third century BCE in Alexandria.[3] However, the Qumran fragments 4QGen[h] and 4QGen[k] attest the existence of the LXX's Hebrew *Vorlage*.[4] As E. J. Revell notes,

textual variants reflected in the Greek are found in the Qumran fragments to such an extent that it is reasonable to argue that any variant reflected in the Greek could have circulated in Palestine.[5]

Thus a Palestinian provenance for the VorLXX cannot be excluded.

Fragments from Qumran that reflect the MT rather than the VorLXX of Genesis 1 are at the time of this study unavailable for examination. Davila mentions the fragment 4QGen[d], which he dates to ca. 50-25 BCE and claims "is identical to the MT."[6] In addition, the Samaritan Pentateuch, which reflects the structure of the MT in Genesis 1, can be traced no earlier than to the Hasmonean period.[7] In addition, prototypes of the SP have also been discovered at Qumran (e.g., 4QpaleoEx[m] and 4QNum[b]).[8] Its text-form, with its more frequent occurrences of vowel letters and *matres lectionis,* is probably later than the MT.[9] It is noteworthy that although the LXX shares approximately 1,600 readings with the SP,[10] it is in the structure of Gen 1:1–2:3 that the latter agrees with the MT. Nevertheless, the question as to whether the Genesis text preserved by the Masoretes was produced in response to the Hebrew VorLXX or the LXX cannot be conclusively settled at this point.

A helpful clue for dating the revision of Gen 1:1–2:3 is evident from a chronological revision having originated evidently from the early Maccabean period that reflects Hasmonean or related interests associated with the rededication of the temple in 164 BCE.[11] Such evidence would serve as a *terminus ad quem* for any revisions of the Hebrew text of Genesis–2 Kings, as reflected in the MT. Whether this chronological revision can be connected to the particular revision in Genesis 1 remains an open question, but it is a possibility that cannot be excluded. Indeed, as suggested in the previous chapter, the ideological interests reflected in the MT of Genesis 1 cohere with the rise of the Maccabees. At the very least, one can say that some time roughly during the 400 years between the Babylonian exile and the mid-second century BCE, an ideological clash occurred regarding the nature of cosmogony and the constitution of a viable social order for Israel.

NOTES

[1] Von Rad, 47-48.

[2] See the introduction to Chapter Three.

[3] See the introduction to Chapter Two.

[4] See Davila, 6-10.

[5] E. J. Revell, "LXX and MT: Aspects of Relationship," in *De Septuaginta: Studies in Honour of John Williams Wevers on his Sixty-fifth birthday,* ed. A. Pietersma and C. Cox (Mississauga: Benben, 1984) 48.

[6] Davila, 5.

[7] Purvis, *The Samaritan Pentateuch,* 86.

[8] Mulder, "The Transmission of the Biblical Text," 96.

[9] Mulder, "The Transmission of the Biblical Text," 96.

[10] Klein, *Textual Criticism,* 17.

[11] Wellhausen comes close to noting this particular schema in the Masoretic chronology (Wellhausen, 308-9). Others who have discerned this are C. Kuhl, *The Old Testament: Its Origins and Compositon,* trans. C. T. M. Herriott (Edinburgh: Oliver and Boyd, 1961) 62; A. Murtonen, "On the Chronology of the Old Testament," *ST* 8 (1954) 137; M. D. Johnson, *The Purpose of the Biblical Genealogies with Special Reference to the Setting of the Genealogies of Jesus* (Cambridge: University Press, 1969) 32; T. L. Thompson, *The Historicity of the Patriarchal Narratives: The Question for the Historical Abraham* (BZAW 133; Berlin: Walter de Gruyter, 1974) 14-15; J. Hayes, *Introduction to*

Old Testament Study (Nashville: Abingdon, 1980) 24-25; and J. Hughes, 243 (note the typographical misprint of 323 years, which should be corrected to 423). All point out that the Masoretic chronological references in the Pentateuch and in Joshua–2 Kings, as opposed to the Greek and Samaritan references, result in a total count that, in light of 2 Chron 36:22 and 1 Macc 4:36-59, place the rededication of the temple (or the first year after its rededication) in the year 4000 after creation. Such evidence strongly suggests that a scribal group allied with the Hasmoneans in the early Maccabean period was responsible for such a chronological revision.

BIBLIOGRAPHY

Aisleitner, J. *Wörterbuch der Ugaritischen Sprache*. Berlin: Akademie-Verlag, 1963.

Albright, W. F. *Archaeology and the Religion of Israel*. Baltimore: Johns Hopkins Press, 1942.

Alexandre, M. *Le commencement du livre Genèse I-V*. CAB 3; Paris: Beauchesne, 1988.

Allen, J. P. *Genesis in Egypt: The Philosophy of Ancient Egyptian Creation Accounts*. YES 2; New Haven: Yale University Press, 1988.

———. *Religion and Philosophy in Ancient Egypt*. YES 3; New Haven: Yale University Press, 1989.

Amiet, P. "The Mythological Repertory in Cylinder Seals of the Agade Period (c. 2335-2155)," in *Ancient Art in Seals*, ed. E. Porada. Princeton: Princeton University Press, 1980, 35-60.

Andersen, F. I. "1 (Ethiopic Apocalypse of) Enoch," *OTP*, vol. 1, 91-222.

Anderson, B. W. "A Stylistic Study of the Priestly Creation Story," in *Canon and Authority*, ed. G. W. Coats and B. O. Long. Philadelphia: Fortress Press, 1977, 148-62.

———. *Creation versus Chaos*. Philadelphia: Fortress Press, 1987.

———. "Introduction: Mythopoeic and Theological Dimensions of Biblical Creation Faith," in *Creation in the Old Testament*, ed. B. W. Anderson. IRT 6; Philadelphia: Fortress Press, 1984, 1-24.

———. *Understanding the Old Testament*, 4th ed. Englewood Cliffs: Prentice-Hall, 1986.

Anderson, G. "The Interpretation of Genesis 1:1 in the Targums," *CBQ* 52 (1990) 21-29.

Andreasen, N.-E. "The Word 'Earth' in Genesis 1:1," *Origins* 8 (1981) 13-19.

von Arnim, I., ed. *Stoicorum Veterum Fragmenta*. 3 vol.; Leipzig: Teubner, 1905-24.

Attridge, H. W., and Oden, R. A., Jr. *Philo of Byblos: The Phoenician History: Introduction, Critical Text, Translation, Notes*. CBQMS 9; Washington: The Catholic Biblical Association of America, 1981.

Bakhtin, M. M./Medvedev, P. N. *The Formal Method in Literary Scholarship: A Critical Introduction to the Sociological Poetics*, trans. A. J. Wehrle. Cambridge: Harvard University Press, 1985.

Barr, J. "Philo of Byblos and his 'Phoenician History,'" *BJRL* 57 (1974) 17-68.

Barthelemy, D. "Text, Hebrew, History of," in *IDBSV*, 878-84.

Bauer, W. *A Greek-English Lexicon of the New Testament*, ed. W. F. Arndt and F. W. Gingrich. Chicago: University of Chicago Press, 1958.

Baumgarten, A. I. *The Phoenician History of Philo of Byblos: A Commentary*. Leiden: E. J. Brill, 1981.

Beauchamp, P. *Création et séparation: Étude exégetique du chapitre premier de la Genèse*. BSR; Aubier Montaigne: Editions du Cerf, 1969.

Begelsbacher-Fischer, B. L. *Untersuchungen zur Götterwelt des alten Reiches im Spiegel der Privatgräber der IV. und V. Dynastie*. OBO 37; Freiburg: Universitätsverlag, 1981.

Beitenhard, H. *Midrasch Tanhuma B*, vol. 1. Bern: Peter Lang, 1980.

Benito, C. A. "'Enki and Ninmah' and 'Enki and the World Order.'" Unpublished Dissertation: University of Pennsylvania (Ann Arbor: University Microfilms) 1969.

Benz, F. L. *Personal Names in the Phoenician and Punic Inscriptions*. Studia Pohl 8; Rome: Biblical Institute Press, 1972.

Bergman, J. "Ancient Egyptian Theogony in a Greek Magical Papyrus," in *Studies in Egyptian Religion*, ed. M. H. van Voss, E. J. Sharpe, R. J. Z. Werblowsky. Leiden: E. J. Brill, 1982, 28-37.

Bertholet, A. "Zum Schöpfungsbericht in Genesis 1," *JBL* 53 (1934) 237-40.

Blenkinsopp, J. "The Structure of P," *CBQ* 38 (1976) 275-92.

Blythin, I. "A Note on Genesis 1:2," *VT* 12 (1962) 120-21.

Böhmer, E. *Das Erste Buch der Thora*. Halle: Buchhandlung des Waisenhauses, 1862.

Brandon, S. G. F. *Creation Legends of the Ancient Near East*. London: Hodder and Stoughton, 1963.

Brett, M. G. "Motives and Intentions in Genesis 1," *JTS* 42 (1991) 1-16.

Brooke, A. E., McLean, N., and Thackeray, H. St. J. *The Old Testament in Greek according to the Text of the Codex Vaticanus, Vol. I, Part I: Genesis*. Cambridge: Cambridge University Press, 1906.

Brueggemann, W. *Israel's Praise: Doxology against Idolatry and Ideology*. Philadelphia: Fortress Press, 1988.

———. "The Kerygma of the Priestly Writers," in *The Vitality of Old Testament Traditions*, ed. W. Brueggemann and H. W. Wolff. Atlanta: John Knox Press, 1975, 101-14.

Burke, K. *A Grammar of Motives*. Berkeley: University of California Press, 1969.

———. "Dramatism," IESS, vol. 7, 445-47.

Burnet, J. *Greek Philosophy, Part 1: Thales to Plato*. London: Macmillan Publishing Company, 1914.

Callinicos, A. *Making History: Agency, Structure and Change in Social Theory*. Ithaca: Cornell University Press, 1988.

Caquot, A., Sznycer, M., and Herdner, A. *Textes Ougaritiques. Tome I: Mythes et Legends*. LAPO 7; Paris: Editions du Cerf, 1978.

Cassuto, U. *Commentary on Genesis: Part I, From Adam to Noah: Genesis I–VI 8*. Jerusalem: Magnes Press, 1961.

Cazelles, H. "*MYN* = espèce, race où ressemblance?" in *Memorial du Cinquantenaire, 1914-1964*. Paris: Boud et Gay, 1964, 105-8.

Cherniss, H. *Aristotle's Criticism of the Presocratic Philosophers*. Baltimore: Johns Hopkins Press, 1935.

Childs, B. S. *Introduction to the Old Testament as Scripture*. Philadelphia: Fortress Press, 1979.

———. *Myth and Reality in the Old Testament*. SBT 27; London: SCM Press, 1960.

Clark, A. C. "The Primitive Text of the Gospels and Acts: A Rejoinder," *JTS* 16 (1915) 225-40.

Clark, K. and Holquist, M. *Mikhail Bakhtin*. Cambridge: Belknap Press of Harvard University Press, 1984.

Clines, D. J. A. *The Theme of the Pentateuch*. JSOTSS 10; Sheffield: Sheffield University Press, 1978.

———. *What does Eve Do to Help? and Other Readerly Questions to the Old Testament*. JSOTSS 94; Sheffield: Sheffield Academic Press, 1990.

Coats, G. W. *Genesis*. FOTL 1; Grand Rapids: William B. Eerdmans Publishing Company, 1983.

Collins, J. J. "Daniel and His Social World," in *Interpreting the Prophets*, ed. J. L. Mays and P. J. Achtemeier. Philadelphia: Fortress Press, 1987, 249-60 (reprinted from *Interpretation* 39, 2 [1985] 131-43).

———. *The Apocalyptic Imagination*. New York: Crossroad, 1987.

———. *The Apocalyptic Vision of the Book of Daniel*. HMS 16; Missoula: Scholars Press, 1977.

Collins, A. Y. "Aristobulus," *OTP*, vol. 2, 831-42.

Conybeare, F. C. and Stock, St. G. *Grammar of Septuagint Greek*. Boston: Ginn, 1905 (Reprint; Peabody: Hendrickson, 1988).

Coogan, M. *Stories from Ancient Canaan*. Philadelphia: Westminster Press, 1978.

Cook, J. "Genesis I in the Septuagint as Example of the Problem: Text and Tradition," *JNSL* 10 (1982) 25-36.

———. "The Exegesis of the Greek Genesis," in *VI Congress of the International Organization for Septuagint and Cognate Studies: Jerusalem 1986*, ed. C. Cox. SCS 23; Atlanta: Scholars Press, 1987, 91-110.

Cooper, J. *The Curse of Agade.* Baltimore: Johns Hopkins University Press, 1983.

Cornford, F. M. *From Religion to Philosophy: A Study in the Origins of Western Speculation.* New York: Harper & Row, 1957.

———. *The Unwritten Philosophy and other Essays.* Cambridge: Cambridge University Press, 1952.

Cotterell, A. *A Dictionary of World Mythology.* Oxford: Oxford University Press, 1986.

Cross, F. M., Jr. *Canaanite Myth and Hebrew Epic: Essays in the History of the Religion of Israel.* Cambridge: Harvard University Press, 1973.

———. *The Ancient Library of Qumran and Modern Biblical Studies.* Garden City: Doubleday & Company, 1958.

———. "The History of the Biblical Text in Light of Discoveries in the Judean Desert," *HTR* 57 (1964) 281-300.

Currid, J. D. "An Examination of the Egyptian Background of the Genesis Cosmogony," *BZ* 35 (1991) 3-17.

Dalley, S. *Myths from Mesopotamia.* Oxford: Oxford University Press, 1989.

Davila, J. "New Qumran Readings for Genesis One," in *Of Scribes and Scrolls: Studies on the Hebrew Bible, Intertestamental Judaism, and Christian Origins*, ed. H. W. Attridge, J. J. Collins, T. H. Tobin. CTSRR 5; Lanham: University Press of America, 1990, 3-12.

Day, J. *God's Conflict with the Dragon and the Sea.* Cambridge: Cambridge University Press, 1985.

Dequeker, L. "Green Herbage and Trees Bearing Fruit (Gen. 1:28-30; 9:1-3): Vegetarianism or Predominance of Man over the Animals," *Bijdragen* 38 (1977) 118-27.

DeRoche, M. "The *Rûaḥ ʾĔlōhîm* in Gen 1:2c: Creation of Chaos?" in *Ascribe to the Lord: Biblical and other Studies in Memory of Peter C. Craigie*, ed. L. Eslinger and G. Taylor. JSOTSS 67; Sheffield: Sheffield University Press, 1990, 303-18.

Diels, H. and Kranz, W. *Die Fragmente der Vorsokratiker, I, II, III.* Berlin-Charlottenburg: Weidmann, 1954, 1952, 1952.

Diemel, A. *Sumerisch-Akkadisches Glossar.* Rome: Verlag des Päpstl. Bibelinstituts, 1934.

Di Lella, A. A. *The Hebrew Text of Sirach: A Text-Critical and Historical Study.* London: Mounton, 1966.

Dillmann, A. *Genesis Critically and Exegetically Expounded*, trans. W. B. Stevenson. Edinburgh: T. & T. Clark, 1897.

Dion, P. E. "YHWH as Storm-god and Sun-god: The Double Legacy of Egypt and Canaan as Reflected in Psalm 104," *ZAW* 103 (1991) 43-71.

Eagleton, T. *Literary Theory: An Introduction*. Minneapolis: University of Minnesota Press, 1983.

Ebach, J. *Weltenstehung und Kulturentwicklung bei Philo von Byblos*. BZWANT 108; Stuttgart: W. Kohlhammer, 1979.

Eichrodt, W. "In the Beginning. A Contribution to the Interpretation of the First Word of the Bible," in *Israel's Prophetic Heritage. Essays in Honor of J. Muilenburg*, ed. B. W. Anderson and W. Harrelson. New York: Harper & Row, 1962, 1-10.

Eissfeldt, O. "Religionsdokument und Religionspoesie, Religions-Theorie und Religionshistorie: Ras Schamra und Sanchunjaton, Philo Byblius und Eusebius von Cäsarea," in *Kleine Schriften* 2. Tübingen: J. C. B. Mohr (Paul Siebeck), 1963, 130-44.

―――. "Zur Frage nach dem Alter der phönizischen Geschichtedes Sanchunjaton," in *Kleine Schriften* 2. Tübingen, J. C. B. Mohr (Paul Siebeck), 1963, 127-29.

Elliger, K. "Sinn und Ursprung der priesterlichen Geschichtserzählung," *ZTK*, 49 (1952) 121-43.

Evans, J. D. G. *Aristotle*. Sussex: Harvester Press, 1987.

Falkenstein, A. *Sumerische Götterlieder*. Heidelberg: Carl Winter, 1959.

Fenton, T. L. "'One Place,' *māqôm ʾeḥād*, in Genesis I 9: Read *miqwim*, 'Gatherings,'" *VT* 34 (1984) 438-45.

Ferguson, J. *Utopias in the Classical World*. AGRL; Ithaca: Cornell University Press, 1975.

Finegan, J. *Encountering New Testament Manuscripts: A Working Introduction to Textual Criticism*. Grand Rapids: William B. Eerdmans Company, 1974.

Fishbane, M. *Biblical Interpretation in Ancient Israel*. Oxford: Clarendon Press, 1985.

―――. "Jeremiah iv 23-26 and Job iii 3-13: A Recovered Use of the Creation Pattern," *VT* 21 (1971) 151-67.

Frame, D. J. "Creation by Word." Unpublished Dissertation: Drew University (Ann Arbor: University Microfilms) 1969.

Frankel, Z. *Vorstudien zu der Septuaginta*. Leipzig: Wilh. Vogel, 1841.

Frankfort, H. *Cylinder Seals: A Documentary Essay on the Art and Religion of the Ancient Near East*. London: Macmillan Publishing Company, 1939.

Freedman, D. N. "Notes on Genesis" *ZAW* 64 (1952) 190-94.

―――. *Pottery, Poetry and Prophecy: Studies in Early Hebrew Poetry*. Winona Lake: Eisenbrauns, 1980.

Freeman, K. *The Pre-Socratic Philosophers: A Companion to Diels* Fragmente der Vorsokratiker. Oxford: Basil Blackwell, 1949.

Furley, D. "The Cosmological Crisis in Classical Antiquity," in *Proceedings of the Boston Area Colloquium in Ancient Philosophy*, II, ed. J. J. Cleary. Lanham: University Press of America, 1987, 1-19.

Gatz, B. *Weltalter, goldene Zeit und sinnerverwandte Vorstellungen.* Spudasmata 16; Hildesheim: Georg Olms, 1967.

Geertz, C. "Ideology as a Cultural System," in *The Interpretation of Cultures: Selected Essays* by C. Geertz. New York: Basic Books, 1973, 193-233.

Geiger, A. *Urschrift und Uebersetzungen der Bibel in ihrer Abhängigkeit von der innern Entwicklung des Judenthums.* Breslau: Julius Hainauer, 1857.

Gibson, J. C. L. *Canaanite Myths and Legends.* Edinburgh: T. & T. Clark, 1978.

Godzich, Wlad. "Foreword" in M. M. Bakhtin/P. N. Medvedev, *The Formal Method in Literary Scholarship: A Critical Introduction to the Sociological Poetics,* trans. A. J. Wehrle. Cambridge: Harvard University Press, 1985, vii-xiv.

Goldstein, J. *II Maccabees.* AB 41A; New York: Doubleday & Company, 1983.

———. "The Origins of the Doctrine of Creation Ex Nihilo," *JJS* 35 (1984) 127-35.

Gooding, D. W. "An Appeal for a Stricter Terminology in the Textual Criticism of the Old Testament," *JSS* 21 (1976) 15-25.

Gordon, C. H. "Khnum and El," *SH* 28 (1982) 203-14.

———. *The World of the Old Testament.* Garden City: Doubleday & Company, 1958.

———. *Ugaritic Literature: A Comprehensive Translation of the Poetic and Prose Texts.* Rome: PIB, 1949.

Görg, M. "*Tōhû wābōhû*—ein Deutungsvorschlag," *ZAW* 92 (1980) 433-34.

Goshen-Gottstein, M. H. "Hebrew Biblical Manuscripts," *Biblica* 48 (1967) 243-90.

———. "Theory and Practice of Textual Criticism: The Text-Critical Use of the Septuagint," *Textus* 3 (1963) 130-58.

Gross, W. "Syntaktische Erscheinungen am Anfang althebräischer Erzählungen: Hintergrund und Vordergrund," *VTS* 32 (1981) 131-45.

Gunkel, H. *Genesis,* 4th ed. GHAT 1; Göttingen: Vandenhoeck & Ruprecht, 1917.

———. *Schöpfung und Chaos in Urzeit und Endzeit.* Göttingen: Vandenhoeck & Ruprecht, 1895.

———. "The 'Historical Movement' in the Study of Religion," *ET* 38 (1926/27) 532-36.

———. "The Influence of Babylonian Mythology upon the Biblical Creation Story," in *Creation in the Old Testament,* ed. B. W. Anderson. Philadelphia: Fortress Press, 1984, 25-52.

Guthrie, W. K. C. *A History of Greek Philosophy,* vol. 1. Cambridge: University Press, 1962.

———. *A History of Greek Philosophy,* vol. 6, Cambridge: University Press, 1981.

———. *In the Beginning.* Ithaca: Cornell University Press, 1957.

Hahm, D. E. *The Origins of Stoic Cosmology.* Columbus: Ohio State University Press, 1977.

Hallo, W. W., and Moran, W. L. "The First Tablet of the SB Recension of the Anzu Myth," *JCS* 31 (1979) 65-115.

Hamilton, V. P. *Genesis 1-17*. NICOT; Grand Rapids: William B. Eerdmans Publishing Company, 1990.

Hanson, J. "Demetrius the Chronographer," in *OTP*, vol. 2, ed. J. H. Charlesworth. Garden City: Doubleday & Company 1985, 843-54.

Hanson, P. *The Dawn of Apocalyptic*. Second ed.; Philadelphia: Fortress Press, 1979.

Hasel, G. F. "Recent Translations of Genesis 1:1," *BT* 22 (1971) 154-66.

Hayes, J. H. *An Introduction to Old Testament Study*. Nashville: Abingdon, 1979.

————. *Introduction to the Bible*. Philadelphia: Westminster Press, 1971.

————. and Irvine, S. A. *Isaiah, the Eighth-Century Prophet: His Times and His Preaching*. Nashville: Abingdon, 1987.

Heidel, A. *The Babylonian Genesis*. 2nd ed.; Chicago: University Press, 1963.

Herrmann, S. *A History of Israel in Old Testament Times*. 2nd ed.; Philadelphia: Fortress Press, 1981.

Herr, M. D. "Mekhilta of R. Ishmael," in *EJ*, vol. 11, 1270-71.

Hesiod. *Theogony and Works and Days*, trans. M. L. West. Oxford: Oxford University Press, 1988.

Hoffmeier, J. K. "Some Thoughts on Genesis 1 and 2 and Egyptian Cosmology," *JANES* 13 (1983) 39-49.

Holmberg, M. S. *The God Ptah*. Lund: CWK Gleerup, 1946.

Holzinger, H. *Genesis*. Freiburg: J. C. B. Mohr, 1898.

Honeyman, A. M. "Merismus in Biblical Hebrew," *JBL* 71 (1952) 11-18.

Housman, A. E. ed. *M. Manilii Astronomicon*, vol. 1. London: Cambridge University Press, 1937.

Howard, G. "The Septuagint: A Review of Recent Studies," in *Studies in the Septuagint: Origins, Recensions, and Interpretations*, ed. S. Jellicoe. New York: KTAV, 1974, 54-66.

Hughes, J. *Secrets of the Times: Myth and History in Biblical Chronology*. JSOTSS 66; Sheffield: Sheffield Academic Press, 1990.

Humbert, P. "Troise notes sur Genesis 1," *NTT* 56 (1955) 85-96.

Hunt, H. A. K. *A Physical Interpretation of the Universe: The Doctrines of Zeno the Stoic*. Carlton, Australia: Melbourne University Press, 1976.

Hurvitz, A. "The Evidence of Language in Dating the Priestly Code," *RB* 81 (1974) 24-55.

————. *A Linguistic Study of the Relationship between the Priestly Source and the Book of Ezekiel*. Cahiers de la Revue Biblique 20; Paris: Gabalda, 1982.

Hyers, C. *The Meaning of Creation: Genesis and Modern Science*. Atlanta: John Knox Press, 1984.

Ilgen, K. D. *Die Urkunden des Jerusalemischen Tempelarchivs in ihrer Urgestalt als Beytrag zur Berichtigung der Geschichte der Religion und Politik*. Halle: Hemmerde und Schwetschte, 1798.

Isaac, E. "1 (Ethiopic Apocalypse of) Enoch," in *OTS*, vol. 1, 5-89.

Isaiah, A. B. and Scharfman, B. *The Pentateuch and Rashi's Commentary: A Linear Translation into English*, vol. 1. Brooklyn: S. S. and R. Publishing, 1949.

Jacob, B. *Das Erste Buch der Tora: Genesis*. New York: KTAV, 1934.

Jacobs, L. *Jewish Biblical Exegesis*. New York: Behrman House, 1973.

Jacobsen, T. *The Harps that Once . . . , Sumerian Poetry in Translation*. New Haven: Yale University Press, 1987.

———. *The Treasures of Darkness: A History of Mesopotamian Religion*. New Haven: Yale University Press, 1976.

———, and Kramer, S. N. "The Myth of Inanna and Bilulu," *JNES* 12 (1954) 160-88.

Jameson, F. *The Ideologies of Theory: Essays 1971-1986, Volume 1 Situations of Theory*. Minneapolis: University of Minnesota Press, 1988.

———. *The Political Unconscious: Narrative as a Socially Symbolic Act*. Ithaca: Cornell University Press, 1981.

Janowski, B. "Tempel und Schöpfung. Schöpfungstheologische Aspekte der priester-schriftlichen Heiligtumskonzeption," in *Schöpfung und Neuschöpfung*. JBTh 5; Neukirchen-Vluyn: Neukirchener Verlag, 1990, 37-70.

Jellicoe, S. *The Septuagint and Modern Study*. Oxford: Clarendon Press, 1968.

Johnson, M. D. *The Purpose of the Biblical Genealogies of Jesus*. Cambridge: University Press, 1969.

Jongeling, B. "Some Remarks on the Beginning of Genesis I,2," *Folia Orientalia*, 21 (19-80) 27-32.

Junker, H. *Die Geisteshaltung der Ägypter in der Frühzeit*. OAW 237; Wien: Hermann Böhlaus, 1961.

———. *Die Götterlehre von Memphis (Schabaka-Inschrift)*. APAW 23; Berlin: Verlag der Akademie der Wissenschaft, 1940.

———. "In Principio Creavit Deus Coelum et Terram: Eine Untersuchung zum Thema Mythos und Theologie," *Biblica* 45 (1964) 477-90.

Kahle, P. E. *The Cairo Genizah*. Oxford: Basil Blackwell, 1959.

Kahn, C. H. *Anaximander and the Origins of Greek Cosmology*. New York: Columbia University Press, 1960.

Kaiser, O. *Die mythische Bedeutung des Meeres in Ägyten, Ugarit und Israel*. BZAW 78; Berlin: Alfred Töpelmann, 1959.

Kampen, J. *The Hasideans and the Origin of Pharisaism: A Study in 1 and 2 Maccabees*. SCS 24; Atlanta: Scholars Press, 1988.

Kapelrud, A. S. "Baʿal and the Devourers," in *Ugaritica VI*. Paris: Mission Archeologi-que de Ras Shamra, 1969, 319-32.

———. "The Date and Origin of the Priestly Code in the Old Testament," *ASTI* 3 (1964) 58-64.

———. "The Mythological Features in Genesis Chapter 1 and the Author's Intentions," *VT* 24 (1974) 178-86.

Katz, M. A. "The Problems of Sacrifice in Ancient Cultures," in *The Bible in the Light of Cuneiform Literature*, ed. W. W. Hallo and G. L. Mattingly. Lewiston: Edwin Mellen, 1990, 89-202.

Kaufmann, Y. *The Religion of Israel: From Its Beginnings to the Babylonian Exile*, trans. M. Greenberg. New York: Schocken, 1972.

Kautzsch, E., ed., *Gesenius' Hebrew Grammar*, trans. A. E. Cowley. Oxford: Oxford University Press, 1910.

Kearney, P. J. "Creation and Liturgy: The P Redaction of Ex 25-30," *ZAW* 89 (1977) 375-87.

Kern, O. *Orphicorum Fragmenta*. Berlin: Weidmannsche, 1922.

Kilian, R. "Gen I, 2 und die Urgötter von Hermopolis," *VT* 16 (1966) 420-38.

Kirk, G. S., and Raven, J. E. *The Presocratic Philosophers: A Critical History with a Selection of Texts*. Cambridge: Cambridge University Press, 1983.

Klein, R. W. *Textual Criticism of the Old Testament: The Septuagint after Qumran*. GBS; Philadelphia: Fortress Press, 1974.

Kleinknecht, H. "*pneuma*" in *TDNT*, vol. 6, 332-59.

Koehler L. and Baumgartner, W., ed. *Lexicon in Veteris Testamenti Libros*. Leiden: E. J. Brill, 1985.

Kramer, S. N. *Enki and Ninhursag: A Sumerian "Paradise" Myth*. BASOR SS 1; New Haven: ASOR, 1945.

———, and Maier, J. *Myths of Enki, the Crafty God*. New York: Oxford University Press, 1989.

———. *Sumerian Mythology*. New York: Harper & Row, 1961.

Kugel, J. "Two Introductions to Midrash," *Prooftexts* 3 (1983).

Kuhl, C. *The Old Testament: Its Origins and Composition*, trans. C. T. M. Heriott. Edinburgh: Oliver and Boyd, 1961.

Lambdin, T. O. *Introduction to Biblical Hebrew*. New York: Charles Scribner's Sons, 1971.

Lambert, W. G. "Old Testament Mythology in Its Ancient Near Eastern Context," in *Congress Volume: Jerusalem 1986*, ed. J. A. Emerton. VTS 40; Leiden: E. J. Brill, 1988, 124-43.

———, and Millard, A. R. *Atra-Hasis: The Babylonian Story of the Flood*. Oxford: Clarendon Press, 1969.

Lane, W. "The Initiation of Creation," *VT* 13 (1963) 63-73.

Langdon, S. *Sumerian Epic of Paradise, the Flood, and the Fall of Man*. Philadelphia: University Museum, 1915.

Lasor, W. S. "Notes on Genesis 1:1-2:3," *Gordon Review* 2 (1956) 26-32.

Lauterbach, J. Z., trans. *Mekilta de-Rabbi Ishmael*, vol. 1. Philadelphia: Jewish Publication Society of America, 1976.

Levenson, J. D. *Creation and the Persistence of Evil: The Jewish Drama of Divine Omnipotence*. San Francisco: Harper & Row, 1988.

Lichtheim, M. *Ancient Egyptian Literature*, vols. 1, 2, 3. Berkeley: University of California Press, 1975, 1976, 1980.

Lloyd, G. E. R. *Aristotle: The Growth and Structure of His Thought*. Cambridge: University Press, 1968.

———. *Early Greek Science: Thales to Aristotle*. New York: W. W. Norton, 1970.

———. *Greek Science after Aristotle*. New York: W. W. Norton, 1973.

Loretz, O. *Schöpfung und Mythos: Mensch und Welt nach den Anfangskapiteln der Genesis*. Stuttgart: Katholisches Bibelwerk, 1968.

Lotman, Y. and Uspensky, B. "On the Semiotic Mechanism of Culture," *New Literary History* 9 (1978) 211-32.

Luyster, R. "Cosmogonic Symbolism in the Old Testament," *ZAW* 93 (1981) 1-10.

Machinist, P. "Assyria and its Image in the First Isaiah," *JAOS* 103 (1983) 719-38.

Mannheim, K. *Ideology and Utopia: an Introduction to the Sociology of Knowledge*, trans. L. Wirth and E. Shils. New York: Harcourt, Brace and World, 1936.

May, G. *Schöpfung aus dem Nichts*. AzKG 48; Berlin: Walter de Gruyter, 1978.

May, H. G. "Some Cosmic Connotations of *Mayim Rabbîm*, 'Many Waters,'" *JBL* 74 (1955) 9-21.

McCarter, P. K., Jr., *Textual Criticism: Recovering the Text of the Hebrew Bible*. GBS; Philadelphia: Fortress Press, 1986.

McClelland, D. *Ideology*. CST; Minneapolis: University of Minnesota Press, 1986.

McKane, W. *Studies in the Patriarchal Narratives*. Edinburgh: Handsel Press, 1979.

Meek, T. J. "Result and Purpose Clauses in Hebrew," *JQR* 46 (1955/6) 40-43.

Metzger, B. M. *The Text of the New Testament: Its Transmission, Corruption, and Restoration*. New York: Oxford University Press, 1964.

Miller, J. M., and Hayes, J. H. *A History of Ancient Israel and Judah*. Philadelphia: Westminster Press, 1986.

Mohr, R. D. "Plato's Theology Reconsidered: What the Demiurge Does," in *Essays in Ancient Greek Philosophy, III: Plato*, ed. J. P. Anton and A. Preus. New York: State University of New York Press, 1989, 293-308.

Morenz, S. *Egyptian Religion*, trans. A. E. Keep. Ithaca: Cornell University Press, 1960.

Morrow, G. R. "Necessity and Persuasion in Plato's *Timaeus*," in *Studies in Plato's Metaphysics*, ed. R. E. Allen. London: Routledge and Kegan Paul, 1965, 427-37.

Mulder, M. J. "The Transmission of the Biblical Text," in *Mikra: Text, Translation, Reading and Interpretation of the Hebrew Bible in Ancient Judaism and Early Christianity*, ed. M. J. Mulder and H. Sysling. Philadelphia: Fortress Press, 1988, 87-136.

Murtonen, A. "On the Chronology of the Old Testament," *ST* 8 (1954) 133-37.

Nickelsburg, G. W. E. "Social Aspects of Palestinian Jewish Apocalypticism," in *Apocalypticisim in the Meditteranean World and the Near East*, ed. D. Hellholm; Tübingen: J. C. B. Mohr (Paul Siebeck), 1983, 641-54.

Niditch, S. *Chaos to Cosmos: Studies in Biblical Patterns of Creation*. SPSH 6; Chico: Scholars Press, 1985.

O'Brien, J. V., and Major, W. *In the Beginnng: Creation Myths from Ancient Mesopotamia, Israel, and Greece*. ASR 11; Chico: Scholars Press, 1982.

Oded, B. "Judah and the Exile," in *Israelite and Judean History*, ed. J. H. Hayes and J. M. Miller. London: SCM Press, 1977, 435-88.

Oden, R. A., Jr. "Philo of Byblos and Hellenistic Historiography," *PEQ* 110 (1978) 115-26.

———. *The Bible Without Theology: The Theological Tradition and Alternatives to It*. San Francisco: Harper & Row, 1987.

Oldfather, C. H. *Diodorus of Sicily*, vol. 1. LCL, Greek Authors; London: William Heinemann, 1933.

Orlinsky, H. "The New Jewish Version of the Torah," *JBL* 82 (1963) 249-64.

———. *Notes on the New Translation of the Torah*. Philadelphia: Jewish Publication Society, 1969.

———. "On the Present State of Proto-Septuagint Studies," in *Studies in the Septuagint: Origins, Recensions, and Interpretations*, ed. S. Jellicoe. New York: KTAV, 1974, 78-109.

———. "The Plain Meaning of *rûaḥ* in Gen. 1.2," *JQR* 48 (1957/8) 174-82.

———. "The Textual Criticism of the Old Testament," in *The Bible and the Ancient Near East*, ed. G. E. Wright. Garden City: Doubleday & Company, 1961, 113-32.

Otzen, B. "The Use of Myth in Genesis," in *Myths in the Old Testament*, ed. B. Otzen, H. Gottlieb, K. Jeppesen. London: SCM Press, 1980, 22-61.

Owens, J. "The Teleology of Nature in Aristotle," in *Aristotle: The Collected Papers of Joseph Owens*, ed. J. R. Catan. Albany: State University of New York, 1981, 136-47.

Paradise, B. "Food for Thought," in *A Word in Season: Essays in Honor of William Mc-Kane*, ed. J. D. Martin and P. R. Davies. JSOTSS 42; Sheffield: University of Sheffield Press, 1986, 177-208.

Parrish, V. S. "The Rhetoric of Creation: Psalm 104 as a Subversive Text." Delivered at the 1991 national SBL meeting. Forthcoming.

von Pauly, A. F. *Paulys Real-Encyclopädie der Classischer Altertumswissenschaft*, vol. 17, ed. G. Wissowa. Stuttgart: J. B. Metzlersche Verlagsbuchhandlung, 1937.

Pope, M. H. "Seven, Seventh, Seventy." *IDB*, vol. 4. Nashville: Abingdon, 1962, 294-95.

Pritchard, J. B., ed. *Ancient Near Eastern Texts Relating to the Old Testament*. 3rd ed., Princeton: Princeton University Press, 1969.

Purvis, J. D. "Exile and Return: From the Babylonian Destruction to the Reconstruction of the Jewish State," in *Ancient Israel*, ed. H. Shanks. Washington D.C.: Biblical Archaeological Society, 1988, 151-76.

————. *The Samaritan Pentateuch and the Origin of the Samaritan Sect.* HSM 2; Cambridge: Harvard University Press, 1968.

von Rad, G. *Genesis: A Commentary,* trans. J. J. Marks. Revised ed., OTL; Philadelphia: Westminster Press, 1972.

Rendtorff, R. *The Old Testament: An Introduction.* Philadelphia: Fortress Press, 1986.

————. *Das überlieferungsgeschitliche Problem des Pentateuchs.* BZAW 147; Berlin: Walter de Gruyter, 1977.

Revell, E. J. "LXX and MT: Aspects of Relationship," in *De Septuaginta: Studies in Honor of John Williams Wevers on His Sixty-fifth Birthday,* ed. A. Pietersma and C. Cox. Mississauga, Ontario: Benben, 1984, 41-52.

Ricoeur, P. *Lectures on Ideology and Utopia,* ed. G. H. Taylor. New York: Columbia University Press, 1986.

Ridderbos, N. H. "Genesis I 1 und 2," *OS* 12 (1958) 214-60.

Robbins, F. E. *The Hexaemeral Literature: A Study of the Greek and Latin Commentaries on Genesis.* Chicago: University of Chicago Press, 1912.

Robinson, J. M. *An Introduction to Early Greek Philosophy: The Chief Fragments and Ancient Testimony with Connecting Commentary.* Boston: Houghton Mifflin, 1968.

Robinson, T. M. "Understanding the *Timaeus,*" in *Proceedings of the Boston Area Colloquium in Ancient Philosophy,* vol. 2, ed. J. J. Cleary. Lanham: University Press of America, 1987, 103-19.

Rose, H. J. *A Handbook of Greek Mythology Including Its Extension to Rome.* New York: E. P. Dutton, 1959.

Saggs, H. W. F. *The Encounter with the Divine in Mesopotamia and Israel.* London: Althone Press, 1978.

Sambursky, S. *The Physical World of the Greeks,* trans. M. Dagut. New York: MacMillan Publishing Company, 1956.

Sandbach, F. H. *Aristotle and the Stoics.* CPSSV 10; Cambridge: Cambridge Philological Society, 1985.

Sarna, N. M. *Exodus.* JPSTCS; Philadelphia: Jewish Publication Society, 1991.

Sasson, J. "A Time . . . to Begin," in " *Sha'arei Talmon": Studies Studies in the Bible, Qumran, and the Ancient Near East, presented to Shemaryahu Talmon,* ed. M. Fishbane and E. Tov. Winona Lake: Eisenbrauns, 1992, 183-94.

————. "Wordplay in the OT," *IDBSV.* Nashville: Abingdon, 1976, 968-69.

Schafer, B. E. "Sabbath," *IDBSV.* Nashsville: Abingdon, 1976, 760-62.

Schäfer, P. "*Bĕrēšît Bārāʾ ʾĔlōhîm*: Zur Interpretation von Genesis 1,1 in der rabbinischen Literatur," *JSJ* 2 (1971) 161-66.

————. "Tempel und Schöpfung. Zur Interpretation einiger Heiligtums-traditionen in der rabbinischen Literatur," *Kairos* 16 (1974) 122-33.

Schaller, J. B. "Genesis 1.2 im antiken Judentum." Unpublished Dissertation; Göttingen Universität, 1961.

Schedl, C. *History of the Old Testament: The Ancient Orient and Ancient Biblical History*, vol. 1. New York: Alba House, 1973.

Schlögl, H. A. *Der Gott Tatenen*. OBO 29; Freiburg: Universitätsverlag, 1980.

Schmidt, W. H. *Die Schöpfungsgeschichte der Priesterschrift*. WMANT 17; Neukirchen-Vluyn: Neukirchener, 1964.

Schürer, E. *The History of the Jewish People in the Age of Jesus Christ (175 B.C.–A.D. 135)*, vols. 1, 2, ed. G. Vermes, F. Miller, M. Black. Edinburgh: T. & T. Clark, 1973, 1979.

Schutt, R. J. H. "Letter of Aristeas," in *OTP*, vol. 2, ed. J. Charlesworth. Garden City: Doubleday & Company, 1985, 12-34.

Schuttermayr, G. "'Schöpfung aus dem Nichts' in 2 Makk 7,28? Zum Verhältnis von Position und Bedeutung," *BZ* 17 (1973) 203-28.

Schwarz, W. "Discussions on the Origin of the Septuagint," in *Studies in the Septuagint: Origins, Recensions, and Interpretations*, ed. S. Jellicoe. New York: KTAV, 1974, 110-37.

Sethe, K. *Amun und die Acht Urgötter von Hermopolis*. APAW 4; Berlin: Verlag der Akademie der Wissenschaften, 1929.

Simpson, C. A. "Genesis: Exegesis," *The Interpreter's Bible*. New York: Abingdon, 1952, 465-829.

Sjorberg, A. W. and Bergmann, E. *The Collection of the Sumerian Temple Hymns*. Locust Valley: J. J. Augustin, 1969.

Skinner, J. *Genesis*. ICC; New York: Charles Scribner's Sons, 1910.

Skinner, Q. "Motives, Intentions, and the Interpretations of Texts," *New Literary History* 3 (1972) 393-408.

Smith, J. M. P. "The Use of the Divine as Superlatives," *AJSL* 45 (1928/29) 212-13.

Smith, J. P. *A Compendious Syriac Dictionary*. Oxford: Clarendon Press, 1903.

Smith, M. S. "The Near Eastern Background of Solar Language for Yahweh," *JBL* 109 (1990) 29-39.

Smith, P. J. "A Semotactical Approach to the Meaning of the Term *rûaḥ ʾĕlōhîm* in Genesis 1:2," *JNSL* 8 (1980) 99-104.

Smyth, H. W. *Greek Grammar*. Cambridge: Harvard University Press, 1920.

von Soden, W. *Grundriss der Akkadischen Grammatik*. AO 47; Rome: PIB, 1969.

Soggin, J. A. *A History of Ancient Israel*. Philadelphia: Westminster Press, 1984.

Solokoff, M. *A Dictionary of Jewish Palestinian Aramaic of the Byzantine Period*. Ramat-Gan: Bar Ilan University Press, 1990.

Speiser, E. A. *Genesis*. AB 1; Garden City: Doubleday & Company, 1964.

de Spinoza, B. *A Theologico-Political Treatise and a Political Treatise*, trans. R. H. M. Elwes. New York: Dover, 1951.

Spurrell, J. *Notes on the Hebrew Text of the Book of Genesis*. Oxford: Clarendon Press, 1887.

Stead, G. "Review of *Schöpfung aus dem Nichts*," *JTS* 30 (1979) 547-48.

Steck, O. *Der Schöpfungsbericht der Priesterschrift: Studien zur literarkritischen und überlieferungsgeschichtlichen Problematik von Genesis 1,1 - 2,4a.* FRLANT 115; Göttingen: Vandenhoeck & Ruprecht, 1975.

Steiner, G. *After Babel: Aspects of Language and Translation.* New York: Oxford University Press, 1975.

Sternberg, M. *The Poetics of Biblical Narrative: Ideological Literature and the Drama of Reading.* Bloomington: Indiana University Press, 1987.

Taber, C. R. "Translation as Interpretation," *Interpretation* 32 (1978) 130-43.

Talmon, S. "The Biblical Understanding of Creation and the Human Commitment," *Ex Auditu* 3 (1987) 98-119.

Tarlin, J. "Thinking in Circles; A Brief Introduction to the Work of Bakhtin and Company," forthcoming.

Taylor, A. E. *Aristotle.* New York: Dover, 1955.

Tcherikover, V. *Hellenistic Civilization and the Jews.* Philadelphia: Jewish Publication Society, 1959.

————. "The Ideology of the Letter of Aristeas," in *Studies in the Septuagint: Origins, Recensions, and Interpretations,* ed. S. Jellicoe. New York: KTAV, 1974, 181-207.

Tengström, S. *Die Toledotformel und die literarische Struktur der priesterlichen Erweiterungsschicht im Pentateuch.* CB OTS 17; Uppsala: CWK Gleerup, 1982.

Teske, R. J. *Saint Augustine on Genesis.* Washington: Catholic University of America, 1991.

Thomas, D. W. "A Consideration of Some Unusual Ways of Expressing the Superlative in Hebrew," *VT* 3 (1953) 209-24.

Thompson, R. C. *The Epic of Gilgamesh: Text, Transliteration and Notes.* Oxford: Clarendon Press, 1930.

Thompson, T. L. *The Historicity of the Patriarchal Narratives.* BZAW 133; Berlin: Walter de Gruyter, 1974.

Tobin, V. A. *Theological Principles of Egyptian Religion.* AUSTR 59; New York: Peter Lang, 1989.

Toeg, A. "Genesis 1 and the Sabbhat," (Hebrew) *BM* 50 (1972) 288-96.

Touitou, E. "Rashi's Commentary on Genesis 1-6 in the Context of Judeo-Christian Controversy," *HUCA* 61 (1990) 159-83.

Tov, E. "The Septuagint," in *Mikra: Text, Translation, Reading and Interpretation of the Hebrew Bible in Ancient Judaism and Early Christianity,* ed. M. J. Mulder. Philadelphia: Fortress Press, 161-88.

————. "The Text of the Old Testament," in *The World of the Bible,* ed. A. S. Van der Woude. Grand Rapids: William B. Eerdmans Publishing Company, 1986, 156-90.

————. *The Text-Critical Use of the Septuagint in Biblical Research.* Jerusalem: Simor Ltd., 1981.

Tredennick, H. *Aristotle: The Metaphysics*, Books I-IX. LCL, Greek Authors, 271; London: William Heinemann, 1933.

Tsumura, D. *The Earth and the Waters in Genesis 1 and 2: A Linguistic Investigation*. JSOTSS 83; Sheffield: Sheffield University Press, 1989.

Van Buren, E. D. *The Flowing Vase and the God with Streams*. Berlin: Hans   Schoetz, 1933.

Van Dijk, J. *Lugal Ud Me-lam-bi Nir-gal: Le recit épique et didatique des Travaux de Ninurta, du Deluge et de la Nouvelle Creation*, I. Leiden: E. J. Brill, 1983.

Van Seters, J. "The Creation of Man and the Creation of the King," *ZAW* 101 (1989) 333-42.

———. "The Primeval Histories of Greece and Israel Compared," *ZAW* 100 (1989) 1-22.

Vawter, B. *On Genesis: A New Reading*. Garden City: Doubleday & Company, 1977.

Vink, J. G. "The Date and Origin of the Priestly Code in the Old Testament," *OS* 15 (1969) 1-144.

Volosinov, V. N./Bakthin, M. M. *Marxism and the Philosophy of Language*, trans. L. Matjeka and I. P. Titunik. New York: Sernium Press, 1973.

Wacholder, B. Z. *Eupolemus: A Study of Judaeo-Greek Literature*. MHUC 3; Cincinnati: Hebrew Union College Press, 1974.

Walcot, P. *Hesiod and the Near East*. Cardiff: University of Wales Press, 1966.

Walters, P. *The Text of the Septuagint: Its Corruptions and Their Emendation*, ed. D. W. Gooding. Cambridge: University Press, 1973.

Waltke, B. K. "The Creation Account in Genesis 1:1-3, Part III: The Initial Chaos Theory and the Precreation Chaos Theory," *BS* 132 (1975) 216-28.

———. and O'Connor M. *An Introduction to Biblical Hebrew Syntax*. Winona Lake: Eisenbrauns, 1990.

Weaver, M. "*Pneuma* in Philo of Alexandria." Unpublished Dissertation: University of Notre Dame (Ann Arbor: University Microfilms) 1973.

Weiss, H.-F. *Untersuchungen zur Kosmologie des Hellenistischen und Palästinische Judentums*. TU 97; Berlin: Adademie-Verlag, 1966.

Welker, M. "What is Creation?" Rereading Genesis 1 and 2," *Theology Today* 48 (1991) 56-71.

Wellhausen, J. *Die Composition des Hexateuchs und der Historischen Bücher des Alten Testaments*. 2nd ed.; Berlin: Georg Reimer, 1889.

———. *Prolegomena to the History of Ancient Israel*. Gloucester: Peter Smith, 1957 (trans. from the 1885 German edition).

Wenham, G. J. *Genesis 1-15*. WBC 1; Waco: Word Books, 1987.

Wente, E. *Letters from Ancient Egypt*. WAW 1; Atlanta: Scholars Press, 1990.

West, M. L., ed. *Hesiod: Theogony*. Oxford: Clarendon Press, 1966.

———, ed. *Hesiod: Works and Days*. Oxford: Clarendon Press, 1978.

———. *The Orphic Poems*. Oxford: Clarendon Press, 1983.

Westermann, C. *Genesis 1-11*, trans. J. J. Scullion. Minneapolis: Augsburg Publishing House, 1984.

Wevers, J. W. "An Apologia for Septuagint Studies," *BIOSCS* 18 (1985) 16-38.

———. *Septuaginta: Genesis*. VTG 1; Göttingen: Vandenhoeck & Ruprecht, 1974.

———. "Proto-Septuagint Studies," in *Studies in the Septuagint: Origins, Recensions, and Interpretations*, ed. S. Jellicoe. New York: KTAV, 1974, 138-57.

———. *Text History of the Greek Genesis*. Göttingen: Vandenhoeck & Ruprecht, 1974.

Wilcke, C. *Das Lugalbandaepos*. Wiesbaden: Otto Harrassowitz, 1969.

Wildberger, H. "Das Abbild Gottes," *TZ* 21 (1965) 245-59.

Williams, R. J. *Hebrew Syntax: An Outline*, 2d ed. Toronto: University of Toronto Press, 1976.

Winston, D. *Philo of Alexandria: The Contemplative Life, the Giants, and Selec- tions*. CWS; New York: Paulist Press, 1981.

———. "Philo's Theory of Cosmogony," in *Religions Syncretism in Antiquity: Essays in Conversation with Geo Widengreen*, ed. B. A. Pearson. Missoula: Scholars Press, 1975, 157-71.

———. "The Book of Wisdom's Theology of Cosmogony," *History of Religions* 11 (1971) 185-202.

Wolfson, H. A. *Philo: Foundations of Religion and Philosophy in Judaism, Christianity, and Islam*, Vol. 1. Cambridge: Harvard University Press, 1947.

Woodbridge, F. J. E. *Aristotle's Vision of Nature*, ed. J. H. Randall, *et al*. New York: Columbia University Press, 1965.

Würthwein, E. *The Text of the Old Testament*, trans. E. F. Rhodes. Grand Rapids: William B. Eerdmans Publishing Company, 1979.

Young, E. J. "The Relation of the First Verse of Genesis One to Verses Two and Three," in *Studies in Genesis One* by E. J. Young. Philadelphia: Presbyterian and Reformed Publishing Company, 1964, 1-14.

———. "The Interpretation of Genesis 1:2," in *Studies in Genesis One* by E. J. Young. Philadelphia: Presbyterian and Reformed Publishing Company, 1964, 15-42.

Zenger, E. *Gottes Bogen in den Wolken*. SBS 112; Stuttgart: Katholisches Bibelwerk, 1983.

DATE DUE

HIGHSMITH 45-220